D0151343

# REGIONAL IDENTITY AND
# ECONOMIC CHANGE

# Regional Identity and Economic Change

## The Upper Rhine, 1450–1600

TOM SCOTT

CLARENDON PRESS · OXFORD

1997

Oxford University Press, Great Clarendon Street, Oxford OX2 6DP
Oxford New York
Athens Auckland Bangkok Bogota Bombay
Buenos Aires Calcutta Cape Town Dar es Salaam
Delhi Florence Hong Kong Istanbul Karachi
Kuala Lumpur Madras Madrid Melbourne
Mexico City Nairobi Paris Singapore
Taipei Tokyo Toronto Warsaw
and associated companies in
Berlin Ibadan

Oxford is a trade mark of Oxford University Press

Published in the United States
by Oxford University Press Inc., New York

British Library Cataloguing in Publication Data
Data available

Library of Congress Cataloging in Publication Data
Scott, Tom, 1947–
Regional identity and economic change : the Upper Rhine, 1450–1600
/ Tom Scott.
p. cm.
Includes bibliographical references (p. ) and index.
1. Breisgau (Germany)—Economic conditions. 2. Rhine River—
Economic conditions. 3. Cities and towns, Medieval—Rhine River.
4. Alsace (France)—Economic conditions. 5. Guilds—Germany—
Breisgau. 6. Guilds—France—Alsace. I. Title.
DD801.B77S36 1997
330.943′46—dc21 97–6897
ISBN 0–19–820644–5

1 3 5 7 9 10 8 6 4 2

Typeset by Graphicraft Typesetters Ltd., Hong Kong
Printed in Great Britain
on acid-free paper by
Biddles Ltd., Guildford & King's Lynn

†AS
†EJS
†WSS

# Acknowledgements

Research for the present work, which has occupied more than two decades, would not have been possible without substantial financial support from the Alexander von Humboldt Foundation, the Leverhulme Trust, the British Academy, the German Academic Exchange Service, and the University of Liverpool, which in addition granted sabbatical leave to allow the book to be completed.

My thanks to these bodies is matched by gratitude to the many archives visited, whose staff were always ready with advice and assistance. The roll-call of scholars who have been generously prepared to share their knowledge with the author and to offer constructive criticism is too long to list. But I would make particular mention of colleagues in Alsace: Francis Rapp and Georges Bischoff in Strasbourg, Odile Kammerer (Colmar/Mulhouse), and Bernhard Metz of the Archives Municipales in Strasbourg. Across the Rhine in the Breisgau I am greatly indebted to Dieter Mertens, Hans Schadek, Willy Schulze, and above all Sabine Wienker-Piepho in Freiburg im Breisgau. In Switzerland, apart from Peter Blickle's help in Bern, I profited from many conversations with Leo Neuhaus, former archivist of the Archives de l'Ancien Évêché de Bâle in Porrentruy.

Further afield, I have received advice and encouragement from Rolf Kießling, Bob Scribner, Jan de Vries, Larry Epstein, Maarten Prak, and Trevor Elliott. The maps were expertly produced on computer by Kay Lancaster of the Department of Earth Sciences, University of Liverpool. Tom Brady nobly took upon himself the task of reading the entire manuscript. His comments and criticism not only ensured that the text was absolved from egregious error: they much improved the shape of the book, though of course he bears no responsibility for its general argument. The book is dedicated to three who did not live to see its unduly protracted completion.

T. S.

*Langholm/Liverpool*
*22 August 1996*

# Contents

# List of Maps

# Note on Usage

Place-names are rendered according to existing political frontiers and styles, as are places of publication in the bibliography. Only the commonest English forms have been employed: Cologne, Munich, but Tirol, Bern, Basel instead of Tyrol, Berne, and (the quite nonsensical) Basle. Place-names in Alsace and francophone Switzerland are cross-referenced in the index in their French and German forms. The names of noble families are given in the language which they spoke: e.g. Kaspar von Mörsberg, not Gaspard de Morimont; Wilhelm von Rappoltstein, not Guillaume de Ribeaupierre, though their lordships and territories are given in the language appropriate to their geography (Morimont, Ribeaupierre). The German style of family titles has been retained where proper, but English style is used for major ruling houses, e.g. margrave Karl of Baden, not Karl von Baden. German Christian names are retained in all cases barring the German emperors and Austrian (arch)dukes.

To avoid confusion, Estates (social corporations, political associations) are distinguished from estates (lands) by rendering the former in upper case. Unless otherwise indicated, measurements and distances are metric. One German mile equates to 4.6 statute miles (7.4 kilometres). The currency of the contemporary coinage leagues was duodecimal: 12*d.* = 1 shilling; 20 shillings = £1.

# *Introduction*

## I

In Europe, we live in an age of regionalism and the reassertion of regional identities. Within the European Union, vast sums are poured into schemes for regional development, mostly channelled towards the poorer member-states or the peripheries of prosperous ones. Much of the force of contemporary regionalism in Europe, indeed, derives from its critique of a hegemonic political culture which characterizes states without a devolved structure of power. Although the debate over models of political integration within Europe has become hopelessly mired in conceptual confusion over what a 'federal' or a 'confederal' Europe might mean, there is now a widespread perception that only a regional framework for political, cultural, and economic activity can overcome the rigidities of the nation-state or, for that matter, of bureaucratic centralism in Brussels, since the region may express an identity which transcends the boundaries of individual states just as much as it gives voice to loyalties which lie at a more local level.

Yet it is no secret that the term 'region' is both ambiguous and imprecise. Therein, perhaps, lies its attraction, since it can embody a diversity of aspirations and identities. In one dimension, the region may be determined by natural features, a landscape bounded by geographical limits or characterized by a uniformity of geology, topography, or ecology; in another, it may reflect the pattern of human settlement, marked by a common language, ethnicity, or culture. But it can also be an artificial construct, a means of identifying social and economic priorities, which can best be addressed by co-operation across existing administrative, territorial, or political divisions. It is this latter usage which informs modern regional planning. Hence the variety of terms which offer themselves as synonyms for or approximations to the region: some are stamped by historical or cultural traditions (the French *pays*, the German *Heimat*); some have political connotations (province, district, the German *Land* or federal state); while others suggest natural landscapes (basins, catchment areas, deltas).[1] In other words, the region is both 'given' and 'created', and its vitality is likely to be greatest where the two elements coincide and interact.

And because regions are as much created as given, their definition is bound to remain both vague and subjective since, as Christopher Harvie observes, it has been 'projected by imagination and poetry as much as by rationalism and legalism'.[2] They exist, therefore, both as a reality and an idea, sustained by the accumulated weight of history and tradition—*Traditionstatbestände*, to use Klaus Graf's phrase—rather than natural-topographical entities.[3] Their very existence, indeed, as Jean-Paul Sorg has argued, presupposes a 'collective regional consciousness': 'La région: une idée, l'objet d'une conscience. Une région existe quand existe une conscience régionale collective. Elle a alors une âme, elle est plus qu'un découpage administratif ou qu'un *niveau politique*.'[4] By the same token, the strength of regionalism as a political and cultural force in contemporary Europe is seen to derive from emotional as well as rational considerations. For political scientists, accordingly, regionalism should be interpreted as a movement of political resistance against the pressure of political homogeneity which develops from 'nationalistically coloured traditions'.[5] However true that may be of Catalunya, or Brittany, or Scotland, such a definition fails to take account of elective affinities which cross political or national frontiers. Within Europe, the Alemannic community on the Upper

---

[1] Cf. Christopher Harvie, *The rise of regional Europe* (London/New York, 1994), 9.

[2] Ibid. 10.

[3] Klaus Graf, 'Das "Land" Schwaben im späten Mittelalter', in Peter Moraw (ed.), *Regionale Identität und soziale Gruppen im deutschen Mittelalter* (*Zeitschrift für historische Forschung*, suppl. 14) (Berlin, 1992), 163.

[4] Jean-Paul Sorg, 'Contribution à la recherche des fondements d'une sociologie régionale', *Revue des sciences sociales de la France de l'Est*, 16 (1988–89), 16. Cf. also idem, 'La Régionalisme comme humanisme', ibid. 20 (1992–93), 98–103. This recognition is almost entirely lacking in a collection of essays by French historians on modern French regions (despite being edited from Alsace!), which tacitly assumes that the latter exist only within known national boundaries and are principally defined by political or jurisdictional allegiance. Cf. Christian Gras and Georges Livet (eds.), *Régions et régionalisme en France du XVIIIe siècle à nos jours* (Publications de la Société Savante d'Alsace et des Régions de l'Est: Grandes Publications, 13) (Paris, 1977).

[5] Cf. Klaus Graf, 'Aspekte zum Regionalismus in Schwaben und am Oberrhein im Spätmittelalter', in Kurt Andermann (ed.), *Historiographie am Oberrhein im späten Mittelalter und in der frühen Neuzeit* (Oberrheinische Studien, 7) (Sigmaringen, 1988), 168.

Rhine, spanning France, Germany, and Switzerland, is a prime example. Here language, culture, and historical tradition bind what politics still divides.

When a regional planning and development association, the Arbeitsgruppe Regio Basiliensis, was formed in 1963 to co-ordinate economic, political, and cultural policy on the southern Upper Rhine, it comes as no surprise to learn that it chose the name Regio to symbolize the essential integrity of an area which for centuries had been caught between competing national interests.[6] But the Regio's remit was never intended to embrace the whole of the Upper Rhine. While to the south, east, and west it is circumscribed by what may loosely be termed natural frontiers (though it extends westwards through the Burgundian Gate to embrace the industrialized district of Montbéliard), to the north it stretches little further than the ancient boundaries between Upper and Lower Alsace on the left bank, and the Breisgau and Ortenau on the right bank, of the Rhine.[7] It ignores—indeed, it deliberately excludes—what historically has been the centrally located and metropolitan capital of the Upper Rhine, namely Strasbourg. In that sense, the Regio is only half a region, or, put differently, it is a region which reflects the centrality and commercial interests of a particular city, namely Basel.

Far from being a transnational association grounded in a partnership of equals and driven by mutual interests, the origins of the Regio, as Alain Howiller has pointed out, lay in the search for solutions to economic problems specific to Basel itself, an industrial metropolis in the heart of Europe, yet outside the European Economic Community: '[The *Regio Basiliensis*] entendait trouver avec les partenaires français et allemands de la région des solutions aux problèmes affrontés par l'économie bâloise: manque des terrains, de main d'œuvre, des logements pour les salariés, défaut de structures de transport adaptées.' But the French and German 'partners' were only ever regarded by the Swiss 'que comme un terrain utilisable en cas de nécessité absolue'.[8] Yet the Regio has subsequently spawned other regional planning associations on the Upper Rhine. First came the Regio du Haut-Rhin, established in 1965, with its headquarters in Mulhouse, to serve southern Alsace, followed twenty years later on the opposite bank of the river by the Freiburger

---

[6] Cf. *Bevölkerung und Wirtschaft der Regio* (Schriften der Regio, 1) (Basel, 1965), 1.
[7] Ibid. 3 (map).
[8] Alain Howiller, *Mémoires de midi: Les Mutations de l'Alsace (1960–1993)* (Strasbourg, 1993), 76.

Regio-Gesellschaft, with a similar function for the Breisgau. It is only more recently, however, that these regional bodies have properly begun to co-ordinate policy across national frontiers. In 1990 a co-ordination committee was at last set up between the three groups, followed by a common association spanning mid-Alsace and the Breisgau (CIMAB).[9] And not until December 1995 was the example of the southern Upper Rhine emulated downriver, with the con-stitution of a forum PAMINA for the frontier region of the south-ern Palatinate, the middle Upper Rhine, and northern Alsace.[10] This proliferation of regional planning associations underscores the two essential features of a *modern* understanding of regional identity: that it may be circumscribed and subdivided according to eco-nomic and structural requirements; and that it is predicated upon the centrality of leading cities—in our case, Basel, Mulhouse, Frei-burg, and (in the case of PAMINA) Karlsruhe. And because no one city today dominates the Upper Rhine, no all-embracing regional planning association exists which would comprehend the region in its entirety.

What we have here, therefore, whatever its historical and cul-tural pedigree, is a region primarily defined by economic central-ity, where the city and its hinterland combine to form an economic unit. This assumption is fundamental to modern regional planning, which takes population density and concentration of economic activ-ity as its starting-point. Hence a recent survey of Baden-Württemberg on the right bank of the Upper Rhine differentiates between regions according to whether they are agglomeration areas (*Ballungsge-biete*), dense clusters of population around one or more large cities; the rural regions lying beyond these; and areas of structural weak-ness (*strukturschwache Gebiete*), those lacking the infrastructure of communications, exchange, distribution, and services which cities can provide.[11] But economic function is crucial to an understanding

⁹ Béatrice Speiser, *Europa am Oberrhein: Der grenzüberschreitende Regional-ismus am Beispiel der oberrheinischen Kooperation* (Schriften der Regio, 13) (Basel/Frankfurt am Main, 1993), 37–48.

¹⁰ Heinrich Hauß, 'Das "alte" Baden und die Regio am Oberrhein', *Badische Heimat*, 76 (1996), 17.

¹¹ Cf. Klaus Kulinat, 'Regional planning in Baden-Württemberg', in Hans-Georg Wehling (ed.), *The German Southwest: Baden-Württemberg: History, politics, economy and culture* (Stuttgart/Berlin/Cologne, 1991), 157–60. Although Kulinat stresses the importance of a precise vocabulary of planning, he never attempts an exact definition of what constitutes a region.

of the historical development of regions and their centres as well. As Stein Rokkan and Derek Urwin have emphasized:

[T]erritorial centres as sites for the provision of services, the processing of information and the control of transactions over long distances cannot be analyzed in isolation. To study hierarchies of centres is to look at the characteristics of the overall linking networks of communication. In other words, centres must be analyzed at two levels: the centrality of the single site, and the degree of centralization within the network of which the site is part. In Western Europe these networks were historically influenced by economic factors . . .[12]

## II

Centrality in this sense is clearly fundamental in determining the character and function of economic regions as a whole, but it offers no immediate clue to the size of such regions. Historians, particularly those associated with the *Annales* school in France, have employed definitions which range from the local—a city and its hinterland, as in Pierre Goubert's classic study of Beauvais and the Beauvaisis in the seventeenth and eighteenth centuries—to the international—as in the many studies of the Mediterranean economy, from Maurice Lombard's Islamic lake of the eighth century onwards to Fernand Braudel's *économie monde* in the sixteenth. Yet only very recently has a preliminary classification of economic regions been attempted for early modern Europe. In his empirical scheme, Maarten Prak proposes three distinct levels or types of economic region, the micro-, meso-, and macro-region. Broadly speaking, these approximate (in his chosen examples) to eastern Swabia in southern Germany; then to the Netherlands, northern Italy, or the Rhône valley; and finally to the Mediterranean or Baltic respectively.[13] For our present purposes it is the micro-region (or 'base-region', as Prak also calls it) which concerns us most. Such a region, he argues, represents an area directly linked to and dependent on a central place, here taken as the hinterland of a medium-sized European city of the day, amounting, in Jan de Vries's definition,

---

[12] Stein Rokkan and Derek W. Urwin, *Economy, territory, identity: Politics of West European peripheries* (London/Beverly Hills/New Delhi, 1983), 11.

[13] Maarten Prak, 'Le regioni nella prima Europa moderna', in *Regioni, culture e ancora regioni nella storia economica e sociale dell'Europa moderna, Proposte e Ricerche: Economia e Società nella Storia dell'Italia Centrale*, 35 (1995), 12–14.

to between 125 and 250 square kilometres. This limited extent, however, is at variance with Prak's own example of such a micro-region, the area of eastern Swabia with its regional centre in Augsburg, whose economic orbit was more like 1,500 to 2,000 square kilometres in the sixteenth century.[14] Yet Prak is quite correct to ascribe a genuine regional economic coherence to eastern Swabia in this period. If we then apply its dimensions to the Upper Rhine in the same period, we find that the regional capital Strasbourg in fact had an economic *rayonnement* even larger than Augsburg's, getting on for 3,000 square kilometres. Should the Upper Rhine, therefore, be regarded as a meso-region, on a par with the Rhône valley, northern Italy, or the Low Countries? Hardly, since Prak defines the meso-region as the core of a macro-region, which scarcely makes sense for the Upper Rhine that, apart from its role as a European crossroads of international trade between the Mediterranean and north-western Europe, lay on the periphery of larger regions, identifiable by the emergence of inchoate national or territorial markets (or, in the case of Germany, the clustering of urban metropolises in Swabia and Franconia). In any case, Prak envisages the meso-region as stretching over 10,000 to 15,000 square kilometres, and attracting immigrant labour from a much wider area still, indicating a quite different order of magnitude from the Upper Rhine.[15]

A further issue concerns the methods most appropriate for calculating economic centrality as a benchmark of regional identity and cohesion in early modern Europe. To project Walter Christaller's famous central-place system, for instance, elaborated for southern Germany in the 1930s, back in time to the pre-industrial age is not without its hazards. Christaller's locational model, based on the marketing principle, not only assumed that population (and therewith purchasing power) was distributed over an undifferentiated and unbounded surface; he also believed that a structured market system, with a regular hierarchy of central places, would maximize profits and minimize costs. But can we realistically suppose that in the sixteenth century peasants sought, or were able, to exploit what is presumed to have been a perfectly functioning market?[16]

---

[14] Prak, 'Le regioni nella prima Europa moderna', 19–21.     [15] Ibid. 13–14.
[16] Cf. Richard Hodges, *Primitive and peasant markets* (Oxford, 1988), 17.

Leaving aside the now somewhat sterile debate on the economic motivation of producers in predominantly agrarian societies—we can quietly agree that peasants will engage in the market provided that the perceived risks are not too great, but that the market itself is subject to social and institutional constraints (or distortions)[17] —the degree and nature of market exchange become decisive. In western Europe from the fourteenth to the nineteenth century peasant markets were partially commercialized, and increasingly exposed to the impact of regional or even international markets, yet market transactions were still controlled or monitored by a non-peasant élite. Characteristic of a partially commercialized economy in these circumstances, Carol A. Smith believes, is that exchange beyond the region is encouraged, but that it is concentrated in a single centre exercising a monopoly of commercial power, which she terms a gateway community or port-of-trade. Because such centres lie on the confines of their hinterlands, Smith terms such a central-place system dendritic, that is, resembling the branches of a tree radiating from its trunk which is the economic conduit to the outside world.[18] The pertinence of the concept of a dendritic system to natural corridors of communication such as waterways seems obvious enough, and gateway communities of the type described by Smith can indeed be found in the early Middle Ages at the mouths of the Rhine and the Rhône.[19]

But does the pattern still hold good, as Richard Hodges has enquired, when economic (and institutional) control is dispersed, rather than concentrated in monopolistic centres?[20] This was the case on the Upper Rhine, politically and territorially fragmented, where the regional capital Strasbourg never achieved a monopolistic position; indeed, it faced constant commercial rivalry from Basel upriver. The experience of sixteenth-century Europe (and elsewhere) reveals numerous overlapping dendritic systems, Hodges has argued, which correspond in effect to Christaller's alternative (and neglected) model of location, predicated upon transport systems.[21] This approach has been taken up by Paul Hohenberg and

---

[17] Cf. ibid. 14–15.

[18] Carol A. Smith, 'Exchange systems and the spatial distribution of elites: The organization of stratification in agrarian societies', in idem (ed.), *Regional analysis*, ii. *Social systems* (New York/San Francisco/London, 1976), 309–74.

[19] Hodges, *Primitive and peasant markets*, 43.　　[20] Ibid. 23.

[21] Ibid. 68.

Lynn Hollen Lees, who suggest that in pre-industrial Europe for regions which are arteries of long-distance trade, especially if river-borne, centrality is less defined by the presence of markets as out-lets for production than by urban networks in which central places are located according to their function as outlets or relay-points of distribution.

# III

The present study applies these insights to investigate whether a sense of regional identity, defined by economic criteria, can be dis-cerned on the southern Upper Rhine in the period from the mid-fifteenth to the late sixteenth century, when the political affiliation and historical lineage of the landscape and the people of the re-gion became the subject of open conflict by the sword and by the pen. For the situation of the Upper Rhine lying on the borderlands of the Holy Roman Empire and France, or the Germanic and Latin worlds, however much it might appear to constitute a natural or self-contained region, rendered it vulnerable to military invasion, political annexation, or cultural appropriation.

During the fifteenth century two developments decisively shaped political consciousness on the Upper Rhine. The first was Burgun-dian expansionism, culminating in the temporary alienation by mortgage of the Austrian Habsburg possessions in Alsace to duke Charles the Bold between 1469 and 1474. The struggle to repulse Burgundy drew the regional powers into close alliance and fos-tered what Claudius Sieber-Lehmann has recently called a sense of genuine nationalism, inasmuch as it was vested in the perception of Charles the Bold as the new 'Turk in the West' and of the Bur-gundians as francophone foreigners.[22] But while those who might increasingly see themselves both by language and tradition as Ger-mans were willing to close ranks against external aggressors, that solidarity was powerless to prevent the growing rift between the princes and feudal nobility of south-west Germany and the repub-lican Swiss, a deep-seated antagonism which discharged itself in the so-called Swiss (or Swabian) War between the Habsburg emperor

---

[22] Claudius Sieber-Lehmann, *Spätmittelalterlicher Nationalismus: Die Burgunder-kriege am Oberrhein und in der Eidgenossenschaft* (Veröffentlichungen des Max-Planck-Instituts für Geschichte, 116) (Göttingen, 1995).

Maximilian and the Confederates in 1499. This conflict, tantamount to a civil war, sealed the *de facto* separation of the Swiss from the Empire, so that the Upper Rhine, for part of its length above Basel, became for the first time a political frontier.[23]

Whether the Rhine below Basel had ever constituted a frontier between Germans and French also became a hotly debated issue in this period. Because in the German lands ethnicity and language defined nationality, chroniclers and humanists had no difficulty in ascribing Germanness to those who lived west of the Rhine, even if the river had historically separated *Germania* from *Gallia*. But to French propagandists, for whom geography determined the bounds of nationhood, the presence of Germans on the left bank of the Rhine served as a perpetual irritation, even if it was only in the later seventeenth century that the Rhine came to be regarded as France's natural eastern frontier.[24] By then, Alsace had been ceded to France in the aftermath of the Thirty Years War, and the uneasy frontier on the Rhine was to become the target of revanchist aspirations whose grim consequences have scarred the history of our own century. These claims, grounded in culture and history, were reinforced by the military significance of the Upper Rhine as a strategic corridor.

In the present study, by contrast, we are concerned to discover whether the cultural integrity of the Upper Rhine was matched by a sense of regional economic identity in our period. What made the Upper Rhine in economic terms a constant object of desire was its peculiar double character: on the one hand, it was a self-subsistent landscape, rich in people and resources, living by exchange between valley and mountain, upland and plain; on the other, it was a transit area, a commercial crossroads north of the Alps, with the river as an artery of long-distance trade to northern Germany and beyond. This suggests that any regional quality inherent in the landscape of the Upper Rhine is likely to have been fluid rather than static, varying according to the shifting pattern of supply and demand, local or international trade. The Upper Rhine, moreover,

[23] Cf. Graf, 'Das "Land" Schwaben', 136.

[24] Rüdiger Schnell, 'Deutsche Literatur und deutsches Nationalbewußtsein in Spätmittelalter und Früher Neuzeit', in Joachim Ehlers (ed.), *Ansätze und Diskontinuität deutscher Staatsbildung im Mittelalter* (Nationes: Historische und philologische Untersuchungen zur Entstehung der europäischen Nationen im Mittelalter, 8) (Sigmaringen, 1989), 259–63.

is far from being an exact geographical description. This study concentrates on the southern reaches of the valley, where mountain and plain do appear to form a natural region, rather than on the more open terrain flanking the river in the Palatinate and in Hesse. By endowment, topography, and location the southern Upper Rhine in the fifteenth and sixteenth centuries displayed a cohesiveness, reflected in the centrality of its chief city Strasbourg, which seems to qualify it as a potential economic region. Yet the study consciously devotes more attention to the Upper Rhine between Basel and Strasbourg than between Strasbourg and Speyer, not only because the greater intensity of economic interchange suggests a more perceptible regional coherence, but because the surviving sources present the historian with fundamental difficulties.

It is one of the besetting problems of a region presently divided between three countries that its archives are scattered and incomplete—indeed, their holdings on occasion have been exchanged between them. Materials relating to the lands on the Upper Rhine formerly under the jurisdiction of the Austrian Habsburgs, in particular, are today located in France (Colmar), and in Germany (Karlsruhe and Freiburg im Breisgau), as well in Austria itself (Innsbruck and Vienna). The archive of the Württemberg administration in Alsace (which survived as a political curiosity until the eve of the French Revolution) is now housed in the Archives Nationales in Paris, having been transported thither on Napoleon's instructions. Only the Swiss archives have survived relatively unscathed over the centuries, thanks to Confederate neutrality which spared Switzerland the ravages of war, but even here the archive of the former bishopric of Basel was the subject of bitter wrangling until finally removed from Bern to its present home in Porrentruy in what is now canton Jura.

Although most archives in the region are nowadays well catalogued, with the exception of Basel they contain only a patchy deposit of economic sources—tax-registers, tariffs, toll-receipts, market-registers, coinage records, and the like. Even demographic sources do not survive in any quantity before the mid-seventeenth century. Price- and wage-series, it is true, were compiled for Alsace in the last century by Auguste Hanauer, but nothing comparable exists on the right bank of the Rhine. Land-transaction deeds, by contrast, are plentiful enough, but are of limited relevance to the present study. In short, an archival basis for the compilation of

reliable statistics on population, domestic productive capacity and
output, imports and exports, investment, and return on capital is
almost entirely lacking. Rather than produce tables or graphs which
would convey a spurious impression of the archival legacy, it was
decided to dispense with quantitative statistics altogether; at various points in the text reference is made to the particular source
problems encountered.

Instead, the study depends to a great extent on institutional
sources: letter-books, minute-books, *aides-mémoires*, reports on
enquiries, proclamations, and court records. The correspondence
between princes and magistracies over issues of economic conflict
and co-operation is surprisingly well preserved, but requires an
exhaustive compilation from the archives of the many authorities
involved. Hence it was necessary to go beyond the principal state
archives to the many local and communal archives on the Upper
Rhine, within whose walls often unsuspected riches were discovered. But any trawl of the archives, however comprehensive,
should not disguise that analysis of a topic as elusive as regional
economic consciousness and identity on the Upper Rhine in the
fifteenth and sixteenth centuries can never aspire to be more than
an approximation to historical reality.

# IV

The analysis is divided into four sections. It begins with an ex-
amination of whether natural regions and frontiers exist at all, and
if so how they should be defined. Here the emphasis is placed on
the contrast between the supposedly natural region of the Upper
Rhine and the historically evolved political-territorial landscape. The
next section examines the economic structure of the Upper Rhine
in the light of competition over resources and their distribution.
It applies theories of centrality to see whether they can explain
the incidence of rural competition in crafts and marketing for the
traditional urban centres. The integration of functions between different rank-size places in a hierarchy of centrality, which central-
place theory posits for an economic region comprising a city and
its hinterland, is shown on the Upper Rhine to break down at the
level of the smallest centres where, in addition, competition between
markets on the right bank of the river was considerably more
intense than on the left.

The focus then switches to patterns of economic co-operation between the authorities in what was a landscape of political and territorial fragmentation. The analysis revolves around the rise of regional coinage associations in the later Middle Ages, whose members on the Upper Rhine came by the sixteenth century to shoulder additional responsibility for public welfare and 'good police' (see Chapter 7), especially the protection of supplies of foodstuffs. Here the trade in meat (largely imports) is contrasted with the trade in grain (often exports) to establish whether differing commercial needs led to a variable geometry of economic regionality. Because of their contrasting structures, the Rappen coinage league, embracing the Breisgau and Upper Alsace, is treated in detail, with only passing reference to the Strasbourg coinage area. The reason is that the latter was dominated by one city, whereas the former rested on a balance between princely and urban interests, so that the Rappen league affords a better insight into the extent of regional economic solidarity. This in turn suggests that regional economic identity may take more than one form: a looser region encompassing the southern Upper Rhine as a whole, and two smaller, more tightly drawn regions, broadly corresponding to the hinterlands of Basel and Strasbourg.

The concluding section draws these strands of analysis together to argue that a regional economic identity on the Upper Rhine cannot be divorced from political and institutional imperatives. The rise of the Upper Rhine as an economic region was succeeded by a fall, as princely territorial consolidation along early absolutist and mercantilist lines began to cut across natural regional affinities. A final chapter then sets the economic history of the Upper Rhine in the fifteenth and sixteenth centuries in the wider context of European economic development. Given the recent emphasis on regional models of explanation for decisive economic transformation towards capitalism from a base of commercialized agriculture and domestic industries, it enquires why the Upper Rhine, despite its favourable economic endowment and commercially strategic location, failed to accomplish that transition. By drawing comparisons with other regions which seemed to fulfil the preconditions for a secular shift towards capitalism, in particular the northern Low Countries and Sicily, the chapter suggests that the Upper Rhine was the victim both of institutional constraints and of underlying structural weaknesses, which the apparent vitality of its regional economy was in the long run unable to conceal.

This study, in sum, lays three claims upon the reader's attention. First, in seeking consciously to write regional economic history, it draws upon interdisciplinary approaches from historical and economic geography. That is particularly the case with theories of location, where the fundamental insights of Christaller, Carol A. Smith, and Hohenberg and Lees are critically applied. Second, it insists that economic identity and change cannot be understood without reference to the social, political, and institutional framework within which they unfolded. A regional economic approach, therefore, requires that politics and power-relations be put back into economics. More generally, any analysis of what constitutes an economic region or regional economic identity must be willing to entertain the possibility that these are not fixed but mutable, subject both to varying perceptions of economic need and to the dictates of wider social and political co-ordinates. And third, the empirical findings for the Upper Rhine are deployed to address the broader question of economic transformation in early modern Europe, by means of a dialogue with the most significant modern research on economic regionality, above all the work of Jan de Vries on the northern Netherlands, and Stephan Epstein on Sicily. Although no new theoretical synthesis is advanced, the study argues that ultimately institutional constraints could never be overridden by natural endowment and strategic location alone. Yet the failure of the Upper Rhine as an economic region to act as an engine of secular economic transformation should not simply be attributed to endogenous structural shortcomings. The wider market, the developing early capitalist world economy, passed the Upper Rhine by because the very feature which had once encouraged the crystallization of regional economic identity in the later Middle Ages—the diffusion of political and economic authority between a multiplicity of centres—in the long run consigned it to the periphery of the nascent early modern states and so prevented it from becoming the core of an emergent national economy.

# PART I

*Regional Identity on the Upper Rhine*

# I

# Regions and Frontiers

## I

In his description of the twelve climes of the globe, drawn from the astrological vision of the pseudepigraphical book of Enoch, the anonymous author of the *Booklet of One Hundred Chapters*, known as the Revolutionary of the Upper Rhine, writing in the decade after 1500, waxed lyrical about the eighth clime:

Further let it be understood that of all climes there is none so prolific in towns and people than the eighth, that is the fairest Alsace, with every-thing aplenty for man to live. The soil is golden. If one washes the soil in the Rhine, one finds in it the best gold. The mountains around Alsace are full of silver and precious stones; many towns and castles filled with valiant people; beautiful fruit, good wine and corn, meat and fish.[1]

The author of this remarkable reforming treatise, himself a native of the Upper Rhine, praised Alsace, which in his diction describes the entire valley of the Upper Rhine from Bingen to Basel,[2] as an 'earthly paradise', and it formed the core of his visionary renewal of the Empire as a whole inspired by late medieval reforming bib-licism.[3] For the 'rosegarden' of Alsace (that is, the Upper Rhine), notwithstanding its bounteous endowment, was overrun with lords ecclesiastical and secular who oppressed the common folk.[4] The author of this treatise—in all likelihood Mathias Wurm von Geuder-theim, burgher of Strasbourg and erstwhile councillor of emperor Maximilian[5]—had every reason to know of what he wrote, for he

[1] Annelore Franke and Gerhard Zschäbitz (eds.), *Das Buch der hundert Kapitel und der vierzig Statuten des sogenannten Oberrheinischen Revolutionärs* (Leipziger Übersetzungen und Abhandlungen zum Mittelalter, A 4) (Berlin, 1967), 229.

[2] Cf. ibid. 186, 220, 226, 246, 289, 370, 512.

[3] Klaus H. Lauterbach, *Geschichtsverständnis, Zeitdidaxe und Reformgedanke an der Wende zum sechzehnten Jahrhundert: Das oberrheinische 'Buchli der hundert Capiteln' im Kontext des spätmittelalterlichen Reformbiblizismus* (Forschungen zur oberrheinischen Landesgeschichte, 33) (Freiburg im Breisgau/Munich, 1985), ch. 3.

[4] Franke and Zschäbitz, *Buch der hundert Kapitel*, 229, 245.

[5] Lauterbach, *Geschichtsverständnis*, 284–98; idem, 'Der "Oberrheinische Revolutionär" und Mathias Wurm von Geudertheim: Neue Untersuchungen zur Verfasser-frage', *Deutsches Archiv für Erforschung des Mittelalters*, 45 (1989), 109–72.

had traversed the district collecting the Common Penny from the imperial Estates in 1495;[6] nevertheless, his panegyric stands four-square in a tradition of hyperbole which had praised the Upper Rhine as a land flowing with milk and honey from the time of the Strasbourg chronicler Jakob Twinger von Königshofen (1346–1420)[7] back to writers of the Carolingian age.[8]

This picture of the Upper Rhine suggests a landscape both self-contained (protected by mountain ranges as natural frontiers) and economically self-sufficient (sustained by the variety of its natural resources). For the southern half of the Upper Rhine with which this study is primarily concerned—Upper and Lower Alsace on the left bank, the Breisgau and Ortenau on the right—this impression is at first glance reasonably accurate: a broad alluvial plain flanked by the Vosges and the Black Forest mountains, both rich in minerals, might well appear to constitute a natural region with abundant resources. But it is quite misleading for the much more open area of the northern Upper Rhine, beyond the rivers Lauter and Murg, where the mountains give way to the rolling uplands of the Palatinate and the Kraichgau, neither blessed with minerals of any note, before the valley broadens into a delta at the confluence of the Main. Modern geographers, indeed, in their search for scholarly precision, classify the Upper Rhine into much smaller divisions, whose topography, geology, and flora are genuinely homogeneous. This *naturräumliche Gliederung*, as it is called in German (there is no satisfactory English equivalent, though 'natural-topographical divisions' comes closest), distinguishes three successive stages of the river plain between Basel and Mainz, together with a similar number of mountain zones; the boundaries of the latter, however, by no means neatly coincide with those on the valley floor.[9]

---

[6] *Deutsche Reichstagsakten*, middle series, 5: *Wormser Reichstag 1495*, i. 2, ed. Heinz Angermeier (Göttingen, 1981), 1218–22 (no. 1663); Lauterbach, *Geschichtsverständnis*, 293; idem, ' "Oberrheinischer Revolutionär" ', 152.

[7] Ibid. 119. Cf. also Graf, 'Aspekte zum Regionalismus', 182.

[8] Heinrich Büttner, 'Geschichte des Elsaß I', in idem, *Geschichte des Elsaß I: Politische Geschichte des Landes von der Landnahmezeit bis zum Tode Ottos III.*, and *Ausgewählte Beiträge zur Geschichte des Elsaß in Früh- und Hochmittelalter*, ed. Traute Endemann (Sigmaringen, 1991), 120–21.

[9] On the *naturräumliche Gliederung* of the Upper Rhine cf. 'Karte der naturräumlichen Gliederung von Baden-Württemberg', in *Historischer Atlas von Baden-Württemberg*, map II. 4, and its accompanying *Beiwort* by Friedrich Huttenlocher (Stuttgart, 1972).

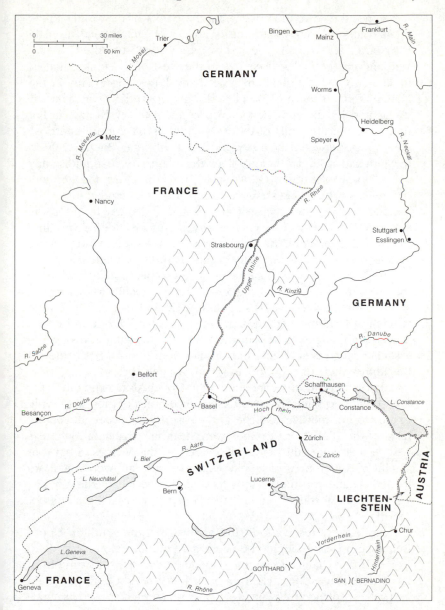

MAP 1. The Upper Rhine in its European context

It is not the case, moreover, that the banks of the Upper Rhine on its southern stretches are mirror images of each other. The plain is by no means equally bisected by the river. Most of the rich alluvial land on the valley floor lies to the west of the Rhine, that is, in Alsace. On the right bank, the Black Forest mountains in the Markgräflerland north of Basel push right up to the river, which is dominated by the Jurassic outcrop of the Isteiner Klotz. Further north, the volcanic hills of the Kaiserstuhl and Tuniberg interpose themselves between the river and the Freiburger Bucht. Only in the Ortenau (Middle Baden) does the plain stretch equidistantly either side of the river. Geologically, too, there are some salient differences. The Vosges are predominantly red sandstone of the Triassic period; older rocks of granite and gneiss are found in the south, with palaeozoic layers as the mountains fold down into the Burgundian Gate. The Black Forest, on the other hand, is more variegated. Red sandstone only occurs on the Enz heights and their eastern escarpment, together with a few other pockets, whereas the proportion of granite and gneiss increases steadily as one moves south, until it gives way to tertiary rock and Triassic limestone where the *Hochrhein* (the Rhine between Schaffhausen and Basel) turns at right-angles to flow northwards.[10] By the same token, while a similar range of mineral deposits can be found on both sides of the Rhine, their distribution is far from even. Precious and base metal ores were mostly concentrated in Upper Alsace and the Black Forest, with no mines of any consequence north of the Val de Villé in the west or the river Bleiche in the east. By the sixteenth century most of the Black Forest mines were nearing exhaustion, whereas new seams were still being discovered in the Vosges. Small but significant differences of climate and exposure allowed viticulture to thrive better on the eastern foothills in the lee of the Vosges, with a modest annual rainfall, than on the west-facing slopes of the Black Forest.

Despite these reservations, the premiss that the southern Upper Rhine can in some degree be seen as a natural region alerts us to its secondary character as an economic landscape, subsisting from its own resources. Because it embraced as a region both mountain and valley, upland and plain, the Upper Rhine predisposed its agrarian economy to diversification based on the exchange of produce

---

[10] Friedrich Metz, *Die Oberrheinlande* (Wrocław, 1925), 32 (map).

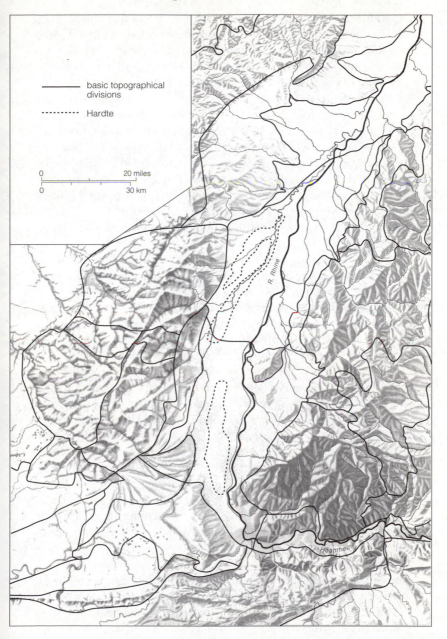

MAP 2. Natural-topographical divisions

and goods within its varying landscapes. Even the valley floor itself was not uniform: it encompassed both wetlands (*Riede*, *Aue*) along the Rhine and its tributaries, and heathlands (*Hardte*) on sand- or gravel-banks left dry as the rivers receded. The wetlands provided a living for fishers, basket-makers, and especially hemp-workers; cattle grazed on the water-meadows, and pigs rootled for beechmast in the forests which also provided hunters with game and wild-fowl. The heaths, too, were extensively wooded (as modern place-names containing the word *hart* demonstrate), but also offered grazing for sheep, whose wool supplied the local textile industry. On the alluvial soils a variety of crops was grown; grain was the staple, be it wheat and rye for bread, oats for bran, or barley for brewing, but in addition industrial crops were planted, such as the red dye-plant madder, widely found in Lower Alsace. Along the foothills of the Vosges and Black Forest orchards and vineyards were strung out, often curling round into the lower reaches of the side-valleys or spilling over on to the plain. Beyond the foothills lay the moister valleys cutting into the mountains, which were largely given over to dairying and cheese-making; on the heights alpine meadows provided pastures for fattening livestock in the summer months. And in the remoter valleys deposits of silver, copper, lead, and iron ore lay waiting to be mined. The picture painted by the Revolutionary of the Upper Rhine seems entirely vindicated. But the Upper Rhine as an economic landscape did not prosper on account of the intensity of regional exchange alone. Because it straddled the major artery of trade in northern Europe, the Upper Rhine as a region lay at the crossroads of commercial traffic which carried its products far beyond the region, even overseas. However diversified its internal economy might be, the efflorescence of the Upper Rhine, one of the most densely urbanized areas of medieval Germany, depended on trade which linked its towns and cities in an urban network stretching downriver to Frankfurt and Cologne, upriver to Switzerland and across the Alps, and over the mountains to both east and west.

These brief observations underscore just how elusive the concept of a 'natural' region as a self-contained entity can be. We must therefore explore in greater detail the configuration of the southern Upper Rhine to discover whether mountain ranges or the river itself acted as barriers or clasps, frontiers or crossing-points.

# II

Jean-Jacques Rousseau, inspired by the precepts of the Enlightenment, believed that political frontiers were in part a work of nature: rivers and mountains could serve as peaceful dividing lines between nations.[11] Rousseau, of course, was writing before the French Revolution and the age of popular nationalism which it unleashed. In our own times, after more than a century of political rivalry during which France and Germany have wrestled for hegemony on the Upper Rhine, the existence of natural frontiers, let alone their capacity to bestow peace, can only arouse the deepest scepticism. Instead, we should ask whether frontiers can be defined satisfactorily at all. Modern political geographers, for their part, are accustomed to distinguish between frontiers and boundaries. The latter, as the etymology implies, mark off territories from each other, whereas the former denote zones, not of separation, but of contact.[12] Boundaries, or borders, can be drawn on maps; frontiers constitute zones of transition between cultural areas—homelands, *pays, Landschaften.* For Europe in the fifteenth and sixteenth centuries, when state formation, the creation of consolidated territories or national monarchies, was underway but far from complete, frontiers better express the imprecise limits of feudal rights and partial jurisdictions than do boundaries which can be plotted areally or spatially as surface measurements (*flächenmäßig*).[13]

This distinction is relevant to any consideration of whether mountains and rivers represented natural dividing lines on the Upper Rhine. At first glance, the Vosges massif to the west does seem to present a formidable obstacle to passage. The peaks fall away sharply to the east into a string of narrow valleys which cut deep furrows

[11] Cf. Hans Conrad Peyer, 'Gewässer und Grenzen in der Schweizergeschichte', in idem, *Gewässer, Grenzen und Märkte in der Schweizergeschichte* (Mitteilungen der Antiquarischen Gesellschaft in Zürich, 48, 3 (= 143. Neujahrsblatt)) (Zürich, 1979), 5.

[12] P. J. Taylor, *Political geography: World-economy, nation state and locality,* 2nd edn. (London, 1989), 145.

[13] In the Enlightenment French thinkers rejected what they saw as a medieval notion of frontiers for the very reason that they were zones rather than exact delimitations. Cf. Odile Kammerer, 'Le Haut-Rhin entre Bâle et Strasbourg: A-t-il été une frontière mediévale?', in *Les Pays de l'entre-deux au Moyen Age; Questions d'histoire des territoires d'Empire entre Meuse, Rhône et Rhin* (Actes du 113e Congrès National des Sociétés Savantes (Strasbourg, 1988), Section d'histoire mediévale et de philologie) (Paris, 1990), 172.

in the landscape. The crest of the range marks a clear watershed between the streams flowing down to the Rhine on the one hand, and the headwaters of the Meurthe and Moselle on the other; today it still constitutes for much of its length the boundary between the *départements* of the Vosges to the west, and the Haut-Rhin and Bas-Rhin 'to the east. But the history of medieval colonization and lordship quickly gives the lie to this simple division. After the millennium several powerful Lorraine abbeys—Remiremont, St-Dié, Moyenmoutier, Senones, and Étival—acquired extensive estates and revenues on the sheltered slopes of the eastern Vosges down to the banks of the river Ill, which furnished them with produce, above all wine, from the fertile basin.[14] By contrast, Alsatian convents, though to a lesser degree, held land in Lorraine and the Franche-Comté, the most notable being the imperial abbey of Murbach with its sister-house of Lure (in German, Lüders) between Belfort and Vesoul.[15] Alsatian peasants, too, had even earlier moved westwards into Lorraine. The dairy-farmers of the Munster valley west of Colmar, who were accustomed to driving their beasts on to the high alpine pastures above the river Fecht, pressed on over the watershed to the uplands of Lorraine, where they cleared the less densely afforested western slopes in order to establish vaccaries or shielings for summer grazing, and even byres for overwintering their cattle.[16] Some Alemannic herders and fishers even established a permanent colony in the Moselotte valley at the village of Woll (now the French town of La Bresse).[17]

This may be no more than an isolated instance of germanophone settlement west of the Vosges, but the complacent view of an older generation of German human geographers, that the crest marked

[14] Hans-Walter Hermann, 'Territoriale Verbindungen und Verflechtungen zwischen dem oberrheinischen und lothringischen Raum im Spätmittelalter', *Jahrbuch für westdeutsche Landesgeschichte*, 1 (1975), 132–37.

[15] Odile Kammerer, 'Le Carrefour alsacien-lorrain dans le grand commerce des XVe et XVIe siècles', in Jean-Marie Cauchies (ed.), *Aspects de la vie économique des pays bourguignons (1384–1559): Dépression ou prospérité?* (Publication du Centre Européen d'Études Bourguignonnes (XIVe–XVIe s.), 27: Rencontres de Douai (25 au 28 septembre 1986)) (Basel, 1987), 85 n. 14.

[16] Büttner, 'Geschichte des Elsaß I', 72; Francis Rapp, 'Routes et voies de communication à travers les Vosges du XIIe au début du XVIe siècle', in *Les Pays de l'entre-deux*, 203; Albert Fischer, 'Die Verdrängung der Münstertäler Melker von den herzoglich-lothringischen Hochweiden am Ende des 16. Jahrhunderts', *Annuaire de la Société d'Histoire du Val et de la Ville de Munster*, 45 (1991), 11. Cf. Karl Kiesel, *Petershüttly: Ein Friedensziel in den Vogesen* (Berlin, 1918), esp. plate 1.

[17] Rapp, 'Routes et voies', 203; Fischer, 'Verdrängung', 11.

a linguistic and ethnic frontier, is open to a more fundamental objection.[18] The colonizing activity of Alsatian convents—Masevaux, St-Amarin, Murbach, and Munster—may have ensured that the limit of German culture extended up the valleys to the watershed in the southern Vosges, but further north, where monastic influence was weak or absent, Romance culture spread eastwards over the crest down the Val d'Orbey to Lapoutroie, into the valley of the Liepvrette, and the upper reaches of the Val de Villé as far as Colroy-la-Roche, and then down the left bank of the Bruche.[19]

Moreover, along their length the Vosges were cut through by numerous passes. Some were little more than defiles, only negotiable on foot or by pack-animals, but others, traversable by carts, carried regional and international trade between the Upper Rhine and Lorraine[20]—the col de Bussang which linked Basel via Thann to the headwaters of the Moselle; the col de Bonhomme, on the route from Colmar via Kaysersberg to the headwaters of the Meurthe; and the col de Saales, from the valley of the Bruche to Raon l'Étape or St-Dié, both important transport routes for salt from the mines of Lorraine to the Upper Rhine; and, broadest of all, the ascent at Saverne (the *Zaberner Steige*), the main highway from Strasbourg to Nancy and Metz. Even in winter the flow of traffic over these passes was not staunched, as the customs rolls of Kaysersberg and Raon l'Étape attest.[21] Towns on both banks of the Rhine became, in Odile Kammerer's phrase, 'economic accomplices' of Épinal, St-Dié, Lunéville, and St-Nicolas-de-Port in Lorraine, for 'Ces montagnes à vaches, surtout le versant lorrain, loin d'être une frontière, représentaient avant le XVIe siècle une véritable colonne vertébrale pour la région mosello-rhénane.'[22] This interpretation echoes the much older argument of Tourneur-Aumont, who stated that 'les Vosges ne sont pas une ligne limite. Elles sont une région

[18] Friedrich Metz, 'Der Südwesten', in idem, *Land und Leute: Gesammelte Beiträge zur deutschen Landes- und Volksforschung* (Stuttgart, 1961), 159.

[19] Büttner, 'Geschichte des Elsaß I', 91; Kammerer, 'Carrefour', 92. What was spoken was not high French but a French-Lorraine dialect. Friedrich Metz, 'Die vorderösterreichischen Lande', in idem, *Land und Leute*, 172. Of course, German had always been the language of northern Lorraine, but there the Vosges no longer constituted a natural barrier.

[20] Especially after the opening of the St Gotthard pass in the early 13th century, though even then neither Alsace nor the Vosges offered necessary transit routes between Italy and Flanders; much trade still passed through Burgundy and Champagne. Rapp, 'Routes et voies', 195.     [21] Kammerer, 'Carrefour', 85.

[22] Ibid. 84.

naturelle',[23] acting 'non comme un monde étranger, comme une barrière, répulsive, mais comme une partie vivante'.[24] Tourneur-Aumont, however, infected by a nationalist strain no less virulent than those of his German counterparts, had gone on to conclude that 'Les Vosges favorisent le retour dans la plaine. Il y a entre la montagne et la plaine une intimité. Le Rhin n'y participe pas. La plaine est plus vosgienne que rhénane',[25] a view understandable in the aftermath of World War I, but otherwise difficult to sustain. Nevertheless, the commercial destinies of Alsace and Lorraine had been inextricably linked throughout the Middle Ages; only in the sixteenth century did they divaricate, as the Habsburg–Valois struggle transformed the Vosges from an economic spine to an arena of political and military conflict.[26]

Even less do the mountains of the Black Forest resemble natural frontiers. Unlike the Vosges, the crest of the Black Forest was not a major watershed; only for a short distance in the Ortenau between the Kniebis pass and the summit of the Hornisgrinde do watershed and crest coincide, and even then they divide, not two separate river systems, but the Rhine and its tributary, the Murg.[27] In any case, in the crowded mountain area which formed the hinterland of Danube, Rhine, and Neckar the watershed underwent considerable geological shifts over the space of millennia. Moreover, on the eastern fringes of the Black Forest—just as happened in the Vosges—convents cleared and settled the densely wooded slopes to the west, while new monasteries were founded across the heights—St Peter in the Dreisam valley above Freiburg, translated from Weilheim unter Teck in Württemberg in 1092,[28] and its neighbour, St Märgen, founded around the same time by Bruno, a canon of Strasbourg cathedral, from the Swabian comital family of Zollern-Haigerloch.[29] For its part, the great Benedictine abbey

---

[23] J. M. Tourneur-Aumont, 'L'Alsace et l'Alemanie: Origine et place de la tradition germanique dans la civilisation alsacienne (Études de géographie historique)', *Annales de l'Est*, 33 (1919), 74. [24] Ibid. 153.

[25] Ibid. 75–76. On the ideologically tainted historiography of the Upper Rhine (to which Lucien Febvre was a shining exception) see now Peter Schöttler, 'The Rhine as an object of historical controversy in the inter-war years: Towards a history of frontier mentalities', *History Workshop Journal*, 39 (1995), 1–21.

[26] Kammerer, 'Carrefour', 91.

[27] Friedrich Metz, *Ländergrenzen im Südwesten* (Forschungen zur deutschen Landeskunde, 60) (Remagen, 1951); idem, 'Die Grenzen im Schwarzwald', in idem, *Land und Leute*, 900. [28] Idem, *Ländergrenzen*, 76.

[29] Wolfgang Müller, 'Studien zur Geschichte der Klöster St. Märgen und Allerheiligen, Freiburg i. Br.', *Freiburger Diözesan-Archiv*, 89 (1969), 13–14.

of St Gallen in eastern Switzerland (to take only the best-known example) received donations of vineyards on the slopes of the Batzenberg, south of Freiburg, where it became a substantial land-owner. In linguistic terms, the peaks of the Black Forest from north to south do mark an approximate boundary between the Swabian and Alemannic dialects, but within the Alemannic region itself dialect variations sometimes follow a west–east axis athwart the mountain range, in particular the line separating Lower from Upper (Swiss) Alemannic, which runs from the Breisgau on a rough latitude to the district above Lake Constance.[30]

Because the Black Forest mountains form a crest less clearly than the Vosges, traffic crossing the heights was less dependent upon certain strategic passes. Only the Kniebis pass at the headwaters of the Rench, linking Oberkirch and Oppenau in the Ortenau with Freudenstadt and the tributaries of the Neckar, marks a significant dividing-point. Elsewhere, merchants could pass easily into Swabia and beyond from Strasbourg via Offenburg and Gengenbach up the river Kinzig to Schramberg and Rottweil, a valley once explicitly described as a 'bridging territory' (*Brückenlandschaft*) between the Rhineland and the Swabian plateau.[31] To the north, the Murg penetrated far into the uplands linking dispersed communities to an important artery of trade, as its boatmen, organized into a local rafting association, carried large quantities of timber downstream to the Rhine and markets beyond. To the south, moreover, Freiburg's and Villingen's control of the Wagensteig and Höllental passes was constantly under threat: at various stages the peasants of the Simonswald, the Prech, and the Glotter valleys built tracks across the Forest which competed with the urban turnpikes.[32]

If the Upper Rhine cannot thus be seen as bounded by its most visible frontiers to west and east, its limits to the south and north are even less precise. From Basel upriver to Schaffhausen the Rhine

[30] Bruno Boesch, 'Der alemannische Sprachraum im Bereich des heutigen Baden-Württemberg: Ein geschichtlicher Überblick', in Günther Haselier, Eberhard Gönner, Meinrad Schaab, and Robert Uhland (eds.), *Bausteine zur geschichtlichen Landeskunde von Baden-Württemberg* (Stuttgart, 1979), 79, 81 (maps); Metz, *Ländergrenzen*, map 50, app. 1 (*Kind/Chind*); Norbert Ohler, *Von Grenzen und Herrschaften: Grundzüge territorialer Entwicklung im deutschen Südwesten* (Themen der Landeskunde: Veröffentlichungen aus dem Alemannischen Institut Freiburg im Breisgau, 4) (Bühl, 1989), 18.

[31] Friedrich Metz, 'Das Kinziggebiet als Brückenlandschaft', in idem, *Land und Leute*, 896–99.

[32] Tom Scott, *Freiburg and the Breisgau: Town–country relations in the age of Reformation and Peasants' War* (Oxford, 1986), 102–5.

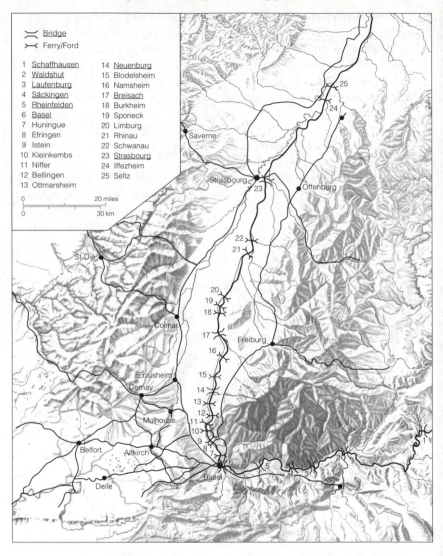

Bridge
Ferry/Ford

| | | | |
|---|---|---|---|
| 1 | Schaffhausen | 14 | Neuenburg |
| 2 | Waldshut | 15 | Blodelsheim |
| 3 | Laufenburg | 16 | Namsheim |
| 4 | Säckingen | 17 | Breisach |
| 5 | Rheinfelden | 18 | Burkheim |
| 6 | Basel | 19 | Sponeck |
| 7 | Huningue | 20 | Limburg |
| 8 | Efringen | 21 | Rhinau |
| 9 | Istein | 22 | Schwanau |
| 10 | Kleinkembs | 23 | Strasbourg |
| 11 | Niffer | 24 | Iffezheim |
| 12 | Bellingen | 25 | Seltz |
| 13 | Ottmarsheim | | |

0            20 miles

0            30 km

MAP 3. Crossing-points and mountain passes on the Upper Rhine

is called in German the *Hochrhein*, to distinguish it from the Upper Rhine proper, which begins at the 'knee of the Rhine', the abrupt right-angle turn to the north which the river takes at Basel. The medieval sources, however, often take the Upper Rhine to stretch as far as the Hauenstein outcrop above Laufenburg, a notable landscape feature halfway to Schaffhausen. That not only marked the south-eastern corner of the Breisgau, but roughly corresponds to the *naturräumliche Gliederung* as well, which follows the line of the river Aare to the south and the boundary of the eastern Black Forest along the river Alb to the north. South of the river, the Jura massif dominates the left bank of the *Hochrhein*, whose deeply cleft valleys of the Birs, Ergolz, and Frick offer no easy passage into inner Switzerland: most trade was carried on the river network of Limmat, Reuss, and Aare, which joined the Rhine further upstream at Koblenz (Aargau). South of Basel, the peak of the Blauen traditionally marked the southern limit of Alsace, while to the west the northern slopes of the Ferrette Jura still broadly speaking trace the modern boundary between France and Switzerland.

Yet the character of the Ferrette Jura as a natural frontier is by no means self-evident. For here the Jura mountains appear on the map as a series of folds running east to west, rather than as a single bold relief. By their course, the rivers Allaine and Lucelle/Lützel defy any simple equation of watershed and crest, while the linguistic frontier between German and French rides roughshod over the horizontal ranges from north to south, on a line from Ferrette (Pfirt) to Delémont (Delsberg) and Moutier (Münster). This helps to explain why the Ajoie (Elsgau), the area south-west of Basel running down to the loop of the river Doubs at St-Ursanne (St Ursitz), which in this period formed the secular territory of the bishops of Basel, was once regarded as the southernmost *Gau* (the ancient Germanic tribal division) of Alsace itself, from which the counties of Ferrette, Montbéliard, and Belfort—the francophone districts spanning the Sundgau and Franche-Comté—later became detached.[33]

---

[33] Otto Stolz, *Geschichtliche Beschreibung der ober- und vorderösterreichischen Lande* (Quellen und Forschungen zur Siedlungs- und Volkstumsgeschichte der Oberrheinlande, 40) (Karlsruhe, 1943), 99, and n. 1. A series of villages around Ferrette in Upper Alsace to the north of the Franco-Swiss frontier and the present-day Ajoie historically formed part of the latter: Bendorf, Bisel, Durlinsdorf, Koestlach, Liebsdorf, Ligsdorf, Levoncourt, Moernach, Mooslargue, Seppois-le-Bas, Oberlarg, Seppois-le-Haut, Ottendorf, Pfetterhouse, Sondersdorf, and Winkel. Ministerium für Elsaß-Lothringen, Statistisches Bureau (ed.), *Das Reichsland Elsaß-Lothringen:*

Further south, however, down through the cantons of Neuchâtel and Vaud, the Jura mountains do indeed present a forbidding barrier which marks the boundary between western Switzerland and the Franche-Comté. But even this frontier was not what it appeared: over the centuries it shifted, and never fully coincided with the crest of the Jura. As Suzanne Daveau has observed,

Tantôt le Haut Jura apparaît comme une frontière, tantôt il ne semble opposer nul obstacle aux acquisitions et aux unions politiques . . . Il n'a peut-être pas été une frontière beaucoup plus étanche quand il n'était un desert que lorsque les défrichements eurent à peu prés supprimé l'obstacle qu'il représentait et eurent fait naître des nouvelles puissances centrées dans la montagne . . .[34]

Gradually this empty landscape was penetrated by human settlement and political authority, but it remains to this day a terrain of forests and summer pastures, with the frontier almost invisible to walkers, except further north where it follows the course of the river Doubs.[35]

The Jura massif and the southern foothills of the Vosges are spanned by the Burgundian Gate, known more commonly in English as the Belfort Gap. Both terms, 'gate' and 'gap', suggest a clearly visible divide, a wall pierced by a narrow entrance, yet nothing could be further from the truth. In one regard, the Belfort Gap did indeed mark a boundary of European significance, for it lay just west of the watershed between the Rhine and the Rhône, and thus between Romance and Germanic culture, the Mediterranean and northern worlds. Any traveller passing from Alsace to Burgundy, however, would be hard put to discern any features of the landscape immediately indicative of a natural frontier. The modern Canal du Rhône au Rhin cuts through the Col de Valdieu, but this is hardly more than a low saddle in otherwise gently undulating terrain. In his geographical account of the Burgundian Gate, published in 1930, André Gibert reproduces a photograph of the landscape between Magny and Valdieu which to the untrained

---

*Landes- und Ortsbeschreibung*, 3 (Strasbourg, 1903), 259. They were all German-speaking into the 17th century.

[34] Suzanne Daveau, *Les Régions frontalières de la montagne jurassienne: Étude de géographie humaine* (Institut des Études Rhodaniennes de l'Université de Lyon: Mémoires et Documents, 14) (Lyon, 1959), 85.          [35] Ibid. 94.

eye appears as pure champaign, broken only by a belt of forest.[36] Here the frontier was in truth not a line but a zone; it remains even today a sparsely populated and extensively wooded area with numerous ponds and marshes.[37] As one might expect in a transitional zone with no obvious natural obstacles, the linguistic frontier showed gains and losses over the centuries, with the germanophone district of the southern Sundgau extending somewhat further westwards until the French acquisition of Alsace in the seventeenth century.[38] Modern place-names, therefore, are no reliable guide to the language of the inhabitants in the sixteenth century. Some communities were certainly bilingual: the official records of Delle (Tattenried) and Florimont (Blumenberg), for instance, two small towns on the southern fringes of the Sundgau, were kept in German (not least because their overlords were German), but a dialect of French may well have been the everyday tongue of their citizens. In one physical respect, none the less, it has been argued that the modern cultural frontier can be identified by the shift in building styles. Around the watershed the gable-ended half-timbered houses of the Sundgau give way to stone-built dwellings facing the road, characteristic of francophone Burgundy.[39] However valid this distinction, it can only be applied with caution to the sixteenth century.

To the north, the Upper Rhine in its full extent stretches as far as Mainz, but the limits of its southern half (with which we are alone concerned in the present study) are by no means straightforward. On the right bank of the river, the tributaries of the Oos and the Murg do mark a natural-topographical division between the Ortenau and the Kraichgau, as the Black Forest mountains begin to flatten into the rolling uplands of the Kraichgau. But both on the valley floor and on the heights the division seems more arbitrary—more the result of human settlement than geographical circumstance. On the left bank, by contrast, matters are at once simpler and more complex. The river Lauter forms the northern boundary of Lower Alsace from Lauterbourg to Wissembourg, and

---

[36] André Gibert, *La Porte de Bourgogne et d'Alsace (Trouée de Belfort): Étude géographique* (Paris, 1930), plate 3 A.

[37] Friedrich Metz, 'Die burgundische Pforte', in idem, *Land und Leute*, 329.

[38] Gibert, *Porte de Bourgogne*, 242–43, and fig. 50; Ohler, *Von Grenzen und Herrschaften*, 19 (map).

[39] Metz, 'Die vorderösterreichischen Lande', 170; idem, 'Die burgundische Pforte', 328.

still constitutes part of the modern political frontier between France and Germany west of the Rhine. But thereafter the Lauter bends north-westwards while the frontier continues on the same latitude due west over the mountain ranges towards Bitche in Lorraine, thereby bisecting the vast Haardt Forest, which today is separated into the forest of the northern Vosges (in France) and the Pfälzerwald (in Germany), the latter blanketing the whole of the southern Palatinate as far as Kaiserslautern. No wonder the linguistic frontier ceases to run northwards; instead, it deflects sharply westwards to include Lorraine, for unity, not diversity, sets its imprint on this landscape.

Even in the valley of the Rhine itself there is uncertainty in identifying features of the landscape which might historically have formed a natural frontier. Although the river Lauter forms the modern boundary, medieval sources frequently mention either the Seltzbach, 10 kilometres to the south, flowing from the hills above Soultz-sous-Forêts to the Rhine at Seltz, because it flanks the northern edge of the Forest of Haguenau, or even the river Sauer which both skirts and bisects it. On occasion they refer to the Forest itself, a belt of dense woodland straddling the highways north of the town of Haguenau, which was difficult to traverse and home to brigands and outcasts. Precisely because of its dangerous and impassable character the Forest was taken loosely to describe the northern limit of Alsace. Between it and the Lauter, therefore, lay something of a no man's land, remote from the centres of early settlement, for which only recently a name has been found—l'Outre-Forêt—a French coinage with no German equivalent. In this no man's land neither rivers nor forest, therefore, marked clear boundaries: it was a classic marcher zone with ambiguous frontiers.[40]

# III

Having beaten the bounds of the southern Upper Rhine, we can no longer be confident that its frontiers were so absolute that they delimited a natural region. Did the course of the river itself, therefore, we must now enquire, serve as a barrier or clasp? Within the river system of southern Germany the Upper Rhine forms a bottle-

---

[40] Heinz Eggers, 'Der Grenzraum Nordelsaß-Südpfalz in Vergangenheit und Gegenwart', *Alemannisches Jahrbuch*, 1991/92, 42, 44–45 (map), 54.

neck between the European watersheds of the Rhône and Danube. Further upstream, the *Hochrhein* and alpine Rhine (*Vorder-* and *Hinterrhein*) are fed by a catchment area which embraces all of northern Switzerland. From this angle the Upper Rhine can be seen as a funnel through which the flow of goods and people from a wide hinterland was squeezed into a narrow channel. But an artery from south to north need not be incompatible with a boundary between east and west. Until the high Middle Ages the Upper Rhine indeed fulfilled that role. For the Romans, the Rhine from Remagen to Constance marked the border between the provinces of Germania Superior and Agri Decumates. And later, in the treaty of Verdun of 843, the Rhine was taken to separate the Frankish lands apportioned between Lothar and Louis the German. But even in the early Middle Ages the Upper Rhine can never have described an exact boundary, easy to survey and to control. For until the Rhine correction of the nineteenth century, begun by colonel Johann Gottfried Tulla, the river meandered between sandbanks and eyots; its side-channels extended over 5 kilometres, with so many inlets and branches that it was hard to know where the main channel lay.[41] Moreover, floods repeatedly altered its course. Only by the treaty of Lunéville in 1801 was the border between France and Germany fixed as the mid-point of the main channel (*Talweg*).[42] As a result of Tulla's feat of engineering, 70 kilometres were lopped off the Rhine's length between Basel and Mainz;[43] the water-table sank, so that many of the previous marshlands along its course were left as dry gravel-banks.

The river, in other words, offered no clear line of demarcation: it was a shifting frontier zone, in the words of Lucien Febvre 'une sorte de jungle en miniature avec ses fourrés fangeux, ses roseraies, ses îles, ses faux bras recourbés en anneaux',[44] and several communities flanking the Rhine once stood on the opposite bank to where they stand today. Breisach, the strategic fortress on the Rhine and outpost of the Breisgau had once lain in Alsace, when the river

---

[41] Peyer, 'Gewässer und Grenzen', 9; Kammerer, 'Haut-Rhin', 173–74.

[42] Peyer, 'Gewässer und Grenzen', 9. The treaty of Karlsruhe of 1840 subsequently defined the mid-point of the main channel: 'On nomme axe du thalweg la ligne de son cours qui est déterminée par la suite non interrompue des sondes les plus profondes.' Cf. Ohler, *Von Grenzen und Herrschaften*, 18.

[43] Metz, 'Südwesten', 155.

[44] Lucien Febvre, *La Terre et l'évolution humaine: Introduction géographique à l'histoire*, 2nd edn. (Paris, 1938 printing), 367.

curled round its eastern ramparts. By 1500 it was still described
by emperor Maximilian as his 'arsenal in Alsace', and the Sélestat
humanist Beatus Rhenanus pondered whether it belonged to the
left or the right bank of the Rhine.[45] The villages of Allmansweier
and Nonnenweier by Lahr had also once been situated on the left
bank, while further south Chalampé (opposite Neuenburg) and
Rosenau below Basel at one time stood on the right bank.[46] It comes
as no surprise, therefore, to find communities reaching across the
river to establish jurisdictional rights and territorial control on the
other side. One striking example is Neuenburg, which acquired
extensive common land for grazing on the maze of eyots and holms
on a stretch of the opposite bank from Ottmarsheim to Blodelsheim,
a distance of 10 kilometres. A long-running dispute over the usufruct of this common between the town and four Alsatian villages
broke out in 1471, and when a provisional settlement was finally
reached in 1517 Neuenburg claimed that it stood to lose around
2,800 hectares of water-meadow and woodland.[47] Another example
is Breisach, which in 1568 bought the village of Biesheim (an imperial mortgage) just across the river to add to its modest rural territory
on the right bank.[48]

In general, however, towns on the Rhine were more concerned
to establish bridgeheads in order to control the flow of commerce
at strategic crossing-points. This was the motive behind Basel's
acquisition of Kleinbasel,[49] which remains to this day an enclave of
Swiss territory on German soil. Where the river ran between steep
slopes rather than through an open plain, as on the *Hochrhein*,
its course was more predictable, so that bridges could be built
with greater confidence that they would not be swept away. That
encouraged Laufenburg to create a dependent settlement on the
north side of the river as a bridgehead to command the rapids
(*Laufen*) which gave the town its name. Another community
on the *Hochrhein*, Rheinfelden, was surrounded by the Austrian

---

[45] Dieter Mertens, 'Reich und Elsaß zur Zeit Maximilians I.: Untersuchungen
zur Ideen- und Landesgeschichte im Südwesten des Reiches am Ausgang des
Mittelalters' (Diss. habil. Freiburg im Breisgau, 1977), 161 and n. 5.

[46] Kammerer, 'Haut-Rhin', 75.

[47] StAFr, C 1 Fremde Orte: Neuenburg 18, nos. 6, 19, 22–29, 32, 41; the loss of
2,800 hectares (7,000 acres), ibid. no. 22, n.d. (1517).

[48] J. B. Ellerbach, *Der dreißigjährige Krieg im Elsaß. (1618–1648)*, i. *Vom Beginn
des Krieges bis zum Abzug Mansfelds. (1618–1622)* (Carspach, 1912), 35.

[49] Peyer, 'Gewässer und Grenzen', 10.

lordship of that name, whose territory in the southern Breisgau, known as the *Landschaft Rheintal*, shielded the town's access to the northern bank.[50]

It is indeed on the steep banks of the *Hochrhein* that the majority of medieval bridges were built. Sebastian Brant, the famous humanist and city syndic of his native Strasbourg, listed in his 'Chronicle of Germany' nine bridges between Constance and Basel alone: at Stein am Rhein, Diessenhofen, Schaffhausen, Eglisau, Kaiserstuhl, Laufenburg, Säckingen, Rheinfelden, and at Basel itself.[51] At Rheinfelden he referred explicitly to a 'stone bridge', that is, a bridge erected on stone piers and arches; its superstructure would have been built of timber and roofed over, as can still be seen in the magnificent bridge which survives at Säckingen. From Basel to Strasbourg, by contrast, on the low-lying banks of the Upper Rhine Brant mentions only two further bridges, at Breisach and at Strasbourg. If his account is taken at face value, it would be easy to regard the Upper Rhine, precisely because of its meandering course, as a veritable hindrance to cross-passage. But the truth is quite the contrary. There is good evidence that Neuenburg possessed not only a customs-post but a bridge as well. In 1471, the same year that its quarrel with the Alsatian villages began, the town council claimed compensation from Peter von Hagenbach, the governor of Outer Austria, then under Burgundian occupation, who, it alleged, had wilfully destroyed its bridge and the workshop next to it.[52] Neuenburg later mentioned having taken timber from the marshy woodlands to repair the damage. Further documents relating to the case make plain what was at stake. The council had dammed the river with a weir, 300 paces wide,[53] thereby channelling its course and presumably laying dry the waterlogged approaches. Over the main channel it had then flung a bridge —or, more likely, a series of pontoons from eyot to eyot. Floods

---

[50] Cf. Anton Senti, 'Die Herrschaften Rheinfelden und Laufenburg', in Friedrich Metz (ed.), *Vorderösterreich: Eine geschichtliche Landeskunde*, 2nd edn. (Freiburg im Breisgau, 1967), 405 (map), 429. The Strasbourg bridgehead in Kehl was not established until the 17th century.

[51] Herbert Krüger, 'Brücke, Fähre und Zoll im Rheinstromgebiet um 1500 (nach Sebastian Brants "Chronik über Teutsch land")', *Elsaß-Lothringisches Jahrbuch*, 21 (1943), 137. Later in the century Daniel Wintzenberger in his *Nuw Reyse Büchlein* (Leipzig, 1579) mentions a bridge at Waldshut. Kammerer, 'Haut-Rhin', 178 n. 14.

[52] StAFr, C 1 Fremde Orte: Neuenburg 18, no. 10, 21 Oct. 1471.

[53] Ibid. no. 22, n.d. (1517).

could easily sweep away, or fires destroy, such rough-and-ready bridges, but with equal speed they could be reinstated. The bridge at Breisach, for instance, first mentioned in 1283 (more than a century before Strasbourg's!)[54] was destroyed by a flood in 1302,[55] but subsequently repaired; at the end of the fifteenth century the council lamented the high cost of maintaining the bridge in good condition in time of war, when scores of soldiers rode over it with horses and artillery.[56]

Recently Odile Kammerer has suggested that more bridges may at one time have existed—possibly a (Roman) bridge at Istein, and another at Kleinkembs. But her essential point is that on the low-lying plain with marshlands bordering the river fords and ferries took the place of bridges. From Basel to Strasbourg she has identified eighteen such crossing-points, and believes that there may well have been more.[57] Below Strasbourg further crossings were possible at Lichtenau, Iffezheim, Seltz, and Lauterbourg, all of which, according to Sebastian Brant, had ferries.[58] Far from being an obstacle, therefore, the river was a zone of constant interchange;[59] it marked no divide in settlement or language, not even in the variants of Alemannic dialect.[60]

It is a modern misconception to imagine that existing political boundaries on the Upper Rhine have their roots in medieval frontiers. The river was yet another marcher zone, where lordship extended over both banks. That is particularly evident in the case of the medieval dioceses on the Upper Rhine: Strasbourg, Speyer, Worms, and above all Mainz, straddled the river and so, at times, did their secular territories—the bishop of Strasbourg, for example, was overlord of much of the southern Ortenau. Only the sees of Basel and Constance were separated by the Rhine, and even then only as far as the confluence of the Aare with the *Hochrhein*.

---

[54] Kammerer, 'Haut-Rhin', 176. The bridge at Strasbourg, first unambiguously attested in 1388, probably superseded earlier, more makeshift constructions.

[55] Krüger, 'Brücke, Fähre und Zoll', 141.

[56] StAFr, L (Deposita) 1: StABr, Akten no. 916, n.d. (late 15th c.), fo. 1ᵛ.

[57] Kammerer, 'Haut-Rhin', 175–76.

[58] Krüger, 'Brücke, Fähre und Zoll', after 128 (map).

[59] This modifies the view expressed by a leading modern French geographer that 'the easily flooded Rhine plain, the Ried, still marshy and wooded until relatively late, constituted a frontier not easily crossed'. Cf. Xavier de Planhol, with Paul Claval, *An historical geography of France* (Cambridge Studies in Historical Geography, 21) (Cambridge/Paris, 1994), 173.

[60] Friedrich Metz, 'Der Oberrhein als Grenze', in idem, *Land und Leute*, 241.

# IV

Both mountains and rivers could on occasion mark boundaries which might appear in some sense to be natural. Their course could then become a matter of vital interest when issues of public peace and regional defence, which transcended the bounds of individual jurisdictions, were at stake. In reaching agreement on the scope (and duration) of such alliances, lords and cities had to consider how their compass was to be defined—should it be seigneurially, areally, or topographically? The treaties of the fourteenth and fifteenth centuries, the great age of public peace alliances (*Landfriedensbündnisse*) in southern Germany, varied widely in their constituency but displayed remarkable constancy in the manner of their description. As a consequence, historians have been tempted to see in them the expression of older landscape affinities (especially in Switzerland),[61] but such seeming affinities were often in fact identical with diocesan boundaries or the limits of late medieval territorial bailiwicks (*Landvogteien*). What appears as a geographical description, therefore, may in reality reflect ancient seigneurial and administrative divisions, though that these, in turn, had been marked out and moulded by natural boundaries need not be doubted.

The earliest treaties in this period concluded by the territorial powers on the left bank of the Rhine—those of 1301 and 1310[62]—proclaimed a public peace stretching along the crest of the Vosges between the rivers Seltz, Birs, and the Rhine itself, taking in the dioceses of Basel and Strasbourg. When that peace was extended to both banks of the Rhine in 1318, however, the bounds had altered slightly: the Lauter now marked the limit of Alsace to the north, while the Hauenstein passes above Basel, on the watershed southwards to Solothurn and the Swiss midlands, replaced the river Birs.[63] The Vosges remained the border to the west, with Ferrette and Montbéliard representing rather imprecisely the boundary at the Burgundian Gate. On the right bank of the Rhine, the peace was to extend only to the river Oos, rather than the Murg (which

---

[61] Josef Köhler, 'Studien zum Problem des Regionalismus im späten Mittelalter' (Diss. phil. Würzburg, 1971), 43–44.

[62] Konrad Ruser (ed.), *Die Urkunden und Akten der oberdeutschen Städtebunde vom 13. Jahrhundert bis 1549*, 2 vols. (Göttingen, 1979–88), i. 344–45 (no. 418), 346–48 (no. 421).                              [63] Ibid. 349–51 (no. 423).

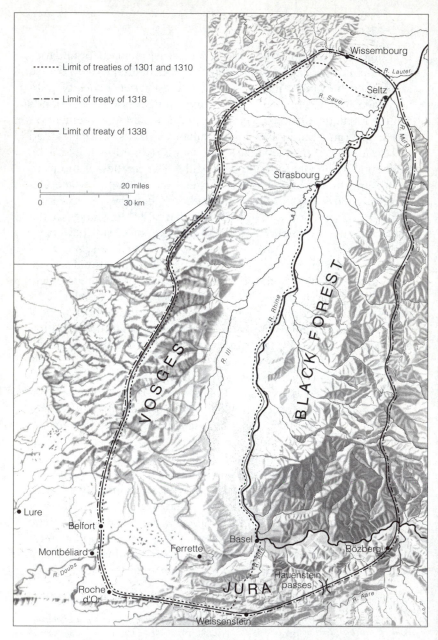

MAP 4. Regional peace alliances of the later Middle Ages

formed a natural counterpart to the Seltz), and followed the ridge
of the Black Forest mountains southwards to the *Hochrhein*. Yet
twenty years later the Murg and the Seltz were paired in a new
treaty, which for the first time gave a clearer indication of the
southern limits of the public peace. From the Hauenstein passes
they stretched to Roche d'Or, the highest point in the west of the
Ajoie, south of Porrentruy, before heading almost due north to
Belfort.[64] An earlier urban league of mutual protection drawn up
between Basel, Strasbourg, and Freiburg in 1326 had set very similar bounds—from the Hauenstein passes to Porrentruy and then
via Rougemont to the crest of the Vosges[65]—while the subsequent
defensive alliance which they concluded with duke Albrecht II of
Austria in 1350 described yet more exactly how far their mutual
commitment ran. It stretched from the fortress of Hauenstein above
Laufenburg (not to be confused with the Hauenstein passes south
of Basel), across the Rhine to the Bözberg mountain west of the
river Aare, and thence via the Hauenstein heights along the peaks
of Leberen, Weissenstein, and Roche d'Or to Lure in southern
Lorraine, that is, 'as far as the territory of the duchess' (Johanna
of Ferrette, Albrecht's wife) extended.[66]

From that it is perfectly clear that in an age which did not think
areally these places were no more than landmarks indicating a
sphere of jurisdiction, rather than marcher-posts staking out precise boundaries. Other later treaties, indeed, preferred to denom-
inate the limits of a public peace in measured distances: either
restrictively—'two [German] miles south of Mulhouse' (as in 1343
and 1347)[67]—or extensively—'four [German] miles above Basel,
four miles below Strasbourg' (as in 1472)[68]—which in that case
would have spanned the Upper Rhine valley from the Ajoie to the
Forest of Haguenau.

What stands out in the wording of these treaties is, in the first
place, the contrast between the unvarying dividing-lines east and
west posed by the Black Forest and the Vosges, and the variable
northern and southern bounds of the region. Here, in the absence
of clear natural frontiers, seigneurial rights were as decisive as

---

[64] Ibid. 355–57 (no. 431).          [65] Ibid. 429–31 (no. 503).
[66] Ruser, *Städtebunde*, ii. 1, 200–4 (no. 153).
[67] Ruser, *Städtebunde*, i. 360–62 (no. 436); Ruser, *Städtebunde*, ii. 2, 811–13 (no. 825).
[68] *Regesten der Markgrafen von Baden und Hachberg 1050–1515*, iv, ed. Albert
Krieger (Innsbruck, 1915), 315 (no. 10,334).

topography. A public peace in 1366, for example, between the bishops of Basel and Strasbourg, the abbots of Murbach and Wissembourg, and the Austrian mortgagee lords of the region, took account of the political claims of the signatories: in the west it embraced Lure (the twin-abbey of Murbach, well outside the compass of the Upper Rhine), while in the north it carefully traced the bounds around Wissembourg, from the Mundat to Schaidt, then through the Bienwald to Neuburg on the Rhine, and thence across to Durmersheim on the right bank and up into the Black Forest.[69] On the Upper Rhine, therefore, frontiers should be seen as an amalgam of natural elements—the crests on either side of the valley 'as the snow melts towards the Rhine' ('als die sneschleiffen gant gegen dem Rine')[70]—and human ones, that is, jurisdictions, or settled landscapes, often of great antiquity. Neither of these was absolute, and each acted upon the other in ways that were neither predetermined nor predictable.

In the second place, however, I would suggest that the treaties do reflect a sense of regional identity on the Upper Rhine in the later Middle Ages, an awareness of mutual needs and interests which was bounded by a sense of place. But the limits of this region were not narrowly circumscribed by the valley itself. What was naturally given—the unity of mountain and plain which spanned the river—must not be ignored; yet to it should be added the legacy of human settlement and political organization, a legacy which ensured that natural frontiers were a great deal more permeable than they seemed (in east and west), and that, where they were weak or absent (to the north and south), a sense of *Landschaft* might extend beyond the valley to embrace both the Ajoie and territories lying in or beyond the Burgundian Gate. And it is to the development of political frontiers that we must now turn.

[69] Ruser, *Städtebunde*, ii. 2, 841–46 (no. 860).
[70] Xavier Mossmann (ed.), *Cartulaire de Mulhouse*, i (Strasbourg, 1886), 163 (no. 194), 337 (no. 355).

# 2

# Territories and Boundaries

The vagueness and permeability of the Upper Rhine's natural frontiers in the later Middle Ages were reflected in the boundaries of
territorial authority. Only the Vosges, separating the lordships of
Alsace from the duchy of Lorraine, constituted in any sense a political frontier. On the right bank of the river, the territories of the
margraves of Baden, the counts of Fürstenberg, and the Habsburg
archdukes all rode effortlessly over the ridges of the Black Forest
mountains. Still less did the river Rhine itself mark a clear political divide. Aside from the enclaves of the secular territory of the
bishops of Basel on the right bank around Schliengen and Istein,
and the district of Beinheim on the left bank opposite Rastatt which
the margraves of Baden had acquired in the fourteenth century, it
was above all the extensive Habsburg possessions on the Upper
Rhine, known collectively as Outer Austria, which spanned the river.
Here the Rhine served only as a convenient distinction between
administrative districts: in contemporary parlance, the Breisgau and
Sundgau banks (*Vorderösterreich breisgauischen und sundgau-
ischen Gestades*).[1]

Either side of the river, it was the lesser tributaries which marked
the oldest human divisions, those between tribal districts (*Gaue*),
dating back to the settlement of the Germanic tribes in the early
centuries AD. On the right bank, the Bleiche (little more than a
stream) to the south, and the Oos and Murg rivers to the north
bounded the Ortenau; on the left, the Lauter and the Seltzbach
marked the frontier between the Nordgau (Lower Alsace) and the
Palatinate; the Birs that between the Sundgau and the Ajoie
(Elsgau). Less obvious, however, was the frontier between the
Sundgau and the rest of Upper Alsace to the north. Reading from
west to east, it was initially marked by the course of the river Thur
downstream from Thann until it flowed into the Ill at Ensisheim;

---

[1] Karl Josef Seidel, *Das Oberelsaß vor dem Übergang an Frankreich. Landesherrschaft, Landstände und fürstliche Verwaltung in Alt-Vorderösterreich (1602–1638)*
(Bonner Historische Forschungen, 45) (Bonn, 1980), 35.

thereafter it seems to have skirted the northern edge of the Harth forest, reaching the Rhine opposite Neuenburg. Yet while no distinction was made in practice under Austrian rule between the Sundgau and the rest of Upper Alsace—the frontier bisected the administrative district of Landser—a consciousness of their separate identity lingers on in the late medieval sources. These could refer to Colmar, Kaysersberg, and Ammerschwihr as 'lower towns' lying beyond the Sundgau,[2] and in one instance even described the diminutive imperial city of Turckheim, west of Colmar, as lying in Lower, rather than Upper, Alsace.[3]

The true frontier between Upper and Lower Alsace was from ancient times the Landgraben, literally the 'rural ditch'. Its origins remain maddeningly obscure. It was certainly man-made; indeed, there may once have been two ditches, separated by a tract of no man's land, north and south of the boggy ground between Sélestat and Guémar running south-eastwards from the river Ill, and it was that strip of land, rather than the ditches themselves, which formed the frontier, in a manner described by Tacitus as typical of the Germanic tribes.[4] Under emperor Diocletian it had marked the boundary between the Roman provinces of Germania Prima and Maximia Sequinorum. After the treaty of Verdun in 843 it divided Alsace as part of Lothar's middle kingdom into the Nordgau and the Südgau (or Sundgau), and later it distinguished the landgraviates of Upper and Lower Alsace. It also marked the northern limit of the diocese of Basel, where it met the diocese of Strasbourg,[5] although the latter's rural deanery of Marckolsheim spilled southwards over the Landgraben to embrace the villages lying on a line from Colmar to the Rhine.[6] Even today, the Landgraben approximates to the boundary between the *départements* of Haut-Rhin and Bas-Rhin.[7] We might therefore expect a division of such an-

---

[2] AMTh, HH 4/1, 3 Jan. 1503.          [3] AMT, AA 19 bis/6, 21 Sept. 1560.

[4] Ministerium für Elsaß-Lothringen, Statistisches Bureau (ed.), *Das Reichsland Elsaß-Lothringen. Landes- und Ortsbeschreibung*, i (Strasbourg, 1898), 257.

[5] Seidel, *Oberelsaß*, 14.

[6] Cf. Georg Wolfram and Werner Gley (eds.), *Elsaß-Lothringischer Atlas: Landeskunde, Geschichte, Kultur und Wirtschaft Elsaß-Lothringens* (Veröffentlichungen des Wissenschaftlichen Instituts der Elsaß-Lothringer im Reich an der Universität Frankfurt) (Frankfurt am Main, 1931), map 16; and its accompanying *Erläuterungsband*, 36.

[7] The present departmental boundary runs north of St-Hippolyte along the Burnenbach close to Orschwiller until it crosses the line of the Landgraben (marked on modern maps as 'Bruch') near the Ill.

tiquity and significance to find visible representation in the landscape. In fact, the course of what Étienne Juillard once termed 'le célèbre et mystérieux Landgraben'[8] is neither straightforward nor distinct. It begins on the heights of the Vosges above the Col de Fouchy, descends to the Val de Lièpvre, rises to the fortress of Haut-Koenigsbourg, and then follows the Eckenbach between St-Hippolyte and Rorschwihr before joining the Ill above Sélestat. Thereafter it proceeds in a series of south-eastward steps until it hits the Rhine opposite castle Sponeck (which may indeed once have stood on the left bank of the river, for it belonged to Württemberg and was administered as part of the duchy's Alsatian county of Horbourg). The most, therefore, that can be said of the Landgraben as a natural frontier is that it marks the narrowest point between mountains and river on the left bank of the Rhine.

It would be easy to imagine that by the sixteenth century the Landgraben had become an obsolete or purely notional boundary, a marcher zone without the military function which its name implied. But there are signs that this was by no means the case. The territorial defensive alliance (*Landsrettung*) drawn up by the Outer Austrian government in 1553 provided that in the event of an attack over the passes of the Vosges subjects were to rally to the Landgraben and pitch camp between the two ditches to await the enemy.[9] A few years later the presence of a picket on the Landgraben is attested,[10] and at the end of the century, in 1592, soldiers were sent to carry out fieldworks;[11] and four years later a 'Frisian' (by then the general name for a dyker) was hired to repair breaches in the rampart near Bergheim.[12] During the Thirty Years War Philipp Truchseß of Rheinfelden reported to the Outer Austrian government in Ensisheim that along the Eckenbach there was no actual ditch-cum-rampart (though it would be easy to throw one up, he added), but that from Bergheim to Guémar there were two ditches, as much as 6 feet deep, of which the outer, or northern, was the older, between which lay indeed a rampart. Although

---

[8] Étienne Juillard, *L'Europe rhénane: Géographie d'un grand espace* (Paris, 1968), 19.

[9] Otto Stolz, 'Die Landsrettungen für Oberelsaß und Breisgau aus dem 16. Jahrhundert', *Elsaß-Lothringisches Jahrbuch*, 20 (1942), 198.

[10] ADTB, E-Dépôt 33: ACD, EE 1/1: 'Quittance du payement fait par la ville de Delle pour les soldat[s] qui estoient sur le Landgraben', 14 Dec. 1558.

[11] ADHR, H 67/6, 4/15 Oct. 1592.

[12] AMBg, AA 3/9, 18 Nov. 1596; cf. ibid. 30 Mar. 1609.

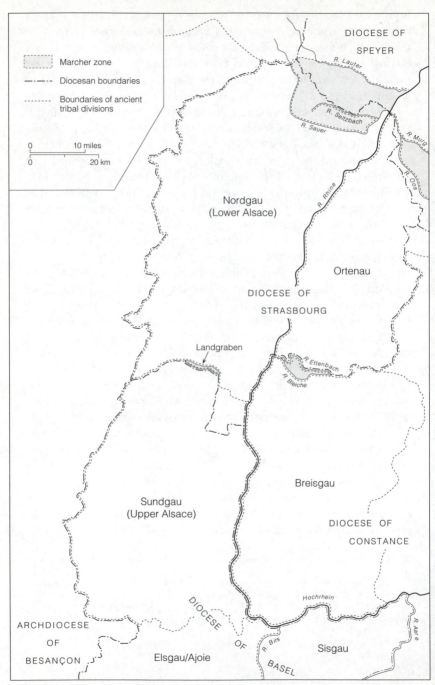

Map 5. Ancient tribal divisions and diocesan boundaries on the Upper Rhine

not in good repair in 1621, the Truchseß felt that they could be put to some defensive use.[13]

The Landgraben offers a highly revealing insight into the relationship between political boundaries and natural frontiers on the Upper Rhine. It was not the major rivers (whose banks were the target of seigneurial control) but the smaller rivers and streams which became the actual frontiers of political authority.[14] Because these streams often flowed through belts of marshy woodland and scrub, it was natural to regard them as marking the limits of landlordships. And along their course marcher associations (*Markgenossenschaften*) came into being, groups of hamlets or villages which banded together to regulate the water-meadows and pastures for communal grazing in these zones of indeterminate lordship. That was true not only along the Landgraben, but on the Bleiche as well, separating the Breisgau from the Ortenau; there it was not so much the stream itself but the forest march of Ettenheimmünster flanking it, the *confinium Alamannorum*, which constituted the frontier with the Ortenau.[15] These observations underscore the point that the search for neat boundaries running along perceived natural divisions projects back into our period the modern misconception that medieval territories should be seen as *Flächenstaate*, occupying a clearly defined surface area. In reality, just as natural frontiers were as often as not zones rather than sharp limits, so too lordships comprised a welter of estates, jurisdictions, customs, stewardships, protective agreements, rights of access, and the like, in other words, a variety of possessions which might overlap or intersect with neighbouring jurisdictions. Where the diversity of titles—to land, to justice, to service, or to tribute—fell together in a process termed by German historians *Besitzverdichtung*, the 'compression' or 'concentration' of possessions, sovereignty might eventually be rounded off within certain bounds to the point where it could be plotted cartographically. But a map can never convey more than a rough expression of the reality and scope of medieval lordship.

---

[13] Ellerbach, *Dreißigjähriger Krieg*, 233–34.
[14] Cf. Mertens, 'Reich und Elsaß', 145 and n. 47.
[15] Klaus Schubring, 'Die Neuformung der Oberrheinlande', in Horst Buszello (ed.), *Der Oberrhein in Geschichte und Gegenwart: Von der Römerzeit bis zur Gründung des Landes Baden-Württemberg* (Schriftenreihe der Pädagogischen Hochschule Freiburg, 1), 2nd edn. (Freiburg im Breisgau, 1986), 47.

In any case, the Upper Rhine was never, in political terms, a closed region before the sixteenth century, in the sense that its natural frontiers marked the perimeter of a concerted territorial authority. Both its position at the crossroads of European routes and the role of the river as an artery of trade ensured that the Upper Rhine remained an open region, one from, through, or into which the tentacles of lordship flowed, reaching out beyond its bounds. In the Middle Ages it never became the core of a territorial principality: instead, it was always part of wider seigneurial or political divisions. That remained true even during the ascendancy of the one dynasty native to the Upper Rhine, the house of Zähringen, in the eleventh and twelfth centuries. Although the Bertoldingen counts (raised to the dukedom of Carinthia in 1061 and from 1190 onwards styling themselves Zähringen after their fortress near Freiburg) strove so vigorously to establish a territorial hegemony that Theodor Mayer was moved to coin the phrase 'the state of the dukes of Zähringen',[16] their power-base never extended over the Upper Rhine as a whole to embrace Alsace. Rather, their original possessions—allodial (patrimonial) estates, stewardships, and comital titles—straddled the Black Forest, reaching in the west no further than the Rhine itself, but stretching instead eastwards into the heartlands of Upper and Lower Swabia along Lake Constance and down the Danube. Yet the most remarkable expansion of the Zähringers' power was directed southwards into Switzerland. There they founded cities at strategic points—the most notable being Freiburg im Üchtland (Fribourg) in 1157 and Bern in 1191—to safeguard their territorial authority. In 1127, moreover, Konrad of Zähringen had been invested with the rectorate of Burgundy, which furnished him with vice-regal powers in one of the Empire's richest lands, adjacent to Switzerland.[17] What stands out from this sketch of the Zähringen dynasty is that its patrimony on the Upper Rhine served essentially as a springboard for expansion beyond the region, rather than as the nucleus of a consolidated territory on the Upper Rhine itself.

---

[16] Theodor Mayer, 'Der Staat der Herzöge von Zähringen', in idem, *Mittelalterliche Studien: Gesammelte Aufsätze* (Lindau/Constance, 1959), 350–64.

[17] Cf. Hans Schadek and Karl Schmid (eds.), *Die Zähringer*, i. *Eine Tradition und ihre Erforschung*; ii. *Anstoß und Wirkung* (Veröffentlichungen zur Zähringer-Ausstellung, 1/2) (Sigmaringen, 1986), esp. i, map 9. Ohler, *Von Grenzen und Herrschaften*, 40–45.

With the extinction of the house of Zähringen in 1218, the Hohenstaufen emperor Frederick II contrived to retrieve the imperial fiefs which the dukes had held, as well as claiming parts of their patrimonial lands for the Empire, but he never succeeded in laying hands on the entire inheritance, which could have formed the basis of a territorial principality in the south-west. In it the Upper Rhine would have played a crucial strategic role in bridging the gap between the extensive Hohenstaufen possessions in Alsace and their own duchy of Swabia. It was left to the Hohenstaufens' successors, the dukes of Habsburg, to attempt to forge that link. Their original patrimony lay in northern Switzerland, but they had at an early stage acquired numerous estates and titles in Alsace. Rudolf of Habsburg made strenuous efforts both before and after his election as German king in 1273 to consolidate these possessions, but he was thwarted by the vigilance of the imperial free cities. On the right bank of the Rhine the Habsburgs had gained a foothold in the thirteenth century by gaining the stewardship of the powerful Benedictine abbey of St Blasien, but it was only in the following century that their major penetration into the Breisgau took place, especially in the wake of their opportunist acquisition of Freiburg in 1368. From that point onwards the Habsburgs remained the dominant power on the Upper Rhine, but even they never succeeded in constructing a consolidated territory out of their disparate possessions. Apart from the opposition of local lords, notably the margraves of Baden, the Habsburgs regarded their western lands on the Upper Rhine as increasingly peripheral to their new-found dynastic interests in the east. Not until archduke Maximilian married Maria, the daughter of Charles the Bold of Burgundy, in 1477 did Outer Austria take on a new dynastic-strategic importance within the Habsburg lands. Here, at last, the possibility beckoned of constructing a closed territory within the confines of the Upper Rhine. Yet even then the Upper Rhine remained only one component, albeit a crucial one, in a much larger system which echoed the Burgundian-Swiss axis of the Zähringers. That is evident from Maximilian's attempts to revive the Lower Union, which finally bore fruit in 1493.

The Lower Union had originally been founded in 1474 as a defensive alliance to repulse the expansionist designs of Burgundy on the Upper Rhine, and specifically to reclaim the Austrian lands which archduke Sigismund of Tirol had wantonly pawned to Charles the Bold. In delimiting the sphere of its actions, the founding treaty gave a vivid sense of the cohesion which the Upper Rhine had acquired as a region in its own right in an age of defensive alliances and public peace ordinances. Its signatories were to render each other aid 'from the forest of Haguenau to the Blauen, and between the mountains on both sides of the Rhine from the Black Forest to the First [the peak Le Climont in the Vosges west of Orbey], together with the four towns, Rheinfelden, Säckingen, Laufenburg, and Waldshut and the forest [the Hotzenwald in the southern Black Forest]'.[18] The members of the Lower Union were drawn from those most immediately under threat: the bishops of Basel and Strasbourg; the cities of Basel, Strasbourg, Colmar, and Sélestat, along with other members of the Decapolis of Alsatian free cities (Kaysersberg, Munster, Rosheim, and Obernai); duke René of Lorraine; the governor of the Württemberg county of Montbéliard beyond the Belfort Gap, and archduke Sigismund himself. Having achieved its aims with the help of the Swiss Confederates—duke Charles the Bold was killed in battle in 1477—the Lower Union's term came to an end in 1484.[19] Maximilian's purpose in reviving it nine years later served quite different ends. He designed to bring the lords and cities of the Upper Rhine into a Habsburg-dominated coalition which would affirm Austrian hegemony in the region and ward off any danger of the Alsatian cities' being lured into an alliance with the Habsburgs' arch-rival, the Wittelsbach elector Palatine.[20] What incentive the local powers had to follow his lead is altogether more questionable, although it has recently been suggested that a growing apprehension of the 'republican' Swiss may have driven them into his embrace.[21] While the Lower Union survived the calamity of the Swiss (or Swabian) War of 1499, which brought the effective secession of the Swiss from the political life of the Empire, Maximilian failed thereafter to turn it to his advantage. His one access of authority and prestige on the Upper Rhine—the successful redemp-

---

[18] ADBR, G 217, fo. 16ʳ; Mertens, 'Reich und Elsaß', 209. The Blauen, the peak south of Basel above the river Birs, seems to have displaced the Hauenstein passes as the southern landmark of the region.

[19] Thomas A. Brady, Jr., *Turning Swiss. Cities and Empire, 1450–1550* (Cambridge, 1985), 49–51.          [20] Mertens, 'Reich und Elsaß', 222.

[21] Brady, *Turning Swiss*, 55. Within the broad framework of mutual suspicion between South German lords and the Swiss, this may well be true, but it ignores the fact that the contracting Alsatian lords and cities had taken the precaution 4 months earlier of renewing their alliance with the Swiss for 15 years. Mertens, 'Reich und Elsaß', 228.

tion of the pawned imperial bailiwicks of Alsace (or Haguenau) and the Ortenau from the elector Palatine[22]—owed more to the involvement of the Swabian League in defeating the Wittelsbachs in the Bavarian War of Succession in 1504 than it did to any intervention of the Lower Union. Indeed, the Swabian League remained a considerable force in South German politics and diplomacy until its dissolution in 1534, whereas the Lower Union, although renewed for fifteen years, drifted into ineffectual obscurity, despite Maximilian's attempts to resuscitate it in 1509 and 1512.[23]

As king and emperor, Maximilian never articulated a clear vision of the Lower Union's function: was it to be a loose protective alliance, or rather the stepping-stone towards a Habsburg territorial power block on the Upper Rhine, a counterweight to the Swabian League (which was showing dangerous signs of independence)? With the outcome of the Swiss War, and Basel's decision to join the Confederation as a full member in 1501, some of the rationale of the Lower Union in any case evaporated. It was only in the preceding decade, before the *débâcle* of the Swiss War, when the Upper Rhine was the launching-pad for his campaigns against France, that the region held the full focus of Maximilian's attention. And it was at the beginning of that decade that the masterful governor of Outer Austria, baron Kaspar von Mörsberg, a Sundgau nobleman whose family had been Austrian partisans for several generations, set forth proposals for transforming Austrian lordship on the Upper Rhine which make manifest the increasing identity of (natural) region with (political) territory.

Invoking the example of the nobility of Lower Alsace, which was well-armed and well-housed in secure castles, von Mörsberg sketched a vision of the Upper Rhine as a region in which the territorial nobility would help create a sovereign principality to which all other princes and cities would be subordinate:

The elector Palatine, the bishop of Strasbourg, the city of Strasbourg, the margrave of Baden; and make out of these same lands, together with his [Majesty's own] lands of Alsace, Sundgau and Breisgau, and the Black Forest, a land which I consider would bear comparison with a powerful

---

[22] Ibid. 165; Brady, *Turning Swiss*, 92.

[23] AMO, AA 61, 23 Apr. 1509; Brady, *Turning Swiss*, 92 n. 55; Mertens, 'Reich und Elsaß', 239–41. The 1512 negotiations proposed to include not only all the major lords on the southern Upper Rhine but in addition the cities of Speyer and Worms, and even envisaged extending its remit into Swabia by including the city of Rottweil and the northern half of the Austrian county of Hohenberg (Horb and Rottenburg). Ibid. 240.

kingdom. If such were brought about, it would beyond doubt serve greatly to advance the holy Empire and the house of Austria. In my opinion, one would not find many powerful kings whose kingdoms had equal might to these lands with all their strength and fruitfulness.[24]

The superficial similarities to the vision of the Revolutionary of the Upper Rhine should not disguise that Kaspar von Mörsberg, a hard-bitten politician to his finger-tips, seriously believed that the Upper Rhine could indeed become the core of a consolidated Habsburg principality under the auspices of the regional nobility. The striking feature of von Mörsberg's proposal was that it ignored —or disdained—any role for urban magistracies in the governance of Outer Austria in what was one of the most densely urbanized areas of Germany. Its tone was one of aristocratic *hauteur*, a contempt for burghers and their pretensions which von Mörsberg had already demonstrated in his dealings with Freiburg im Breisgau.[25] No doubt he hoped to strike a sympathetic chord with Maximilian, whose apparent benevolence towards the Austrian territorial towns masked motives of naked fiscality.[26] Yet von Mörsberg's scheme remained a blueprint, largely because the process of territorialization on the Upper Rhine was almost complete by 1500.

When we come to examine that process, two distinct patterns of territorial development can be traced in the course of the later Middle Ages. The northern half of the Upper Rhine (in our restricted definition), in effect the Ortenau and Lower Alsace, was a kaleidoscope of diminutive jurisdictions, where Austria had no

---

[24] Mertens, 'Reich und Elsaß', 224. The document, unearthed by Mertens, is in TLA, Maximiliana XIV, 1491, fo. 2ʳ⁻ᵛ.

[25] Scott, *Freiburg and the Breisgau*, 149. StAFr, B 5 III c 10, fo. 5ʳ⁻7ᵛ: 'Vnfruntlicheit her Caspar von Morspergs, landvogts'. Cf. Tom Scott, 'Der "Oberrheinische Revolutionär" und Vorderösterreich: Reformvorstellungen zwischen Reich und Territorium', in Norbert Fischer and Marion Kobelt-Groch (eds.), *Außenseiter zwischen Mittelalter und Neuzeit: Festschrift für Hans-Jürgen Goertz zum 60. Geburtstag* (Studies in Medieval and Reformation Thought, 61) (Leiden/New York, 1997), 47–63.

[26] It should not be forgotten, however, that Maximilian, as well as summoning the only imperial diet outside an imperial free city to Freiburg in 1498, contemplated convoking further imperial diets there in 1511 and 1515, thereby underscoring the strategic significance which he attached to the outer lands. Cf. Steven W. Rowan, 'A Reichstag in the reform era: Freiburg im Breisgau, 1497–98', in idem and James A. Vann (eds.), *The old Reich: Essays on German political institutions 1495–1806* (Studies presented to the International Commission for the History of Representative and Parliamentary Institutions, 48) (Brussels, 1974), 33–57; HHSA, Maximiliana 23, fo. 122ʳ–123ᵛ; 33, fo. 27ʳ.

patrimonial stake except for the Val de Villé. In the Ortenau the only major territory was the margraviate of Baden, though it was finally partitioned into two lines in 1535, Baden-Durlach and Baden-Baden (having initially been divided into three on the death of margrave Christoph in 1515), and was destined to remain partitioned until 1771. Baden-Durlach ruled the northernmost lands stretching across the Black Forest to Pforzheim; Baden-Baden the middle lands in the Ortenau. The southern part of the Ortenau contained a profusion of lesser jurisdictions: the various possessions of the bishopric of Strasbourg (a block of land on the headwaters of the Rench, centred upon Oberkirch, and a strip along the march of Ettenheimmünster bordering the Breisgau); the Hanauer Land opposite Strasbourg, ruled by the counts of Hanau-Lichtenberg; the county of Hohengerolds-eck; the imperial territories comprising the bailiwick of the Ortenau, the free cities of Offenburg, Gengenbach, and Zell, and the free imperial valley of Harmersbach (a constitutional curiosity as a free peasant 'republic' under the Empire), as well as many petty lord-ships belonging to imperial knightly families; and the lordship of Hausen up the Kinzig valley, which belonged to the counts of Fürstenberg.[27]

In Lower Alsace no one prince or magistracy dominated the landscape, which was an irreducible patchwork of interlocking and overlapping jurisdictions. The bishopric of Strasbourg controlled several sizeable tracts of territory, principally around Molsheim, Ben-feld, Erstein, and Saverne. These were rivalled in size by the city of Strasbourg's holdings, extensive but scattered rural dependencies, divided into seven administrative districts, including lands on the right bank of the Rhine (though the city divested itself of the mort-gaged lordship of Kürnberg with the town of Kenzingen in 1515).[28] The imperial bailiwick of Alsace was centred upon Haguenau, while the other imperial cities of Lower Alsace—Wissembourg, Rosheim,

---

[27] For a detailed list cf. Wilhelm Melcher, 'Die geistlichen und weltlichen Territ-orien in der Ortenau: (Ihre Geschichte bis zur Auflösung 1803 bis 1806)', in Kurt Klein (ed.), *Land um Rhein und Schwarzwald: Die Ortenau in Geschichte und Gegenwart* (Kehl, 1978), 65–79.

[28] For Strasbourg cf. Gerhard Wunder, *Das Straßburger Gebiet: Ein Beitrag zur rechtlichen und politischen Geschichte des gesamten städtischen Territoriums vom 10. bis zum 20. Jahrhundert* (Schriften zur Verfassungsgeschichte, 3) (Berlin, 1965), 115 (map); idem, *Das Straßburger Landgebiet: Territorialgeschichte der einzelnen Teile des städtischen Herrschaftsbereichs vom 13. bis zum 18. Jahrhundert* (Schriften zur Verfassungsgeschichte, 5) (Berlin, 1967).

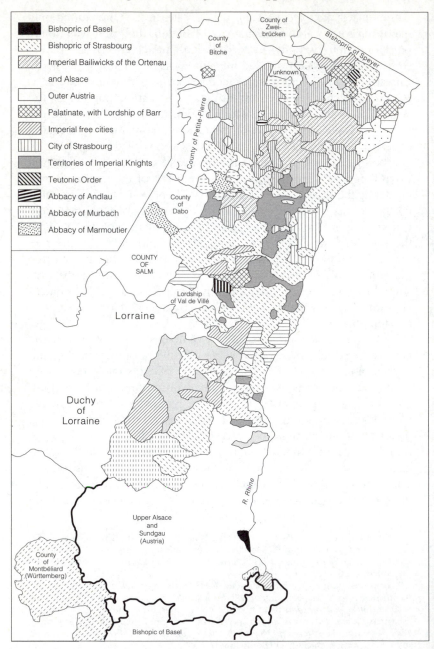

Map 6. Territories on the Upper Rhine, *circa* 1500

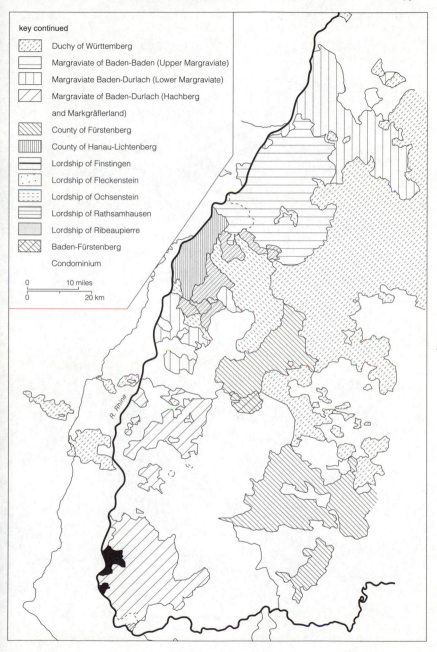

**key continued**

| | |
|---|---|
| | Duchy of Württemberg |
| | Margraviate of Baden-Baden (Upper Margraviate) |
| | Margraviate Baden-Durlach (Lower Margraviate) |
| | Margraviate of Baden-Durlach (Hachberg and Markgräflerland) |
| | County of Fürstenberg |
| | County of Hanau-Lichtenberg |
| | Lordship of Finstingen |
| | Lordship of Fleckenstein |
| | Lordship of Ochsenstein |
| | Lordship of Rathsamhausen |
| | Lordship of Ribeaupierre |
| | Baden-Fürstenberg Condominium |

0    10 miles
0    20 km

R. Rhine

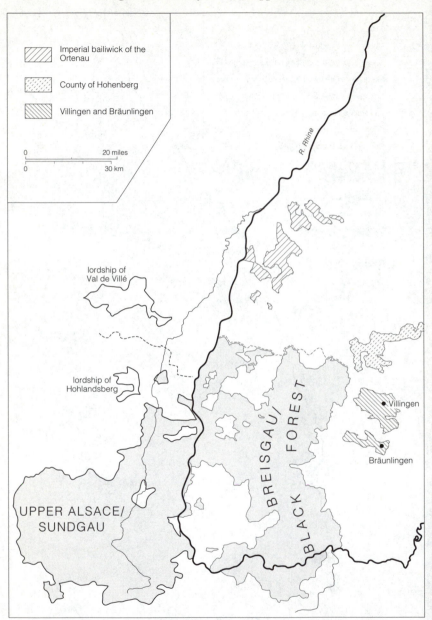

MAP 7. The Austrian outer lands on the Upper Rhine, *circa* 1500

Obernai, and Sélestat—all had small rural territories of their own. As in the Ortenau, many villages belonged to imperial knights. Among the major feodaries were the electors Palatine, who owned the county of Petite-Pierre (Lützelstein), the counts of Hanau-Lichtenberg (with a block of territory around Ingwiller and Bouxwiller), and the counts of Bitche-Zweibrücken bordering the Palatinate; among the lesser feodaries were the lords of Fleckenstein (with four pockets of land above Wissembourg), the lords of Rathsamhausen, and the lords of Barr.

In the southern half of the Upper Rhine the picture changes dramatically. Austria held sway on both banks of the river. Its control of the Breisgau, however, was restricted by the territories of the margraves of Baden-Durlach, which held it in a pincer: to the north lay the ancient margraviate of Hachberg, with its administrative seat in Emmendingen;[29] to the south stretched the so-called Markgräflerland, comprising the adjacent lordships of Rötteln and Sausenberg below Basel, and the exclave of Badenweiler. Apart from the two tiny exclaves of the bishopric of Basel mentioned at the outset, no other lords claimed territorial rights in the Breisgau. Upper Alsace, by contrast, fell into two distinct halves. In the south, Austria owned the county of Ferrette and the lordship of Belfort, which together made up the bulk of the Sundgau. Apart from the territories of the imperial free cities of Basel and Mulhouse (the latter became an external, or associate, member of the Swiss Confederation in 1515), this was the closest the Habsburgs came to constructing a *territorium clausum* on the Upper Rhine; significantly, it was divided into administrative districts (*Ämter*), each governed from a small provincial town, whereas the Breisgau was never the subject of reorganization into *Ämter*; in the latter, authority remained vested in the local nobility or was exercised in conjunction with the magistracies of the territorial towns.

The rest of Upper Alsace lying to the north was as politically variegated as Lower Alsace. It contained the Austrian *Ämter* of Ensisheim (the capital of Outer Austria) and the lower part of Landser, as well as the lordship of Hohlandsberg, with its impressive fortress perched above Colmar, and the district around Ammerschwihr. The bishopric of Strasbourg owned the so-called

---

[29] Baden also ruled the Prech valley to the north-east as a condominium with the counts of Fürstenberg.

Upper Mundat, with its bailiwicks of Eguisheim, Rouffach, and (detached to the south) Soultz.[30] Two imperial abbeys had sizeable dependencies: the larger, Murbach, held the bailiwicks of St-Amarin, Guebwiller, and Wattwiller; the smaller, Munster, controlled its eponymous valley, although the imperial free city of Munster was nominally independent. The remaining imperial free cities of Upper Alsace—Colmar, Turckheim, and Kaysersberg— each had rural territories (although Kaysersberg was subsumed within a small imperial bailiwick). The villages of the imperial knights, however, were much less numerous than in Lower Alsace. In addition, there were two important secular lordships. The lords of Ribeaupierre (Rappoltstein), imperial vassals who found themselves sucked into dependence on Austria, controlled a swathe of territory spanning the Landgraben (the bailiwicks of Ste-Marie-aux-Mines, Ribeauvillé, Bergheim, and Guémar), as well as the lordship of Orbey on the heights of the Vosges, and the bailiwick of Heiteren in the plain east of Rouffach.[31] Finally, the dukes of Württemberg possessed territories west of the Rhine: the county of Horbourg just across the Ill from Colmar, and the lordship of Riquewihr. These were accountable, not to the government in Stuttgart, but to Württemberg's principal French territory, the county of Montbéliard, between Alsace and the Franche-Comté, all of which (since the dukes were not signatories to the treaty of Westphalia in 1648) remained sovereign enclaves on French territory until the eve of the French Revolution.[32]

The southern Upper Rhine as a region was therefore in no sense coterminous with Outer Austria—but, equally, Outer Austria was not coterminous with the Upper Rhine. The 'outer lands', strictly speaking, comprised all the various Habsburg territories from the Tirol westwards to the Rhine, that is to say, the Vorarlberg lordships, the margraviate of Burgau on the Danube, the imperial bailiwick

---

[30] It also owned the district around Marckolsheim, which lay either side of the Landgraben.

[31] A more detailed list is given in Emile Herzog (ed.), *Inventaire sommaire des archives départementales antérieur à 1790: Archives civiles: Série I E, Seigneuries* (Colmar, 1952), 103–4. Ribeaupierre also shared jurisdiction of two villages west of the watershed in Lorraine, Fraize and Saulcy-sur-Meurthe. Benoît Jordan, *Entre la gloire et la vertu: Les Sires de Ribeaupierre 1451–1585* (Publications de la Société Savante d'Alsace et des Régions de l'Est: Recherches [Textes] et Documents, 44) (Strasbourg, 1991), 68.

[32] A detailed list, ibid. 83. Württemberg was obliged to recognize French suzerainty over Montbéliard in 1743–48.

of Swabia, the landgraviate of Nellenburg at the western end of
Lake Constance, and the county of Hohenberg on the river Neckar.
The final authority for these territories remained the Upper Austrian
government in Innsbruck, which administered the scattered Swabian
possessions—Swabian Austria, as they were known—by direct rule.
But the lands on the Upper Rhine itself had their own regional government with its seat in the small Alsatian town of Ensisheim, until
it was transferred to Freiburg im Breisgau with the loss of Alsace
to France in the aftermath of the Thirty Years War. This was the
government of Outer Austria in the narrower sense, responsible
for Alsace and the Sundgau (treated as a single entity), the Breisgau,
and the Black Forest (the lordship of Triberg and the county of
Hauenstein), as well as the four Forest towns on the *Hochrhein*.
At first glance, Outer Austria in this restricted sense was bounded
more or less by the frontiers of the Upper Rhine basin, but there
were some significant anomalies. The two towns of Villingen and
Bräunlingen with their dependent territories (both in Austrian hands
from the early fourteenth century) lay separate from the rest of
Outer Austria east of the Black Forest on the rolling uplands of the
Baar. Although they were subject to the government in Ensisheim,
they could just as easily have been integrated into the neighbouring county of Hohenberg and ruled from Rottenburg.[33]

To the south, on the *Hochrhein*, the Outer Austrian territories not
only included the four Forest Towns, three of which—Waldshut,
Laufenburg, and Säckingen—had been founded by the Habsburgs,[34]
but rural lordships as well, which extended over some distance
into Switzerland. The lordship of Laufenburg ran for 16 kilometres
along the south bank of the Rhine, but it was overshadowed by the
lordship of Rheinfelden which, apart from the district of Rheintal
north of the Rhine, encompassed the districts of Möhlinbach and
the Frick valley south of the river, the latter stretching well inland.
Remarkably, the Frick valley was administered as part of the
Breisgau (with which it had no obvious connection), rather than
with the Black Forest lordships.[35] To regard these districts in any
way as intruders on Swiss soil would be to commit the double

---

[33] Maximilian's plans to extend the Lower Union in 1512 to embrace part of the
county of Hohenberg show that, in political and administrative terms, there was
no clearly perceived divide between the Upper Rhine and Swabia. Cf. above n. 23.
[34] Rheinfelden was held as an imperial pawn from 1330 onwards.
[35] Senti, 'Die Herrschaften Rheinfelden und Laufenburg', 407, 408–9.

error of imagining territorial authority areally rather than seigneuri-ally, and of regarding the Rhine as a natural frontier. These lord-ships remained Austrian until the Napoleonic Wars, and in the town halls of Laufenburg and Rheinfelden portraits of the Habsburgs still hang to this day.[36]

In Alsace, the position of the Val de Villé (in German, the Weilertal or Albrechtstal) within the corpus of Outer Austrian sub-jects became a matter of dispute. It controlled an important trade route over the Vosges from Sélestat up the Giessen, with the castle of Ortenbourg dominating the narrow entrance to the valley, which then forked above Villé to Colroy-la-Roche in the north or the Col de Saales further west. Although it lay north of the Land-graben in Lower Alsace, it was under the jurisdiction of Ensisheim, but its inhabitants were not members of the third Estate of towns and rural districts (*Städte und Landschaften*) of Outer Austria. Having been pawned in 1551 to the powerful Alsatian noble fam-ily von Bollweiler,[37] the subjects of the Val de Villé made repeated efforts between 1553 and 1575 to be admitted to the Outer Austrian Estates. The motives they advanced were twofold: they lay precari-ously close to France and Lorraine at a time when the Habsburg–Valois struggle was intensifying, and their mortgagee lord, Nikolaus von Bollweiler, they alleged, was oppressing them.[38] The Ensisheim government was keen enough to accept them, but the Estates, par-ticularly the towns, demurred, fearing that the valley's proximity to France would drag them into additional military burdens and expense.[39]

In the Burgundian Gate the Austrian lordship of Belfort defies easy categorization. It lay west of the Rhine–Rhône watershed, and was in language and culture Burgundian rather than Alsatian. Yet because it formed part of the Austrian Sundgau, it may be regarded in this period to all intents and purposes as Alsatian, and there-fore territorially part of the Upper Rhine. The same cannot be said,

---

[36] Metz, 'Vorderösterreichische Lande', 175. It should not be forgotten, however, that in the last stages of Habsburg lordship in Switzerland in the 15th century, which culminated in the loss of the Thurgau in 1460, both Bern and Basel had explicit designs upon the Fricktal, which contained important iron-workings. Cf. Karl Schib, 'Die vier Waldstädte', in Metz, *Vorderösterreich*, 388.

[37] Seidel, *Oberelsaß*, 40.

[38] StAFr, C 1 Landstände 9, 4 Jan. 1563; Dieter Speck, *Die vorderösterreichischen Landstände im 15. und 16. Jahrhundert: Entstehung, Entwicklung und Ausbildung bis 1595/1602* (Veröffentlichungen aus dem Archiv der Stadt Freiburg im Breisgau, 29), 2 vols. (Freiburg im Breisgau/Würzburg, 1994), i. 265.

[39] StAFr, B 5 IXa i, fo. 194ʳ; Speck, *Landstände*, i. 265 and n. 230.

however, for the castle and town of Héricourt, west of Belfort, which belonged to Austria until the early sixteenth century. Héricourt was described in 1481 as lying in Burgundy, and two years later archduke Sigismund of Tirol warned his nephew, the future king Maximilian, that he had no intention of letting Austrian possessions in Burgundy—not only Héricourt but Châtelot and L'Isle-sur-le-Doubs as well—pass into foreign hands. Indeed, Austrian lordship was augmented in 1524, when count Wilhelm of Fürstenberg sold his rights and estates in these and neighbouring places to arch-duke Ferdinand (only to receive them back as a pawn).[40] None of these places (as far as one can tell) was ever administered from Dôle as part of the Franche-Comté (Austrian Burgundy), and yet they were not included in the list of Outer Austrian districts either. Héricourt remained in Austrian hands, it seems, until 1525, when it was sold to archduke Ferdinand's minister, Gabriel Salamanca, count of Ortenbourg. His family held it until 1560, when it passed to the duchy of Württemberg and was absorbed into the county of Montbéliard which surrounded it.[41]

The only major additions to Austrian power in our period res-ulted from Maximilian's success in reclaiming the imperial baili-wicks in Alsace and the Ortenau from the elector Palatine in 1504. The king ensured that they were henceforth administered by his trusted lieutenants in the Outer Austrian government. The baili-wick of Haguenau was given to Kaspar von Mörsberg (after 1502 the deputy governor of Outer Austria), who was named first as imperial, and then, in a significant change of title, Habsburg ter-ritorial bailiff in Lower Alsace, until he was succeeded by his son, Hans Jakob, in 1511. The bailiwick of Alsace thus remained under direct Austrian control—it was administered from Ensisheim, but with its own officials separate from those of the Outer Austrian government[42]—until it was briefly remortgaged to the Palatinate in 1530, before being restored to Austria in 1558.[43] The Palatine half of the bailiwick of the Ortenau (the other half continued to be

---

[40] Franz Ludwig Baumann and Georg Tumbült (eds.), *Mitteilungen aus dem f. fürstenbergischen Archive*, i. *Quellen zur Geschichte des f. Hauses Fürstenberg und seines ehedem reichsunmittelbaren Gebietes. 1510–1559* (Tübingen, 1894), 99–101 (no. 171).     [41] Stolz, *Geschichtliche Beschreibung*, 123–25.

[42] Wolfgang Hans Stein, 'Formen der österreichischen und französischen Herr-schaftsbildung im Elsaß im 16. und 17. Jahrhundert: Ein Vergleich', in Hans Maier and Volker Press, *Vorderösterreich in der frühen Neuzeit* (Sigmaringen, 1989), 298.

[43] Mertens, 'Reich und Elsaß', 165, 168; Paul Stinzi, 'Die Habsburger im Elsaß', in Metz, *Vorderösterreich*, 560–62; Seidel, *Oberelsaß*, 46.

held by the bishop of Strasbourg) was entrusted to count Wolfgang of Fürstenberg, Maximilian's marshal, who was at that time the Outer Austrian governor, as compensation for arrears of pay and undischarged loans to the monarch. The Ortenau remained pawned until archduke Ferdinand redeemed both halves, from Fürstenberg in 1551 and from Strasbourg in 1556, not into the hands of the Empire but to the house of Austria.[44]

The fragmentation of lordship in the north and the sprawling character of the Outer Austrian lands in the south cannot conceal that around 1500 signs of a new sense of territoriality were emerging on the frontiers of the Upper Rhine which began to mark off the region more distinctly from its neighbours. Two significant developments provide evidence of this change. The peace of Basel on 22 September 1499 not only put an end to the ruinous and ill-fated war with the Swiss Confederates; it at last established a firm frontier between Switzerland and Outer Austria which ensured that both sides abandoned claims on each other's territory for good (though it could not stop Basel and later Mulhouse from turning Swiss).[45] The boundary between Upper Alsace and the duchy of Lorraine (which jutted into Alsace over the Vosges in the Val de Lièpvre) was likewise fixed after hundreds of hearings of the affected parties by the imperial court of justice in Rottweil in 1521.[46]

On the other hand, the frontier between Outer Austria and the Württemberg county of Montbéliard remained contentious from the later fifteenth century onwards.[47] These boundary disputes acquired a new dimension after 1519, once duke Ulrich had been expelled from his duchy and an Austrian government of occupation installed in Stuttgart. Plans were drawn up to annex by force not only Montbéliard but Horbourg and Riquewihr as well, but they came up against the constitutional stumbling-block that the Alsatian and Burgundian patrimony of the house of Württemberg

[44] Otto Kähni, 'Die Landvogtei Ortenau', in Metz, *Vorderösterreich*, 492–94; Seidel, *Oberelsaß*, 46.

[45] Brady, *Turning Swiss*, 63; Georges Bischoff, *Gouvernés et gouvernants en Haute-Alsace à l'époque autrichienne: Les États des pays antérieurs des origines au milieu du XVIe siècle* (Publications de la Société Savante d'Alsace et des Régions de l'Est: Grandes Publications, 20) (Strasbourg, 1982), 104.

[46] Ibid. 132 and 147 n. 37, citing documents in ADMM, B. 9648.

[47] AN, K 2017/III. 'Contestations avec les seigneurs de Belfort et de Delle au sujet des limites du Comté de Montbéliard pour le territoire de Bethoncourt, Nom[m]ay, Dambenois, Fesches [Fêche-l'Église], Dampierre et Badevel, 1470–1539'.

was ruled, not by Ulrich, but by his younger brother Georg. More-over, the Outer Austrian Estates, who were instructed to provide the necessary troops, evinced reluctance, perhaps being chary of provoking Basel,[48] which at that time held Montbéliard in mort-gage. After duke Ulrich's restoration in 1534 the frontier remained un-settled, but it was Württemberg rather than Austria which appeared as the aggressor. In the 1540s Württemberg laid claim to the castle of Morvillars (Morschweiler) and the district of Méziré (Miserach) south of Belfort,[49] while in 1564 the Outer Austrian government had to rebut an attempt by the lords of Franchemont to assert jur-isdiction over Châtenois-les-Forges north-east of Montbéliard as a Württemberg fief, although it lay on Belfort territory.[50]

Within the region, however, the Habsburgs were able to pursue their aim of subordinating their rivals, although the territorial equi-librium was never seriously upset. Their purpose, in fact, was rather to assert sovereignty than to acquire territory—*arrondissement* rather than expansion. Those who were immediate vassals of the Empire were particular targets of attack. The imperial abbey of Murbach repeatedly protested its independence, but found itself assessed for military taxes in 1536 by the Outer Austrian govern-ment, which it was required by treaty to pay.[51] Later in the cen-tury, though, the abbey refused to pay the Austrian excise called the Evil Penny on the grounds that it was earmarked not for (im-perial) defence but for the redemption of Austrian mortgages.[52] While Murbach never sank to the level of a territorial subject, sit-ting on the prelates' bench of the Outer Austrian Estates, it was in general obliged after 1536 to contribute one-twentieth of any tax voted by the Outer Austrian nobility.[53]

The lords of Ribeaupierre (Rappoltstein) were rather less fortu-nate. Although both Wilhelms von Rappoltstein, father and son, had served long spells as Outer Austrian governor either side of 1500 (the latter during the turbulent days of the Peasants' War), their loyalty to the Habsburgs was not rewarded in the way that the

---

[48] Bischoff, *Gouvernés et gouvernants*, 132; ADHR, 17 J 19 (11/22 Feb. 1525).
[49] ADD, E 5067 (4 July 1542); E 5094/6 (4 Nov. 1545 ff.); E 5094/18 (1545).
[50] ADHR, 1 C 149/6 (1564).     [51] ADHR, 10 G 10/13–15 (1 June 1536).
[52] ADHR, 1 C 929/1 (1566–75).
[53] Seidel, *Oberelsaß*, 47. He refers to Murbach as a 'peculiar hybrid', which seems a more accurate verdict than Bischoff's, who describes the treaties of 1536 and 1539 as amounting to Murbach's effective integration into Outer Austria. Bischoff, *Gouvernés et gouvernants*, 141.

von Mörsbergs' was. The latter were, after all, originally territorial knights with a small lordship (Morimont) on the borders of Alsace and the Ajoie, who used their partisanship to acquire fiefs and, in 1488, a baronage, whereas the von Rappoltstein were imperial vassals commanding an important territory in the heart of Alsace, which contained significant reserves of silver. It was Austria's stake in the silver-mines (jointly exploited with Ribeaupierre) which gave the Habsburgs a strategic interest in tying the von Rappoltstein to their territorial jurisdiction.[54] In 1521 the family was still listed in the imperial registers (*Matrikeln*), that is, having the right to attend imperial diets as a member of second Estate, but by 1544 they were described as a 'vacated Estate' (*ausgezogener Stand*) under Austrian protection.[55] In fact, the von Rappoltstein had already contributed to the Austrian military levy of 1519, while their subjects lost their right of appeal to the imperial court of justice in Rottweil and had to take suit in Ensisheim (unlike the subjects of Murbach, who retained their access to the imperial courts).[56]

These were minor instances of attrition, however, compared with the long-standing rivalry between Habsburg and Wittelsbach on the Upper Rhine. In September 1497 these tensions turned an otherwise minor incident in the Upper Mundat into an open declaration of war by the Outer Austrian governor, Kaspar von Mörsberg, on the bishop of Strasbourg, the Wittelsbach Albrecht of Bavaria. The town of Soultz in the southern part of the Upper Mundat had taken reprisals against a local lord, Claus von Schauenburg, an episcopal and Austrian vassal, who had imprisoned two of its inhabitants. Before the matter could be settled by the mediation of the Lower Union, a rapidly assembled Austrian expeditionary force captured Soultz, plundered its way through the Upper Mundat, and laid siege to Rouffach. That wider political issues were at stake is evident not only from the fact that the citizens of Soultz were required to swear an oath of loyalty to Austria, but also that the armistice concluded on 15 September stipulated that fiefs of noble

---

[54] Bischoff, *Gouvernés et gouvernants*, 141.

[55] Seidel, *Oberelsaß*, 59; Rudolf Brieger, *Die Herrschaft Rappoltstein: Ihre Entstehung und Entwicklung* (Beiträge zur Landes- und Volkskunde von Elsaß-Lothringen, 31) (Strasbourg, 1907), 75.

[56] Bischoff, *Gouvernés et gouvernants*, 246; Seidel, *Oberelsaß*, 60, 47. For an account of the von Rappoltsteins' struggle to preserve their immediacy, see now Jordan, *Entre la gloire et la vertu*, 97–100, who gives a different interpretation, however, of exemption from the Rottweil court.

vassals in the Upper Mundat which had been alienated by Austria should revert to the bishop. The peace treaty finally signed in August 1498 cancelled any Austrian territorial gains—Soultz was handed back—but, more importantly, guaranteed safe conduct through the Upper Mundat, military aid from its subjects, and free access (*Öffnung*) for Austrian troops to Soultz in time of need. Any threat from the Wittelsbachs to the heart of Outer Austria had been banished,[57] though disputes continued throughout the sixteenth century on whether the nobility resident in the Upper Mundat should swear allegiance to the bishop or to Austria.[58]

On the right bank of the Rhine, the Habsburgs faced a somewhat lesser threat from the margraves of Baden, an altogether second-rate power alongside the Wittelsbachs. And yet Baden consistently managed to thwart their efforts to round off their territorial authority at every turn. Although on the diplomatic level relations between the two powers were generally cordial during the fifteenth century,[59] long-running conflicts over the residence of Austrian subjects in the margravial Breisgau as outburghers of Freiburg soured relations at a local level.[60] A more general conflict, however, broke out over the landgraviate of the Breisgau. In its original frontiers, the landgraviate encompassed all the territory on the right bank of the Rhine between the 'four walls' of the Bleiche stream in the north, the river Wiese bounding the Sausenhart in the south, the Rhine and the ridge of the Black Forest,[61] that is, the ancient lands of the dukes of Zähringen, the margraves of Hachberg, and the counts of Freiburg. Although the margraves had inherited the legal title to the landgraviate from the Zähringers, part of it had passed as a pawn to the counts of Freiburg. When Austria took possession of

---

[57] Bischoff, *Gouvernés et gouvernants*, 98; idem, 'La Guerre du Haut-Mundat: Un épisode oublié de l'histoire d'Alsace', *Annuaire de la Société d'Histoire des Régions de Thann-Guebwiller*, 13 (1979–80), 77–89, esp. 80–81, 85.

[58] Cf. ADHR, 3 G 3, 1545. The bishop attempted to tax Austrian vassals who had estates in the Upper Mundat, and in the Thirty Years War the Outer Austrian government claimed sovereignty over the convents of St Valentin in Rouffach, and Lautenbach, as well as over Austrian vassals, on the grounds that the Upper Mundat was a 'vacated Estate' of the landgraviate of Upper Alsace; but these were conflicts below the level of territorial integrity. Seidel, *Oberelsaß*, 79.

[59] Cf. Konrad Krimm, *Baden und Habsburg um die Mitte des 15. Jahrhunderts: Fürstlicher Dienst und Reichsgewalt im späten Mittelalter* (Veröffentlichungen der Kommission für geschichtliche Landeskunde in Baden-Württemberg, B 89) (Stuttgart, 1976), 49–50, 66–67. [60] Scott, *Freiburg and the Breisgau*, 36–37.

[61] Franz Kreutter, *Geschichte der k. k. Vorderösterreichischen Staaten*, i (St Blasien, 1790), pp. xiii–xiv. For the 'four walls' cf. GLA 229/8577, n.d. (1511).

the lordship of Badenweiler from count Konrad of Freiburg in 1398, it immediately laid claim to the landgraviate. The title constituted rights of territorial jurisdiction over the Breisgau, but in contrast to Upper Alsace, where the Habsburgs had deployed the landgraviate as an instrument to territorialize their authority in the fourteenth century, the Breisgau title seemed for much of the fifteenth century an empty formula (especially after Austria lost Badenweiler in 1444). Nevertheless, Maximilian chose to revive it in 1490 by attaching strings to his confirmation of the dynastic treaty between margraves Christoph of Baden and Philipp of Hachberg. These would have required Baden to hold Rötteln castle and the town of Schopfheim from Austria in fee, revocable at will, and to place the lordships of Badenweiler and Sausenberg under Austrian landgravial jurisdiction. For more than thirty years Baden was able to ignore these onerous provisions. But in 1524 Austria began a long legal battle over the landgraviate, eventually gaining judgement in 1565. This was not the end of the affair by any means. Baden refused to accept the ruling, and the case dragged on in a desultory fashion, earning rich pickings for the lawyers, for another 200 years, until Austria at last abandoned its claim in 1741.[62]

Although Habsburg lordship in Outer Austria remained essentially pre-territorial—a congeries of rights and protective alliances —the consolidation of the Sundgau and, to a lesser degree, the Breisgau went further than anything the Habsburgs achieved in Swabia. On the Upper Rhine prelates and nobles became subject to territorial authority (*landsässig*), whereas in Swabia they were able successfully to resist integration under Austrian jurisdiction.[63] Yet even within Outer Austria proper the Habsburgs' administrative writ did not run entirely unchallenged by the end of the Middle Ages. Despite their solid block of territory in the Sundgau, it remained pock-marked with towns and lordships under the jurisdiction of the nobility which were exempt from the system of district administration. Most of these nobles held land on the edges, rather than at the heart, of the Sundgau, but they included such powerful

---

[62] Martin Wellmer, 'Der vorderösterreichische Breisgau', in Metz, *Vorderösterreich*, 285–88. Cf. Karl Josef Seidel, 'Die Landgrafschaft im Breisgau und die Häuser Habsburg und Baden', *Zeitschrift für die Geschichte des Oberrheins*, 125 (1977), 381–87.

[63] Volker Press, 'Vorderösterreich in der habsburgischen Reichspolitik des späten Mittelalters und der frühen Neuzeit', in Maier and Press, *Vorderösterreich*, 13–16.

families as the von Mörsberg, von Andlau, and von Hattstatt.[64] To a vital extent, Austrian power in Alsace rested upon the support of the nobility, whose families in several cases—the von Reinach and von Hallwyl, for instance—had resettled from Switzerland and thrown in their lot with a dynasty more sympathetic to their aristocratic status than the republican Swiss. In return, the Habsburgs were keen to harness them to their cause—several families served the Austrian administration in Ensisheim, notably the von Hallwyl and von Mörsberg—and could not afford to treat them in a cavalier fashion.[65] Agreements brokered by the bishop and the city of Basel in 1494 and 1495 sought to regulate relations between the nobles and their dependants, and the Austrian districts. The nobility was obliged to render military service and other customary territorial obligations to Austria, but that was not the same as integrating their subjects into the *Ämter*,[66] that is, making them directly subordinate to Austrian provincial jurisdiction. In the first decades of the sixteenth century, the third Estate in Alsace, voicing the anger of cameral subjects who bore the brunt of taxation, waged a constant campaign to this end which, in Georges Bischoff's words, poisoned debates in the diets and threatened to paralyse an effective regional defence (*Landsrettung*). Complaints about the anomalous status of nobles' subjects continued to be voiced at territorial diets throughout the sixteenth century.[67] Here lay the Achilles' heel of the Habsburgs' preference for seigneurial lordship, ruling in concert with a trusted group of local nobility, rather than constructing a closed principality with visible and defined areal boundaries—as, for example, Bavaria.

The position of the Outer Austrian lands on the Upper Rhine within the Habsburg diplomatic system took an entirely new turn after 1519, with the Austrian annexation of Württemberg and the dynastic vision of the new emperor, Charles V. Control of Württemberg reopened the possibility of creating a Habsburg realm across south-west Germany which would forge the disparate outer

---

[64] Bischoff, *Gouvernés et gouvernants*, 238. He lists: in the Jura, the von Eptingen, von Mörsberg, Reich von Reichenstein; in the francophone Sundgau, the von Roppe and von Montreux (Münsterol); around Mulhouse, the zu Rhein, von Hans, von Andlau, and von Reinach; and at the edges of the Upper Mundat and the abbacy of Murbach, the von Stör, von Waldner, and von Hattstatt.

[65] Idem, 'Die markanten Züge des österreichischen Elsaß', in Maier and Press, *Vorderösterreich*, 276. [66] ADHR, 16 J 175 (1494/95).

[67] Bischoff, *Gouvernés et gouvernants*, 118; Speck, *Landstände*, i. 333, 335.

lands into some semblance of a coherent territorial entity. Building upon Maximilian's stillborn plan at the end of his reign for administrative centralization, a blueprint drawn up in 1520—probably the work of Charles V's Brabantine councillor, Maximilian van Bergen—advocated an integrated Austrian principality, governed by an aulic council (*Hofrat*) and central treasury, with four seats of justice based in Wiener Neustadt, Innsbruck, Stuttgart, and Ensisheim, with appellate jurisdiction over Württemberg and Outer Austria reserved to Innsbruck. In Tom Brady's words: 'The project presents an alternative . . . to the Empire as a republic of princes: an Imperial monarchy based on a centralized Austria, allied to the financially potent free cities and the other smaller southern princes.'[68] The blueprint was never converted into official policy, partly because of the dramatic swings of political fortune in the east: the Ottoman advance, culminating in 1526 in the battle of Mohács, in which king Louis of Hungary was killed; and then the succession to the crowns of Hungary and Bohemia by archduke Ferdinand. But another reason may lie in Charles V's ambivalent attitude towards his Austrian patrimony and his brother Ferdinand. The treaties of Brussels on 30 January and 7 February 1522, by which Charles assigned the governance of the Austrian lands to Ferdinand, contained several secret clauses of unusual interest. Not only was the transfer to be kept dark for six years (Ferdinand was merely described as Charles' deputy, *Statthalter*), but the emperor reserved certain Habsburg jurisdictions in Alsace—the county of Ferrette and the imperial bailiwick of Haguenau, including Breisach in the Breisgau on the right bank of the Rhine—to himself, or whoever should inherit the Burgundian lands, by reversion on Ferdinand's death.[69] Why Charles was moved to align Outer Austria with the

[68] Brady, *Turning Swiss*, 113–14; text 235–41.

[69] Alfons Dopsch, 'Die Weststaatspolitik der Habsburger im Westen ihres Großreiches (1477–1526)', in *Gesamtdeutsche Vergangenheit. Festgabe für Heinrich Ritter von Srbik zum 60. Geburtstag am 10. November 1938* (Munich, 1938), 60. Cf. Alphons Lhotsky, *Das Zeitalter des Hauses Österreich: Die ersten Jahre der Regierung Ferdinands I. (1520–1527)* (Österreichische Akademie der Wissenschaften: Veröffentlichungen der Kommission für Geschichte Österreichs, 4 [Schriften des DDr. Franz-Josef Mayer-Gunthof-Fonds, 7]) (Vienna, 1971), 114–15. Wilhelm Bauer, *Die Anfänge Ferdinands I.* (Vienna/Leipzig, 1907), 151–52. The inclusion of Breisach, as the arsenal of Outer Austria, is not mentioned in the secret treaty (cf. Bauer, *Anfänge*, 252), but is referred to in Loys [i.e. Louis] Gollut, *Les Mémoires historiques de la république séquanoise et des princes de la Franche-Comté de Bourgogne*, ed. C. Duvernoy and E. Bousson de Mairet (Arbois, 1846), 1544: 'l'empereur voulut retenir la Ferrette, Suntgaw, et tout ce que passe iusques au Rhin et Brissac inclusivement.'

Burgundian lands (the Netherlands and the Franche-Comté) will never be known for certain, though the Upper Rhine was later to form an indispensable link in the 'Spanish road' of military provisioning downriver to the Low Countries. Yet the link had always been at the heart of Maximilian's strategic vision, even if it was never translated into any kind of administrative reality. Charles's Burgundian councillors on the eve of the Brussels treaties, however, had seemingly drafted a plan for a new regional power block, comprising the Franche-Comté and Alsace, to act as a buffer between France and the Empire.[70] Nothing came of these designs for the time being, as Charles V in 1540 eventually renounced his original proviso and confirmed Outer Austria in its entirety as an inheritance of the Austrian Habsburg line.[71]

But the temptation remained, for towards the end of his reign in 1551 Charles V, it transpired, reverted to the idea of bequeathing the territories west of the Rhine to his son, Philip II of Spain. This reversal of policy encountered stiff opposition, however, from archduke Ferdinand, and was never carried through.[72] Four years later, indeed, a counter-proposal was apparently under discussion, whereby the Franche-Comté should be divorced from the Netherlands and attached to Outer Austria. The scheme seems to have emanated not from Ferdinand himself (who was in any case far too canny to lend it any overt support), but from the secretary of the imperial ambassador, Simon Renard, a native of Besançon in the Franche-Comté by the name of Quiclet, who commented:

Qu'il sçavoit que ce pais-cy [Franche-Comté] portait à S. M. et au Roy de Bohème sons fils bonne dévotion; et luy sembloit que l'on l'aymeroit mieulx . . . que led. sr roy d'Angleterre [Philip II], [adding that] si led. Comté estoit joinct avec celluy de Ferrette, il luy sembloit que ceulx de ced. Comté en seroient plus fortz et asseurez.[73]

Quiclet also urged Ferdinand to send a representative to the Estates of the Franche-Comté at Dôle 'pour parler de quelque confédération

---

[70] Seidel, *Oberelsaß*, 27; Bischoff, *Gouvernés et Gouvernants*, 132–33.
[71] Franz Huter, 'Vorderösterreich und Österreich. Von ihren mittelalterlichen Beziehungen', in Metz, *Vorderösterreich*, 78.
[72] Hans Kramer, 'Die Beziehungen zwischen Vorderösterreich und Österreich in der Neuzeit', in Metz, *Vorderösterreich*, 103; Stolz, *Geschichtliche Beschreibung*, 88.
[73] 'He knows that this land holds His Majesty and the king of Bohemia his son in good devotion, and, it seems to him, loves them more than the king of England . . . If the county were to be joined with that of Ferrette, it seems to him that those in the county would be stronger and more secure.'

avec le pais de Ferrette'.[74] This astonishing suggestion reveals how contradictory the strategic perceptions of the role of Outer Austria in the Habsburg international system had become. Was a frontier to be drawn at the Rhine, thereby truncating a long-standing political entity with its own government, or was part of Burgundy to be joined to a territory which already spilled over the natural frontiers of the Upper Rhine, and with which it would have been contiguous but for the intervening Württemberg county of Montbéliard? The balance of advantage between preserving the integrity of Outer Austria, where political and regional identities were closely though not completely aligned, or sundering the Upper Rhine for the sake of wider dynastic ambitions, was never satisfactorily resolved.

These uncertainties, indeed, continued to dog Habsburg policy into the seventeenth century. Rivalries over the succession to the imperial throne among the various branches of the Austrian Habsburgs led emperor Ferdinand II to make overtures to Philip III of Spain, whereby the latter, as compensation for renouncing any claims to the crowns of Bohemia and Hungary, would receive not only the landgraviate of Alsace and the bailiwick of Haguenau, but the imperial bailiwick of the Ortenau on the right bank of the Rhine as well. Although archduke Maximilian, as ruler of Tirol and the outer lands, protested vigorously, arguing that any diminution of the Empire required the consent of the electors, and that such a deal would never be tolerated by the Swiss or by France, the provisions were incorporated into the (second) secret treaty of Oñate on 20 March 1617.[75] Spain's interest in such a *quid pro quo* was manifest: the Upper Rhine, with its impregnable fortress of Breisach, was an essential corridor between Milan and the Spanish Netherlands, as the European balance of power collapsed in the turmoil of the Thirty Years War. The onset of hostilities put the treaty of Oñate on ice, but Spain still clung to its aspirations on the Upper Rhine, even after a new Austrian treaty of inheritance in 1630 had attempted to resolve the internal dynastic bickerings.

---

[74] 'To treat of a confederation with the land of Ferrette'. Both quotations are to be found in Lucien Febvre, *Philippe II et la Franche-Comté*, new edn. (Paris, 1970), 79, where his name is given as Quichet. On Quiclet's activities as a spy in France cf. Jean-Daniel Pariset, *Humanisme, réforme et diplomatie: Les Relations entre la France et l'Allemagne au milieu du XVIe siècle d'après des documents inédits* (Publications de la Société Savante d'Alsace et des Régions de l'Est: Grandes Publications, 19) (Strasbourg, 1981), 117–18 n. 23.

[75] Stolz, *Geschichtliche Beschreibung*, 88–89; Seidel, *Oberelsaß*, 32–33.

Spain even tabled its demands during the peace negotiations of 1648, but with the cession of Alsace to France under the terms of the treaty of Westphalia, the issue became a dead duck.[76]

This survey of territories and their boundaries makes plain how much the Upper Rhine remained a patchwork quilt of diminutive and often intersecting jurisdictions throughout the period with which we are concerned. The mixed political fortunes of Outer Austria from the late fifteenth to the early seventeenth century demonstrate, moreover, how little distance even the one major regional power, the Habsburgs, had travelled—or, perhaps, had sought to travel—in turning their scattered inheritance on the Upper Rhine into a closed territorial principality with established and identifiable borders. The result can be described as a territorial balance—or as a stalemate. The one immediate consequence of this jumble of frontiers and jurisdictions was that any attempt to pursue territorial autarchy or autarky was bound to lead to economic conflict. Co-operation across political, judicial—and, by the sixteenth century, confessional—frontiers was essential if the basic requirements of economic life, and therewith human survival, were to be met. The discrepancy between economic needs and political facts within the Upper Rhine, a region determined by the uneasy interplay of natural frontiers and human boundaries, gave rise both to competition and to coexistence. The investigation of the patterns of economic conflict and co-operation, and the balance between them, forms the subject of the chapters which follow.

[76] Ibid. 33.

# PART II

*Economic Competition and Conflict*

# 3

# Central Places and Urban Networks

## I

Human geographers have commonly defined a region in terms of the relations between a city and its hinterland. In R. E. Dickinson's classic formulation the region is

a geographical unit of economic and social activity and organization . . . It is an entity of human space relationships, which are effected through the medium of the route pattern and the urban centres . . . This conception does not involve the idea of a water-tight compartment, nor does such integration mean that the linear boundaries can be defined in reality. It does maintain that such a region has a core and that it is normally centred upon the principal cities. Such a region is a unit in the sense that its people are bound together economically and socially far more than with adjacent areas. This unity is due to three sets of conditions: first, the predominance of a group of activities—agriculture, industry, commerce and service—that are the same or complementary and interdependent through the interchange of goods and services; second, the dominance of both movements and activities by one or more great cities, that are at once the chief centres of affairs and the chief centres of radial routes and traffic; third, a common bond of historical development . . . both in the economic and cultural senses, in spite of the fact that these associations often cut across old-established political boundaries.[1]

What stands out in this definition is that its criteria are primarily economic and commercial. Cultural identity and historical tradition play a part, but political divisions are of little account.

This approach is clearly attuned to modern urbanized industrial society; whether the influence of cities over their hinterlands was as dominant in pre-industrial society is open to question. To describe the Rhineland in the late Middle Ages as densely urbanized, when the population of its largest city, Cologne, never exceeded 40,000,

---

[1] R. E. Dickinson, *The regions of Germany* (London, 1945), 23. This definition is also taken as his starting-point by J. C. Russell, *Medieval regions and their cities* (Newton Abbot, 1972), 15–16.

is, as J. C. Russell has reminded us, to arouse false expectations.[2] French and German human geographers have preferred to define medieval regions by geography and by shared linguistic usage and social custom. They speak of the *pays*, or the *Landschaft*, though therein lurks the danger of creating a romantic illusion of a landscape with unchanging values and traditions.[3] Nevertheless, it was the greatest of the French historical geographers, Paul Vidal de la Blache, who in the early years of this century pioneered the notion of the *ville-maîtresse*, or regional capital, which served as the administrative, cultural, and political focus for its *pays*, as well as the centre of its economic life.[4]

The importance of the city as a centre of marketing and distribution for its surrounding countryside has been a fundamental assumption in the work of economic geographers. For them, the common cultural and historical ties which shape regional identity recede before the role of the market area radiating out from a central place. For J. H. von Thünen, writing in the early nineteenth century, distance from the market was the criterion by which the distribution of agricultural zones could be predicted. In his ideal-typical model, which he termed the 'isolated state', von Thünen posited a series of concentric circles around a central place of exchange, which were determined by the type of cultivation (in terms of seed cost and yield), the cost of working the land, and the cost of transport. In a simplified form, the circle closest to the market would engage in market gardening and dairy produce; the next would be given over to various types of cereal agriculture, and the outermost circle devoted to pastoralism, though von Thünen in fact proposed a more elaborate hierarchy of six circles all told.[5]

<hr />

[2] Russell, *Medieval regions*, 78.

[3] Cf. Frank Göttmann, Horst Rabe, and Jörn Sieglerschmidt, 'Regionale Transformation von Wirtschaft und Gesellschaft. Forschungen und Berichte zum wirtschaftlichen und sozialen Wandel am Bodensee vornehmlich in der frühen Neuzeit, 1: Theoretische und methodische Grundprobleme', *Schriften des Vereins für Geschichte des Bodensees und seiner Umgebung*, 102 (1984), 117–18.

[4] Paul Vidal de la Blache, 'Régions françaises', *Revue de Paris*, 15 Dec. 1910, 821–49, esp. 838; R. E. Dickinson, *City region and regionalism: A geographical contribution to human ecology* (London, 1947), 12; idem, *City and region: A geographical interpretation* (London, 1964), 8. Cf. Russell, *Medieval regions*, 18.

[5] J. H. von Thünen, *Der isolirte Staat in Beziehung auf Landwirthschaft und Nationalökonomie oder Untersuchungen über den Einfluß, den die Getreidepreise, der Reichthum des Bodens und die Abgaben auf den Ackerbau ausüben*, pt. 1, 2nd edn. (Rostock, 1842), 2–5, 171–95, 219–22, 222, 222–23, 228–45. Cf. Peter Hall (ed.), and Carla M. Wartenberg (trans.), *Von Thünen's isolated state: An English*

It was not until the 1930s, however, that another German economic geographer, Walter Christaller, systematized the links between market centres of different sizes into a rank-order based on a predictable dispersion of central places. These he assigned to seven categories, ranging in size from settlements with a typical population of around 1,000 up to metropolises with 500,000 inhabitants. He asserted that the range of centrality of each tier of central places proceeds in a logarithmic ratio of the square-root of 3 (1.732), so that his smallest central place served a radius of 4 kms., the next 6.9 kms., then at intervals of 12 kms., 20.7 kms., 36 kms., 62.1 kms. up to the metropolis with a centrality of 108 kms.[6] But the key to Christaller's theory of centrality lay not in population size as such, but in the extent to which each level of central place provided a surplus of goods and services over and above the next level down the rank-order. Christaller, moreover, avoided describing the hinterland of a central place as its market region, for he was fully aware that the provision of goods and services extended well beyond the narrowly economic. Instead, he talked of a complementary region, which he thought better expressed the mutual relationship between town and country.[7] Affirming that centrality was more a question of function than of location,[8] he concluded: 'Remembering the meaning of *centrality*, we find that the complementary region is that region in which an importance-deficit exists. This importance-deficit is counterbalanced by the importance-surplus of the central place. Thus the region and the central place together make up an entity.'[9]

The advantages of Christaller's approach are manifest. Using the terminology of central places, he was able to dispense with the artificial distinction between town and country. At the lowest level of settlement, therefore, whether a community of a thousand souls

---

edition of Der isolierte Staat by *Johann Heinrich von Thünen* (Oxford, 1966), 9–11 (first ring: free cash cropping [*freie Wirtschaft*]); 106–23 (second ring: forestry [*Forstwirtschaft*]); 140–41 (third ring: crop alternation system [*Fruchtwechselwirtschaft*]); 142 (fourth ring: improved system [*Koppelwirtschaft*]); 143 (fifth ring: three-field system [*Dreifelderwirtschaft*]); 149–58 (sixth ring: stock farming [*Viehzucht*]).

[6] Walter Christaller, *Central places in Southern Germany*, trans. Carlisle W. Baskin (Englewood Cliffs, NJ, 1966), 67. The German original appeared under the title *Die zentralen Orte in Süddeutschland: Eine ökonomisch-geographische Untersuchung über die Gesetzmäßigkeit der Verbreitung und Entwicklung der Siedlungen mit städtischer Funktion* (Jena, 1933). [7] Idem, *Central places*, 20.

[8] Ibid. 19. [9] Ibid. 22.

had been granted an urban franchise to distinguish it from a mere village or market settlement becomes otiose: what matters is the centrality of the place in question in regard to its surrounding area —and that place need not be a town. Moreover, Christaller stressed that centrality was a two-way process: the central place ('town') cannot be understood in isolation from its complementary region ('countryside'). This recognition, which underlies modern regional planning, has only gradually been absorbed by urban historians, who have tended to treat towns as fish out of water.

Yet the drawbacks of Christaller's methodology in constructing a modern central-place network were also well recognized at the time; they need not detain us here.[10] What matters is how far his theory can be made fruitful for pre-industrial Europe. Both in terms of size and of location certain reservations must be entered. Any attempt to construct a system with seven levels of centrality in a society which was, by modern standards, sparsely urbanized seems doomed to failure. Towns of up to 30,000 inhabitants occupy the first five rungs of Christaller's modern system, but historians of late medieval and early modern Europe have found in practice that very few towns exceeded that size and that, in reality, only a total of three, or at the most four, levels of centrality can confidently be distinguished. Writing on English towns in the early modern period Peter Clark and Paul Slack have put forward a fourfold division between market town, county town, provincial capital, and national capital, though the last category would clearly be inapplicable to Germany.[11] Their scheme has recently been adopted in broad outline for Europe as a whole in the early modern period by Paul Hohenberg and Lynn Hollen Lees. In their analysis, the first group, that is, market towns, comprised settlements with fewer than 2,000 inhabitants; these, they argue, probably made up more than 75 per cent of towns in France, Germany, and Switzerland. To the second group, county towns, there is no obvious equivalent outside England, though Hohenberg and Lees suggest that in France it took in centres below the level of regional capitals of up

---

[10] Cf. for the Upper Rhine Wilfried Dege, *Zentralörtliche Beziehungen über Staatsgrenzen untersucht am südlichen Oberrheingebiet* (Bochumer Geographische Arbeiten) (Paderborn, 1979), 8–12.

[11] Peter Clark and Paul Slack, *English towns in transition 1500–1700* (London/Oxford/New York, 1976), 8–9.

to 10,000 inhabitants.[12] In Germany these towns have also been identified as a distinct group by Hektor Ammann;[13] they may be termed subregional centres, sometimes (but by no means always) the old *chef-lieux* of the Roman *pagi* or the subsequent German *Gaue*. The third category describes centres whose hallmark is a multiplicity of functions, not simply economic, with populations of between 10,000 and 25,000.[14]

A more substantial revision to Christaller's theory seems to be required over the issue of location. The rank-order distribution of central places in early modern Europe does not, empirically, correspond to his predicted logarithmic progression. Certain areas of Europe either experienced the dominance of overlarge centres (London in relation to the rest of England is the classic example), or else clusters of medium-ranking cities which would appear to have encroached upon each other's complementary regions (as in the case of Flanders, or Lombardy and Tuscany).[15] To explain this discrepancy Hohenberg and Lees have proposed a system of urban networks, predicated upon long-distance trade, instead of the impetus to urban development deriving from a town's immediate market area, which underlies central-place theory as elaborated by Christaller. In this trading network the goods exported are not luxury items but the basic commodities of a predominantly agrarian economy, grain and cloth. Towns drew upon agricultural surpluses and processed rural commodities such as wool not only for domestic consumption but for re-export as well. Towns, therefore, were certainly market centres for their regions, but at the same time they were 'nodes, junctions, outposts or relays' of a trading network. 'In this light', argue Hohenberg and Lees, 'a primarily agricultural region may develop its urban array in a way almost opposite to the process implied by central place theory', by which the initial point of distribution is located not at the centre of a region but at

---

[12] Paul L. Hohenberg and Lynn Hollen Lees, *The making of urban Europe 1000–1950* (Cambridge, MA/London, 1985), 51–53.

[13] Cf. Hektor Ammann, *Wirtschaft und Lebensraum der mittelalterlichen Kleinstadt, i. Rheinfelden*, n.p., n.d. [Aarau, 1947], 5.

[14] Hohenberg and Lees, *Making of urban Europe*, 54. It should be noted, however, that their categories differ somewhat from Clark and Slack's. The latter proposed (1) market centres of 600–1,500 inhabitants; (2) county centres of 1,500–5,000 inhabitants (on occasion more); (3) provincial capitals, with populations of 7,000 or more in 1500.    [15] Ibid. 56.

its periphery, as the gateway which links it to a further-flung network. Thus, lesser centres serve primarily to gather and ship the staple or export crop, and secondarily to distribute a return flow of goods, in this way stimulating the production of still larger surpluses.[16] Such a system is clearly likely to develop most readily where convenient arteries of transport, above all rivers, exist.

The existence of gateway cities (or ports-of-trade) has already been emphasized in the work of Carol A. Smith from her studies of central America, who developed what she terms a dendritic theory of location for predominantly agrarian societies whose peasant economy was still only partially commercialized.[17] But whereas her gateway communities dominate their attenuated hinterlands, and may not apply to an economy as specialized and export-oriented as the Upper Rhine in the early modern period, Hohenberg and Lees propose a much less deterministic system, in which the dispersion of settlements and the interaction between them is capable of much greater variation. As a result, the participants in such an urban network may each benefit from its existence, rather than contributing to the economic hegemony of a gateway centre. At the same time, however, Hohenberg and Lees overlook Christaller's own observations on alternative patterns of centrality. He was well aware of the importance of communications in determining the location of central places, whether they lay along rivers, roads, or, in his own day, railways. This he termed the 'traffic principle', whereby 'the distribution of central places is most favorable when as many important places as possible lie on one traffic route between two important towns, the route being established as straightly and as cheaply as possible'.[18] For our period, and especially for the Upper Rhine, Christaller's remarks on river systems are particularly enlightening. Comparing places which lie on, or at a certain distance from, the river, he states:

The range of goods offered at the place next to the river is consequently larger than the range of goods offered at the other place. Accordingly, the

---

[16] Hohenberg and Lees, *Making of urban Europe*, 62. Cf. Tom Scott and Bob Scribner, 'Urban networks', in Bob Scribner (ed.), *Germany: A new social and economic history*, i. *1450–1630* (London/New York/Sydney/Auckland, 1995), 129 ff.

[17] Smith, 'Exchange systems', 309–74. It should be added that J. C. Russell also drew attention to the existence of gateway or 'portal' cities, though his observations remained empirical, rather than resulting from any theoretical insight. Russell, *Medieval regions*, 231.          [18] Christaller, *Central places*, 74.

complementary region of the place next to the river is larger, and this place enjoys a more favorable develoment. Its larger complementary region, however, does not extend equally to all its sides; its largest extension is vertical to the river, because the neighboring central places also lying on the river enjoy the same advantages of cheaper river transportation . . . The complementary region is accordingly not an ellipse the long axis of which is formed by the river, but an ellipse the short axis of which is formed by the river. In fact, the towns generally lie on the rivers, i.e. they are lined up densely like pearls on a string . . .[19]

One way of visualizing such a central-place system based on the traffic principle would be to imagine the sails of a schooner mirrored in the water, projecting both skywards and downwards in a series of ellipses. That Christaller's recognition of the possibility of urban networks stretching along perceived lines of communication has been overlooked by historians and geographers can be attributed to his failure to elaborate the results of these theoretical insights into an alternative system of central places alongside the honeycomb of hexagonal interlocking marketing regions for which he is famous. And even when he returned to the theme after World War II in a study which accorded the traffic (*Verkehr*) principle equal weight alongside the supply or market (*Versorgung*) or administrative (*Zuordnung*) principle, Christaller remarked that *Versorgung* reflected the medieval unity of market and *Umland*, whereas *Verkehr* was confined to periods of frantic expansion of the traffic network, notably the nineteenth century.[20]

# II

In order to discover how well these theoretical approaches explain the rank-order of communities on the Upper Rhine, four variables have been chosen to illustrate the range of central functions and the intensity of relations with the surrounding countryside. They are (1) population size; (2) the principal economic activity within the town and its diffusion through exports and at fairs and markets; (3) the range of economic activity beyond the town which

[19] Ibid. 57–58.

[20] Idem, *Das Grundgerüst der räumlichen Ordnung in Europa: Die Systeme der europäischen Zentralen Orte* (Frankfurter Geographische Hefte, 24. 1) (Frankfurt am Main, 1950), 8–12; B. J. L. Berry and Allan Pred, *Central place studies: A bibliography of theory and applications* (Philadelphia, 1961); Dickinson, *City region and regionalism*, 54–56.

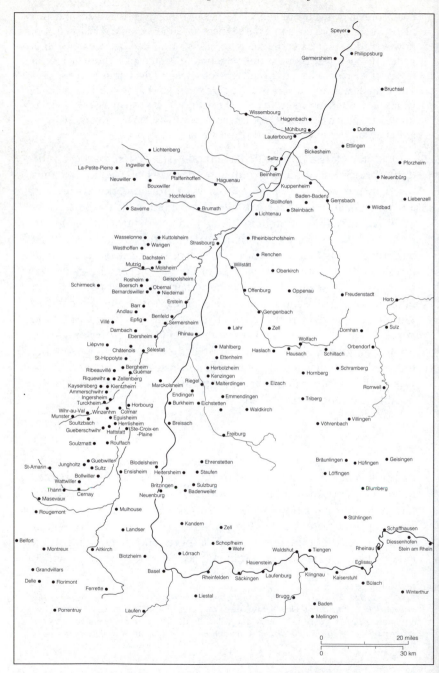

MAP 8. Towns and markets on the Upper Rhine, 1400–1600

was controlled entirely or in part by the town's businessfolk (the extent of outwork, and share-cropping); (4) the provision of merchant capital in credit and banking.

These criteria require elucidation and justification. Hektor Ammann originally advocated five variables: the penetration of urban capital into rural property; the circulation of coinage; the use of weights and measures; the market area; and the catchment area of visitors to the town's markets and fairs.[21] In themselves, these are useful indications of centrality (assuming that the sources allow us to plot them), but not all of them lend themselves to clear or consistent mapping. It is much easier, as Michael Mitterauer has pointed out, to trace a market area in terms of coinage circulation, or of weights and measures, than by investment or mercantile activity.[22] For our present purposes we need variables that will show not only the relationship of a central place to its hinterland but, even more importantly, the relationship of central places to each other, down to the smallest tier. At that level, criteria such as coinage areas or weights and measures barely apply, as does patronage of annual fairs. Instead, population size must be taken into consideration (while avoiding J. C. Russell's mistake of facilely equating it with centrality *per se*). Moreover, the general configuration of the urban economy—whether craft or industrial, diversified or specialized, regulated or unrestricted—is clearly of more use in identifying its dynamics than the essentially unvarying indicators of coinage or weights and measures. Here, too, the role of outwork in the putting-out system (*Verlagssystem*) as the vital link between urban investors and dependent rural labour needs to be included. And that, in turn, raises the question of the availability of capital for investment. These variables (however difficult it may be to glean satisfactory quantitative data from the sources) are likely to reveal whether towns were primarily centres of local exchange or relay-points along an urban network better than Ammann's more static approach.

---

[21] Cf. Peter Schöller, 'Stadt und Einzugsgebiet: Ein geographisches Forschungsproblem und seine Bedeutung für Landeskunde, Geschichte und Kulturraumforschung', in idem (ed.), *Zentralitätsforschung* (*Wege der Forschung*, 301) (Darmstadt, 1972), 285.

[22] Michael Mitterauer, 'Das Problem der zentralen Orte als sozial- und wirtschaftsgeschichtliche Forschungsaufgabe', in idem, *Markt und Stadt im Mittelalter: Beiträge zur historischen Zentralitätsforschung* (Monographien zur Geschichte des Mittelalters, 21) (Stuttgart, 1980), 43.

On these criteria, Strasbourg stands out as the regional capital beyond peradventure. It was by far the largest city in the region, with a population of around 18,000 in the mid-fifteenth century, rising to 25,000 by 1580 and 29,000 in the early seventeenth century.[23] Its growth depended upon its location at the confluence of the river Ill with the Rhine, where it acted as a loading-point for cargoes of Alsatian wine, which were carried downriver to the staging-posts of Frankfurt and Cologne for onward shipment to markets in northern Germany, Scandinavia, and England.[24] In addition, it exported certain staples—wheat and barley—down the Rhine to Cologne, as well as more unusual specialized crops such as onion seeds,[25] while madder, grown as an industrial crop between Wissembourg and Haguenau, was distributed from Strasbourg southwards into Switzerland.[26] Strasbourg also developed a modest manufacturing sector in textiles, producing mostly lesser-quality undyed woollen, linen, and fustian cloths (*Grautuch*), as well as linings and ticking, for a regional market, including Switzerland, but with some exports further afield, chiefly to Cologne.[27] Efforts were also made to promote the manufacture of high-quality Ypres cloth in the early sixteenth century.[28] Strasbourg's textile industry was closely linked

[23] Knut Schulz, *Handwerksgesellen und Lohnarbeiter: Untersuchungen zur oberrheinischen und oberdeutschen Stadtgeschichte des 14. bis 17. Jahrhunderts* (Sigmaringen, 1985), 29–30.

[24] Philippe Dollinger, 'La Ville libre à la fin du Moyen Âge (1350–1482)', in Georges Livet and Francis Rapp (eds.), *Histoire de Strasbourg des origines à nos jours*, ii. *Strasbourg des grandes invasions au XVIe siècle* (Strasbourg, 1981), 153–55. Cf. Hektor Ammann, 'Von der Wirtschaftsgeltung des Elsaß im Mittelalter', *Alemannisches Jahrbuch*, 1953, 11–63; Médard Barth, *Der Rebbau des Elsaß und die Absatzgebiete seiner Weine: Ein geschichtlicher Durchblick*, i (Strasbourg/Paris, 1958), 365–407.

[25] François-Joseph Fuchs, 'L'Espace économique rhénan et les relations commerciales de Strasbourg avec le sud-ouest de l'Allemagne au XVIe siècle', in Alfons Schäfer (ed.), *Festschrift für Günther Haselier aus Anlaß seines 60. Geburtstages am 19. April 1974* (Oberrheinische Studien, 3) (Bretten, 1975), 303–4; cf. François-Joseph Fuchs, 'Les Foires et le rayonnement économique de la ville en Europe (XVIe siècle)', in Livet and Rapp, *Histoire de Strasbourg*, ii. 269, 276, 287–88.

[26] Dollinger, 'La Ville libre', 157.

[27] Ibid. 156; Fuchs, 'Espace économique', 294–95, 308–10; Hektor Ammann, 'La Place de l'Alsace dans l'industrie textile du Moyen Âge', in *La Bourgeoisie alsacienne: Études d'histoire sociale* (Publications de la Société Savante d'Alsace et des Régions de l'Est: Grandes Publications, 5) (Strasbourg, 1967), 80, 88.

[28] Gustav Schmoller, *Die Strassburger Tucher- und Weberzunft: Urkunden und Darstellungen nebst Regesten und Glossar: Ein Beitrag zur Geschichte der deutschen Weberei und des deutschen Gewerberechts vom XIII.–XVII. Jahrhundert* (Strasbourg, 1897), 131 (no. 65).

to what Hektor Ammann has dubbed a Lower Alsatian 'textile group' of towns and villages, comprising Wissembourg, Pfaffenhoffen, Haguenau, Saverne, Sarrebourg, and Obernai, whose production, geared for export, was handled by a small number of merchants employing weavers in town and country by the putting-out system.[29] Strasbourg's month-long annual fair was re-established in the early fifteenth century, when it was transferred from late October to mid-June and restricted to a fortnight; only in 1570 was it joined by another fair at Christmas.[30] Though Strasbourg, in common with other cities in Upper Germany, notably Zürich and Nuremberg, or indeed Basel, tried to upgrade its annual markets to genuine international fairs on the scale of Frankfurt, Nördlingen, or Zurzach, neither Strasbourg nor Basel ever became a true *Messestadt*: their annual fairs remained regional rather than international.[31] Strasbourg's cattle-market, too, met more than local needs. Although it was mainly concerned to supply the citizenry with meat from abroad (since few cattle were raised in Lower Alsace), it also served as a point of redistribution, for butchers from the right bank of the Rhine in the Ortenau frequented the market to buy up cattle brought from Montbéliard and Burgundy, even on occasion from as far afield as Poland and Hungary.[32]

Strasbourg's wealth derived not only from wine but from the silver deposits in the Vosges mountains, especially in the Val de Lièpvre. The leading merchant families, such as the Ingold, Minckel, and Prechter, used the profits from their investment in silver-mining to establish general trading companies with branches throughout

---

[29] Ammann, 'La Place de l'Alsace', 75 (map), 80–89; idem, 'Wirtschaftsgeltung', 72; Schulz, *Handwerksgesellen und Lohnarbeiter*, 61; Schmoller, *Strassburger Tucher- und Weberzunft*, 105 (no. 50), 521–22.

[30] Dollinger, 'La Ville libre', 150; Fuchs, 'Espace économique', 289; idem, 'Foires', 259.

[31] Hektor Ammann, 'Die deutschen und schweizerischen Messen des Mittelalters', in *La Foire* (Recueils de la Société Jean Bodin, 5) (Brussels, 1953), 171. In German it is possible to distinguish between the *Jahrmarkt* and the *Messe*, the latter being the true international fair, held at most twice a year (as in the case of Leipzig or Frankfurt). Because the distinction has no equivalent in English usage, there has been a tendency to restrict the term 'fair' unduly. Cf. John Gilissen, 'The notion of the fair in the light of the comparative method', ibid. 333–42. For recent criticism of this and other attempts to downplay the importance of regional fairs see S. R. Epstein, 'Regional fairs, institutional innovation, and economic growth in late medieval Europe', *Economic History Review*, 2nd series, 47 (1994), 459–60.

[32] Fuchs, 'Foires', 301–2; idem, 'Espace économique', 319; Dollinger, 'La Ville libre', 147.

Europe.[33] The Ingold, a partnership of five brothers, set up companies in 1532 and 1551 to deal chiefly in spices and precious metals, which had factors abroad in Antwerp, Lyon, Venice, Milan, and Genoa, as well as at home in Frankfurt and Nuremberg.[34] Alongside the sale of silver ore in several European cities, the Prechter specialized in the paper-trade, and likewise maintained branches in Venice, Antwerp, and Lyon.[35] As the Strasbourg merchant houses diversified their activities into banking and credit, however, they sowed the seeds of their own downfall. Imprudent loans, especially to monarchs, precipitated a crisis in mid-century. The bankruptcy in 1559 of the Grand Parti, a consortium of financiers to the French crown, hit the Ingold hard, who became effectively insolvent by 1571. A string of bankruptcies followed over the next few years: the houses of Mesinger, Minckel, Braun, Engelmann, and Marstaller all collapsed, thereby putting an abrupt end to Strasbourg's role as a European centre of finance.[36]

The only city to rival Strasbourg as a regional capital for the Upper Rhine was Basel. Its population, however, was considerably smaller. The most reliable recent estimate, which emphasizes the peaks and troughs caused by epidemics, suggests that Basel numbered 10,400 inhabitants in the late 1420s, though the figure was undoubtedly swollen by those attending the Council of Basel. By the mid-fifteenth century the population had fallen back to 9,000, and remained at that level, apart from periodic slumps due to the plague, until 1500. Thereafter severe and repeated epidemics may have reduced the population to 5,000 at its lowest, in 1525, though it recovered quickly to a normal level of 7,000 to 8,500. By 1590 it had once again reached 9,000, and as many as 12,000 by 1609.[37]

---

[33] Fuchs, 'Foires', 277, 313.

[34] Idem, 'Richesse et faillite des Ingold, négotiants et financiers strasbourgeois du XVIe siècle', in *La Bourgeoisie alsacienne*, 204–5.

[35] Idem, 'Foires', 310–12; idem, 'Une famille de négotiants banquiers du XVI siècle: Les Prechter de Strasbourg', *Revue d'Alsace*, 95 (1956), 159, 166–72.

[36] Idem, 'Richesse et faillite', 210–11, 215–16; idem, 'Foires', 331–33. On the Grand Parti cf. Roger Doucet, 'Le Grand Parti de Lyon au XVI siècle', *Revue historique*, 171 (1933), 473–513; 172 (1933), 1–41. The Prechter, who never lent to the French crown, survived, but were weakened by family deaths. Fuchs, 'Les Prechter', 160–61, 180.

[37] Franz Gschwind, *Bevölkerungsentwicklung und Wirtschaftsstruktur der Landschaft Basel im 18. Jahrhundert: Ein historisch-demographischer Beitrag zur Sozial- und Wirtschaftsgeschichte mit besonderer Berücksichtigung der langfristigen Bevölkerungsentwicklung von Stadt (seit 1100) und Landschaft (seit 1500)* Basel (Quellen und Forschungen zur Geschichte und Landeskunde des Kantons Baselland, 15)

Like Strasbourg, it was an entrepôt, not as the outlet for a thriving and diversified commercialized agriculture, but rather as the point of intersection of international routes across the Alps and between Upper Germany and Burgundy and Lorraine. Nevertheless, its size enabled it to dominate the agricultural production of the surrounding area—the Markgräflerland on the right, the Sundgau on the left bank of the Rhine—whose peasants were dependent on the city as a market for their produce.[38] Neither in Basel nor in Strasbourg, however, is there any evidence of urban landowners seeking to exploit the market in foodstuffs by entering into share-cropping agreements with the surrounding peasantry, as occurred in the much larger Tuscan and Lombard cities.[39]

The economic history of Basel in the fifteenth and sixteenth centuries was stamped, as in so many other German cities, by a running struggle for ascendancy between the merchant and the craft guilds. The latter complained of the former's monopolistic practices and of competition from craftsmen outwith the city, employed in many cases as outworkers by its merchants. The promulgation of a new craft constitution (*Gewerbeordnung*) in 1526 finally appeared to seal the victory of the artisans over the four patrician merchant guilds by forbidding trade in goods which could be produced in Basel itself and by granting the craftsmen a sales monopoly within the city and its territory.[40] How strictly these provisions could be enforced was, of course, another matter; in 1552 the craft constitution of 1526 was revoked on the grounds that it had never been fully effective, and had given rise to conflict and dissent among

(Liestal, 1977), 172–74. Cf. Markus Mattmüller, *Bevölkerungsgeschichte der Schweiz*, pt. 1: *Die frühe Neuzeit, 1500–1700*, 2 vols. (Basel/Frankfurt am Main, 1987), i. 199; ii. 699. These figures lie somewhat higher than the older estimates; cf. Schulz, *Handwerksgesellen und Lohnarbeiter*, 30–31.

[38] Dorothee Rippmann, *Bauern und Städter: Stadt-Land-Beziehungen im 15. Jahrhundert. Das Beispiel Basel, unter besonderer Berücksichtigung der Nahmarktbeziehungen und der sozialen Verhältnisse im Umland* (Basler Beiträge zur Geschichtswissenschaft, 159) (Basel/Frankfurt am Main, 1990), 161.

[39] Cf. S. R. Epstein, 'Cities, regions, and the late medieval crisis: Sicily and Tuscany compared', *Past and Present*, 130 (1991), 39–40.

[40] Hans Füglister, *Handwerksregiment: Untersuchungen und Materialien zur sozialen und politischen Struktur der Stadt Basel in der ersten Hälfte des 16. Jahrhunderts* (Basler Beiträge zur Geschichtswissenschaft, 143) (Basel/Frankfurt am Main, 1981), 272–92. Cf. Schulz, *Handwerksgesellen und Lohnarbeiter*, 21, 121–22; Rippmann, *Bauern und Städter*, 186; Hans R. Guggisberg, *Basel in the sixteenth century: Aspects of the city republic before, during and after the Reformation* (St Louis, MO, 1982), 26–27.

the guilds.[41] Yet there is no parallel after 1526 to the activities of a merchant such as Ulrich Meltinger, active from the 1470s onwards, who traded throughout the Upper Rhine in wool, leather, and wine, as well as supplying wool to weavers in Alsatian towns and villages by the putting-out system. Meltinger and other burghers of Basel invested in silver-mining, too, both in the mines of the Sundgau and in the Black Forest on the Schauinsland at Todtnau, as well as taking stakes in iron-ore mining in eastern Switzerland around Sargans.[42] The imposition of ceilings on production and higher entry-fines for guild membership ensured that Basel in the sixteenth century sacrificed its role as a centre of export manufacturing and mercantile enterprise: in Traugott Geering's harsh verdict, its once important textile industry, which had specialized in luxury cloths, unlike Strasbourg, declined into insignificance through its own fault.[43] The city's two fairs, at Whitsun and in late October, did attract visitors from its wider hinterland—as far as Colmar and Strasbourg on the left bank, and Offenburg on the right bank of the Rhine—but they were not frequented by most Lower Alsatian towns, which were drawn instead to Strasbourg's much busier fairs; in 1494 the Whit fair was abolished because it clashed with the genuinely international fairs at Zurzach and Nördlingen.[44] It is questionable, therefore, whether Basel's annual markets deserve the epithet of fairs at all, especially once the city had clipped the wings of its mercantile élite.

Basel's decision to join the Swiss Confederation in 1501 entailed an economic as well as a political reorientation. Whereas its natural hinterland had been Alsace, after 1501 the city's economic links with Switzerland intensified.[45] This is particularly evident in the growth of banking and credit. Basel became the leading provider of finance to the Swiss cantons, both Protestant and Catholic. Between 1500 and 1610, Martin Körner has calculated, almost 59

[41] Füglister, *Handwerksregiment*, 281–82.

[42] Franz Ehrensperger, 'Basels Stellung im internationalen Handelsverkehr des Spätmittelalters' (Diss. phil. Basel, 1972), 350–51; Rippmann, *Bauern und Städter*, 180–86, 231–33.

[43] Traugott Geering, *Handel und Industrie der Stadt Basel: Zunftwesen und Wirtschaftsgeschichte bis zum Ende des 17. Jahrhunderts* (Basel, 1886), 313; Rippmann, *Bauern und Städter*, 186.

[44] Ehrensperger, 'Basel Stellung', 337; Rippmann, *Bauern und Städter*, 57.

[45] Guggisberg, *Basel in the sixteenth century*, 4. Basel's links to the secular territory of the bishopric of Basel in the Ajoie continued. Cf. ibid. 47.

per cent of private finance for public loans was raised on the Basel capital market.[46] Moreover, archduke Ferdinand raised loans from Basel financiers almost every year until 1551, whilst the powerful abbey of St Blasien in the Black Forest began to borrow enormous sums after 1574.[47] As well as securing supplies of essential foodstuffs for the cantons, which were lacking in cereals, several Swiss cities used their credit capacity to bolster indigenous manufacturing, and that was true of Basel also, which encouraged religious refugees from France, the Spanish Netherlands, and Italy to bring their skills in lace-making and velvet- and silk-weaving to the city.[48] These immigrants began to breathe new life into Basel's languishing trade towards the end of the sixteenth century, and helped restore some of the centrality which a protectionist artisan economy had squandered.

The second category of urban settlements proposed by Hohenberg and Lees includes what may be called in the German context subregional centres, that is, towns which acted primarily as markets for their surrounding districts, but which in addition possessed, however modestly, wider economic significance within and beyond the region as a whole. On the southern Upper Rhine these comprised towns which all boasted fair-sized populations of around 5,000. In Alsace, Colmar, Sélestat, and Haguenau fit this bill. Colmar, the largest, may have had anything between 6,000 and 6,800 denizens in 1500, though this figure dropped back below 6,000 in the mid-sixteenth century due to plague.[49] Sélestat's population may have totalled 5,500 in 1400, but thereafter experienced a steep decline to little more than 4,000 by 1450, a figure which remained static for the next century; only in 1600 had its population recovered to around 5,000.[50] Haguenau is reckoned to have had a population in excess of 5,000 in the fifteenth century, but data for the sixteenth are very scant.[51] To this triad Wissembourg can perhaps be added, since it had 4,000 inhabitants (or just under) in this period.[52] On the right bank of the Rhine, however, only Freiburg im Breisgau could match these Alsatian cities by the sixteenth century. However, the town had much earlier experienced a veritable boom on the back

[46] Martin H. Körner, *Solidarités financières suisses au seizième siècle* (Bibliothèque Historique Vaudoise, 66) (Lausanne, 1980), 440.     [47] Ibid. 400–1.
[48] Guggisberg, *Basel in the sixteenth century*, 39–40; Körner, *Solidarités*, 436–37.
[49] Schulz, *Handwerksgesellen und Lohnarbeiter*, 33.     [50] Ibid. 34.
[51] Ibid. 35.     [52] Ibid.

of the lucrative mining industry in the Black Forest, and its population may have touched 10,000 in the mid-fourteenth century.
Thereafter its demographic profile showed a sharp decline, though
historians are by no means agreed on its rapidity or on an eventual recovery. The most recent estimates suggest a population of
around 7,200 in 1385, which had slumped to little more than 5,000
by 1450. It then achieved a precarious stability at around 6,000 by
the turn of the century, only to be hit by further bouts of plague
in the first decades of the sixteenth century. Thereafter it appears
to have recovered quite strongly in the second half of the century, perhaps reaching 7,000 by 1600, and 8,000 on the eve of the
Thirty Years War.[53]

It is striking that all four Alsatian towns mentioned were imperial free cities within the Decapolis, the Alsatian urban league which
had been founded in 1354 to protect their independence against
neighbouring princes and to safeguard the public peace. But their
constitutional status had little bearing upon their economic fortunes,
for other members of the Decapolis were much smaller, some,
such as Munster and Turckheim, being little more than villages.
Rather, they owed their prominence to their function as relay-points
for the export of Alsatian wine—both Colmar and Sélestat were
strategically situated on the river Ill—or, in the case of Haguenau,
to its role in the local textile industry. Wissembourg, though at times
in danger of losing its independence to the electors Palatine, was
an outlet on the river Lauter for the viticulture of the northernmost

---

[53] For 1385 and 1450 see Rosemarie Merkel, 'Bemerkungen zur Bevölkerungsentwicklung der Stadt Freiburg zwischen 1390 und 1450', *Zeitschrift des Breisgau-
Geschichtsvereins ('Schau-ins-Land')*, 108 (1989), 83–91. Merkel exposes the
methodological inadequacies of Peter-Johannes Schuler, 'Die Bevölkerungsstruktur
der Stadt Freiburg im Breisgau im Spätmittelalter—Möglichkeiten und Grenzen einer
quantitativen Quellenanalyse', in Wilfried Ehbrecht (ed.), *Voraussetzungen und
Methoden geschichtlicher Städteforschung* (Städteforschung: Veröffentlichungen des
Instituts für vergleichende Städtegeschichte in Münster, A 7) (Cologne/Vienna, 1979),
139–76. Schuler, however, correctly advocates using a multiplier of 4 rather than 5,
as used by Hermann Flamm, so that his figures are more likely to give the correct
order of magnitude in what, because of the patchy archival record, can never be
more than estimates. For 1500 cf. Scott, *Freiburg and the Breisgau*, 123 and n. 38,
124 and n. 42. For 1600 cf. Schulz, *Handwerksgesellen und Lohnarbeiter*, 32; Horst
Buszello and Hans Schadek, 'Alltag der Stadt—Alltag der Bürger: Wirtschaftskrisen,
soziale Not und neue Aufgaben der Verwaltung zwischen Bauernkrieg und Westfälischem Frieden', in Heiko Haumann and Hans Schadek (eds.), *Geschichte der
Stadt Freiburg im Breisgau*, ii. *Vom Bauernkrieg bis zum Ende der habsburgischen Herrschaft* (Stuttgart, 1994), 70 and 519 n. 9.

reaches of Lower Alsace; wines were grown there much more extensively than today, and Wissembourg had in fact the oldest recorded vineyards in Alsace.[54]

Colmar's economy, it should be stressed, was not solely based on the wine trade; on the rich alluvial soil along the Lauch and the Ill its inhabitants engaged in commercial market-gardening, including the export of onion seeds, just as in Strasbourg.[55] It also sheltered a modest textile industry which manufactured cheaper cloths, such as linings, for export—again, a scaled-down version of Strasbourg's economy.[56] But unlike Strasbourg or Haguenau there is no evidence that production was organized by the putting-out system using local villagers as outworkers. The radius of visitors to Colmar's three annual fairs (at Corpus Christi, Ascension, and Martinmas) and to the four ember-day fairs cannot readily be determined, but is unlikely to have extended beyond the Upper Rhine. This, at least, may be inferred from a demand by Colmar's own merchants in the early seventeenth century that the ember-day fairs be abolished, since they were overrun by merchants from Strasbourg, Basel, Freiburg, and Breisach, who were stealing their trade![57] Although it had the right to strike its own coinage from silver mined in the Vosges, Colmar never developed as a financial or mercantile centre; what wealth its citizens possessed was likely to be invested in civic annuities rather than commercial ventures.[58] About the economic centrality of the other medium-sized

---

[54] Christian Wolff, 'Le Vignoble', in Jean-Michel Boehler, Dominique Lerch, and Jean Vogt (eds.), *Histoire de l'Alsace rurale* (Publications de la Société Savante d'Alsace et des Régions de l'Est: Grandes Publications, 24) (Strasbourg/Paris, 1983), 448.

[55] Lucien Sittler, 'Landwirtschaft und Gartenbau im alten Kolmar', *Elsaß-Lothringisches Jahrbuch*, 20 (1942), 71–94, esp. 88.

[56] Ammann, 'La Place de l'Alsace', 90. On Colmar's guilds, cf. Lucien Sittler, 'Les Corporations et l'organisation du travail à Colmar jusqu'au début du XVIIe siècle', in *Artisans et Ouvriers d'Alsace* (Publications de la Société Savante d'Alsace et des Régions de l'Est: Grandes Publications, 9) (Strasbourg, 1965), 47–77; Auguste Scherlen, *Das Zunftwesen Colmars und der Umgebung* (Colmar, 1923).

[57] Ibid. 16–17.

[58] Cf. Odile Kammerer, 'Richesses publiques et capitaux privés: l'Exemple de Colmar à l'entrée des temps modernes (1350–1560)', *Revue d'Alsace*, 112 (1986), 83–106, esp. 99 ff. On the lords of Ribeaupierre's loans in Colmar cf. eadem, 'Colmar ville-état et la puissante seigneurie des Ribeaupierre avant le XVIe siècle', in Jean-Marie Cauchies (ed.), *Les Relations entre États et principautés des Pays-Bas à la Savoie (XIVe–XVIe s.)* (Publication du Centre Européen d'Études Bourguignonnes, 32: Rencontres de Montbéliard (26 au 29 septembre 1991)) (Neuchâtel, 1992), 104.

Alsatian towns it is impossible to gain much information because of the paucity of the sources.

On Freiburg im Breisgau, by contrast, we are much better informed. The wealth generated by silver-mining in the fourteenth century had partly been reinvested by merchants in cloth manufacturing. Although Freiburg experienced a prolonged economic, as well as demographic, decline in the fifteenth century, which gave rise to a predictable clamour on the part of the surviving craftsmen for protectionist legislation to safeguard their shrunken market and employment, the town council was reluctant to accede to their demands. In 1472, it is true, the council introduced restrictions on competition in the textile industry, but within four years it had largely abandoned this policy. Compulsory guild membership, hitherto strictly enforced, was abandoned, employment deregulated, and new types of woollen cloth introduced. Thereafter cloth-making in Freiburg remained an open trade with elements of early capitalist organization, notably the putting-out of piecework by entrepreneurs to wage-working weavers, as was already the case with linen-manufacturing.[59] Limits on production were not enforced, despite requests from the clothmakers' guild, even in the face of competition from rural wool- and linen-weavers in the later sixteenth century.[60] Moreover, a new craft of cutting and polishing precious stones was built up after 1450 which, despite restrictions on output and pricing, still permitted masters to raise capital from foreign merchants and to employ guild members on piecework in what rapidly became an export-oriented enterprise.[61]

Freiburg's economy, therefore, was by no means solely devoted to domestic consumption or exchange with its immediate environs. But its relatively weak centrality can none the less be observed from the catchment area of visitors to its annual markets. These had originally been held at midsummer and at Martinmas, but a third, in the early spring, was added in 1516 because, as the diploma tellingly reveals, the summer fair was losing trade to Strasbourg's, held at the same time;[62] indeed, it was subsequently abandoned. Although they were patronized by merchants from the length and

[59] Scott, *Freiburg and the Breisgau*, 65–66, 136; Theophil Frank, 'Das Textilgewerbe der Stadt Freiburg i. Br. bis zum Ausgang des 16. Jahrhunderts' (Diss. phil. Freiburg, 1912), 30, 92–93.                                   [60] Ibid. 35, 38, 39–40.
[61] Scott, *Freiburg and the Breisgau*, 136.
[62] StAFr, A 1 I d 52, 20 Apr. 1516; Scott, *Freiburg and the Breisgau*, 64 and n. 64.

breadth of Upper Germany and the Rhineland, with some visitors from as far afield as Geneva, Savoy, and Lombardy to the south, the annual markets attracted custom mainly from the Upper Rhine, and preponderantly from Strasbourg.[63] By contrast, few Baslers visited the Freiburg markets, whose own fair was frequented by merchants on the right bank of the Rhine as far north as Offenburg, a clear indication that they saw Basel as a stronger economic magnet than Freiburg.[64] Whatever wider mercantile activity had once developed on the back of silver-mining, by the sixteenth century Freiburg's few remaining merchants no longer possessed the capital or displayed the flair to be entrepreneurs or financiers on a large scale. Much more typical of their horizons were the dealings of haberdashers such as Marx Hoff in the 1480s, who traded chiefly in wine-stone from the Breisgau villages which he sold at the Frankfurt fairs in exchange for cloth.[65]

The third category of central places, with populations of 2,000 or less—called market towns by Hohenberg and Lees—comprises local centres of exchange living in symbiosis with their surrounding countryside. The German term for these, *Ackerbürgerstädte*, or peasant burgher towns, highlights the predominantly agricultural character of such communities. Yet this description threatens to obscure significant variations within what otherwise might be regarded as an undifferentiated mass of minor central places, albeit that the sources rarely afford us any detailed insight into their economic and social structure. Mulhouse, for example, benefiting from its traffic advantage on the river Ill, may have topped 2,000 inhabitants in the early fifteenth century, even if the population sank back to 1,700 in 1512, though it then recovered to reach 2,600 by 1600.[66] It is therefore unclear whether it should be assigned to the second or third level of centrality. Breisach, too, may have had a

[63] Berent Schwineköper, 'Beobachtungen zum Lebensraum südwestdeutscher Städte im Mittelalter, insbesondere zum engeren und weiteren Einzugsbereich der Freiburger Jahrmärkte in der zweiten Hälfte des 16. Jahrhunderts', in Erich Maschke and Jürgen Sydow (eds.), *Stadt und Umland: Protokoll der X. Arbeitstagung für südwestdeutsche Stadtgeschichtsforschung Calw 12.–14. November 1971* (Veröffentlichungen der Kommission für geschichtliche Landeskunde in Baden-Württemberg, B 82) (Stuttgart, 1974), 44–53.

[64] Rippmann, *Bauern und Städter*, 57.

[65] Steven W. Rowan (ed.), 'Die Jahresrechnung eines Freiburger Kaufmanns 1487/88: Ein Beitrag zur Handelsgeschichte des Oberrheins, mit einem Nachwort von Berent Schwineköper', in Maschke and Sydow, *Stadt und Umland*, 227–77.

[66] Schulz, *Handwerksgesellen und Lohnarbeiter*, 35.

population of more than 2,000 in our period,[67] but as a vantage-point on the Rhine with bridge and toll-station it exercised central functions well beyond its actual population size.

It is true that the profusion of small towns along the foothills of the Vosges stemmed directly from the burgeoning of viticulture, but wine-growing in Alsace, unlike other regions of south-west Germany such as the Neckar valley in Württemberg,[68] cannot be seen as satisfying merely local or regional consumption. On the contrary, most of these wine villages would never have acquired urban franchises in the first place had it not been for the supraregional, indeed, international, demand for Alsatian wine which encouraged foreign merchants to invest in vineyards or to buy up vintages *sur souche* before the harvest, thereby creating employment opportunities in a labour-intensive industry and bestowing an unusual, if hazardous, prosperity upon the region.[69] Had not most Alsatian wine gone for export, in fact, it is hard to see how so many communes could have existed in close proximity without economically cutting each other's throats. Some were huddled so close together —Ammerschwihr, Kaysersberg, and Kientzheim—that they were within gunshot of each other, as Sebastian Münster observed in his *Cosmographei.*[70] Moreover, some small towns in Alsace that were not engaged in viticulture still managed to acquire an influence which belied their size. Of the members of the Lower Alsatian textile group, for instance, Pfaffenhoffen on the river Moder, which during the Middle Ages had been no more than a village with market rights, seems to have been granted urban privileges in the sixteenth century, when it was fortified by its overlord, the count of Hanau-Lichtenberg, as acknowledgement of its standing in the regional production of woollen cloth.[71] Masevaux, a small Outer Austrian town in the Doller valley in the southern Vosges, was a noted centre for the manufacture of linen-twill, which it regularly traded at the Frankfurt fairs.[72] Even though restrictions on produc-

---

[67] A population of 3,000 has been suggested for the beginning of the 17th century by Günther Haselier, *Geschichte der Stadt Breisach am Rhein*, i. 1: *Von den Anfängen bis zum Jahr 1700* (Breisach, 1969), 306, without any supporting evidence.

[68] Cf. Scott and Scribner, 'Urban Networks', 130–31.

[69] Barth, *Rebbau des Elsaß*, i. 365 ff.; Ammann, 'Wirtschaftsgeltung', 18, 30–40; Franz Irsigler, 'Kölner Wirtschaft im Spätmittelalter', in Hermann Kellenbenz (ed.), *Zwei Jahrtausende Kölner Wirtschaft*, i (Cologne, 1975), 287.

[70] Sebastian Münster, *Cosmographei* (Basel, 1550), 526.

[71] Ammann, 'La Place de l'Alsace', 82.        [72] Ibid. 91.

tion and a prohibition on outwork were imposed by a new weaving ordinance in 1527,[73] Masevaux's producers, both weaver and drapers, continued to patronize the Frankfurt fairs throughout the century, even maintaining their own factor there.[74] Furthermore, the advantages of location on a particular trade route could pitch a small community into fulfilling specific central functions altogether out of proportion to its general economic significance or population size. That was the case with Cernay in Upper Alsace, which was the scene of an international cattle-mart at the gateway to the rich pasturelands of the Franche-Comté and Burgundy.[75] Merchants from the whole of Upper Germany thronged to the Ochsenfeld outside Cernay's walls, a mart privileged by emperor Frederick II, the importance of which was overshadowed in the Empire only by the cattle-market at the otherwise equally insignificant commune of Buttstädt in Thuringia.[76] Cernay's thriving cattle-trade stands in marked contrast to the administratively and strategically more central Belfort, situated at the entrance to the Burgundian Gate, which might also have been expected to develop as a commercial node between Burgundy and the Upper Rhine. But Belfort was only 'un carrefour des routes secondaires'; traffic passed to the south via Montbéliard or else to the north via Thann over the col de Bussang.[77] Although the town had four annual fairs, and its inhabitants were craftsmen and merchants rather than agriculturalists, the radius of Belfort's economic influence was limited. Its merchants, according to a guild statute of 1462, were permitted to trade freely throughout Upper Alsace and as far south as Pontarlier, but westwards only up to the line of the rivers Lisaine and Luze, and eastwards to the Largue, a maximum of 20 kilometres.[78]

---

[73] AMMx, HH 1/3, 12 June 1527, §§ 25, 30.

[74] AMMx, BB 5, pp. 51–52 (1531); HH 3/19 (1580).

[75] Jean Vogt, 'Grandeur et décadence du marché de bétail de Cernay (Deuxième moitié du XVIe et début du XVIIe siècle)', *Annuaire de la Société d'Histoire des Régions de Thann-Guebwiller*, 1970–72, 131–38.

[76] Tom Scott, 'Economic landscapes', in Scribner, *Germany: A new social and economic history*, 23, 25, and 24 (map); cf. Ian Blanchard, 'The continental European cattle trades, 1400–1600', *Economic History Review*, 2nd series, 39 (1986), 436, 443.

[77] Bruno de Villèle, 'Belfort à la fin du Moyen Âge' (Diss. phil., Besançon, 1971), i. 89 (map), 90; Georges Bischoff, 'Belfort au XVe siècle—une duchesse et des comptes', in Yvette Baradel, Georges Bischoff, André Larger, Yves Pagnot, and Michel Rilliot, *Histoire de Belfort* (Roanne/Le Coteau, 1985), 95.

[78] De Villèle, 'Belfort', 90; Bischoff, 'Belfort', 93–95.

By comparison with Alsace, the Breisgau and Ortenau were thinly strewn with market towns. Wine-growing towns and villages along the slopes of the Black Forest hills and the Kaiserstuhl never attained the demographic concentration or commercial significance of their Alsatian counterparts; it is doubtful whether much of their harvest was sold beyond south-west Germany. The Ortenau could boast three imperial cities—Offenburg, Gengenbach, and Zell—but they lay too much in the lee of Strasbourg to develop more than a modest centrality. In the Breisgau, however, Waldkirch was set somewhat apart from its neighbours on account of its involvement as an ancillary centre of cutting and polishing; the town benefited from its location on the river Elz, which provided plentiful water to drive the grinding-wheels. Of the four Forest Towns on the *Hochrhein*, Rheinfelden stood out (even with a population of little more than 1,000)[79] because of its stake in commercial salmon fishing, whilst Laufenburg's access to water power from the fast-flowing rapids enabled it to become a metallurgical centre for iron-ore mining in the Frick valley.[80]

Most difficult of all to classify is the welter of mining communities in the valleys of the Black Forest and the Vosges. Exhaustion of seams or technical obstacles to their working—flooding, and the collapse of shafts—made mining a precarious business: settlements could spring up almost overnight, only to become ghost towns within a generation. The crassest example on the Upper Rhine is Ste-Marie-aux-Mines in the Val de Lièpvre west of Sélestat, where new reserves of silver were discovered in the early sixteenth century. By 1525 Ste-Marie-aux-Mines is supposed to have given shelter to 3,000 miners; 1,200 new houses—shacks, more likely—were run up in quick order, while its suburb of Fortelbach—a squatter camp—allegedly supported 72 inns.[81] By mid-century, however, the heyday of the Val de Lièpvre mines had already passed; no other mining settlement on either bank of the Rhine (as far as the sources reveal) ever approached the size and activity of Ste-Marie-aux-Mines, though Sulzburg in the Markgräflerland and a cluster

---

[79] Schulz, *Handwerksgesellen und Lohnarbeiter*, 44–45; Ammann, *Rheinfelden*, 14.

[80] Rudolf Metz, 'Bergbau und Hüttenwesen in den Vorlanden', in Friedrich Metz, *Vorderösterreich*, 151, 153. In the 16th century the *Hochrhein*'s hammersmiths' league encompassed 36 iron-founders. Ibid. 154.

[81] Friedrich Metz, 'Die elsässischen Städte. Die Grundlagen ihrer Entstehung und Entwicklung', in idem, *Land und Leute*, 320.

of mining towns in the western Sundgau around Giromagny produced commercially significant quantities of ore.

# III

It therefore remains to be seen how far these three categories of town on the southern Upper Rhine can be accommodated into a hierarchy of central places with a regular dispersion. Because rank-order determines their dispersion on Christaller's hexagonal grid, it is necessary to begin by identifying groups of towns according to their size. There is no difficulty in designating Strasbourg as the regional capital, both by population and location, as well as by economic and commercial function. It was the only undisputed metropolis on the southern Upper Rhine. The status of Basel, however, is much more equivocal, falling as it does on the borderline between two categories, regional capitals and 'county towns' (or subregional centres, as we have to say for Germany). Clearly it would be absurd to lump Basel together with the other members of a category whose towns ranged in size from 10,000 down to a mere 2,000, even if its economic centrality was on the wane up to the mid-sixteenth century. Basel's reorientation towards the Swiss Confederation seems latterly to have compensated for the constraints of an economic regime hostile towards entrepreneurialism by encouraging the development of a banking sector which served the whole of Switzerland. It seems more appropriate, therefore, to regard Basel as a subregional metropolis, on the fringe of Strasbourg's wider orbit; at the same time, it was the pre-eminent city between Upper Rhine and *Hochrhein*, and certainly the dominant power within the regional coinage association of that area, the Rappen league, evincing a size and a centrality perceptibly greater than the next tier of central places within its complementary region.

Within the group of subregional centres arrayed around Basel and Strasbourg, what stands out is the spread of towns with populations of 4,000 to 6,000, half the size of Basel, and yet with clear water between themselves and the remaining communes, few of which ever exceeded 2,000 inhabitants (or only briefly). This suggests that the limits of the second category have been set too widely by Hohenberg and Lees; in terms of a rank-order progression, one might indeed expect a cluster of subregional centres to be dotted around the submetropolis with populations half its size, and clearly distinct from the next category down, namely genuinely local centres. Clark and Slack's slightly narrower bands for England— 600–1,500; 1,500–5,000 +; 7,000 +—seem to fit the bill rather better, but even they fail to pick up the unmistakable separation of the subregional centres (their 'county towns') around 4,000–6,000 in size from the mass of lesser market towns. To describe this final and largest category as market towns, however, raises certain difficulties. While it is true, for instance, that the petty capitals of the Austrian administrative districts in Alsace were indeed centres of distribution and exchange for their respective *Ämter*—and how jealously they guarded their urban privileges against rural encroachment we will discover in the next two chapters—their centrality derived as much from administrative and judicial as from purely economic functions. Again, it is not at first evident that the string of wine-growing communes along the Vosges should be called market towns, for their hinterlands were so compacted as hardly to constitute distinct market areas at all; rather, their centrality stemmed from their place in an urban network tied to long-distance trade.

In social and economic terms, we have observed, many towns in this last group were indistinguishable from villages. Although the Upper Rhine—or more properly Alsace—was by medieval standards quite densely urbanized, the total given by Hektor Ammann of eighty-five towns founded in Alsace alone up to 1,500 seems pitched far too high; a figure in the mid-sixties may be somewhat nearer the mark.[82] He includes, for instance, several villages which had been fortified, as if circumvallation were a sufficient badge of urban status. The textile centre of Pfaffenhoffen mentioned earlier may, in fact, never have received a charter of liberties raising it from a village to a town. Some villages in Alsace—Wasselonne and Kuttolsheim—stood under the direct protection of the Empire, just as the cities of the Decapolis did, with privileges to match, but that did not make them towns.[83] More significant is the number of market franchises which were granted to villages for both weekly and annual markets in the later Middle Ages. Although many of these charters may have been inspired by political and territorial rather than purely economic motives, they nevertheless give some

---

[82] Hektor Ammann, 'Das Städtewesen des Mittelalters. Erläuterungen zu Karte 34', in *Erläuterungsband zum Elsaß-Lothringischen Atlas*, 124–25. Cf. Henri Dubled, 'Ville et village en Alsace au Moyen Âge: Essai de definitions, critères de distinction', in *La bourgeoisie alsacienne*, 64–65.  [83] Ibid. 65.

indication of the level of economic activity on the Upper Rhine, which was reflected in the proliferation of such lesser central places.

The next step is to examine whether these three levels of centrality can be reconciled with the intervals between the five levels which Christaller originally posited for centres up to a population of 30,000. According to the marketing principle, upon which his central-place system was essentially based (despite his various disclaimers), the rank-order dispersion is in threes, and at first sight this seems to hold good for the major centres on the Upper Rhine. As the regional metropolis, Strasbourg lies almost equidistant between the submetropolises of Basel (115 kms. upriver) and Worms (125 kms. downriver), thereby describing a region which comes close to the range of 108 kms. which Christaller in modern times predicted for the apex of his system, the L-place, a vast metropolitan city of half-a-million inhabitants. The next circle has a notional radius of 62.1 kms., which in fact corresponds to Colmar and Freiburg's distance from Strasbourg in one direction and Basel in the other, each at around 60 kms. distant from the metropolis or submetropolis, or of Wissembourg and Pforzheim in relation to Worms and Strasbourg. But from this point onwards the discrepancies between theory and reality begin uncomfortably to intrude. Although Wissembourg is near the mark at 55 kms. from Strasbourg, Pforzheim, over the first range of Black Forest hills, is both too far away, at 75 kms., and somewhat eccentric, moreover, to the Upper Rhine valley. Furthermore, Freiburg's and Colmar's complementary regions with a radius of 36 kms. fit this theoretical grid only if they are placed at a distance of 60 kms. from each other, whereas they lie a mere 38 kms. apart, so that their hinterlands would appear to collide. Further down the scale such overlaps become even more obtrusive if the many lesser towns and villages in Alsace are assumed to be located according to the marketing principle.

This suggests that the system of central places on the Upper Rhine owes more to the transport (or traffic) principle, which Christaller broached in his classic study, but never satisfactorily developed. This system assumes that the largest number of central places will be situated along a direct route between two cities, spaced at equal intervals, rather than being dispersed radially, as in the marketing pattern. Here the interlocking hexagons are arranged differently and the intervals progress not by threes but by fours. The hexagon itself is somewhat smaller, and the central places are situated not at its corners but midway along its sides. In practice, the grids on the transport principle of dispersion are squeezed into lozenges, rather than forming isometric hexagons.[84] This would accommodate the relationship of Freiburg to Colmar much better; it would more plausibly imply that Wissembourg's counterpart across the Rhine was Ettlingen and Durlach taken together as a twin central place, rather than Pforzheim; and it would help to account for the number and spacing of communes at regular intervals along the Rhine and the Ill. Moreover, by distinguishing between primary and secondary routes, which run parallel to each other, the lozenge grid may explain the tracking of wine-growing towns and villages along the present-day *route du vin* in Alsace, which shadows the course of the Ill and the Rhine for much of its length, and to a certain extent their equivalents along the foothills of the Black Forest through the Breisgau and the Ortenau, linked by the modern federal highway, the *Bundesstraße* 3.

The transport principle echoes Hohenberg and Lees' system of urban networks, but in seeking to construct a model appropriate to early modern Europe they refrain, unlike Christaller, from proposing a preordained dispersion based on mathematical formulae. Rather, they stress the flexibility and adaptability of urban networks in contrast to the perceived rigidities of a central-place system. Moreover, their analysis does not require the regional capital Strasbourg to be interpreted as the gateway community of a dendritic system, holding its hinterland in economic thrall. They draw particular attention to the importance in pre-industrial Europe of river systems, a point recognized by Christaller, but never used fruitfully in his theoretical analysis.[85] The relevance of this approach to the Upper Rhine is immediately apparent. The wine-growing communes of Alsace, for instance, delivered their casks to boatmen and brokers at points along the Ill, especially the entrepôts of Colmar and Sélestat, for onward shipment to Strasbourg and thence down the Rhine to foreign markets. Along the Ill subsidiary centres sprang up for the distribution of wine and other agrarian produce at fairly regular intervals between the main centres—Mulhouse, Ensisheim, Benfeld, Erstein. On the Rhine itself towns were more densely clustered on the *Hochrhein* above Basel, where the vagaries of the river's channel were less acute, than below Basel, where the river

---

[84] Cf. Berry and Sked, *Central place studies*, 7; Dickinson, *City and region*, 54–56.
[85] Cf. Scott and Scribner, 'Urban networks', 131.

meandered through marshland and gravelbanks. But in either case the spacing of towns was remarkably regular—intervals of around 15 kms. on the *Hochrhein* between Waldshut, Laufenburg, Säckingen, and Rheinfelden, and approximately 30 kms. on the Upper Rhine from Basel to Neuenburg, Breisach, Rhinau, and Strasbourg—which implies that the traffic principle of centrality has some bearing upon their location.

On the right bank, two important tributaries fed into its riverine transport network. On the Kinzig, whose valley formed the main artery over the Black Forest to central Swabia, Offenburg served as an entrepôt for a chain of smaller towns upstream—Gengenbach, Zell am Harmersbach, Haslach, and Hausach, with further settlements on the rivers Wolfach (Wolfach itself) and Gutach (Hornberg, and Triberg)—which rafted timber from the afforested slopes downstream to the Rhine. But the Kinzig was overshadowed by rafting on the Murg from the heights above Gernsbach down to Rastatt, where the boatmen formed themselves into a powerful cartel, the Murg rafting association (*Murgschiffergesellschaft*), which dominated the supply of timber throughout the whole of the northern Upper Rhine.

A further advantage of Hohenberg and Lees' approach is that they recognize, as Christaller barely did, that competition between centres in an urban network might occur as readily as complementarity: it could be brought about by political conflict—the pressure towards *arrondissement* within the early modern territorial principalities—or by shifts in economic activity, as one centre displaced another through changing patterns of trade or innovations in manufacturing (especially in textiles). However, the drawback inherent in their search for a model flexible enough to do justice to the early modern European economy is that the system of urban networks may end up as pure description, imposing retrospectively a pattern upon historical reality, rather than as a predictive explanation of the location, function, and dispersion of central places, as in Carol A. Smith's dendritic system. Urban networks, therefore, should be used as an additional tool of analysis, not as a substitute for central-place theory.[86] Both approaches must be borne in mind when we examine the nature and extent of economic conflict within the region of the Upper Rhine in the fifteenth and sixteenth centuries.

[86] Hohenberg and Lees, *Making of urban Europe*, 72.

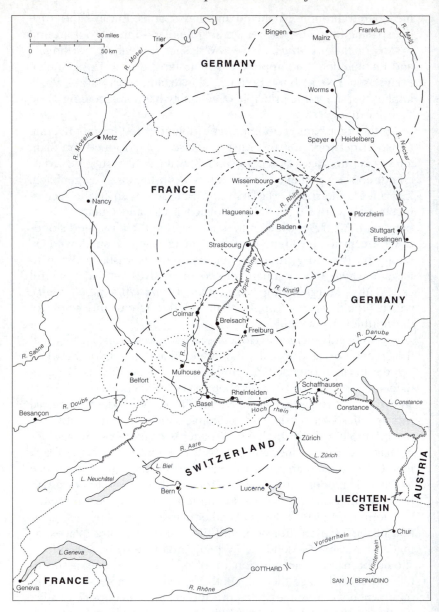

MAP 9a. Central places on the Upper Rhine, according to the marketing principle

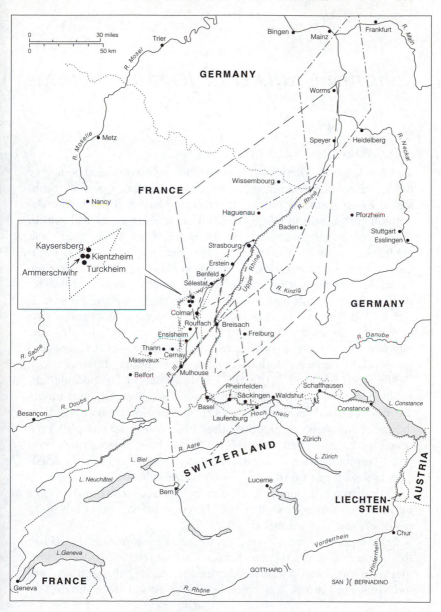

MAP 9b. Central places on the Upper Rhine, according to the
traffic/transport principle

# 4

# *Country Crafts and Regional Guilds*

## I

The fundamental premiss of the historical-geographical study of the location of central places is that the network is a perfect mesh, that is to say, on the one hand, a central place will not face competition in the supply of goods and services from a rival within its complementary area and, on the other hand, its centrality will contribute to, or be absorbed by, the centrality of the next highest place in the rank order, in what has been termed the 'nesting' principle, reminiscent of a Russian doll. In other words, a perfect dispersion of central functions is posited, based on the pattern of supply and demand, and calculated by time–cost effectiveness, that is, *not* the distance travelled to market as such, but the distance which it is worth a consumer's while travelling to obtain a particular good or service. Modern central-place theory, however, has rightly been sceptical about the extent of rational economic calculation on the part of the consumer. Even modern consumers are not regarded as driven by pure economic rationality but by 'bounded rationality', limited by their ability to grasp complex economic linkages.[1] Even in modern market-based economies with good communications, the ideal-typical pattern is often falsified. This is *a fortiori* true of early modern pre-industrial societies with weaker market integration, slower communications, and poorer information networks, so that the choice of market was both more restricted and less informed.

Central-place theories based on the marketing principle also run the danger of assuming that markets are purely economic instruments of distribution and exchange. In reality, throughout pre-industrial Europe markets were privileged foundations created by

---

[1] Cf. Allan Sked, *Behavior and location: Foundation for a geographic and dynamic location theory*, i (Lund Series in Geography, B 27) (Lund, 1967), 26, cited in Dege, *Zentralörtliche Beziehungen*, 12.

their overlord's grant of a franchise, rather than the spontaneous outflow of economic opportunity or necessity. This imparted an artificial character to markets, so that, in Robert Dodgshon's words, their impact on the economy of their environs was likely to be 'stilted'.[2] In areas of territorial fragmentation (of which the Upper Rhine was one, though not the most extreme, example in Germany) lords bent upon territorial consolidation (autarchy) might found markets, not only as a device to augment their seigneurial revenues, but as a means of making their territories economically self-sufficient (autarky). Seen from this perspective, the distribution of markets might be deliberately skewed, with rival markets set up in close proximity to existing ones, as lords sought to compel their subjects to frequent only home markets and shun foreign ones. None of the systems of centrality put forward by Christaller, whether based on the marketing, traffic, or administrative principle, take account of this possibility. Only Hohenberg and Lees, in their discussion of urban networks, have acknowledged in broad terms that towns and markets were as much manifestations of political and seigneurial interests as they were of economic: in medieval Europe they were established to secure control of territory or to promote colonizing ventures (the many 'Newtons', 'Villeneuves', and 'Neuburgs' testify to this).

Furthermore, in Hohenberg and Lees's system the spatial distribution of towns is much less regular and more flexible than in a predictive rank-order hierarchy. 'Since cities are links in a network, often neither the first source nor the ultimate destination of goods, they are in some measure interchangeable as are the routes themselves. Marketing shifts, political conflicts and policies, even innovations in shipping and banking can lead to the displacement of one center by another.'[3] The marketing shifts which they have in mind are the rivalries which develop between urban centres linked by a long-distance trading network, as one mercantile capital dislodged another from its pre-eminence—Regensburg by Nuremberg and then the latter by Augsburg between the fourteenth and the sixteenth centuries, or Erfurt by Leipzig after 1500, in what Robert-Henri Bautier, observing the eclipse of Flemish by Brabantine cities

---

[2] Robert A. Dodgshon, *The European past: Social evolution and spatial order* (Houndmills, Hants/London, 1987), 238–39; cf. Mitterauer, 'Problem der zentralen Orte', 41; Scott, 'Economic landscapes', 2.

[3] Hohenberg and Lees, *Making of urban Europe*, 64.

in the later Middle Ages, memorably called a 'relay-race'.[4] For Hohenberg and Lees, the network system 'testifies to the mercurial force of movable wealth and universal ideas', at whose heart lay an 'internationale of cities . . . more concerned with the world at large than with its own backyard'.[5]

The experience of the Upper Rhine in the fifteenth and sixteenth centuries was utterly different. The two metropolises, Strasbourg and Basel, faced no sustained challenge to their ascendancy, even if they competed for commercial control of the southern stretch of the Upper Rhine (though Basel's economy, as we have seen, underwent a significant reorientation). Rather, the centrality of the regional 'county' and lesser market towns was repeatedly challenged by economic competition in their own backyard. That competition took three principal forms: the towns resented the rise of craft production in the countryside, which eroded the traditional function of urban centres; they objected to the establishment of rural salt-chests, which infringed the lucrative urban monopoly on stapling salt; and they feared competition from new rural markets, some in franchised villages, others held informally at church-ales or at weddings, which undermined the autonomy of borough markets. The towns' litany of grievances was plangent and sustained, and their detail is often difficult to absorb. For the sake of clearer presentation therefore, the grievances concerning country crafts and staples, and the possible countermeasures open to towns or territorial rulers, will be examined in the remainder of this chapter, with the conflicts over markets reserved for the following chapter. It is hardly necessary to stress, however, that these issues often overlapped and intersected.

## II

Of the three heads of grievance, the rise of rural crafts is the most difficult to document and interpret with accuracy. Unless they were practised within the towns' market precinct (*Bannmeile*), there was rarely a pretext for legal redress, which might leave an archival deposit in the form of records of a court case. Instead, we are largely reliant on indirect evidence, particularly urban protests,

---

[4] Robert-Henri Bautier, *The economic development of medieval Europe* (London, 1971), 176.        [5] Hohenberg and Lees, *Making of urban Europe*, 70.

whether individual or collective. On the Upper Rhine specific complaints at the threat posed by the spread of country crafts are in fact not all that numerous. One of the earliest occurred in 1476, when amidst deliberations on how to get the town's economy on the mend Freiburg's magistrates noted that, apart from the long-standing burden of civic debt, the town's 'trades [and] useful imports have markedly declined because all trades and crafts in the countryside have increased'.[6] And in 1518 the four Forest Towns on the *Hochrhein* bemoaned the competition they allegedly faced from rural crafts.[7] The only other specific reference, albeit a most suggestive one, to the threat emanating from rural handicrafts was made by Villingen in the eastern Black Forest in the mid-sixteenth century. In a series of submissions, mostly connected with Austria's intention of raising the mortgage sum on the lordship of Warenberg which was held by the town, Villingen pleaded poverty on the grounds that craftsmen who had earlier resided in the town had emigrated to hamlets and villages within a radius of 1 German mile (that is, 4.6 statute miles, or 7.4 kms.). They included millers, smiths, bakers, cartwrights, cobblers, and clothiers.[8] There they were being actively encouraged to ply their trade by the local lords to whom the villages belonged, in direct competition with Villingen and its market.[9]

It would be easy to dismiss these as isolated instances—or indeed as special pleading—were it not for the string of anguished pleas collectively submitted by members of the Outer Austrian third Estate from the late fifteenth century onwards at territorial, imperial, and general Austrian diets. Although the protests often originated from the Breisgau Estates, they were by no means confined to the right bank of the Rhine, and by the mid-sixteenth century had slipped

---

[6] StAFr, A 1 VII b 14, 1443? [*recte*: 1476]: 'und dennocht an gewerben, nuczlichem züfaren mercklich zü abgang komen sigen durch das, das alle gewerb und handtwerck uff dem land geuffet werden'. Cf. Tom Scott (ed.), *Die Freiburger Enquete von 1476: Quellen zur Wirtschafts- und Verwaltungsgeschichte der Stadt Freiburg im fünfzehnten Jahrhundert* (Veröffentlichungen aus dem Archiv der Stadt Freiburg im Breisgau, 20) (Freiburg, 1986), 4.

[7] StAFr, C 1 Landstände 3: particular complaints of the Breisgau towns at the general Austrian diet in Innsbruck, drawn up 14 Mar. 1518, presented 4 May 1518, § 7.

[8] StAVl, H 37 [no. 2969]: 'verzaichnus vnnd be schreybung der pfandbrieffen vnd versazungen Warenberg . . . de Aõ 1556 [?]', fo. 7ʳ; cf. H 36 [no. 2968], 1553–11 July 1562, fo. 46ᵛ; Speck, *Landstände*, i. 331.

[9] StAVl, H 37 [no. 2969], fo. 7ʳ; W 2 [no. 1974], 11 Aug. 1515–18 July 1558: n.d. (*circa* 1560).

into the bloodstream of Outer Austrian urban grievances as a whole. A string of petitions in 1483,[10] 1517/18,[11] 1524,[12] and 1557[13] paints a vivid picture of a flourishing rural petty-capitalist economy, in which villagers were busy trading in salt, iron, cloth, and preserved goods, alongside the burgeoning crafts which once had been located *intra muros*—tailors, cobblers, cartwrights, ropemakers, smiths, saddlers, butchers.[14] Rather touchingly (but disingenuously), the towns lamented that the peasants, too, were suffering from these developments, inasmuch as they were so overwhelmed by the range of goods available in the countryside that they could no longer save any money![15]

To estimate the challenge posed by these rural craftsmen—given the obviously *parti pris* nature of the towns' reaction—it would be necessary to offer some quantitative evidence of their distribution. But that is precisely where, as Francis Rapp has observed, the sources are found wanting;[16] nevertheless, they do offer some hints. Crafts and petty trading crop up frequently in the Black Forest valleys. In 1483 they were recorded in the lordship of Triberg,[17] and

[10] TLA, Kanzleibücher, ältere Reihe, Lit. D. Embieten, fo. 163ʳ, 6 June 1483. The context suggests that this instruction emanated from a submission by the Outer Austrian Estates.

[11] StAFr, C 1 Landstände 1: grievances of the third Outer Austrian Estate, n.d. (1517), § 3; C 1 Landstände 3: instruction by the Breisgau and Black Forest towns for their emissary, Ulrich Württner, at the imperial diet in Donauwörth, 5 Dec. 1517; ibid.: particular complaints of the Breisgau towns (as n. 7), § 2.

[12] GLA 79/1657: grievances of the towns, districts, and jurisdictions in Alsace, Sundgau, Breisgau, and the Black Forest, n.d. (*circa* 1524), § 3; BNUS, MS. 845, fo. 10ʳ: protocol of the Outer Austrian Estates at the diet in Breisach, 22 May 1524. Cf. Günther Franz (ed.), *Der deutsche Bauernkrieg: Aktenband*, 2nd edn. (Darmstadt, 1968), 133.

[13] StAFr, B 5 IXa i. fo. 287ᵛ ff.: petition of the Outer Austrian towns and districts in Alsace, Sundgau, Breisgau, and the Black Forest to king Ferdinand, n.d. (1557); ibid. fo. 307ʳ: legal opinion on the same; ibid. fo. 322ᵛ–323ʳ: decision of the Upper Austrian government, 9 Jan. 1558.

[14] Cf. Tom Scott, 'Economic conflict and co-operation on the Upper Rhine', in E. I. Kouri and Tom Scott (eds.), *Politics and society in Reformation Europe: Essays for Sir Geoffrey Elton on his sixty-fifth birthday* (London, 1987), 218.

[15] StAFr, C 1 Landstände 3: particular complaints of the Breisgau towns (as n. 7), § 2.

[16] 'Les forgerons, les potiers, les charpentiers ou les tailleurs qui vivaient et travaillaient dans le plat-pays n'apparaissent guère dans nos textes.' Francis Rapp, 'La Guerre des Paysans dans la vallée du Rhin supérieur: quelques problèmes d'interprétation', in *Charles-Quint, le Rhin et la France: Droit savant et droit pénal à l'époque de Charles-Quint* (Publications de la Société Savante d'Alsace et des Régions de l'Est: Recherches et Documents, 17) (Strasbourg, 1973), 144.

[17] TLA, Kanzleibücher, ältere Reihe, Lit. D. Embieten, fo. 163ʳ, 6 June 1483.

their presence is subsequently borne out by the occupations of witnesses in a court case in Triberg in 1505: among those called to testify were four tailors, six carpenters, two butchers, two weavers, one cartwright, and one draper.[18] If such a fortuitous listing can reveal sixteen craftsmen in a small lordship at one go, it is not altogether fanciful to conjecture that there may have been many more. When this evidence is taken together with the grievances of the Forest Towns in the southern Black Forest a decade later, and Villingen's predicament in the eastern Black Forest in mid-century, a picture emerges of rural crafts as by-employments in marginal upland areas where low returns from poor agricultural land forced peasants into taking up supplementary occupations in order to eke out a living.

This interpretation would fit well with the prevailing view of the late medieval agrarian crisis and its consequences, but there is good reason to doubt its general validity. The spread of crafts and petty dealing was not confined to upland areas, but extended throughout the fertile plain of the Upper Rhine. This can be demonstrated not merely by the indirect evidence of the Outer Austrian Estates' *gravamina* (expressed with tendentious exaggeration in order to rebuff demands for increased taxes or military levies), but directly as well, by the existence of regional craft associations in the valley of the Upper Rhine spanning town and country, and from edicts intended to confine or suppress the activities of rural craftsmen. Most commonly it was journeymen and apprentices who were gathered into the regional confraternities which pullulated on the Upper Rhine from the fifteenth century onwards. Whether they encompassed potters, saddlers, tinsmiths, coppersmiths, ropemakers, or cartwrights, the ordinances regulating their conduct and welfare presumed, without exception, the diffusion of the craft in question throughout town and country. When a fraternity of master tilers and their journeymen, for instance, was established in 1443, its charter referred explicitly to masters and apprentices 'in the towns, villages, or in the countryside between Strasbourg and Basel'.[19] Certainly, the urban authorities were alarmed by the spread of rural crafts from the early fifteenth century, as Knut Schulz's extensive researches on the fate of apprentices and wage-labourers in the

---

[18] StAFr, C 1 Fremde Orte: Triberg 23a, n.d. (1505).
[19] Schulz, *Handwerksgesellen und Lohnarbeiter*, 175–76.

leading Upper Rhenish cities have demonstrated. He instances urban guilds increasing entry-fines and imposing stricter qualifications on applicants in an effort to safeguard the livelihood of existing guildsmen and to deter immigration by less-qualified rural artisans. In the case of Basel, that applied to the bakers and butchers and, by the later sixteenth century, to the linen-weavers as well.[20] Where princes rather than urban magistrates addressed themselves to the issue, they inclined to tackle the problem of country crafts in the context of their territory's economy as a whole. One striking example is the ordinance issued in 1495 by the margraves of Baden:

> Item, in all our villages and also in all villages within our principality all trades [*gewerbe*], haberdashery, butchery, bathhouses, and other such things which appertain to towns shall henceforth be entirely abolished and no longer carried out or practised, with the exception of Oberbühl, Rastatt, Graben, and Stein, which are deemed to be markets, and similarly several other villages which we have allowed [to do so] for their convenience and for reason of necessity . . .[21]

While the various measures to combat rural crafts—whether designed to suppress, repulse, or integrate them—are undoubted testimony to the existence of artisanal activity in the countryside, how effective they were is another matter, which will be considered below. What the edicts of themselves cannot do, of course, is to offer any insight into the origins and development of country crafts and petty dealing on the Upper Rhine.

# III

Traditional accounts of the rural economy in pre-industrial Europe have always accepted that some handicrafts and indeed manufacturing took place beyond town walls. Bathhouse-keepers, innkeepers, charcoal-burners, fishers, millers, smiths, fullers, hemp-bleachers, basket-makers, even butchers were by the nature of their occupation as likely to be resident, temporarily or permanently, in the countryside as in towns, and there is no difficulty in tracing such artisans in medieval village custumals in Germany or elsewhere.[22]

---

[20] Schulz, *Handwerksgesellen und Lohnarbeiter*, 216 and n. 22; 225, 253.

[21] Wolfgang Leiser, 'Zentralorte als Strukturproblem der Markgrafschaft Baden', in Maschke and Sydow, *Stadt und Umland*, 8.

[22] Cf. Hermann Duncker, 'Das mittelalterliche Dorfgewerbe (mit Ausschluß der Nahrungsmittel-Industrie) nach den Weistumsüberlieferungen' (Diss. phil. Leipzig, 1903).

By the early modern period glassworks, brickyards, and sawmills with their attendant labour should be added to the list, as the emphasis began to shift from household crafts and cottage industries to early manufactories. Yet the growth of village crafts throughout late medieval Europe has been particularly associated with the development of the textile industry, above all with its diffusion by means of the putting-out system (*Verlagssystem*), whereby urban merchants and richer masters with spare capital to invest first brought their poorer fellows into wage dependence and subsequently, in order to evade the regulations on competition imposed by guild protectionism, diverted some or all of their enterprise to the countryside, where they hired peasants (often women) as outworkers on piece-rates, supplying them with raw materials (wool, linen, cotton, unspun or as yarn), or tools (spinning-wheels, cards, shuttles, looms) in return for delivering semi-finished cloths. In southern Germany the economy of Swabia from Lake Constance to the Allgäu was dominated by linen-, fustian-, and wool-weaving, whose manufacturers all resorted to *Verlag* in varying degrees. The country weavers (*Gäuweber*) were seen as a serious threat by the urban weavers from the mid-fifteenth century in cities such as Nördlingen and Memmingen, which were seized by periodic outbursts of artisan discontent.[23]

On the Upper Rhine, however, the incidence of rural crafts can be attributed only at the margins to the rise of cottage textile industries and the deployment of *Verlag*. Indeed, of the many areas of Germany where the putting-out system in textiles, or mining and metallurgy, was commonplace, the Upper Rhine is conspicuous by its rarity.[24] Only the textile group of Lower Alsatian towns and villages offers a close parallel to the pattern of cloth manufacturing in Swabia;[25] the Strasbourg council placed no restraints on the use of rural weavers, but it had to face frequent complaints from its

[23] Cf. Scott, 'Economic landscapes', 13, 15–17, and 14 (map). The most exhaustive recent study is by Rolf Kießling, *Die Stadt und ihr Land: Umlandspolitik, Bürgerbesitz und Wirtschaftsgefüge in Ostschwaben vom 14. bis ins 16. Jahrhundert* (Städteforschung: Veröffentlichungen des Instituts für vergleichende Städtegeschichte in Münster, A 29) (Cologne/Vienna, 1989), esp. 178–79, 224, 228, 482–85, 488–90.

[24] Cf. the comprehensive study by Rudolf Holbach, *Frühformen von Verlag und Großbetrieb in der gewerblichen Produktion (13.–16. Jahrhundert)* (*Vierteljahrschrift für Sozial- und Wirtschaftsgeschichte*, suppl. 110) (Stuttgart, 1994).

[25] Ibid. 128–29. Cf. Roman Heiligenthal, *Grundlagen der Regionalplanung, Raumplanung und Staatsplanung* (Siedlungsstudien, 10) (Heidelberg, 1940), 23.

own guildsmen, especially around 1500, at competition from serge-weaving outworkers in the employ of the city's merchant drapers.[26] In the case of Basel, Rippmann believes that rural competition from spinners, dyers, and weavers—such as those put out by the entrepreneur Ulrich Meltinger—must have been considerable, given that Basel's textile guilds increasingly drew in their horns to shelter behind protectionist legislation.[27] But this is something of a *post hoc ergo propter hoc* argument, since it could be maintained, in company with Traugott Geering, that it was the restrictive tendencies of the guilds themselves which prompted the decline of the city's cloth industry, rather than the fact of rural competition. Freiburg im Breisgau's wool- and linen-weavers also complained at the activities of foreign drapers, pedlars, and country weavers;[28] but as the council's attempt to snuff out rural linen-weaving in 1495 revealed the problem lay partly with urban drapers who wished to supply yarn to outworkers in the countryside for weaving. The 1495 prohibition does not seem to have been enforced very strenuously, which is not surprising, inasmuch as the council had already committed itself to a free market in cloth manufacturing.[29] Despite these instances, the Upper Rhine was never a classic textile landscape on the lines of Swabia, parts of Württemberg, Thuringia, or Lower Saxony. The references to village craftsmen in our area do mention clothiers and weavers, but the preponderant trades were genuine handicrafts, very few of which lent themselves readily to adaption to the putting-out system, and among which was a fair sprinkling of master craftsmen rather than dependent wage-labourers.

On the reasons for the growth of country crafts on the Upper Rhine the sources are silent, so that we must fall back on hypotheses. The flourishing and commercialized rural economy of the region, driven by the export of wine and other produce, certainly required a constant supply of tools and casks from the workshops of coopers, smiths, and carpenters. The Upper Rhine, moreover, was an area of partible inheritance, where subdivision of tenancies into holdings of uneconomic size may have forced some peasants into by-employments, especially if, as is commonly supposed,

[26] Schmoller, *Strassburger Tucher- und Weberzunft*, 521–22.
[27] Rippmann, *Bauern und Städter*, 185–87.
[28] Frank, 'Textilgewerbe', 35, 39–40.          [29] Ibid. 40.

the population began to swell again from the 1470s onwards.[30] However, both the labour-intensive character of viticulture (vineyards required eight times the manpower of cereal agriculture), and the known references to master craftsmen suggest that by-employment can be no more than a partial explanation, more applicable to the pastoral economy of the uplands. That might well account for the complaints at rural crafts voiced by the Forest Towns, or by Villingen, though it needs to be remembered that the uplands of the eastern Black Forest were areas of mixed inheritance patterns, both partible and impartible, and in that sense cannot be compared directly with the Rhine valley proper. On the lower slopes of the flanking hills and on the valley floor it is more likely that the diversification and specialization of agriculture in an area of monocultures and industrial crops (not only vines, but dyestuffs such as madder, hemp, and saffron) yielded sufficient surpluses to allow some of the rural population to concentrate on the secondary (craft) or even tertiary (service) sector in the form of village oil- and wine-dealers, mercers, haberdashers, clothiers, and pedlars. The very density of settlements—particularly in Alsace—may indicate that land was too scarce to support purely agricultural livelihoods, or, to put it another way, that land had become so valuable that the returns from working it could support a substantial number of craftsmen by creating a demand for consumer goods and services. In this context it is worth noting that the entrepreneur Ulrich Meltinger's stake in the economy of Basel's hinterland was not simply in supplying raw materials to outworkers but in satisfying the demand which existed in the countryside for commodities.[31] With the paucity of quantitative data in this period there is no way of knowing which explanation, supply-side or demand-side, is the more plausible, and in any case Francis Rapp's observations about the apparent lack of population pressure in Lower Alsace should make us wary

---

[30] This argument, however, needs to be approached with some caution. Anything resembling a reliable statistical basis for such an assertion is entirely lacking. Francis Rapp, moreover, has shown that parts of the valley plain in Alsace—in an area of allegedly high population density throughout the Middle Ages—were attracting immigrants from Swabia and beyond on the eve of the Peasants' War of 1525, which presumably indicates that land was still available for settlement. Francis Rapp, 'Die soziale und wirtschaftliche Vorgeschichte des Bauernkriegs im Unterelsaß', in Bernd Moeller (ed.), *Bauernkriegs-Studien* (Schriften des Vereins für Reformationsgeschichte, 82, 2/83 [no. 189]) (Gütersloh, 1975), 30–32.

[31] Rippmann, *Bauern und Städter*, 237–38.

of accepting uncritically a hypothesis predicated on settlement density. At all events, there is little reason to think that rural craftsmen on the Upper Rhine were no more than peasants with insufficient land to feed their households, and obliged to take up a secondary occupation in order to supplement their livelihood, in a pattern so vividly depicted by Pierre Goubert for the *manouvriers* or cottagers of the region of the Beauvaisis north of Paris in the seventeenth century.[32]

# IV

With the issue of salt-chests we are on much firmer ground. Salt was not a commodity freely available on the open market, but was sold at franchised salt-staples located in towns, whose councils guarded their monopoly in salt as jealously as their market privileges. They had good reason to: the sale of salt, an essential food preservative, was highly lucrative. It is reckoned, for instance, to have made up around one-quarter of Belfort's municipal revenues in the fifteenth century; in 1450 the town secured from emperor Frederick III the confirmation of its monopoly, which extended beyond the immediate territory of Belfort itself (that is, the lordship of la Roche de Belfort and the provostry of l'Assise de Belfort) to embrace the whole of the Rosemont valley to the north and the parish of Phaffans.[33] The administrative districts of Outer Austria in Alsace and the Sundgau are known to have had salt-chests in their chief towns—Ensisheim, Thann, Masevaux, Altkirch, Ferrette, Landser, and Habsheim,[34] along with Dannemarie[35] and Florimont.[36] Already in the mid-fifteenth century the Outer Austrian government had issued a proclamation that salt was only to be sold in towns or at recognized (franchised) markets.[37] Yet complaints at competition from unlicensed salt-chests went hand-in-hand with those concerning village crafts and rural markets, and can be found in

---

[32] Pierre Goubert, 'The French peasantry of the seventeenth century: A regional example', *Past and Present*, 10 (1956), 55–77, esp. 60.

[33] Bischoff, 'Belfort', 91.

[34] Wilhelm Beemelmans, *Die Verfassung und Verwaltung der Stadt Ensisheim im sechzehnten Jahrhundert* (Beiträge zur Landes- und Volkskunde von Elsaß-Lothringen, 35) (Strasbourg, 1908), 66 n. 142.

[35] Mossmann, *Cartulaire de Mulhouse*, iii. 509 (no. 1544).

[36] ADTB, E-Dépôt 46: ACF, AA 3, 20 Aug. 1520 (confirmation of privilege).

[37] Ammann, *Rheinfelden*, 22.

the same lists of grievances submitted by the Outer Austrian third Estate from 1483 onwards.[38] But not until the 1550s does the archival record allow a fuller insight into the grievances of individual *Ämter*. These reveal that competition was rife not merely between the town and villages of one district, but between the administrative towns themselves. While Landser and Altkirch both complained of salt-chests in the surrounding villages (in Altkirch's case, within its one-mile market precinct), Masevaux objected to its neighbouring district town of Rougemont setting up its own chest.[39] Belfort, despite its privilege of 1450, found itself exposed to subjects in the Rosemont valley buying up salt outside the territory for resale in Rosemont itself, thereby bypassing Belfort's staple, but Rosemont, for its part, resented Belfort's attempt to enforce a monopoly.[40] These internal rivalries were papered over by the submission of a list of general grievances to a diet in 1557, which blandly referred to the proliferation of salt-chests in the countryside.[41] After discussion these were referred upwards to Innsbruck. The Upper Austrian government, perhaps understandably, evinced only lukewarm sympathy for the Outer Austrian third Estate's difficulties. A legal opinion on the problem maintained that anyone should be free to buy or sell salt unless a particular liberty or indefeasible usage spoke against it.[42] Armed with that judgement, the Upper Austrian government declared that nothing could be done without full details of the whereabouts of the salt-chests and copies of the towns' franchises being submitted to the government in Ensisheim for further deliberation.[43] The matter does not seem to have been brought to a satisfactory outcome, for eleven years later the town of Ensisheim was protesting at the installation of more salt-chests within a half-mile radius at Battenheim, Wittenheim, Issenheim, Meyenheim, and Reguisheim.[44]

[38] TLA, Kanzleibücher, ältere Reihe, Lit. D. Embieten, fo. 163ʳ, 6 June 1483; StAFr, C 1 Landstände 3: particular complaints, 1518 (as n. 7), §§ 2, 7; Speck, *Landstände*, i. 331, 333–34.

[39] StAFr, C 1 Landstände 7; 'Der Statt Massmünster Beschwerden', n.d. (*circa* 1554), § 2; Speck, *Landstände*, i. 331, 333.

[40] StAFr, C 1 Landstände 7: 'Beschwernus . . . der Statt Beffort', n.d. (*circa* 1554); ibid.: 'Beschwerden . . . der herrschafft Rosenfels', 22 Jan. 1554, § 5; Speck, *Landstände*, i. 331, 333.

[41] StAFr, C 1 Landstände 7: Generalia, n.d. (1557), § 5; B 5 IXa i. fo. 287ᵛ; cf. C 1 Landstände 9.         [42] StAFr, B 5 IXa i. fo. 305ᵛ–306ᵛ.

[43] Ibid. fo. 322ᵛ–323ʳ; cf. king Ferdinand's response, 9 Jan. 1558. HSA, B 17 4*, fo. 67ᵛ.

[44] ADHR, C 674. Ensisheim to the Upper Austrian government, n.d. (1568).

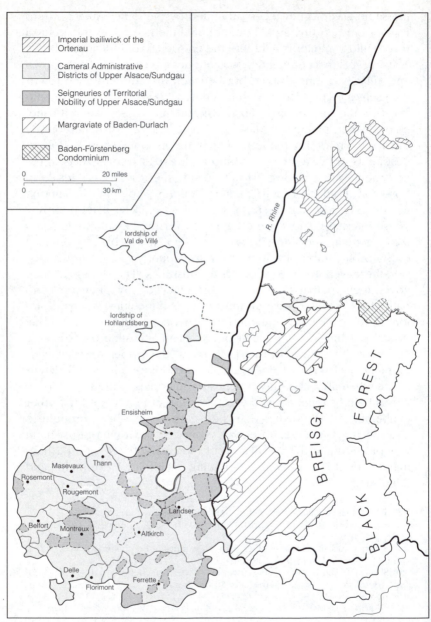

Map 10. The administrative districts of Outer Austria

If the issue in Alsace turned mainly on competition within the Outer Austrian administrative districts themselves, on the right bank of the Rhine territorial rivalries were at stake. Although overshadowed by a series of bitter conflicts over village markets, the Austrian towns in the Breisgau found their salt monopolies challenged by new salt-chests in the margraviate of Baden. In 1547 Endingen, Kenzingen, and Waldkirch lodged a protest with the authorities in Ensisheim that their livelihood was being undermined by newly established markets and salt-chests in villages throughout the margraviate of Hachberg.[45] In the ensuing negotiations the margravial representatives averred that Baden had the sovereign right to install salt-chests if it so chose; in any case, they were patronized by Austrian subjects as well, from the Breisgau and beyond.[46] Nine years later Breisach, too, complained on behalf of itself and other (unspecified) towns at the infringement of its salt-staple, though the council did not make clear whether the competition was coming from Austrian or margravial villages (or indeed both).[47] On the Black Forest uplands the situation of Villingen and Bräunlingen as Austrian outposts amidst foreign lordships made them particularly vulnerable to concerted efforts to promote territorial autarky. Complaints at the establishment of salt-chests were part and parcel of Villingen's wider struggle in the mid-sixteenth century to ward off competition from rural crafts and village markets. After being raised at the same Outer Austrian diet in 1557 which had considered the Sundgau communes' complaints, the issue of salt-chests was discussed in protracted bilateral negotiations throughout the 1560s and 1570s with the counts of Fürstenberg, whose lands lay mostly to the south.[48] But Villingen also faced a challenge from the duchy of Württemberg, which had installed a salt-staple at Schwenningen to the north-east around 1560, which continued to annoy the town throughout that decade.[49]

# V

From the constant chorus of complaints it is beyond doubt that rural crafts and staples were perceived as a threat to the livelihood

---

[45] GLA 229/64261, n.d. (after 13 Mar. 1547); cf. 74/9618, n.d. (1550).

[46] GLA 74/9620, n.d. (1550).

[47] StAFr, C 1 Landstände 7: Breisach's grievances, 27 June 1556, § 9; Speck, *Landstände*, i. 331. [48] StAVI, H 36 [no. 2968], fo. 46ᵛ; H 37 [no. 2949]; W 2 [no. 1974].

[49] GLA 81/47, 18 Nov. 1567; ibid. 18 Sept. 1568.

both of towns as privileged corporations and of individual urban craftsmen, but competing voices argued over the best means of combating them. Should rural artisans be kept at arm's length and if possible suppressed, or should they rather be lumped together with the urban guilds, perhaps with lesser rights, in order to be kept under supervision and control? Regulation and restriction were everywhere the goal, but achieving them could take very different paths. The Austrian towns in the Breisgau and the Sundgau, confronted with butchers trading in their hinterlands, may illustrate the contrast. During the sixteenth century Freiburg limited the number of days on which the butchers of its rural territory in the Dreisam valley could slaughter or bring their beasts to the civic market. Although the butchers demanded parity with their urban counterparts, the council refused them entry to the town guild;[50] instead, they were subject to a separate set of regulations,[51] even though they had to abide by the same price tariff as the Freiburg butchers.[52] At the end of the previous century, by contrast, Belfort had encouraged the butchers and leather-dealers from its hinterland to join the civic guilds. As a result, one-quarter of the town's tanners and cobblers (*escoffiers-courvoisiers*) and just under half— 45 per cent—of its butchers and meat-traders were in fact countryfolk, mostly living within a 20-kilometre radius of Belfort.[53] Some towns had franchises which explicitly required rural craftsmen to join the appropriate urban guild—Florimont on the southern margins of the Sundgau, for instance, had the right according to its urban charter to incorporate rural petty traders (*Grempler*)[54]—but it is difficult to see how such privileges could be readily enforced.

Easier by far was to establish regional or territorial guilds which embraced both town and country. These were commonplace on the Upper Rhine. For Alsace, Anne-Marie Imbs has compiled a list of lordships and administrative districts whose guilds embraced both urban and rural artisans. Although her research has several weaknesses—too much material is undated, and too much reliance placed on printed sources—some of her evidence should not be discounted out of hand. The town and lordship of Masevaux, for instance, boasted eight guilds from 1399 through to the eighteenth century; the county of Hanau-Lichtenberg (with its scattered pos-

[50] StAFr, F B 27/21, 13 June 1567.       [51] StAFr, F A 15/1, 6 Feb. 1579.
[52] StAFr, A 1 VIe ε 54, 1558.       [53] Villèle, 'Belfort', 96–97.
[54] ADHR, C188/27, 4 Feb. 1511.

sessions in Lower Alsace, including the Hanauer Land across the Rhine in the Ortenau) twenty-nine guilds from 1571 onwards; and the district of Altkirch ten guilds between 1584 and 1704.[55] Moreover, some guilds only recorded after 1600 had assuredly been in existence in the previous century. Imbs also draws attention to looser forms of association—where rural or village crafts were affiliated to urban corporations—though her examples are probably quite late; in any case, she does not spell out how affiliation differed in practice from territorial guild membership.[56]

On the right bank of the Rhine, the margraviate of Baden quickly abandoned its efforts—such as the ordinance of 1495 which we have already cited—to restrict crafts and trading to the chartered boroughs and a few villages in favour of a series of ordinances regulating crafts on a territorial basis. In the case of potters, as provisions in 1512 made clear, they were at liberty to settle wherever they chose, but might sell their wares at the chartered markets and nowhere else.[57] This ordinance remained in force throughout the century, even after the division of Baden territory in 1535,[58] with annual joint conventions of the potters in Baden-Baden and Baden-Durlach.[59] The potters allow us to observe the changing emphasis of margravial policy. If it was powerless to restrict crafts to the chartered boroughs, then at least it might protect the integrity of urban markets, upon whose revenues from tolls and excises the principality was in part dependent. The best that individual crafts in the towns could expect was that their rural competitors at least be required to submit their wares to quality control by civic inspectors

---

[55] Anne-Marie Imbs[-Obermuller], 'Tableaux des corporations alsaciennes XIVe–XVIIIe siècles', in *Artisans et Ouvriers d'Alsace*, 43. Certainly a territorial guild of carpenters, spanning the whole of the Upper Rhine, including both subjects of imperial cities and villages as well as dependants of the bishop of Strasbourg in the Upper Mundat, is recorded from 1518. Ernest Wickersheimer, 'La Corporation des maçons et charpentiers du bailliage du Kochersberg', ibid. 199.

[56] Imbs, 'Tableaux des corporations', 44. She cites coopers in villages around Colmar who were so affiliated, but since one of these was Neuf-Brisach, the evidence can hardly stem from the sixteenth century! Interestingly, however, some of the affiliations cut across territorial–political allegiances.

[57] GLA 36/286, 3 June 1512; cf. 74/10487.

[58] GLA 67/215, fo. 67ʳ, 27 May 1585.

[59] Cf. GLA 74/10487, 29 May 1538. On potters in south-west Germany and Alsace cf. in general now Susanne Eules, *'der hafner gesellen lobliche bruderschaft.' Organisation der Hafnerbruderschaft und Erzeugnisse der Hafner des 15. bis 18. Jahrhunderts im Elsaß, Sundgau und Breisgau* (Artes Populares. Studia Ethnographica et Folkloristica, 22) (Frankfurt am Main/Bern/New York/Paris, 1991).

—as with crafts as varied as tinsmiths[60] and wool-weavers[61]—if they wished to gain access to urban markets. But that in itself could not prevent unregulated artisans from continuing to ply their trade beyond the supervision of mastercraftsmen in their workshops, either in the countryside or in their own homes (as the master tailors of the district of Baden complained in 1579).[62]

At first glance, these examples seem to confirm the stock image of rural craftsmen as largely unskilled or at best semi-skilled, producing inferior wares of lesser value for immediate consumption or use in their localities, either within their own family groups or else for sale at village markets and church-ales. If that had been the whole truth they would scarcely have presented a serious challenge to urban craftsmen. But there is little doubt that some rural craftsmen had acquired qualifications. A sixteenth-century weavers' ordinance, for instance, from the district of Ettenheim, part of the secular territory of the bishops of Strasbourg in the southern Ortenau, provided for a committee to supervise quality and to settle disputes, which was to comprise two guildmasters from Ettenheim itself and seven further masters from the surrounding villages.[63] It is hard to conceive where these latter might have learnt their trade, except in the towns. Here Anne-Marie Imbs's evidence for Alsace, although tainted by fatal imprecision, at least offers a clue. She adduces the tiny imperial free city of Turckheim, which served as a training centre for the craftsmen of the surrounding villages. Master craftsmen (their trades, alas, unspecified) from Eguisheim, Herrlisheim, Ingersheim, Katzenthal, Niedermorschwihr, Soultzbach, Voegtlinshofen, Wihr-au-Val, Wintzenheim, and Zimmerbach—a total of ten villages ranged in an arc around the city—apparently all sent their apprentices to complete a masterpiece in Turckheim.[64] Notwithstanding the folly of building castles in the air, it is at least permissible to speculate that the district guilds attested for Altkirch and Masevaux, or the territorial guilds of Hanau-Lichtenberg, may have enabled their country members to undergo a full apprenticeship up to master's status.

Taken together, these observations mark out the Upper Rhine as a landscape where country crafts had entrenched themselves to the point where they were frequently absorbed into regional craft

---

[60] GLA 74/10497, n.d. (1564).     [61] GLA 74/2872, 11 June 1527.
[62] GLA 74/10579, n.d. (Dec. 1579).     [63] GLA 138/97, n.d. (16th c.).
[64] Imbs, 'Tableaux des corporations', 45.

associations, some of which included master craftsmen. Whether separate rural guilds, independent of the towns, ever developed cannot be determined with any confidence on the evidence available. In order, therefore, to assess the economic and commercial challenge which rural crafts and staples undoubtedly presented to the traditional artisan and market towns, the Upper Rhine needs to be set in a wider context. Late medieval Germany, along with many other parts of western Europe, witnessed a proliferation of handicrafts and petty trading in the countryside after 1400.[65] Indeed, there is scarcely a region, from Mecklenburg or Saxony in the north to Bavaria or germanophone Switzerland in the south, where the threat posed by country crafts did not exercise urban magistrates and territorial rulers. But it is generally agreed that the greatest concentration was in south-west Germany and Switzerland, an area of relatively dense population but with few obvious signs (at least until the later sixteenth century) of rural immiseration.[66] The sources for Switzerland, however, are more plentiful than for the Upper Rhine, and have been correspondingly studied in greater depth. They bear out the picture of a burgeoning and diversified rural economy, with artisanal production, unlicensed markets, rural staples, and the spread of commerce and credit, which the Swiss cities were at pains to contain. Here country crafts were not confined to textile workers producing linen, cotton, fustian, or woollens within the putting-out system (though certain cities such as St Gallen dominated the textile manufacturing of their hinterlands), but embraced cobblers, tailors, smiths, fishers, joiners, and ropemakers, as well as a variety of petty traders (to cite the evidence assembled for Lucerne).[67] By the later sixteenth century some of these craftsmen

---

[65] Cf. Hermann Kellenbenz, 'Ländliches Gewerbe und bäuerliches Unternehmertum in Westeuropa vom Spätmittelalter bis ins XVIII. Jahrhundert', in *Deuxième Conférence Internationale d'Histoire Économique, Aix-en-Provence 1962* (École Pratique des Hautes Études—Sorbonne, Sixième Section: Sciences Économiques et Sociales, Congrès et Colloques, 8) (Paris/The Hague, 1965), 377–427. This wide-ranging survey, however, places its main emphasis on rural crafts from the later 16th century onwards. Cf. also idem, 'Rural industries in the West from the end of the Middle Ages to the eighteenth century', in Peter Earle (ed.), *Essays in European economic history* (Oxford, 1974), 45–88.

[66] Cf. Wilfried Reininghaus, *Gewerbe in der frühen Neuzeit* (*Enzyklopädie Deutscher Geschichte*, 3) (Munich, 1990), 65 ff., 70.

[67] Anne-Marie Dubler, *Handwerk, Gewerbe und Zunft in Stadt und Landschaft Luzern* (Luzerner Historische Veröffentlichungen, 14) (Lucerne/Stuttgart, 1982), 198, 393.

were beginning to organize themselves into independent guilds beyond civic control, possibly, as Anne-Marie Dubler has conjectured for Lucerne, as a means of self-protection in the face of a worsening economic climate.[68]

The cities' response to the rise of crafts and craft associations was anything but uniform. In the Swiss midlands, Bern and Lucerne tried to restrict major crafts to the existing towns and franchised markets, but tolerated jobbing artisans in villages and at informal rural markets.[69] The same went for the much smaller territory of Solothurn. Here integration into urban guilds held out the only hope of containing aspirations towards the setting up of independent rural corporations. By contrast, the northern cities on the Rhine, Basel and Schaffhausen, as well as Zürich, contrived to stamp out rural guilds altogether,[70] though that, of course, was not the same as eliminating country crafts as such. To underscore that point we need only recall the well-known rising in canton Zürich in 1489, the Waldmann affair. It had broken out precisely on account of the peasantry's anger at attempts by the city to suppress the manifestations of a flourishing rural economy—expanding viticulture, oil-presses, salt-chests, a range of crafts, and informal marketing —but ended in far-reaching concessions to the rural population.[71] Switzerland was by no means the only area in the German-speaking lands where rural guilds can be identified. According to Helga Schultz, they sprang up both in central Germany (Hesse and Saxony) and in the south-west (Württemberg and Baden),[72] but her evidence, which in any case only dates from the late sixteenth century, in fact suggests that such guilds were rarely separate corporations, but rather territorial guilds spanning urban and rural craftsmen. At all events, outright attempts at suppression gave way to limited toleration. In Saxony, as Gerhard Heitz has argued in his study of rural

---

[68] Dubler, *Handwerk*, 193.

[69] Hans Conrad Peyer, 'Die Märkte der Schweiz in Mittelalter und Neuzeit', in idem, *Gewässer, Grenzen und Märkte*, 29–30.

[70] Dubler, *Handwerk*, 184–85; cf. Reininghaus, *Gewerbe*, 72.

[71] Christian Dietrich, *Die Stadt Zürich und ihre Landgemeinden während der Bauernunruhen von 1489 bis 1525* (Europäische Hochschulschriften, 3rd series, 229) (Frankfurt am Main/Bern/New York, 1985), 22 ff., 44–45, 49–50, 53 ff., 90.

[72] Helga Schultz, *Landhandwerk im Übergang vom Feudalismus zum Kapitalismus. Vergleichender Überblick und Fallstudie Mecklenburg-Schwerin* (Forschungen zur Wirtschaftsgeschichte, 21) (Berlin, 1984), 28.

linen-manufacturing, craftsmen after 1550 were allowed to settle and ply their trade in villages under loose princely supervision.[73]

That supports the impression conveyed by the Upper Rhine, at least where territorial or district guilds held sway. Yet the very existence of territorial guilds was calculated to erode the autonomy of the *Amtsstädte*, in that they placed urban craftsmen on almost the same footing as rural artisans, thereby diluting the function of the lesser or district towns as central places. The issue then switched to how far princes and magistrates were capable of defending the corporate liberties of towns against market competition from the countryside. Once we have reviewed these disputes, it should then be possible to assess the ability of the Upper Rhine as an economic region to balance and integrate the activities of central places and their hinterlands.

---

[73] Gerhard Heitz, *Ländliche Leinenproduktion in Sachsen (1470–1555)* (Deutsche Akademie der Wissenschaften zu Berlin: Schriften des Instituts für Geschichte, 2nd series: Landesgeschichte, 4) (Berlin, 1961), 105, 107.

# 5

# Village Markets and Informal Marketing

## I

In the previous chapter we have argued that both the spread of handicrafts and of salt-chests to the countryside testify to the growing commercialization of the Upper Rhenish economy in the later Middle Ages. But nowhere was this transformation more vividly apparent than in the proliferation of village markets which challenged the autonomy of long-established urban central places, particularly when the former encroached upon the town's privileged market area or precinct (*Bannmeile*).[1] Since market franchises appertained to the regalian rights of the emperor, new foundation charters were diplomas of great significance and value to the recipient; as such they were jealously preserved in civic muniment rooms and so number among the best-surviving documents of the age. By the same token, any infringement of market rights or precincts was a matter of legal as well as economic import, so that conflicts between town and country markets have left a substantial archival deposit.

While village markets are a direct testimony to the needs of a commercialized economy for additional points of distribution and exchange at closer intervals than the existing urban network provided, it can, of course, be argued that their establishment owed as much to territorial–political as to economic ends. It is hard to believe, none the less, that princes would have promoted new markets unless they supposed that the markets would prove to be viable, either in catering for an existing demand or by creating a new one. From the ensuing conflicts, however, it is clear that not

---

[1] On market areas and their privileged status cf. the case study by Eugen Ehmann, *Markt und Sondermarkt: Zum räumlichen Geltungsbereich des Marktrechts im Mittelalter* (Nürnberger Werkstücke zur Stadt- und Landesgeschichte: Schriftenreihe des Stadtarchivs Nürnberg, 11) (Nuremberg, 1987).

all new foundations prospered: markets were refounded (or trans-lated), their market-days altered, or the number of annual markets augmented, which indicates that some foundations had either petered out or else required additional promotion. For that reason it has been questioned whether the new markets can have posed a genuine threat to established urban markets. Here it was not so much the sheer number of markets but their location and period-icity in relation to existing ones which were decisive. The real chal-lenge to the prosperity of urban markets came far less from the proliferation of annual fairs (at which foreign merchants might offer exotic or luxury goods for sale) than from new weekly markets, which absorbed the bulk of inner-regional commerce, especially the exchange of agricultural produce and craft goods, that is, the necessities of daily life.[2] Even so, it might be argued that a village market held once a week was hardly likely to jeopardize a large urban market held twice-weekly, or even daily. But that is beside the point: it was the accumulation of many small village markets in the towns' immediate hinterland (or precinct) which represented the real danger, especially if their market-days clashed. For the vil-lage markets had several advantages over urban foundations: they usually imposed lower or even no tolls or stallage, and often used lesser weights and measures. Moreover, a simple tabulation of vil-lage market foundations may well understate their true impact, for informal marketing—that is, without charter—on Sundays, holi-days, church-ales, or at weddings lured urban craftsmen to hawk their wares beyond the town walls; indeed, if they were to remain in business, they had to engage the rural population, which in-creasingly shunned the more expensive urban markets at which they had traditionally purchased craft goods.[3]

Structurally, the rise of village markets can be seen as the next stage of growth in the European economy after the many urban

[2] This might appear to reflect the distinction found in Austria between *Bann-märkte*, franchised markets, usually privileged to deal in merchant's goods (cloth, salt, grain, iron), and *Gäumärkte*, rural markets supplying only local needs such as foodstuffs and wine, often held informally on Sundays or at church-ales, and with-out the right to trade in merchant's goods. But on the Upper Rhine the village and informal markets were *not* restricted to a range of purely local commodities, hence the incidence of conflict. Cf. Michael Mitterauer, 'Typen und räumliche Verbreitung der mittelalterlichen Städte und Märkte in den österreichischen Ländern', in idem, *Markt und Stadt*, 299–300.

[3] Scott, 'Economic conflict and co-operation', 220–24.

foundations of the high and late Middle Ages. The latter, as Hohenberg and Lees argue, were inspired by many needs besides the purely economic—defensive, judicial, administrative—whereas village markets essentially developed in response to economic and commercial pressures. Hence there was no compelling reason for them to be elevated into towns. For Switzerland, Hans Conrad Peyer has pointed out that in the four centuries between 1400 and 1800 no villages received urban privileges, but from the mid-fifteenth century onwards village markets burgeoned. Compared with a figure of ninety towns, which remained constant, the number of markets in villages and hamlets increased from 30 to 300![4] For the Upper Rhine the figures are rather less dramatic. On the right bank eight new towns were founded between 1400 and 1800, though only one of these falls into the period up to 1600—the elevation of the administrative seat and market centre of the margraviate of Hachberg, Emmendingen, to full urban status in 1590.[5] Over the same time-span fifty-four village markets were established, with just under half (twenty-six) of these before 1620, though that total includes several which subsequently disappeared or had to be revived.[6] For the left bank comparable statistics are less readily available. In view of the plethora of medieval urban charters there would have been little scope for further urban foundations by the sixteenth century. On the question of village markets, however, the sources are strangely silent. Rural craft production, as we have already seen, undoubtedly proliferated, but the village markets which could have acted as local and convenient centres of exchange have left very little trace in the records. Three villages under the jurisdiction of the abbey of Murbach—Wattwiller, Uffholtz, and St-Amarin—are known to have received franchises from emperor Frederick III between 1464 and 1480 for both weekly markets and annual fairs.[7] But thereafter there is barely a reference to village markets until a

---

[4] Peyer, 'Märkte der Schweiz', 22.

[5] Cf. Hansjörg Englert, 'Das Emmendinger Stadtrecht von 1590' (Diss. phil. Freiburg im Breisgau, 1973).

[6] Figures compiled from *Historischer Atlas von Baden-Württemberg*, map XI. 2: 'Marktorte des Spätmittelalters und der frühen Neuzeit 1250–1828'.

[7] ADHR, 10 G 8, pp. 159–60; Dubled, 'Ville et village', 69 nn. 31, 33. Georges Bischoff, *Recherches sur la puissance temporelle de l'abbaye de Murbach (1229–1525)* (Publications de la Société Savante d'Alsace et des Régions de l'Est: Recherches et Documents, 22) (Strasbourg, 1975), 147. St-Amarin and Uffholtz were entered as towns by Hektor Ammann on map 34 ('Das Städtewesen im Mittelalter') in Wolfram and Gley, *Elsaß-Lothringischer Atlas*.

century later, when the Basel merchant Andreas Ryff (1550–1603) composed his travel journal. In his description of the Upper Rhine he listed the annual markets, chiefly in Alsace, which lay on his itinerary. They included such tiny fairs as Buhl near Guebwiller,[8] the church-ale fair at Gallenberg by Didenheim south of Mulhouse, and the annual cloth fair at Kingersheim north of Mulhouse, which flourished from the patronage of pilgrims visiting the shrine there of bishop Adelphus of Metz.[9] Unfortunately Ryff did not record any weekly markets he may have visited. Whether the meagre references indicate that weekly markets and annual fairs were indeed rare in Alsatian villages, or that they simply failed to offer sufficient competition to their numerous urban neighbours to unleash disputes which left a legal record, will be considered later. For the moment, the argument will concentrate on the long-running conflicts between Baden and Austria over competing markets, played out principally in the Breisgau, which are richly documented.

## II

The earliest signs of conflict can be traced to the beginning of the fifteenth century, as margrave Bernhard I strove to exploit the political instability caused by the temporary alienation of the Breisgau from Habsburg overlordship in order to set about consolidating his weak, fragmented, and economically backward lands.[10] His main target was the Breisgau towns, all hitherto subject to Austria, whose markets offered the only outlet for the produce of margravial villages. In 1418 he established fairs and weekly markets for the margraviate of Hachberg at Eichstetten and Emmendingen,[11] which,

---

[8] It was already in existence in the mid-14th century. Bischoff, *Recherches*, 146.

[9] Friedrich Meyer and Elisabeth Landolt (eds.), 'Andreas Ryff (1550–1603), Reisebüchlein', *Basler Zeitschrift für Geschichte und Altertumskunde*, 72 (1972), 36, 110 n. 31.

[10] Cf. Richard Fester, *Markgraf Bernhard I. und die Anfänge des badischen Territorialstaates* (Neujahrsblätter der Badischen Historischen Kommission, 6) (Karlsruhe, 1896).

[11] GLA D 619, 10 Aug. 1418. Two months earlier count Konrad of Freiburg had acquired a similar franchise for his village of Badenweiler. GLA D 613, 15 June 1418. When his line died out in 1444, the lordship of Badenweiler reverted by descent to Baden, which thereby acquired two markets in the northern Markgräflerland, the other being at Sulzburg (geographically contiguous but dynastically an exclave of the margraviate of Hachberg), which received its charter in 1442 from emperor Frederick III. GLA 229/103818, 8 Sept. 1442.

together with the introduction of tolls and customs-posts, were designed to curb the towns' commercial monopoly by drawing trade away from their markets.[12] In addition, he sought to quash the judicial immunities of the many rural burghers of these towns (especially Freiburg) resident in margravial villages and, ideally, to purge his territory of these outburghers altogether. In 1424 the Breisgau communes allied to launch a campaign against the margrave, in which their troops burnt down the recently established market at Emmendingen, before pressing on to harry the Ortenau. Peace was finally achieved in the treaty of Mühlburg in July that year, by whose terms the towns were required to divest themselves of all outburghers in margravial territory, in return for the lifting of economic sanctions.[13] This was the only occasion on which conflict between the towns of the Austrian Breisgau and Baden erupted into a shooting war; it was superseded by a string of legal battles which exercised officials on both sides, often for years on end. The first Breisgau town to feel the brunt of what amounted to an economic boycott was Neuenburg on the Rhine, which was particularly vulnerable, being all but surrounded by the margravial lordship of Badenweiler.

In November 1462 a comprehensive settlement between Neuenburg and margrave Rudolf IV of Hachberg was brokered by the city council of Basel. Its provisions covered many contentious issues which had soured relations between the town and its hinterland for several years, above all, the perpetual quarrels over forest and pasture rights along the banks of the Rhine, and the use of foreign courts to settle them. Matters came to a head when margrave Rudolf resorted to banning his subjects from frequenting Neuenburg's market. This, it transpired, was in fact a reprisal for the town's previously having captured a clutch of margravial subjects on market-day as hostages to be used as a bargaining counter in negotiations. Basel's arbitration restored free access to the town market, but at the same time required the council to desist from arbitrary arrests.[14] The mediation appears to have been successful:

[12] Jürgen Treffeisen, 'Aspekte habsburgischer Stadtherrschaft im spätmittelalterlichen Breisgau', in idem and Kurt Andermann (eds.), *Landesherrliche Städte in Südwestdeutschland* (Oberrheinische Studien, 12) (Sigmaringen, 1994), 213.

[13] Scott, *Freiburg and the Breisgau*, 36–37; Treffeisen, 'Aspekte', 213–14.

[14] StANb, AA, A 77, 16 Nov. 1462, pp. 10, 11, 17; cf. F. Huggle, *Geschichte der Stadt Neuenburg am Rhein* (Freiburg im Breisgau, 1876–81), 140–50.

although Neuenburg became embroiled over the next half-century in repeated quarrels over the usufruct of common in the Rhine's *Auwäldern* with the bishop of Basel's subjects in Schliengen and Steinenstatt,[15] and more especially with the villages on the left bank in Alsace (as we noted in a previous chapter),[16] any disputes with Baden appear to have been confined to the two villages of Hügelheim and Zienken immediately to the north of Neuenburg.[17]

In Neuenburg's dispute with Baden in 1462 market competition in the countryside was not, it seems, directly at issue; yet the logic of a boycott of the urban market was that the peasantry could find other outlets for its produce and meet its requirements for goods and services elsewhere. Three-quarters of a century later, a new conflict between Neuenburg and Baden was to reveal that commercial relations between town and country were much more complex than the simple exchange of agrarian produce for craft goods might imply. Amidst a raft of complaints advanced against Baden by Austrian subjects in the Breisgau in the years after 1549, Neuenburg presented its own separate list of grievances. The town's craftsmen and traders objected to having to pay stallage when they set up their stalls at the annual fair in margravial Sulzburg, whereas the Malterdingen market in the lordship of Hachberg to the north—already a thorn in the flesh of the northern Breisgau towns—imposed none.[18] Moreover, when the Neuenburgers visited church-ales in nearby margravial villages, they were also dunned for stallage, as if these villages enjoyed full market rights.[19] The margravial official in Badenweiler recalled that at church-ales it had long been customary to demand a payment of a dozen *Schleifrie-men* (abrading-belts used in stone-polishing) but that in return the Neuenburgers could sell freely in the territory on other holidays.[20] Neuenburg's potters then added their own two-ha'pence-worth by complaining that the peasants in Auggen would not sell them clay;[21] as a reprisal the council was denying the villagers access to fishing in the Rhine.[22] For their part, the margravial subjects protested that Neuenburg had increased its tolls, and was levying them

---

[15] StANb, AA, A 92, 28 Mar. 1477; StAFr, C 1 Fremde Orte: Neuenburg 18, no. 21, 8 Jan. 1516.

[16] Ibid. no. 6, n.d. (1471); no. 7, n.d. (1471); no. 22, n.d. (1517); C 1 Landstände 1, n.d. (1511).          [17] StANb, AA, A 108, 14 Jan. 1507; A 109, 14 Nov. 1510.

[18] GLA 74/9619, n.d. (Aug. 1549).          [19] GLA 74/9618, 1 Feb. 1550.

[20] GLA 74/9619, 23 Aug. 1549.          [21] GLA 74/9618, 1 Feb. 1550.

[22] Ibid. n.d. (1550).

on foodstuffs (butter, cheese, onions, salt) and goods (skins and leather) which the villagers bought at the town market,[23] at the same time as the council was preventing its butchers and traders from selling candles and tallow in the countryside.[24]

What these tit-for-tat reprisals reveal is that the margravial villagers had overcome the rudimentary provision of chartered markets in the Markgräflerland by informal marketing at church-ales and other festivals. Neuenburg's craftsmen and traders visited these to ply their wares, only to find that they faced stallage charges (for the best booths, at any rate).[25] The council's response was distinctly short-sighted. On the one hand, it tried to prevent its traders selling certain essential goods to the villagers (who were thereby encouraged to buy them elsewhere); on the other, if the council hoped that the peasants would consequently be obliged to visit the town market, it did its best to deter them by imposing higher tolls. Significantly, the peasants declared that they used the Neuenburg market to purchase certain foodstuffs—dairy produce, mostly —which they presumably could not supply themselves: these were wine- and grain-growing villages which depended on a regionally integrated market system to satisfy all their requirements. As later disputes were to show, the exchange of arable and pastoral produce between the valley floor and the Black Forest uplands was an essential feature of the economy on the right bank of the Rhine. Neuenburg, commanding one of the few bridges on the river, which linked the Breisgau to trade routes into Alsace and Burgundy, should have been a natural entrepôt for the exchange of goods across the Rhine, yet the council allowed its economic gaze to be clouded by a few commercial pinpricks from its margravial hinterland. Certainly it was vulnerable to the economic strangulation which a boycott of basic foodstuffs might effect, in a way that Breisach, a much more important crossing-point on the Rhine, was not, since it was less hemmed in by foreign territory. But no such threat appears to have been uttered in 1549/50: this time the margraves did not ban their subjects from visiting Neuenburg's market, as they had done ninety years earlier; their officials were merely

---

[23] GLA 74/9620, 20 Mar. 1550. Neuenburg's 1-[German]mile salt franchise, which Maximilian had confirmed in 1493, does not seem to have been challenged during this dispute. Cf. StANb, AA, A 97, 21 Apr. 1493.

[24] GLA 74/9620, 20 Mar. 1550; 74/9618, n.d. (1550); 74/9615, n.d. (1550).

[25] GLA 74/9619, Aug. 1549.

trying to make the most out of the few fairs or marketing opportunities that existed in the Markgräflerland.[26] Rather, it was the
Neuenburg council which did its unwitting best to deter visitors to
its market. A calculated policy of commercial rivalry over market
share and market access was indeed being pursued by Baden at that
time, but it centred not on the relatively consolidated Markgräflerland but on the more fragmented lands of the margraviate of
Hachberg to the north.

The district north of Freiburg, stretching from the volcanic slopes
of the Kaiserstuhl eastwards through alluvial flatlands, watered by
the Dreisam, Glotter, and Elz, to the foothills of the Black Forest
in the *Freiamt*, was split between three territorial lords. The ancient
margraviate of Hachberg, centred on the fortress of Hochburg by
Emmendingen (now a ruin), controlled the core of the district,
though it had outliers to the west and south, and was itself pock-
marked by several Habsburg lordships. Austria dominated the
western fringes as well as the routes northwards flanking the tributary rivers from its towns of Endingen, Riegel, and Kenzingen.
On the borders of the Ortenau the bishop of Strasbourg held the
administrative district of Ettenheim. Up to the sixteenth century the
only markets on Hachberg territory had been in the villages of
Emmendingen and Eichstetten, both founded in 1418, each with
an annual fair and a weekly market, on Wednesdays and Saturdays
respectively. In 1510, however, the margraves of Baden added a
third market at Malterdingen, eccentric to the margraviate proper,
but well placed to deflect trade from nearby Austrian Endingen,
Riegel, and Kenzingen. Its foundation, indeed, immediately evinced
a protest from Endingen.[27] It also caused Waldkirch, the Austrian
commune guarding the mouth of the Elz valley, which possessed
an extensive market precinct of 2 German miles (nearly 15 kms.) for
its own Saturday market, to petition to have Malterdingen's market
abolished. This request was in fact partially conceded by emperor
Charles V, who confirmed Waldkirch's liberties, but allowed Malterdingen to hold a market on any other day of the week.[28]

---

[26] At that time the only chartered markets were at Lörrach (a fair and a weekly
market founded in 1403); Badenweiler (the same, founded in 1418, but transferred
to Britzingen in 1498); and Sulzburg (a weekly market, which seems to have petered
out, and two fairs, founded in 1442). Scott, 'Economic conflict and co-operation',
222.          [27] GLA 229/64261, 1 Apr. 1510.
[28] StAFr, C 1 Fremde Orte: Waldkirch, 26, 3 Feb. 1528. When Waldkirch's privilege was confirmed two years later by the government in Innsbruck, the latter

The immediate cause of fresh hostilities amongst these parties in mid-century is not known for certain, but from the subsequent course of events it appears that Malterdingen's market had been restored to its slot on Saturdays. In 1547, at any rate, Endingen, Kenzingen, and Waldkirch sent a joint petition to the government in Ensisheim, complaining about the establishment in Malterdingen both of a weekly market on Saturdays and of an annual fair instituted on St Catherine's day (25 November), which were each attracting numerous patrons at the expense of the Austrian towns' customs revenues. At the same time, several margravial church-ales had been granted full market rights: Emmendingen now had one fair on St Martin's day (11 November), and Eichstetten two, one on St James's day (25 July), and the other on St Matthew's day (21 September). The three towns also objected to the installation of salt-chests in margravial villages.[29] We can tell that more than casual competition was at stake from the Austrian government's reaction. When such grievances cropped up at territorial diets (as part of the to-and-fro of negotiating subsidies) the government's usual tactic was to play for time by requesting further and better particulars of the alleged infringements. But in the case of Endingen, Kenzingen, and Waldkirch, the government backed their plea that the matter be referred to king Ferdinand (as ruler of the 'outer lands'),[30] who in turn charged the authorities in Innsbruck with pursuing the case.[31] They recommended—especially in the light of Waldkirch's successful intervention against Malterdingen in 1528—that the matter be taken up directly with margrave Ernst of Baden.[32] Ferdinand did so, simultaneously alerting his brother Charles as emperor not to grant Baden any market privileges which might infringe those of the Austrian towns.[33] Entrusting the case to Innsbruck rather than to Ensisheim was an earnest of how gravely Austria viewed the threat, but it did not make for the speedy despatch of business, as all the relevant papers and instructions had to be sent to Tirol from the Upper Rhine, a journey there and back of almost a

referred only to a possible overlap with other *Austrian* markets, indicating that the threat from Malterdingen had, temporarily at least, receded. HSA, B 17 1*, fo. 175$^{r-v}$: the Upper Austrian government to the Outer Austrian government, 13 Oct. 1530.

[29] GLA 229/64261, 13 Mar. 1547.     [30] Ibid. 5 Oct. 1547.
[31] TLA, Kanzleibücher: Von der königl. Majestät, 1547–49, fo. 95$^v$–96$^r$, 4 Nov. 1547.
[32] TLA, Kanzleibücher: Gutachten an Hof, 1546–48, fo. 380$^{r-v}$, 24 Nov. 1547.
[33] TLA, Kanzleibücher: Von der königl. Majestät, 1547–49, fo. 111$^v$–112$^r$, 15 Dec. 1547.

fortnight. By March the following year all that had been accomplished was to elicit from margrave Ernst the information that the only weekly market on Hachberg territory was indeed at Malterdingen, and that it had received its charter a long time ago,[34] along with the three fairs which (he claimed) had so far failed to arouse any ill-will. In fact, urban craftsmen such as cobblers and locksmiths were, he asserted, frequenting margravial villages in order to sell their wares outside church on Sundays, just as was the custom in Outer Austria.[35] Clearly convinced that it was too far removed from the scene of action to intervene effectively, the Innsbruck government eventually proposed in 1550 that the matter be referred for arbitration to the bishop of Strasbourg, to whom Ensisheim was to forward the relevant documents, though it was careful to add that the Outer Austrian government should reach no decisions without reference to Innsbruck.[36] Negotiations took place at the bishop's residence at Saverne in Alsace, where the parties rehearsed the arguments they had advanced over the preceding three years.[37]

Here the margravial defence—hitherto obscured by a largely Austrian run of documents—at last emerged with greater clarity. The Malterdingen market and fair, Baden's officials contended, were already in existence in emperor Frederick's day (emperor Frederick III, one supposes!); they had never levied tolls, customs, or stallage. If they were flourishing, that was because the (Austrian) towns had increased toll-charges. Waldkirch had nothing to complain about, they insisted, since it lay three hours' distant (on foot) from Malterdingen (the Baden officials seem to have been very slow walkers). The church-ales had also long been upgraded to full fairs—but that applied equally to the one at Heimbach (just to the east of Malterdingen), an Austrian village held by Konrad Stürtzel, son of Maximilian's chancellor, about which no complaints had been voiced![38]

The margravial representatives then turned the tables on Austria by producing grievances of their own. Margravial subjects in the Kaiserstuhl were now being required to pay tolls at the full rate, instead of the customary half-rate, on produce brought to the Endingen market. That went particularly for corn, which the town

---

[34] Ibid. fo. 154ᵛ–155ʳ, 11 Feb. 1548; HSA, B 17 3*, fo. 64ʳ, 1 Mar. 1548.
[35] GLA 74/9619, Aug. 1549.     [36] HSA, B 17 3*, fo. 131ᵛ–132ʳ, 12 Feb. 1550.
[37] GLA 74/9618, n.d. (1550); cf. 74/9620, n.d. (1550); 74/9615, n.d. (1550).
[38] GLA 74/9620, n.d. (1550).

was insisting should be sent there for milling, after which the peasants could collect it only on paying a toll and having to leave the
husks (useful as fodder) behind.[39] For its part, Riegel, strategically
situated just downriver from Malterdingen, had begun to impose
toll-charges on produce brought back from the Malterdingen market by margravial subjects, which hit the Kaiserstuhl peasants and
those to the north in Weisweil and Hausen.[40] Kenzingen, too, was
the target of margravial complaints: Weisweil's tiler, who was
accustomed to fetch limestone for his kilns from the district around
Herbolzheim, was now being required to pay a 'sand-toll' in
Kenzingen, which forced him to make an hour's detour via the
town.[41] Lastly, and most serious of all, Eichstetten protested that
Freiburg and other Austrian Breisgau towns had combined to
destroy its bridge over the river Dreisam,[42] which may indicate that
rivalry over markets and turnpikes was just as intense in Eichstetten
as in the much better-documented Malterdingen.

The outcome of these negotiations is unknown, but it is worth
remembering that the bishop of Strasbourg was himself not an
entirely disinterested party to the mediation, since his own district
of Ettenheim was also affected by margravial competition, as a
fleeting reference in the Freiburg archives to legal proceedings
between Hachberg and the bishopric over the Malterdingen market reveals.[43] Unlike the case of Neuenburg, it is clear that the
Austrian towns of the northern Breisgau did face a deliberate challenge from Baden: the restoration of Malterdingen's Saturday market after the climb-down of 1528 is evidence enough of that. It is
much harder, naturally, to assess how grave the threat was, though
the Austrian towns, given their strategic location, at least had the
chance to mount reprisals. A nagging doubt remains, none the less,
that the Austrian towns may have brought their predicament upon
themselves by increasing toll-charges at their own markets, just as
shortsightedly as Neuenburg a century earlier: the exact chronology of their introduction—provocation or riposte—cannot now
be reconstructed. Although the general threat of market competition throughout Outer Austria did not abate (as the submissions to

---

[39] GLA 74/9618, n.d. (1550); cf. 74/9615, n.d. (1550).
[40] GLA 74/9618, n.d. (1550); cf. 74/9615, n.d. (1550).
[41] GLA 74/9618, n.d. (1550); cf. 74/9615, n.d. (1550).
[42] GLA 74/9618, n.d. (1550).
[43] StAFr, B 5 IXa i, fo. 155ʳ–157ᵛ; ibid. fo. 158ʳ–161ᵛ, n.d. (1551).

the 1557 territorial diet testify),[44] the immediate conflict with Baden seems to have subsided, an indication, perhaps, that the margrave had been forced to back down. It was to recur twenty years later, however, in the most extensive and protracted quarrel of all, but in the intervening period the question of tolls and customs continued to exercise the Breisgau towns greatly.

Whatever dues the Austrian towns might themselves choose to levy at markets or on turnpikes, they had no means of preventing their Habsburg overlords from inflicting additional customs and excise duties throughout Outer Austria to raise general revenue, and these were bound to drive up the cost of the goods on sale in the towns. Although there is no indication that such a measure underlay the difficulties of the late 1540s, the Outer Austrian Estates were certainly confronted in 1560 with a general toll to be levied on all goods, except foodstuffs, entering or leaving Outer Austria unless intended for domestic consumption, alongside a separate 'Turkish tax' (*Türkensteuer*) to help finance the defensive campaign against the Ottomans on Austria's eastern frontier. That autumn Freiburg took the lead in opposing the impost, claiming that already the weekly and annual markets were suffering loss of trade and a shortfall in revenue.[45] Moreover, it alleged, the Austrian customs officials were collecting the new impost even on goods not destined for commercial exchange. Though the Breisgau towns fell in behind Freiburg's draft petition, not all the Black Forest communes or the Forest Towns on the *Hochrhein* did so;[46] nevertheless, Freiburg pressed ahead and ensured that the towns' grievances were forwarded to Innsbruck.[47] The Upper Austrian authorities voiced some scepticism over the extent of any commercial damage caused by the impost, but were willing to offer some concessions. Henceforth, goods coming from or going abroad (by which was meant Italy, the Swiss cantons, France, Burgundy, and Lorraine) should only pay the impost once, and then pass freely throughout the whole of Outer Austria; if the goods were destined for internal consumption, then no impost was liable.[48] These concessions were

---

[44] Ibid. fo. 287ᵛ ff., n.d. (1557).

[45] StAFr, B 5 XI xix, fo. 55ʳ, 20 Sept. 1560; ibid. fo. 58ʳ⁻ᵛ, n.d. (Sept. 1560); B 5 IXa i, fo. 432ᵛ–433ᵛ. [46] StAFr, B 5 XI xix, fo. 61ʳ⁻ᵛ, 7 Oct. 1560.

[47] TLA, Kanzleibücher: Gemeine Missiven 1560, fo. 989ᵛ, 9 Nov. 1560.

[48] Ibid. fo. 1049ʳ–1053ᵛ, 21 Nov. 1560; StAFr, B 5 IXa i, fo. 442ʳ–443ʳ; cf. TLA, Kanzleibücher: Missiven an Hof 1560, fo. 568ᵛ–571ᵛ, 21 Nov. 1560.

approved by emperor Ferdinand (as he had then become) and were confirmed in writing to Freiburg with the instruction to summon the Breisgau Estates to consider them.[49]

The Estates expressed considerable relief that the impost would now apply only to foreign imports and exports, so that goods from within the Empire or the other Austrian territories (as they understood the concessions) were exempt. None the less, there were some commodities such as iron and certain fancy cloths obtainable only from abroad, on which the full impost would still be levied.[50] It is not entirely clear whether the new provisions really did indicate that the impost would no longer constitute a tariff barrier between the various territories on the Upper Rhine: a subsequent plea on behalf of the imperial and territorial enclaves in the largely Austrian Upper Alsace—the imperial free cities, the bishop of Strasbourg's Upper Mundat, the Württemberg county of Horbourg —that they should only be required to pay a reduced impost suggests that they were indeed regarded as foreign territory.[51] The Breisgau towns, at any rate, were not happy, and continued to badger both Ensisheim and Innsbruck for further concessions.[52]

The internal bickering within Outer Austria over territorial imposts is anything but tangential to the disputes between Austria and Baden over market competition, since it provides the context for the renewed conflict at the end of the decade. For whatever concessions the Breisgau towns might have wrung from their rulers could not conceal that the impost placed Kenzingen's and Endingen's markets at an even greater disadvantage over against Malterdingen's, given that the latter had already dispensed with market fees and of course did not levy the Austrian impost. It was (understandably enough) not the apparent handicap of the impost but the threat to Austrian markets which prompted the government in Innsbruck to launch an on-the-spot enquiry, but the two issues cannot in

---

[49] TLA, Kanzleibücher: Geschäft vom Hof 1560, fo. 385ᵛ–386ʳ, 9 Dec. 1560; StAFr, B 5 IXa i, fo. 437ᵛ, 10 Dec. 1560; cf. B 5 XI xix, fo. 72ᵛ–73ʳ, 16 Dec. 1560. Cf. Speck, *Landstände*, i. 245.          [50] StAFr, B 5 XI xix, fo. 81ʳ–83ʳ, n.d. (27 Jan. 1561?).
[51] StAFr, B 5 IXa i, fo. 470ᵛ (1562).
[52] StAFr, B 5 XI xix, fo. 167ᵛ–168ʳ, 23 Feb. 1562; ibid. fo. 169ᵛ–171ʳ, n.d. (2 Mar. 1562?); ibid. fo. 176ʳ⁻ᵛ, n.d. (Mar. 1562?); TLA, Kanzleibücher: Gemeine Missiven 1562, fo. 465ᵛ–466ʳ, 11 Apr. 1562. They also complained at the behaviour of the Austrian customs official at Kenzingen, who was seeking to levy the impost on goods not included in the customs tariff. In the end, the Innsbruck government proposed sending the comptroller-general of customs in Outer Austria, Georg Tiffer, to investigate the matter. TLA, Kanzleibücher: Gemeine Missiven 1561, fo. 650ʳ⁻ᵛ, 13 June 1561; Gemeine Missiven 1562, fo. 456ᵛ–457ʳ, 10 Apr. 1562.

reality be divorced. The enquiry—a wide-ranging affair—was to be conducted by the bailiff of the four lordships (that is, Kenzingen, Kürnberg, Kastelberg, and Schwarzenberg), Georg Gaudenz von Blumeneck, the comptroller-general of customs, Georg Tiffer, and the Austrian officials in the towns of Kenzingen and Waldkirch, in consultation with the mayors of Kenzingen and Endingen, with the purpose of devising suitable countermeasures.[53] What Tiffer (the most senior official engaged on the enquiry) ended up doing was in fact investigating a fresh margravial turnpike toll at Teningen on the Elz, cunningly positioned to catch traffic passing from Freiburg and Waldkirch to Kenzingen and further north. Though not spelt out in the sources, the new toll-rates—4*d.* a cart, 2*d.* a handcart, and 1*d.* a horse—can only have been designed to be levied on non-margravial subjects, or else they would have made a nonsense of Baden's customs policy of deliberately undercutting Austria; the toll-post was, perhaps, a belated *revanche* for Riegel's and Kenzingen's tolls earlier in the decade.[54] This time, however, the authorities in Innsbruck, worried by the threat of war with France, shied away from a direct confrontation with Baden (as advocated by their subordinates in Ensisheim); instead, archduke Ferdinand of Tirol (emperor Ferdinand's successor) was to urge emperor Maximilian II to order the abolition of the toll.[55] Even though such an edict was duly issued, Innsbruck was still trying to find out in the autumn of 1569 whether the customs-post had in fact been destroyed.[56] The stage seemed set for another major confrontation between Baden and Outer Austria. But the conflict, though engendering much bitterness at the grass-roots, was to prove how little room for manœuvre either side had in a district whose economy was integrated, commercialized, and geared to regional markets, in defiance of political and territorial frontiers.

## III

By the 1570s, recurrent subsistence crises on the Upper Rhine—as elsewhere in Germany, or for that matter, Europe—encouraged

---

[53] TLA, Kanzleibücher: Missiven an Hof 1568, fo. 524ʳ–528ʳ, 29 May 1568, esp. fo. 524ᵛ–526ʳ; cf. Geschäft vom Hof 1568, fo. 177ʳ–178ʳ, 10 June 1568; Gemeine Missiven 1568, fo. 1309ᵛ–1310ᵛ, 28 July 1568.

[54] TLA, Kanzleibücher: Gemeine Missiven 1569, fo. 205ᵛ–206ʳ, 10 Feb. 1569; Missiven an Hof 1569, fo. 82ʳ–84ʳ, 12 Feb. 1569.     [55] Ibid.

[56] HSA, B 17 5*, fo. 226ʳ⁻ᵛ, 19 Sept. 1569; TLA, Kanzleibücher: Gemeine Missiven 1569, fo. 1738ʳ–1739ʳ, 31 Oct. 1569.

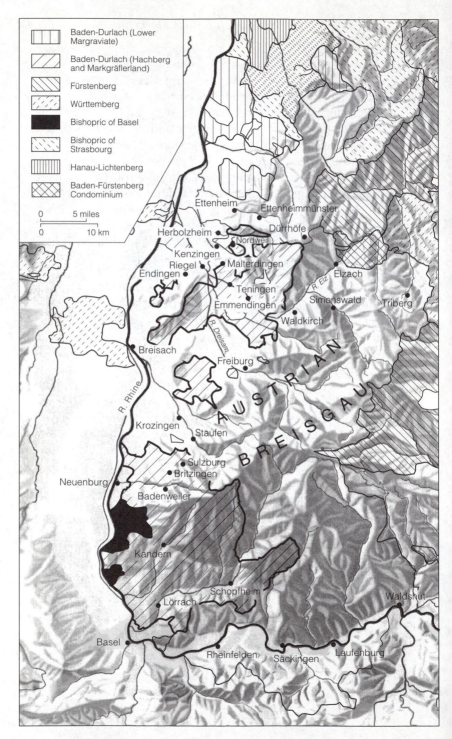

MAP 11. Market competition in the Breisgau, 1400–1600

Legend:
- Baden-Durlach (Lower Margraviate)
- Baden-Durlach (Hachberg and Markgräflerland)
- Fürstenberg
- Württemberg
- Bishopric of Basel
- Bishopric of Strasbourg
- Hanau-Lichtenberg
- Baden-Fürstenberg Condominium

0   5 miles
0   10 km

Ettenheim
Ettenheimmünster
Herbolzheim
Nordweil
Dürrhöfe
Kenzingen
Riegel
Malterdingen
Elzach
Endingen
R. Elz
Teningen
Simonswald
Triberg
Emmendingen
Waldkirch
R. Dreisam
Breisach
Freiburg
A U S T R I A N
R. Rhine
Krozingen
Staufen
B R E I S G A U
Sulzburg
Britzingen
Neuenburg
Badenweiler
Kandern
Schopfheim
Waldshut
Lörrach
Basel
Rheinfelden
Säckingen
Laufenburg

the authorities to look to their own. Whatever grain was available, they believed, should be kept within the territory to supply the needs of their own subjects. Prohibitions were therefore placed on foreigners buying at local markets, and on subjects supplying markets in neighbouring territories. Such prohibitions could easily have escalated into a full-scale economic war, but the political and commercial realities on the Upper Rhine—interlocking and over-lapping jurisdictions on the one hand, interdependent economic zones, on the other—ensured that the conflicts were never allowed to get out of hand. Instead, they simmered for years, producing flurries of correspondence, accusation and counter-charge, between local officials, with governments sometimes struggling to keep abreast of what was happening on the ground. Indeed, the conflicts were so protracted precisely because the authorities favoured contain-ment rather than a show-down.

Baden, always the economic inferior of Austria, began the attack on two flanks, in the lordships of the Markgräflerland—Badenweiler, Rötteln, and Sausenberg—and in the margraviate of Hachberg, by adopting measures to promote its indigenous markets at Sulzburg and Malterdingen. As twenty years before, Malterdingen presented a more insidious threat than Sulzburg. Before the harvest of 1571, when grain was already scarce, the margravial official in Badenweiler, Hartmann von Habsberg, fearing another crop failure, had for-bidden his subjects to sell grain outside the territory, as well as imposing a price ceiling. In fact, the harvest that year in the Mark-gräflerland turned out reasonably well, but that only allowed mer-chants to replenish their depleted stocks and store fresh grain, so that prices remained high. Because Austria had also imposed an export ban on foodstuffs from its own territories, Baden's subjects, even though they could still visit Austrian markets such as Staufen, were prevented from carting any produce brought there home. The need for a weekly market in the Markgräflerland itself, von Habsberg concluded, had therefore become acute. Of the various possible locations, including Müllheim and Auggen, Sulzburg would be the most suitable, he thought, not least because it was convenient for peasants from the Black Forest valleys as well.[57]

Because Sulzburg had previously had a weekly market, and in view of the sizeable mining community there, the margravial councillors

---

[57] GLA 229/103820, 28 Sept. 1571.

approved the plan,[58] and the market was duly restored on Saturdays, with subjects forbidden to sell produce elsewhere.[59] These provisions applied *pari passu* to the Hachberg markets at Malterdingen and Eichstetten. Foreigners were to be allowed to purchase foodstuffs at these margravial markets, provided they could show that they were for personal consumption and not for resale.[60] This may have met the needs of the moment as far as the northern Markgräflerland (the lordship of Badenweiler) and the margraviate of Hachberg were concerned, but it pitched the southern districts of Rötteln and Sausenberg into a quandary.

The bailiff of Rötteln pointed to the danger of a reciprocal ban by Basel, Rheinfelden, or Neuenburg; around 100 margravial peasants regularly sold their crops at these three urban markets (chiefly in Basel, it must be said), whereas only a handful of foreign subjects offered any produce in Rötteln in exchange, at a time when there were already insufficient reserves of grain in the two southern lordships. Austria, moreover, had also banned its subjects from supplying Basel's market, so that the city had been forced to buy 1,000 quarters (*Malter*) of wheat from Strasbourg. It is evident, therefore, that peasants in the south of the Markgräflerland expected to be able to satisfy their grain requirements at urban markets outside the territory. The explanation is simple: within Rötteln and Sausenberg the agrarian economy was largely given over to viticulture (with pastoralism on the higher slopes). If the Basel market were closed, remarked the bailiff, where else could his subjects dispose of their wine? Certainly not to local inn-keepers, who simply could not absorb the quantity. Without the necessary cash from sales, the wine-growers would be unable to buy steel, ironware, cloth, or leather (and, by implication, the economy would stagnate). Whilst not opposing the market at Sulzburg, the bailiff urged that it impose no export restrictions; far better to punish any natives who exported scarce goods than to provoke reprisals from territorial neighbours. As a parting shot, the bailiff mentioned the considerable irritation among the Swiss which Austria's ban on its subjects' patronizing the markets of Basel and Mulhouse had provoked.[61]

It would be absurd to depict the bailiff of Rötteln as an enlightened apostle of free trade: he merely saw who had the whip-hand in his neck of the woods. By contrast, in the north of the Markgräflerland,

[58] GLA 229/103820, 3 Oct. 1571.        [59] GLA 229/103819, 15 Oct. 1571.
[60] GLA 229/103820, 29 Oct. 1571; 229/103819, 3 Nov. 1571.
[61] GLA 229/103820, 5 Nov. 1571.

his counterpart in Badenweiler, Hartmann von Habsberg, was altogether more sanguine. A market at Sulzburg, he argued, would not infringe Neuenburg's precinct of 1 German mile (thereby displaying a rather vague sense of distance), and in any case there were long-standing free-trade agreements between Basel and the Baden jurisdictions. As far as Austrian territory went, margravial subjects were already experiencing discrimination at Neuenburg's and Staufen's markets, where produce bought by Baden peasants was subsequently knocked down to natives prepared to match their price (a practice known as *Auslosung*). The case for establishing a local market at Sulzburg, however, was not helped (as von Habsberg conceded) by complaints from his own subjects at poor sales; they preferred to hawk their produce at the much larger and busier market in Freiburg.[62]

Yet even the Hachberg officials, invited to estimate the likely consequences of promoting markets in their own jurisdiction, urged caution. Certainly the Malterdingen market was flourishing, but the weekly market at Eichstetten, they lamented, had collapsed. Any ban on subjects' visiting Austrian markets would elicit countermeasures, whilst a ban on exports would also hurt them since they depended on the urban markets (all Austrian) to supply craft goods. In turn, any Austrian interdict on its subjects' visiting Malterdingen would not only cost the margrave dear in lost excises, but make it hard for the Hachbergers to sell their wine, which, the officials observed, was traded with peasants from the (largely Austrian) Black Forest (who also brought cheese to market) against boards, laths, vine-props, and the like. Moreover, faced with the shortage of grain, margravial bakers were already having to cross over to Alsace to obtain supplies; any attempt, therefore, to impose unilateral price ceilings on foodstuffs would simply drive even more customers away.[63]

The councillors at margrave Karl's court recognized the force of these objections. As a stop-gap measure, they suggested stockpiling salt, cloth, iron, ropes, and leather at Sulzburg (a curious piece of quasi-mercantilism), and allowing produce to be sold both at Sulzburg and abroad at Freiburg.[64] Karl himself promised to keep the matter under review,[65] but in the meantime the ban promulgated the previous month was to remain in force. Faced with predictable

---

[62] Ibid. 9 Nov. 1571.     [63] Ibid. 8 Nov. 1571.     [64] Ibid. n.d. (Nov. 1571).
[65] GLA 229/103819, 18 Nov. 1571; cf. 229/103820 (draft).

outrage from Neuenburg, the official in Badenweiler denied any
infringement of the 1462 treaty,[66] dismissed any talk of trespassing
on its market precinct, and asserted that Neuenburg would not dare
extend the scope of priority sales to natives (*Auslosung*), since it
depended on margravial subjects to supply it with produce. In turn,
von Habsberg declared, the Sulzburg market, after a slow start, was
beginning to pick up, attracting custom from its environs, including the nearby Austrian villages in the plain and in the Black Forest,
because it was seen to levy no tolls.[67] At first, this optimism seemed
to be warranted. Although Neuenburg continued to fire volleys
of complaints in the direction of margrave Karl,[68] it was the town
which offered the first glimpse of compromise. It refused to send
an attested copy of the 1462 treaty to Hartmann von Habsberg and
parried all subsequent requests from Baden to do so,[69] but then
changed tack on the question of the Sulzburg market itself. If it
were moved to Thursday, Neuenburg suggested, it would be possible in a circuit to visit Staufen on a Wednesday, Sulzburg the
next day, and Neuenburg's own market on a Saturday.[70] Margrave
Karl's councillors (in an untabled memoir) were not averse to the
idea, even though they accepted von Habsberg's point that a
Saturday market suited Sulzburg's miners better, for they received
their weekly wages that day. They were also willing to let margravial subjects take their corn to the nearest mill, regardless of
overlordship, hitherto another source of friction with Neuenburg,
Staufen, and Heitersheim.[71]

At this point the sources fall annoyingly silent for a whole
year. Any idea that the situation had been resolved, however, is
dispelled by a brief but telling sequel in 1573. Far from Neuenburg beating a retreat, it transpired that the Sulzburg market was
by then in serious decline. The reasons for this sudden reversal

---

[66] GLA 229/103819, 14 Nov. 1571.
[67] Only rope-makers and saddlers apparently were lacking amongst those who
frequented the Sulzburg market. Ibid. 16 Nov. 1571.
[68] Ibid. 20 Feb. 1572 (draft); ibid. 26 Feb. 1572; ibid. 5 Mar. 1572 (draft); ibid. 6?
Mar. 1572 (draft).
[69] Ibid. 20 Mar. 1572; ibid. 14 Apr. 1572; ibid. 9 May 1572; ibid. 17 May 1572.
Neuenburg claimed to have shown the draft to Ludwig Wolf von Habsberg
(Hartmann's father), when he was the official in Badenweiler. Margrave Karl
ordered a search in the chancery for Baden's own copy. Ibid. 26 Mar. 1572. None
could be found. Neuenburg's defiance should be seen as a mark of weakness, not
strength: the 1462 treaty contained no reference to rival Baden markets.
[70] Ibid. 20 Mar. 1572.          [71] Ibid. 27 Mar. 1572 (draft).

are completely obscure: had Neuenburg at last succeeded in enforcing its privileges? Had the restrictions on margravial access to Austrian markets begun to bite? It does at least appear that Karl's councillors in Karlsburg finally undertook a thorough investigation of the distribution of chartered markets in the Markgräflerland and surrounding districts. At the end of February, the magistrate of Sulzburg, Mattheus Wertz, submitted a list of markets in the environs of Sulzburg to the chancery in Karlsburg, which could not help revealing the preponderance of Austrian markets and fairs in both towns and villages. Apart from Sulzburg's weekly market, the remainder were located in Breisach (Tuesday), Staufen (Wednesday), Freiburg (Thursday and Saturday), and Neuenburg (Saturday). The only annual fairs on Baden territory in the southern Breisgau, apart from the two at Sulzburg and one at Ballrechten, were one at Kandern and three at Schopfheim (the only town in the lordship of Rötteln), whereas Freiburg had six (including four ember-day fairs), Breisach five, Staufen four, Neuenburg two, and Heitersheim and Offnadingen one each.[72] This survey, to judge by the correspondence crossing the desk of Egidius Castner, the margravial councillor responsible, was prompted by Sulzburg's lament that its weekly market and fairs were languishing. For that reason, it had petitioned the margrave to reconfirm its market privileges, but in its submission it referred to its weekly market 'traditionally held on a Monday'![73] When Karl's councillors met to consider the request, they discovered—two years after the event!—that Sulzburg's Saturday market indeed contravened the imperial charter conferred by emperor Frederick III;[74] they therefore decided that instead of moving it to Thursday, as Neuenburg had proposed, it should be restored to its rightful place on Mondays.[75] This suggestion was accepted by the margrave, and a new edict to that effect promulgated on 21 March 1573.[76]

By any standards this is a bizarre chain of events. The margravial chancery certainly had copies of Sulzburg's market privilege of

---

[72] GLA 229/103819, n.d. (1573); cf. 229/103820, 27 Feb. 1573. There were attempts to revive the fair and weekly market at Ehrenstetten in 1563, but it seems that these Austrian efforts were unsuccessful. HSA, B 17 4*, fo. 389ᵛ, 6 Feb. 1563.

[73] GLA 229/103820, n.d. (1573); cf. ibid. 11 Mar. 1573.

[74] Cf. GLA 229/103818, 8 Sept. 1442 (copy) and 229/103819, 8 Sept. 1442 (copy).

[75] GLA 229/103820, 20 Mar. 1573.

[76] GLA 229/103818, 21 Mar. 1573; cf. 229/103819, 21 Mar. 1573; 229/103820, 21 Mar. 1573; ibid. 4, 7, and 14 Apr. 1573.

1442 (though these do not survive in a contemporary hand, and may therefore only have been transcribed in 1573 from the original diploma, presumably deposited in Sulzburg).[77] It is remarkable, none the less, that the chancery should belatedly have discovered that it had been in the wrong all along, and that it made no attempt to brazen the matter out. This points to some Austrian intervention at a high level—perhaps by emperor Maximilian II himself—though the Upper Austrian government was only alerted to the renewed conflict over markets following the Outer Austrian diet in July that year, which had principally identified the competition emanating from the margraviate of Hachberg, rather than from the Markgräflerland. It is strange, too, that Neuenburg did not make more of the issue: Sulzburg's weekly market lay well within the radius of Neuenburg's *Bannmeile* of 2 German miles, and it is hard to believe that the Austrian town neglected to enquire about its legitimacy after it was revived in 1571. Most remarkable of all, the list of local markets compiled by Mattheus Wertz completely failed to record the annual fair and Tuesday market in the margravial village of Britzingen, whither it had been transferred from Badenweiler in 1498.[78] No doubt it had petered out—but why were no attempts made to revive it alongside Sulzburg's, if the Markgräflerland was so starved of indigenous markets? It lay more centrally in the territory than did Sulzburg—and would have offered a greater rivalry to Neuenburg. A verdict on these questions will be reserved until the more complex and protracted rivalries in the margraviate of Hachberg have been considered.

# IV

Market competition in the northern Breisgau presents a vivid contrast to the local difficulties encountered in the Markgräflerland. Although the margraviate of Hachberg was considerably smaller and seemingly less significant than the block of territory in the southern Breisgau which made up the Markgräflerland, Baden displayed a much more urgent concern for its commercial welfare.

---

[77] See above, n. 73.

[78] GLA D 1052, 11 Sept. 1498; cf. 229/12838. The failure to mention the market in Lörrach, founded in 1403 (cf. GLA D 477), is less puzzling. It is unlikely that the market had disappeared altogether (despite lying in Basel's shadow); rather, its location made it remote from the issue of local competition which exercised Wertz. Lörrach did not receive its urban charter until 1682.

By mid-century Malterdingen had been successfully revived, having seen off attempts to shift its market-day from Saturday. Then, in 1572, the bailiff of Hachberg, Peter Efferhard von Reeß, proposed restoring Emmendingen's weekly market, which had been abandoned (though its fair was still held). He suggested holding it on Fridays, rather than on Wednesdays, as the original privilege of 1418 had ordained,[79] in order that it should not clash with other local markets. Thereby, the bailiff confidently predicted, Emmendingen 'would not only flourish with fine buildings, but therein every kind of trader, merchant, and craftsman would seek lodging and recourse as in a town, so that in time it would become a fine little town itself'.[80] The intention to make a town out of Emmendingen was therefore evident from the outset, even if it was only to be realized eighteen years later in 1590. Margrave Karl accepted the proposal, and the market charter was proclaimed on 23 May 1572.[81]

By the following summer the Breisgau towns were up in arms. At an Outer Austrian diet they lodged vehement protests over the market in Malterdingen, now joined by those in Emmendingen and Sulzburg,[82] and petitioned archduke Ferdinand of Tirol for help. The threat to Austrian toll revenues once again prompted Innsbruck to take the matter seriously, and the archduke promised to intervene. But the difficulty of co-ordinating a response over such a long distance bedevilled the authorities' efforts; by November, only Freiburg and the Outer Austrian treasury (newly instituted three years previously) had submitted memoranda on the issue, as requested.[83] In the meantime, the situation had deteriorated, as Georg Gaudenz von Blumeneck, bailiff of the four lordships, and Hans Andreas Halbmair, the Kenzingen official, reported to Ensisheim in September. Margravial subjects were now being prevented from visiting Austrian markets unless they had obtained a

---

[79] GLA D 619, 10 Aug. 1418.
[80] GLA 198/203, fo. 40ʳ, n.d. (before 20 May 1572); Englert, 'Emmendinger Stadtrecht', 47–48; Ludger Hünnekens, 'Neue Beiträge zur Emmendinger Stadtgeschichte', *Zeitschrift des Breisgau-Geschichtsvereins ('Schau-ins-Land')*, 105 (1986), 11–12.
[81] GLA 198/203, fo. 41ʳ⁻ᵛ (draft); Englert, 'Emmendinger Stadtrecht', 48–49.
[82] Cf. GLA 229/64262, 14 July 1573.
[83] TLA, Kanzleibücher: Gemeine Missiven 1573, fo. 1210ʳ–1211ʳ, 15 July 1573; Embieten und Befelch 1573, fo. 456ʳ–457ʳ, 3 Nov. 1573. Freiburg's response, however, was a collective one on behalf of the leading Breisgau towns. StAFr, B 5 XI xx, fo. 492ʳ⁻ᵛ, 12 Sept. 1573; cf. B 5 XI xxii (unfoliated), 28 July 1574.

token showing that they had offered their goods for sale at a margravial market first. The principal victim was Waldkirch, because its market trade depended on the exchange of grain and other crops, including wine, brought by margravial subjects, for dairy produce, livestock, and timber brought down from the Black Forest valleys by Austrian peasants from the lordship of Triberg. Von Blumeneck recommended that the latter be allowed to use only Austrian markets, whereby not only Waldkirch but Kenzingen and Endingen, too, would soon see a revival in their commercial fortunes, since the latter two communes had enough wine and corn to supply all the needs of Triberg, Kastelberg, and Schwarzenberg.[84] From margravial protests six months later it appears that von Blumeneck's advice had been taken, for the authorities in the county of Tübingen (whose lords were Austrian vassals) and in Kenzingen, Riegel, and Endingen had banned their subjects from visiting any but Austrian markets in the district, namely those at Kenzingen and Endingen.[85]

The protests by the two Austrian officials left their margravial counterparts in Hachberg decidedly unimpressed.[86] They pointed out (correctly) that all the margravial markets had ancient charters, and that it was only negligence on the part of the subjects themselves that had caused some of them to wither and die. No prohibition, they insisted, had been placed on visiting Austrian markets, merely priority accorded to native ones; by contrast, the officials noted with regret that the lord of Staufen in the Austrian Breisgau had banned his subjects from patronizing any other local (i.e. margravial) market.[87]

Throughout the autumn and winter the Austrian authorities were still trying to glean more information, including how far the construction of gates and towers at Emmendingen had progressed.[88] By February 1574, however, von Blumeneck and Halbmair had changed their tune. They conceded that the Austrian ban on visiting margravial markets should remain in place (since it was in response to Baden's initial restrictions), but observed that good neighbourly relations were not well served by such bans. It would

---

[84] GLA 229/64261, 3 Sept. 1573.　　[85] GLA 229/64262, 12 Feb. 1574 (draft).
[86] Ibid. 9 Oct. 1573; cf. GAEm, Akten V, 2 166, no. 3.
[87] GLA 229/64262, 15 Oct. 1573; cf. GAEm, Akten V, 2 166, no. 4.
[88] GLA 229/64262, 4 Dec. 1573; HSA, B 17 5*, fo. 380ʳ–381ʳ, 4 Dec. 1573; GLA 229/64262, 6 Feb. 1574. On 22 Feb. 1574 von Blumeneck reported that common rumour had it that a town was in the making. Ibid.

be far better, they argued, to erect customs-posts on the routes leading to the margravial markets. In that fashion, money could be creamed off from the many Alsatian visitors as they crossed the Rhine at Limburg, while a new post should be established at the Dürrhöfe in the Biederbach valley above Elzach[89] (a seemingly remote location, it might be thought, until one realizes that it was designed to catch the Triberg and Elzach peasants as they headed over the hills to Emmendingen and Malterdingen in order to evade the Austrian controls in the Elz valley at Waldkirch). This was certainly regarded as a feasible option by the government in Innsbruck, especially as a means of deterring those Austrian peasants not directly subject to the ban, namely those who were ruled by mortgagee lords, such as the inhabitants of Elzach under Hans Raphael von Reischach, or of Triberg under Lazarus von Schwendi.[90] As usual, however, a decision fell foul of the interminable delays between Tirol and the Upper Rhine, and by the summer matters were no nearer a resolution.[91]

Another device to clip the wings of the Baden markets, of course, was to promote well-situated Austrian markets to deflect traffic away from Malterdingen and Emmendingen. It is surprising, therefore, that the two officials based in Kenzingen, von Blumeneck and Halbmair, made no mention of the establishment the previous October of a weekly market on Tuesdays at Elzach, which should have proved attractive to the Black Forest peasantry, though nothing further is known of its development.[92] They certainly recognized what

---

[89] Ibid. 15 Feb. 1574 (draft).

[90] TLA, Kanzleibücher: Embieten und Befelch 1574, fo. 136ᵛ–137ᵛ, 21 Apr. 1574.

[91] GLA 229/64261, 22 May 1574; TLA, Kanzleibücher: Embieten und Befelch 1574, fo. 278ʳ⁻ᵛ, 26 June 1574; cf. HSA, B 17 5*, fo. 390ʳ–391ʳ, 26 June 1574.

[92] GLA 229/24537, 25 Oct. 1573. The founding of a market at Elzach appears to have been part of a strategy by Hans Raphael von Reischach to increase income from the mortgage, for he had become embroiled in a dispute with the lordships of Kastelberg and Schwarzenberg over the building of new roads over the Black Forest, which had hit the toll and market revenues of Waldkirch whilst abetting the rise of Malterdingen. TLA, Kanzleibücher: Missiven an Hof 1573, fo. 44ᵛ, 16 Feb. 1573. Four years later his request to construct a road through the Yach valley (a shortcut to Triberg which would have obviated the need to follow the Elz up the Prech valley) was dismissed on the grounds that it contravened Freiburg's liberties, would diminish Breisach's bridge-toll revenues, and would harm Kenzingen and Endingen's markets. TLA, Kanzleibücher: Embieten und Befelch 1577, fo. 51ʳ–55ʳ, 6 Feb. 1577, esp. fo. 54ʳ⁻ᵛ. Against this background it is perhaps understandable that von Blumeneck, as bailiff of Kastelberg and Schwarzenberg, was inclined to suppress all reference to von Reischach's activities.

impact the revitalized weekly market at Kenzingen was having,[93] for, as von Blumeneck and Halbmair proudly reported to Ensisheim in the summer of 1574, it had led to a precipitous decline in trade at the Hachberg markets. This was the effective response to the bleatings of Kenzingen, Endingen, and Waldkirch that one Hachberg market was equal to three Outer Austrian ones! The three towns even had the nerve to play the religious card, complaining that as loyal Catholic subjects they were disadvantaged at margravial markets on Fridays and Saturdays because on those days they could not sell meat, unlike the evangelical peasants of Baden.[94]

Throughout this war of attrition over markets in the northern Breisgau remarkably little was heard from the leading Austrian town of the district, Freiburg, apart from championing its fellows' grievances at the 1573 diet and its role in drawing up a joint memorandum to Innsbruck. When Freiburg finally got round to replying to a string of enquiries from Ensisheim in July 1574 (its excuse was that its town clerk had quit), the town adopted a very aloof tone indeed. Its market had not suffered; no complaints had been received; the markets at Sulzburg and Emmendingen were on the point of collapse; many inhabitants of Kenzingen, Endingen, and Waldkirch maintained that they could not do without the Malterdingen market; and so it had nothing to add to its earlier submission, to wit: the government should make further enquiries of those more directly affected.[95] This dismissive attitude helps put the competition from margravial markets into a more sober perspective. Already in the spring of 1574 there had been hints (nothing more) that the Kenzingen official and the bailiff of the four lordships did not see eye-to-eye over the correct response to the margravial threat. Georg Gaudenz von Blumeneck, less persuaded of the efficacy of a market ban than of toll-stages, was inclined to admit that the margravial ban had been prompted by grievances that Freiburg was denying margravial subjects access to its market to sell their produce and wine, a point which he made in a letter to Hans Andreas Halbmair stressing the need to avoid misunderstandings

---

[93] Although Kenzingen was recorded as having two fairs and a market by the end of the 14th century, the only subsequent references are to the confirmation of its fair privileges in 1496. GLA 208/425, 6 July 1495; cf. StAKz, Urk. 70; GLA 21/257, 15 Jan. 1496; cf. StAKz, Urk. 71, and TLA, Maximiliana, XIV/43, fo. 2<sup>r–v</sup>, 15 Jan. 1496.

[94] GAEm, Akten V, 2 166, no. 1, 1573 (*recte*: May 1574: cf. GLA 229/64262, 16 May 1574); cf. also GLA 198/203, and Englert, 'Emmendinger Stadtrecht', 49.

[95] StAFr, B 5 XI xxii (unfoliated), 28 July 1574.

in their response to enquiries from on high.[96] For his part, Halbmair was in favour of a tougher line: banning any contact with margravial markets and forbidding Austrian craftsmen from seeking work in margravial villages.[97] But they could at least agree on one thing, namely that if the reciprocal bans were to be maintained, then Baden (without strong urban markets) would come off worse.[98]

It appears that the Austrian ban was in fact suspended (or else restricted to the export of foodstuffs), for in April 1575 Halbmair was seeking to persuade the Ensisheim procurator-fiscal, Dr Michael Textor, of the need to reintroduce a general prohibition on frequenting margravial markets as the only way of crushing the trade of Malterdingen.[99] But Textor recommended instead urging the local Austrian lords individually to hold their subjects in check.[100] The danger was that they might then take the law into their own hands, for within weeks Strasbourg was accusing Halbmair of having exceeded his authority by banning its subjects in Niederhausen north-west of Kenzingen from visiting margravial markets[101] (though from 1573 Strasbourg in fact no longer held the village as an immediate imperial overlord, but as a territorial vassal of Austria).[102] Although Halbmair stressed that he had no desire to sour relations with the city council of Strasbourg, he then prepared to act in an identical way towards the village of Nordweil, likewise under Austrian sovereignty, but administered by Württemberg on behalf of the abbey of Alpirsbach.[103]

When the Outer Austrian ban was renewed in the autumn, Baden's patience began to wear thin. The Hachberg officials suggested to margrave Karl that a corresponding ban on margravial subjects should now be accompanied by the threat of the death penalty!—or (perhaps more efficaciously) by mutual agreement with Baden's neighbours, such as the Swiss, over market access.[104] Even

---

[96] GLA 229/64262, 22 Feb. 1574.
[97] GLA 229/64261, 7 Mar. 1574; cf. GAEm, Akten V, 2 166, no. 7.
[98] GLA 229/64261, 8 Apr. 1574.   [99] GLA 229/64263, 30 Apr. 1575.
[100] Ibid. 17 May 1575.   [101] Ibid. 11 June 1575.
[102] Wunder, *Straßburger Gebiet*, 52–53; idem, *Straßburger Landgebiet*, 124–25.
[103] GLA 229/64263, 20 June 1575. Halbmair observed that Nordweil's Lutheran preacher had just died, so that there was hope the village might return to the old faith as well as forsake Malterdingen's market (on evangelical territory). In fact, Württemberg installed another Lutheran incumbent, Georg Henninger, whereupon Halbmair was instructed to arrest him. Both he and a replacement preacher were taken prisoner, but in 1578 they managed to escape. Speck, *Landstände*, i. 470–71.
[104] GLA 229/64262, 3 Sept. 1575 (draft); ibid. 12 Sept. 1575.

Freiburg, otherwise so aloof, claimed to have heard rumours that it was to be a target this time.[105] In fact, Baden's response turned out much more mildly: renewed objections to Austria's ban, and restrictions on margravial peasants visiting Austrian markets before their own, as well as formal representations to the government in Ensisheim.[106]

Reviewing developments over the previous four years early in 1576 Hans Andreas Halbmair (standing in for the indisposed Georg Gaudenz von Blumeneck) put his finger on the nub of the problem. In a time of dearth, both Baden and Austria had issued partial market bans from 1573 onwards relating to grain and other foodstuffs; once supplies (and prices) had stabilized, these could then be suspended, only to be reintroduced or reinforced whenever shortages loomed.[107] Such bans seem never to have been universally applied throughout the Breisgau—witness Freiburg's detached attitude, and Breisach's bald statement in mid-1576 that a new margravial edict had left it entirely unscathed.[108] Moreover, the bans were extremely difficult to police, even when scouts were sent to rival market-days to keep a look-out for foreign subjects.[109] Not surprisingly, the authorities cast around for other means of exerting pressure. In Baden's case that involved (for instance) prohibiting its subjects in Ottoschwanden from selling timber from the forest which they shared with Kenzingen at the latter's market,[110] or withholding various dues, such as those owed by margravial (and therewith evangelical) villages to the church at Bombach in the (Catholic) Austrian Breisgau.[111] For their part, the Austrian officials in Kenzingen and Waldkirch sought to deny free passage to foreign subjects bent on visiting margravial markets.[112]

In the spring of 1576 the Outer Austrian government at last offered to lift its ban if Baden followed suit (all previous suggestions to that end by Baden had been brushed aside),[113] though when

---

[105] StAFr, B 5 XI xxiv, fo. 134$^v$–135$^v$, 7 Sept. 1575. The rumours may have had some substance, though. Cf. ibid. fo. 137$^v$–139$^r$, 22 Sept. 1575; GLA 229/64262.

[106] Ibid. 8 Sept. 1575; ibid. 12 Sept. 1575; cf. GAEm, Akten V, 2 166, no. 12.

[107] GLA 229/64262, 29 Feb. 1576 (draft); cf. ibid. 29 Mar. 1576.

[108] GLA 229/64261, 30 June 1576.          [109] GLA 229/64262, 29 Mar. 1576.

[110] Ibid. 29 Feb. 1576; cf. GLA 229/64261, 13 Mar. 1575. This quarrel lasted another seven years until the forest was finally divided between the two communes. GLA 115/613; 208/636; StAKz, Urk. 97, 10 Aug. 1583.

[111] GLA 229/64262, 29 Mar. 1573.

[112] Ibid. 19 Sept. 1575; cf. ibid. 8 Sept. 1575, 29 Feb. 1576, 29 Mar. 1576.

[113] Ibid.; cf. ibid. 7 Aug. 1576.

Kenzingen got wind of this *démarche* it moaned that its market had only been able to flourish behind the security of protectionist walls.[114] The margravial councillors gratefully accepted Ensisheim's proposal, provided that Austrian subjects would again be free to bring their wares into margravial territory.[115] All seemed settled—until Baden once again revived the toll-post at Teningen in 1577.[116] From 1568 the wheel had come full circle! But by now both sides no longer had the stomach for a fight; the subsistence crises of the early 1570s had eased. The Innsbruck government proposed to archduke Ferdinand that for the sake of good neighbourliness he should tolerate the bridge-toll at Teningen, so long as the toll-rates were not increased on Austrian subjects unilaterally and the road was kept in good condition.[117] And there matters finally rested.

# V

This detailed analysis of market competition between Baden and Austria on the right bank of the southern Upper Rhine during the fifteenth and sixteenth centuries does not make for easy reading, but it is only by tracing the twists and turns of a conflict which was fought out at grass-roots level that the significant contours in the pattern of competition can be discerned. Baden's abiding interest was to promote markets which would serve the domestic needs of its territories, yet the margraves—unlike their predecessors, the dukes of Zähringen, four centuries earlier—had never relied on towns as economic reservoirs or administrative headquarters. And even though their officials openly admitted that the inhabitants of the Markgräflerland and Hachberg were all too dependent on the goods and services which the numerous Austrian towns in the Breisgau provided, no attempt was made until late in the sixteenth century (with Emmendingen) to embrace an urban policy which might have offered a counterweight to Austrian dominance. Hence, with the exception of Sulzburg, and Schopfheim in the south of the Markgräflerland, the margravial markets were perforce confined to villages which, however much their trade might annoy their Austrian neighbours, never developed into centres of craft or manufacturing

---

[114] GLA 229/64263, 26 May 1576.    [115] GLA 229/64262, 19 Sept. 1576.
[116] GLA 229/64261, 11 Apr. 1577.
[117] TLA, Kanzleibücher: Missiven an Hof 1577, fo. 272$^v$–275$^v$, 23 May 1577.

production in their own right. As central places, they remained stunted. Contrary to first impressions, that applies to Sulzburg as well, for its status as a town had very little to do with the promotion of its market. It was chosen in preference to the otherwise inconsequential villages of Auggen and Müllheim because of its location as a hinge between valley and plain, and because of the consumption needs of its mining community. If the margraves had been genuinely concerned to further the growth and prosperity of the one town in the north of the Markgräflerland, then it is hard to see why, after a brief flourish, it was allowed to languish.

It is location which holds the key to understanding the margraves' market policy. The revenues from excises which would flow into the margravial coffers from well-situated and well-patronized markets and fairs (as opposed to tolls and stallage which, if they had been levied, would have accrued to the communes themselves) were what mattered, as the Hachberg officials well knew. That is why Baden was eager to promote both Emmendingen and Malterdingen as markets, despite their close proximity, because they both lay on a major artery of trade leading northwards from the Breisgau, with links eastwards into the Black Forest and westwards to Alsace; this strategy was all of a piece with the efforts to establish a customs-post at Teningen. The fiscal imperative presumably also explains why Baden was prepared to let the less favourably situated Britzingen and Eichstetten wither. This in turn accounts for the curiously lopsided treatment of the Markgräflerland and the margraviate of Hachberg. Despite its lamentations, the threat facing Neuenburg from the market at Sulzburg was far less immediate than the challenge to Kenzingen, Endingen, or Waldkirch. Margravial policy was much more strongly committed to exploiting the potential of the Hachberg markets than that of Sulzburg, as the longer duration of conflict there indicates. Compared with the locational advantage of Malterdingen and Emmendingen, Sulzburg was a backwater, situated in a valley which was a cul-de-sac. Without its mineral resources, the community would have been hard put to survive. Whatever interest Baden had in the commerce of the Markgräflerland lay in ensuring that the export market for its wine in Basel and elsewhere was not disrupted, as the bailiff of Rötteln pointed out; there was no compelling reason to promote further internal markets or fairs apart from those which already existed in Schopfheim, Kandern, and Lörrach. The Markgräflerland, as a virtually unbroken tract of territory, faced no economic threat from territorial intruders and, by the same token, presented few opportunities for diverting commerce from foreign rivals, with the one exception of Neuenburg.

By contrast, the possibilities of making mischief in the much less consolidated Hachberg possessions were far greater. Yet any assessment of the commercial threat posed by margravial village markets must conclude that it was sporadic and of limited impact. The lesser market towns of the Austrian Breisgau, rather than the 'county towns', or subregional centres, such as Freiburg (or even Breisach), were those worst affected. Partly, it is true, that stemmed from their unfortunate location, clustered on or near the same trade routes for whose commercial traffic Malterdingen and Emmendingen were also competing. But it is equally clear that these lesser urban centres were peculiarly vulnerable by virtue of their restricted size, or, as we might say, of their weak centrality. The tenor of the submissions by the Austrian bailiffs and officials, and of the town councils themselves (leaving aside the tone of wounded pride that chartered boroughs should be challenged by upstart villages in the first place) leaves little doubt that their livelihood would be imperilled if the economic balance were radically upset: they were communities geared to a commercialized and specialized agriculture which depended on the exchange of basic commodities between plain and uplands—wine and corn for dairy produce, timber, livestock, and animal products.

In a world of plenty it made little difference to them (if not to their overlords) at which markets the exchange took place. But at a time of increasing dearth, as the sixteenth century wore on, access to markets, both to sell and to buy goods, became an existential issue. This is evident from a comparison of the conflicts in mid-century and those in the 1570s. In mid-century the source of friction was the competition for a share of existing trade posed by rival markets as such. By the 1570s bans or restrictions on market access to safeguard essential supplies of foodstuffs were complicating the equation. That is why the latter conflicts were so intractable: until the subsistence crisis (the worst on record, lasting nearly four years) had eased, the authorities felt bound to protect their own subjects as best they could.

At the same time, it was clear to all concerned that economic boycotts *à l'outrance* were senseless where territories and jurisdictions

lay hugger-mugger. Coexistence was imperative (the belated attempt
by several Austrian towns to plead religious discrimination can in
this regard only elicit a wry smile). Against this background it may
seem surprising that no effort was made to resolve the conflict of
the 1570s by mediation, as had occurred in mid-century. But what
was there to mediate? Once it was established that all the markets
had charters (even if their pedigree was occasionally in doubt),
there was no hope of consigning them to oblivion. The only alternative was to adjust the periodicity of the markets to enable subjects to visit them *seriatim* (though that left the clash between
Waldkirch and Malterdingen unresolved). As for the restrictions on
market access, these were clearly imposed and suspended according to the needs of the moment; increasingly the authorities resorted
to partial or local bans, policed by the local lords or officials themselves, rather than blanket prohibitions. The aim was to contain a
conflict for which, in times of dearth, there was no ready or general solution. In the end, the dictates of coexistence—good neighbourliness—had to prevail.

That leaves a question-mark over the true gravity of the competition faced by Austrian communes from margravial markets.
With no statistics to measure the volume or value of trade, we are
forced to fall back on indirect evidence. Perhaps the most striking
feature of the competition is how rapidly the fortunes of individual
markets could soar or plummet, as the reports by officials on the
spot bear out, which makes an accurate assessment no easier.
The issue is further complicated by the rise of informal marketing,
whose impact is altogether unquantifiable (though at least we
know that it was perceived as a threat). To advert to the repeated
grievances expressed by the third Estate at Outer Austrian diets is
not particularly enlightening, since the grievances were submitted
as pleas for the remission of Austrian taxes and war levies. To read
the sweeping claims of economic misery voiced by the Outer Austrian towns *unisono*, when in reality only the Breisgau and Black
Forest communes on the right bank of the Rhine were seriously
affected, is to register some degree of scepticism. It also suggests
that the conflict between Baden and Austria in the Breisgau needs
to be set in the context of the Upper Rhine as a whole, where the
economic relations between town and country could follow widely
differing configurations.

## VI

The intensity and duration of Baden's conflict with Austria over markets in the Breisgau might give the impression that the economy of the right bank of the Upper Rhine was circumscribed by exchange between the valley floor and the western slopes of the Black Forest mountains. But we have argued in an earlier chapter that the Black Forest ranges in no sense formed a natural barrier between the Rhine valley and the Swabian uplands. Politically, Outer Austria extended its grasp eastwards to embrace the outposts of Villingen and Bräunlingen; economically, the links between the Breisgau and the Baar were scarcely less important than those which led upstream to Basel or downstream to Strasbourg and Frankfurt. Freiburg's commercial pre-eminence in the Middle Ages, for instance, had derived more from its vantage-point on a major west–east route from the Rhine over the Black Forest to the cities of Upper Swabia than from any involvement in the axis of north–south trade along the Rhine, especially since the preferred overland route clung to the west bank of the river in Alsace.

When Freiburg set about constructing a rural territory in the later fifteenth century, it chose to buttress its control of the Dreisam valley at the foot of the Wagensteig and Höllensteig passes leading over to Swabia, rather than expand into the Breisgau plain.[118] Its territorial gaze subsequently remained firmly directed eastwards to the Black Forest, not westwards towards the valley of the Upper Rhine. Together with its counterpart Villingen, which was responsible for maintaining the greatest stretch of roads,[119] Freiburg fought a series of running battles with peasants from the Black Forest foothills who strove to construct rival turnpikes over the mountains and so bypass the existing toll-stages and reduce traffic at the towns' markets. Of these, the routes over the Simonswald and Glotter valleys caused repeated trouble throughout the fifteenth and sixteenth centuries.[120]

---

[118] Scott, *Freiburg and the Breisgau*, 41–44; idem, 'Die Territorialpolitik der Stadt Freiburg im Breisgau im ausgehenden Mittelalter', *Zeitschrift des Breisgau-Geschichtsvereins ('Schau-ins-Land')*, 102 (1983), 7–24.

[119] Cf. StAVl, N 13 [no. 408], 4 Nov. 1443; N 17 [no. 2031], 4 Feb. 1570–22 Nov. 1571; N 18 [no. 1512], 22 May 1571.

[120] Scott, *Freiburg and the Breisgau*, 102–5.

Not only Villingen and Bräunlingen, but the towns of the Rhine valley, too, regarded the Black Forest uplands as part of their wider market area, and were accordingly vulnerable to competition from rival markets set up by the local lords. This is apparent from the grievances presented by the Breisgau towns to the Outer Austrian government in 1550. They, along with Villingen, and the four Forest Towns on the *Hochrhein*, protested that count Friedrich of Fürstenberg had established a string of new weekly markets in his territories stretching across the southern Black Forest and the Baar at Vöhrenbach, Löffingen, Lenzkirch, and Neustadt, and was forcing his subjects to use them first on pain of a 10-florin fine. Although at a meeting called to Freiburg on 29 October that year some towns professed themselves unaffected by Fürstenberg's actions, it was decided to draw up a collective submission, pointing out the danger of diminished toll revenues and the loss of Fürstenberg peasants' custom at Austrian markets, which once they had regularly frequented.[121] Price rises were the upshot, for, as the government explained to king Ferdinand, the peasants' produce—cheese, butter, eggs—was being bought up by third parties who visited the market to regrate stocks: the gloomy prospect beckoned that 'the markets [*Flecken*] and villages will grow and the towns will decline and go to ruin'.[122] Initial attempts to persuade count Friedrich to abandon his endeavour got nowhere,[123] but in the autumn of 1561 in a conciliatory gesture he offered to suspend the markets, provided that Austria and Fürstenberg could agree on joint measures to combat forestalling.[124] But later he seems to have reneged on his promise, for during the conflicts of the early 1570s over the Baden markets Villingen complained that forestallers were buying up dairy produce at Fürstenberg markets for resale at Malterdingen, Emmendingen, and Sulzburg.[125] This permits the conclusion that the Fürstenberg threat was not so much direct (would peasants from the Baar regularly have travelled well over 50 kilometres to sell their wares at Breisach, Endingen, or Neuenburg—though Freiburg was within striking distance?) as oblique, whereby their existence impinged less on a perceived market area than it offered an unprecedented opportunity for itinerant petty traders to drive up prices at the Breisgau markets.

[121] StAFr, B 5 IXa i, fo. 155ʳ–157ᵛ (1550).     [122] GLA 229/64261, 15 Nov. 1550.
[123] StAFr, B 5 IXa i, fo. 158ʳ–161ᵛ (1551).     [124] Ibid. fo. 162ʳ–163ᵛ, 11 Aug. 1551.
[125] GAEm, Akten V, 2 166, no. 2, 17 Feb. 1573.

Villingen, of course, was quite another matter—a classic instance of a town marooned in hostile territory, with Fürstenberg to the south and Württemberg to the north, while Bräunlingen, on the doorstep of the counts' residence at Donaueschingen, was completely surrounded by Fürstenberg territory. We have already encountered Villingen's complaints at the proliferation of rural crafts and salt-chests, but the town was also exposed to direct market competition at various times from the 1490s right through to the late 1580s. Bräunlingen faced similar difficulties in 1550, at the time of the Breisgau towns' grievances.

The first phase of friction concerned mutual access to markets. Although an agreement guaranteeing free access was reached in 1491,[126] the provisions of subsequent treaties in 1501[127] and 1516[128] make it clear that Fürstenberg was still trying to prevent its subjects from visiting Villingen to sell produce or to avail themselves of the services of its urban craftsmen. Apart from a brief skirmish with Rottweil in 1545,[129] the next phase of aggression began in the 1560s, when Villingen was beset by burgeoning handicrafts in its surrounding villages.[130] The church-ales in these villages were being patronized by cobblers, bakers, tanners, and the like from Rottweil, Schaffhausen, and elsewhere to such a degree that they had become chartered fairs in all but name, whose profusion was detrimental to Villingen's weekly market.[131] Then, in 1567, count Heinrich of Fürstenberg, mindful of the prevailing dearth, issued fresh injunctions to his subjects to shun Villingen, unless they had gone first with their produce to the revived markets at Vöhrenbach and Geisingen, the latter held twice-weekly on Wednesdays and Saturdays.[132] Despite Villingen painting the situation in the blackest hues—it could not, it alleged, even afford to repair the town

---

[126] StAVl, E 7 [no. 692], 27 Oct. 1491; Siegmund Riezler (ed.), *Fürstenbergisches Urkundenbuch*, iv (Tübingen, 1879), 131–32 (no. 134).

[127] StAVl, E 13a [no. 2942], 11 Jan. 1501; Riezler, *Fürstenbergisches Urkundenbuch*, iv. 184–86 (no. 200/2).        [128] GLA 184/479, 14 July 1516.

[129] StAVl, AAAb/1 [no. 2963], fo. 142ᵛ, 9 Mar. 1545. The imperial free city was preventing its subjects in Weilerbach, Mühlhausen, and Dauchingen, immediately to the north-east of Villingen, from having recourse to Villingen's market.

[130] A stray encounter in 1561, when Georg Meyenberg, Villingen's mayor, came across count Friedrich out hunting, indicates, however, that the Fürstenberg market bans may still have been in force, for Friedrich promised to lift them if approached by the Ensisheim authorities. GLA 184/479, 9 Aug. 1561.

[131] StAVl, W 2 [no. 1974], 11 Aug. 1513–18 July 1558: *circa* 1560.

[132] GLA 184/479, 24 July 1567; 184/478, 9 July 1567.

wall—the Outer Austrian government failed to offer much sympathy,[133] though at least archduke Ferdinand was informed via the government in Innsbruck.[134]

Count Heinrich refused an offer of mediation by Überlingen (the traditional recourse; no doubt he suspected it of partiality towards a fellow-commune) and instead proposed calling up two independent judges.[135] Meanwhile, archduke Ferdinand tried to exert pressure on Fürstenberg to withdraw, but without success.[136] Innsbruck racked its brains for a way out of the impasse,[137] but the best it could come up with was to ask the neighbouring Austrian officials in Hauenstein, Stockach, Waldkirch, and Kenzingen for their suggestions.[138] Then Freiburg, which had an axe to grind because its own market was suffering from higher dairy prices and a lack of poultry and hares, advocated a public decree, backed by stiff penalties, prohibiting Austrian subjects from selling wine, corn, and fruit to the Fürstenbergers. This strategy, it conceded, was not without risk, for Fürstenberg might then bar Freiburg from buying cattle in its territory.[139] The proposal was not taken up. Rather, by the autumn the Innsbruck authorities were taking the Ensisheim administration to task (with their usual disdain) for having failed to come up with an answer,[140] whereupon the latter rounded on Villingen for not having hit back with its own market ban. With some justice the town retorted that, given its exposed position, it was much more dependent on support for its own market from those around it than vice versa.[141] In September 1569 two imperial commissioners, Sigmund von Hornstein and Wilhelm Böcklin von Böcklinsau, were

---

[133] GLA 184/479, 9 Aug. 1567; ibid. 16 Aug. 1567; ibid. 20 Sept. 1567; ibid. 24 Sept. 1567; ibid. 27 Sept. 1567.

[134] GLA 184/479, 21 Oct. 1567; cf. HSA, B 17 5*, fo. 131$^{r-v}$. The Innsbruck government added with some asperity that the bailiff of Triberg—an Austrian subject! —had likewise barred his peasants from Villingen's market, but it was uncertain whether the ban was as extensive as Fürstenberg's. TLA, Kanzleibücher: An die königl. Majestät oder fürstl. Durchlaucht 1567, fo. 1416$^r$–1418$^v$, 27 Oct. 1567.

[135] GLA 184/478, 12 Nov. 1557 (*recte*: 1567).

[136] GLA 184/479, 3 Nov. 1567; ibid. 22 Nov. 1567; ibid. 2 Jan. 1568; ibid. 6 Jan. 1568.

[137] TLA, Kanzleibücher: Embieten und Befelch 1568, fo. 63$^{r-v}$, 22 Jan. 1568; HSA, B 17 5*, fo. 150$^r$–151$^r$, 22 Jan. 1568; GLA 184/479, 23 Jan. 1568 (cf. HSA, B 17 5*, fo. 154$^v$–155$^r$); TLA, Kanzleibücher: An die königl. Majestät oder fürstl. Durchlaucht 1568, fo. 44$^r$–46$^v$, 23 Jan. 1568; Embieten und Befelch 1568, fo. 91$^{r-v}$, 12 Feb. 1568.

[138] HSA, B 17 5*, fo. 156$^v$–157$^r$, 19 Feb. 1568.

[139] StAFr, B 5 XI xix, fo. 693$^v$–694$^v$, 8 Apr. 1568.

[140] GLA 184/479, 14 Oct. 1568; cf. HSA, B 17 5*, fo. 209$^{r-v}$.

[141] GLA 184/479, 29 Nov. 1568.

appointed to mediate in the conflict,[142] but it took another two and a half years to achieve a settlement which restored the free access that had been guaranteed in the 1516 treaty.[143] Count Heinrich, however, appears only to have beaten a tactical retreat, for in 1574 Villingen pressed Ensisheim to have the accord properly ratified.[144] While the ensuing silence in the records indicates that Villingen may at last have shaken off the shackles of its economic beleaguerment, there are signs in 1587 that Fürstenberg was once again up to its old tricks.[145]

Villingen faced identical competition to the north from the duchy of Württemberg. This, however, appears to have been less sustained, though that may be due to a patchy archival deposit.[146] From protests in 1568 it emerged that as early as 1552 Württemberg had prohibited its subjects to the north-east of Villingen from delivering produce to the town's market,[147] and around 1560 it had set up a salt-chest in Schwenningen.[148] Though both Ensisheim and Innsbruck intervened, the conflict never became as acute as the differences with Fürstenberg, probably because no rival markets were involved, which would have touched on regalian rights and presented a serious commercial threat to Villingen.

The contrast with the situation in the Rhine valley is manifest. The intensity of the conflict between Baden and Austria was determined by the precarious balance of geography and territoriality. Each side claimed a stake in the commerce of the Freiburg basin, at the node of exchange between upland and plain, where their territories intersected. Neither was powerful enough to suppress the other's competition. In Villingen, by comparison, the issue was not so much commercial rivalry as sheer survival. The town controlled only a modest rural hinterland, and the latter was beginning to usurp the town's traditional urban functions.[149] Surrounded by hostile territories, Villingen had no bargaining counter: it needed the custom

---

[142] HSA, B 17 5*, fo. 228ʳ–229ʳ, 22 Sept. 1569.

[143] StAVl, E 18 [no. 1516], 9 Apr. 1572; Baumann and Tumbült, *Mitteilungen aus dem f. fürstenbergischen Archive*, ii. *Quellen zur Geschichte des f. Hauses Fürstenberg und seines ehedem reichsunmittelbaren Gebietes, 1560–1617* (Tübingen, 1902), 165–66 (no. 286). The settlement referred to a subsequent treaty in 1567, but whatever it may have contained, it cannot have held for very long, in view of Villingen's protests from the summer onwards.     [144] GLA 184/479, 17 Feb. 1574.

[145] Ibid. 6 Nov. 1587.     [146] GLA 81/47, 18 Nov. 1567.

[147] HSA, B 17 5*, fo. 197ᵛ–198ʳ, 3 June 1568.     [148] GLA 81/47, 18 Sept. 1568.

[149] Cf. Villingen's complaints against Fürstenberg weavers and saddlers plying their trade in villages under Villingen's jurisdiction. FFA, Jurisdictionalia C, xii, 3, 1588.

of its neighbours more than they needed the town's. It was therefore peculiarly vulnerable to market competition from Fürstenberg, but could hardly dare impose market bans of its own. That competition, however, revealed how interconnected were the economies of the Rhine valley and the Swabian uplands, for Fürstenberg's actions threatened not only the Austrian outpost of Villingen but the Breisgau capital, Freiburg, as well, which only a few years later was professing itself aloof from the market competition afflicting the lesser towns of the Austrian Breisgau.[150]

Competition over economic resources and their distribution was an obvious concomitant of the process of territorial consolidation, but it would be misleading to infer that market rivalries were only likely to occur between sovereign principalities. The collective grievances of the Outer Austrian third Estate in 1557 had not specified whether the competition that was threatening its livelihood was located within or without Austrian jurisdiction; some salt-chests, as we have remarked, were set up in the countryside of the Austrian *Ämter*. There are, in fact, several instances within Outer Austria where a local lord tried to promote a market against the interests of his Austrian neighbours. That was the case in Krozingen, halfway between Breisach and Neuenburg, where in 1576 Hans Friedrich von Landeck launched a weekly market, provoking the wrath of his neighbour, baron Georg Leo von Staufen, who was simultaneously striving to ward off Sulzburg's challenge to his urban market at Staufen.[151] Neuenburg was quick to join the protest,[152] but Breisach was more cautious, though it agreed that the market should be opposed.[153] What accounted for Breisach's hesitation, it transpired, was the fact that Hans Friedrich von Landeck was one of its town councillors![154] Nothing more was heard of the Krozingen market: Austria had the power to call one of its own vassals to heel in a way that was impossible with Baden.

---

[150] They also gave rise to conflict with the lords of Schellenberg, whose market at Hüfingen was harmed by the promotion of Geisingen, and with Schaffhausen, whose supply-lines of agrarian produce were being correspondingly squeezed. Cf. August Vetter, *Geisingen: Eine Stadtgründung der Edelfreien von Wartenberg* (Constance, 1964), 125–31, and idem, *Hüfingen* (Hüfingen, 1984), 119–22. These conflicts lie outside the scope of the present study. For Villingen's assertion of its priority ranking at the Hüfingen weekly markets and fairs cf. StAVl, QQ 1 [no. 2020], 15 Oct. 1559–17 May 1793: 15 Oct. 1559; G 20 [no. 1480], 15 Oct. 1559.
[151] GLA 229/56506, 24 Feb. 1576.    [152] Ibid. 3 Mar. 1576.    [153] Ibid.
[154] Cf. StAFr, B 5 XI xxiv, fo. 222$^{r-v}$, 3 Apr. 1576.

Krozingen was not the only instance of an attempted market foundation by a local lord after the mid-sixteenth century in the Austrian Breisgau. But elsewhere the initiative came from mort-gagee lords, keen to extract the greatest economic return from their pawns. We have already noted the efforts of Hans Raphael von Reischach in Elzach in 1573. The following year, Lazarus von Schwendi sought to revive the weekly Saturday market in Triberg, originally franchised in 1481,[155] which had been allow to fall into desuetude, but Villingen objected that it would damage its own market and encourage forestalling.[156] Eight years later, as lord of the *Kirchspiel*, the district south of Freiburg comprising Ambringen, Ehrenstetten, and Kirchhofen, which had been repeatedly mort-gaged throughout the century, von Schwendi tried to restore the St Laurence's fair on 10 August in Ehrenstetten,[157] after a previous mortgagee twenty years previously had seemingly failed to have the village's fair and market charter reconfirmed.[158] There is no evid-ence that any of these efforts bore fruit, at least more than tem-porarily. The only successful new foundation came in 1589 when Herbolzheim, in the formerly mortgaged lordship of Kürnberg (redeemed by Austria in 1564),[159] was granted three fairs and a weekly market on Thursdays by archduke Ferdinand of Tirol.[160]

In Baden, by contrast, which all but lacked a territorial nobility and was administered directly through *Ämter*, each with its own district seat of justice and market, there should, in principle, have been no likelihood of chartered markets being confronted with upstart competitors from within the territory. In the southern lands, Hachberg and the Markgräflerland, that was largely the case. But because Baden had acquired its northern territories piecemeal over the centuries from existing lords—the Hohenstaufen, the counts of Hohenberg and Eberstein, the lords of Fleckenstein and Windeck—it inherited towns and markets often lying in close proximity across the Upper and Lower Margraviates. By the closing decades of the sixteenth century local communities, particularly in the margravi-ate of Baden-Baden, were making determined efforts to safeguard

[155] GLA 21/427, 30 Apr. 1481; cf. 122/84; 122/85; 122/307.
[156] StAVl, QQ 2 [no. 2039], 16 July 1574.
[157] StAFr, C 1 Fremde Orte: Kirchhofen 17, 18 May 1582.
[158] HSA, B 17 4*, fo. 389ᵛ, 6 Feb. 1563.
[159] Wellmer, 'Der vorderösterreichische Breisgau', 308; Wunder, *Straßburger Landgebiet*, 122.　　　　　　　　　[160] GLA 21/223, 13 Oct. 1589.

or reassert lapsed or endangered market franchises. A comical, but telling, instance concerned Rastatt, whose market privilege dated from 1404. Although the market had not collapsed, the commune requested a reissue of its charter because part of its seal had broken off.[161] Margrave Philibert's councillors responded in tones of derision: there was no real threat to the market, and the diploma was still perfectly valid.[162] But Rastatt would not let go: it petitioned Philibert directly, and indeed with success, for a new charter was duly conferred by emperor Maximilian II.[163] The fear of losing its economic pull, in a territory plentifully supplied with markets, must have sat deep in the bones of Rastatt's council to provoke such an agitated reaction. Steinbach, which had received its urban privilege and market franchise as early as the mid-thirteenth century,[164] petitioned in 1587 to have its Wednesday market revived as a means of preventing the informal trading of goods on Sundays and holidays.[165] In 1576 Kappelwindeck by Bühl hoped to safeguard the future of its fair on the Monday before the Nativity of the Virgin by having it moved to the Wednesday before, in order to avoid a clash with Bühl's weekly Monday market, which had brought about the former's decline.[166]

But the most revealing submission was Kuppenheim's in 1580, which complained that its Tuesday market had languished since an outbreak of plague at the beginning of the century and competition from markets in neighbouring territories.[167] Margrave Philibert's invitation to the other markets of the Upper Margraviate to comment on Kuppenheim's wish to hold two horse-fairs in addition to its weekly market[168] provoked a unanimously hostile response from Bühl (governed in condominium by Baden-Baden and the lords of Windeck), Ettlingen, Gernsbach, Baden, and Rastatt.[169] Gernsbach's and Baden's comments, in particular, show how jealously they guarded their market area. Gernsbach controlled the upper reaches

---

[161] GLA 220/792, 21 Feb. 1570.          [162] Ibid. 23 Feb. 1570.
[163] Ibid. 3 Aug. 1570.
[164] GLA D 79, 23 Aug. 1258 (cf. 229/100736; 229/100737). On the twilight existence of this diminutive town with the widest civic liberties of any Baden commune, see Rüdiger Stenzel, 'Die Städte der Markgrafen von Baden', in Treffeisen and Andermann, *Landesherrliche Städte*, 101–2 and n. 16.
[165] GLA 229/100737, 26 Feb./5 Mar. 1587.
[166] GLA 229/51503, n.d. (3 Sept. 1576).          [167] GLA 229/56808, n.d. (Feb. 1580).
[168] Ibid. 22 Feb. 1580.
[169] Ibid. 27 Feb. 1580 (Georg von Windeck in Bühl; Ettlingen); 1 Mar. 1580 (Bühl); 2 Mar. 1580 (Gernsbach); 4 Mar. 1580 (Baden); n.d. (1580) (Rastatt).

of the Murg valley and poured scorn on Kuppenheim's claim that the upland villagers and even Gernsbach's own bakers were keen to patronize it: for the remoter Murg communes that would involve a journey of anything between 15 and 23 kilometres (passing Gernsbach on the way), a distance there and back difficult to achieve in one day. In Baden's case, Kuppenheim's request directly collided with its own Tuesday market. The town pointed out that merchants (in this case Jews) already had their fixed itinerary —Mondays in Bühl and Gernsbach, Tuesdays in Baden, Wednesdays in Ettlingen (for Steinbach's market was still in abeyance), Thursdays in Rastatt, and Saturdays back to Baden. Moreover, there were fairs enough in the Upper Margraviate (at Bickersheim and Rastatt), though if Kuppenheim were to get its way, then the fairs would be at least less damaging to Baden's livelihood than another weekly market. Faced with this barrage of protest, margrave Philibert not surprisingly turned Kuppenheim down, though after renewed pleas he granted two fairs for a trial period of up to two years.[170]

While the density of markets in the Upper Margraviate, many of some antiquity and several located in chartered boroughs,[171] reflects the fragmentation of medieval lordship, of which Baden was the beneficiary, the foundation of market centres was itself a response to the commercial opportunities which the Ortenau as a wine-growing region flanking the Rhine, with easy access to outlets such as Strasbourg, afforded. This is well illustrated by a deposition concerning Rastatt's market in 1555, which recorded that merchants from Sélestat in Alsace maintained wine warehouses in Rastatt, whose stocks were sold on commission by locals, thereby evading any restrictions on foreigners' access to the market.[172] Jockeying to defend existing market areas on occasion even spilled over into friction between adjacent communes in the Upper and Lower Margraviates. In 1567 Ettlingen claimed that its market was threatened by the setting up of a second weekly market in Durlach, particularly since subjects in the Lower Margraviate were then forbidden

---

[170] Ibid. n.d. (April 1580); 21 May 1580.

[171] Politically, this fact does not contradict the view of margravial policy as generally lukewarm towards towns, since most of the boroughs in the Upper and Lower Margraviates (Baden-Baden and Baden-Durlach) were inherited or acquired from previous overlords. Cf. Stenzel, 'Städte der Markgrafen', 90 ff.

[172] GLA 220/792, n.d. (1555).

to sell their produce at Baden-Baden markets.[173] *Per contram*, the village of Stupferich in the Upper Margraviate objected in 1578 that it was being prevented from frequenting the Durlach market, even though it lay closer than Ettlingen's.[174] Though these were no more than isolated incidents, they do show that the authorities' desire in both margraviates to control economic resources by preventing a free market in goods and services might be no respecter of geographical convenience, let alone a common dynastic and political heritage. A sense of solidarity, it should be added, was yet further eroded after mid-century by the split in confessional allegiance between Lutheran Baden-Durlach and—after many vicissitudes—Catholic Baden-Baden.

Although rivalry between the two margraviates was kept reasonably in check, the unholy combination of competing markets and restrictions on free trade, which so bedevilled relations between Baden and Austria in the Breisgau, can also be observed (albeit nowhere near as vehemently) in the Ortenau in the tensions which arose between Baden-Baden and its southern neighbour, the county of Hanau-Lichtenberg. By the 1570s signs that the counts were inclining towards territorial autarky were there for all to see: the promotion of a weekly market in Lichtenau was accompanied by prohibitions on subjects in the Hanauer Land visiting the Baden-Baden markets at Bühl and Steinbach.[175] These were indeed the developments which formed the backdrop to Kuppenheim's actions in 1580. One might have expected an even more aggressively autarkic policy from the counts, given that their territory was effectively an exclave of their principal possession in Alsace, being hemmed in by Baden-Baden to the north and the imperial bailiwick of the Ortenau to the south. Why that did not happen is suggested by a supplication in 1580 from the villagers of Rheinbischofsheim to count Johann Reinhart of Hanau-Lichtenberg. Although he had imposed an export ban on produce, the villagers pointed out that it could not possibly all be sold within the Hanauer Land at the existing markets in Lichtenau and Willstätt. This was in fact a pretext for demanding their own market at Rheinbischofsheim, but, as the villagers themselves acknowledged, the produce was chiefly sent to Strasbourg, just across the river.[176] The situation, in other

[173] GLA 74/5114, 17 Nov./4 Dec. 1567.    [174] Ibid. 26 Sept. 1578.
[175] GLA 229/60778, 16 Jan. 1574.    [176] ADBR, E 2926, n.d. (*circa* 1580).

words, was analogous to that in the southern Markgräflerland, where a local economy geared to exporting its surpluses to an urban entrepôt (Basel) could not afford to contemplate too great a regulation of markets and access thereunto.

On the left bank of the Rhine the picture is altogether—and puzzlingly—different. Neither in the consolidated Austrian lordships of Upper Alsace, whose division into *Ämter* resembled Baden's, nor in the fragmented and often diminutive jurisdictions to the north is there any evidence, on an appreciable scale, of new or revived market foundations,[177] still less of competition between markets (though restrictions on the marketing of foodstuffs were, as we shall explore in Part III, part-and-parcel of governments' concern for public welfare as the sixteenth century wore on).

Within the Austrian part of Upper Alsace, it is true, both Ensisheim and Delle—each a district seat with its own chartered market and salt-chest—in the 1560s petitioned to be allowed to set up corn-exchanges, but this was in effect a plea to staple corn against the threat of bad harvests, rather than the outflow of an active desire to stimulate commerce in the hope of profit.[178] The exception which proves the rule was Giromagny in the southern foothills of the Vosges, on the western flank of the Austrian Sundgau. Here the motive was quite straightforward: the burgeoning population of the mining districts in the Rosemont and Rougemont valleys, which after mid-century began to overshadow the increasingly worked-out mines of the Val de Villé and the Val de Lièpvre, had created a consumer demand which was not conveniently met by the market at Belfort, nearly 13 kilometres away. In 1563 various suitable sites for a new weekly market were discussed: Auxelles-Bas was ruled out as lying too close to Plancher-les-Mines,[179] but

---

[177] Worth mentioning, if only on account of its rarity, was the bishop of Strasbourg's revival of the weekly market at Stotzheim, west of Benfeld, in 1563. ADBR, 8 E 481, A 9, 23 July 1563.

[178] ADHR, C 674, n.d. (1564/68); C 406/23, 2 Apr. 1563; ADTB, E-Dépôt 33: ACD, HH 1/1, 20 Mar. 1568. In the case of Ensisheim, the intent was made plain by its request that subjects within a radius of 2 German miles (9 statute miles, or 15 kms.) should be obliged to bring their grain to Ensisheim rather than sell it in foreign territory at Colmar, Kaysersberg, Ammerschwihr, Guebwiller, or in the Upper Mundat at Rouffach or Soultz.

[179] Plancher-les-Mines was the most westerly Outer Austrian mining community, a German-speaking commune amidst a francophone landscape. Rudolf Metz, 'Bergbau und Hüttenwesen', 167. It is marked on map 9 of the *Elsaß-Lothringischer Atlas*, however, as lying just over the border in the Württemberg county of Montbéliard.

Vescemont, Rougegoutte, or Giromagny were all possibilities.[180] The choice of the Innsbruck authorities (this was too serious a matter for their country cousins in Ensisheim) fell upon Giromagny as the most central location—which would thereby be elevated to a district market and seat of the inspector of mines.[181] This did nothing to mollify Belfort, which objected that foodstuffs were being diverted from its own market to Giromagny's.[182] Yet the establishment of the latter's market was clearly not intended as an act of commercial piracy but as a response by the Austrian authorities to a perceived local need. Much the same presumably applied to the weekly market further east at Haut-Etueffont, about which Masevaux had complained in 1557.[183] Iron-ore mining had developed separately from the silver-, copper-, and lead-mines around Giromagny, and Haut-Etueffont, centrally placed, offered the obvious site for a market to supply the miners' needs.

Elsewhere in Alsace, the profusion of central places and the fragmentation of political authority might have seemed an ideal breeding-ground for market competition. Yet the archival sources (dispersed, but by no means deficient) tell us next to nothing. The most that comes to light are some traces of rivalry in the very north of Lower Alsace around Wissembourg, initially stemming from the imperial free city's desire to institute an annual fair in 1570 on All Saints (1 November).[184] When word got about, the officials of the surrounding Palatine districts were asked for their assessment of its likely impact by elector Friedrich.[185] Given the long history of strained relations between the Palatinate and Wissembourg, the replies were remarkably unruffled. The customs-receiver at Seltz on the Rhine did observe that the fair would encroach on one of Seltz's own fairs, held in the week before Martinmas,[186] but the bailiff of Altenstadt, on Wissembourg's own doorstep, saw this as a positive advantage, since it would make it worthwhile for merchants to visit each in succession, and hence bring additional custom to Seltz, always provided that Wissembourg's fair did not extend

[180] ADHR, C 406/23, 2 Apr. 1563.     [181] Ibid. 12 Aug. 1563.
[182] ADHR, C 588/1, 5 Dec. 1563.
[183] StAFr, C 1 Landstände 7, n.d. (*circa* 1557).
[184] This appears to have been to compensate for falling business at the fair held around Vincula Petri (1 Aug.), which, the council suggested, should be reduced to one week's duration instead of two. ADBR, C 38/37, fo. 47ʳ–48ʳ, n.d. (1570).
[185] Cf. ADBR, C 38/35; 38/36; 38/37.     [186] ADBR, C 38/35, 22 Oct. 1570.

beyond All Saints.[187] These views did not carry the day, and three years later Wissembourg tried instead to secure a fair at Martinmas itself, that is, after Seltz's fair, but the elector was advised to tread cautiously.[188] It had emerged in the course of the Palatine enquiries that Seltz's fair was already suffering competition from a fair at Hatten, a short distance to the west, on Hanau-Lichtenberg territory.[189] There are no signs, however, that these occasional irritations gave rise to prolonged conflict. That applies equally to Munster's promotion of a market upstream on the Fecht at Muhlbach in 1573, designed to evade the abbey of Munster's own chartered market,[190] or to the bishop of Strasbourg's efforts to establish a weekly market at Châtenois, at the mouth of the important passes over the Vosges through the Liepvrette and Villé valleys, in 1601, which would have cut off trade from Sélestat. After the city had obtained a legal opinion from the faculty of law in Freiburg, declaring illegal any market within 2 German miles of Sélestat, the matter was dropped.[191]

# VII

So far our analysis has concentrated on the proliferation of central places with overlapping hinterlands as the prime cause of competition faced by established chartered markets on the Upper Rhine. In so doing we have uncovered a striking discrepancy between the right and the left banks of the river. On the right bank, a spate of new market privileges can be traced throughout the fifteenth and sixteenth centuries in what Meinrad Schaab has called a 'euphoria' of new foundations, culminating on occasion in a profusion of mutually paralysing little central places[192]—hence the disappearance and subsequent revival of many smaller markets. But on the left bank, in Alsace, where urban charters, to which market rights were

---

[187] ADBR, C 38/37, fo. 51ʳ⁻ᵛ, 17 Oct. 1570; cf. C 38/35.
[188] ADBR, C 38/37, fo. 53ᵛ–54ʳ, 4 June 1573.
[189] ADBR, C 38/35, 22 Oct. 1570.
[190] ADHR, 1 H 19/59, no. 110, n.d. (1573).
[191] AMSé, HH 128/2 & 3, 31/27 Mar. 1601.
[192] Meinrad Schaab, 'Städtlein, Burg-, Amts- und Marktflecken Südwestdeutschlands in Spätmittelalter und früher Neuzeit', in Emil Meynen (ed.), *Zentralität als Problem der mittelalterlichen Stadtgeschichtsforschung* (Städteforschung. Veröffentlichungen des Instituts für vergleichende Städtegeschichte in Münster, A 8) (Cologne/Vienna, 1976), 265.

invariably attached, had been granted *ad libitum* during the Middle Ages to communes situated cheek by jowl, the evidence of commercial conflict over the protection of market areas is remarkably meagre.

Before addressing this problem directly, however, we would do well to enquire whether the threat to market privileges may have taken other forms, which did manifest themselves without distinction throughout the Upper Rhine. The short answer is to point to the universal complaints about foreign pedlars and petty traders, the ubiquitous *welsche Krämer*. These men (for they were rarely women) hailed mostly from upland or mountainous regions where employment, especially in the winter months, was scarce, so that they took to the road as hawkers, selling a variety of cheap wares not only at chartered markets but informally in the countryside as well on Sundays, holidays, or at weddings. On the Upper Rhine these pedlars were frequently described as Savoyards, but they might come from anywhere in the Alps, or even from overseas. Consequently, attempts to curb their activities can be found from Tirol (where in the Peasants' War of 1525 the Merano articles demanded their curtailment)[193] throughout the Upper Rhine in Outer Austria[194] and Baden,[195] and as far as the county of Montbéliard[196] in the fifteenth and sixteenth centuries. Less clear-cut, though, are the reasons why they were hounded. Certainly town councils saw hawking (*Hausieren*) outside the regular market days or fairs as leaching trade and revenues from the chartered markets, but another objection was not so much commercial as legal or political, namely that the hawkers avoided paying civic taxes or performing military service.[197] Repeated ordinances at territorial[198] or urban[199] level only testify to the impossibility of policing the informal marketing of goods.

---

[193] Tom Scott and Bob Scribner (eds.), *The German Peasants' War: A history in documents* (Atlantic Highlands, NJ/London, 1991), 90.

[194] Cf. GLA 79/1702: Grievances of the Outer Austrian Estates, 13 May 1573; StAFr, C 1 Landstände 11, 1573.          [195] Cf. GLA 74/10501, n.d. (*circa* 1538 and 1553).

[196] AN, K 1901/I: 'Touchant les estrangers merciers vendant leur[s] espiceries aux villages', 1560 ff.

[197] Cf. Albert Jäger, 'Der Engedeiner Krieg im Jahre 1499, mit Urkunden', *Neue Zeitschrift des Ferdinandeums für Tirol und Vorarlberg*, iv (1838), 212.

[198] Cf. GLA 21/2, 31 Jan. 1584: Archduke Ferdinand's ordinance for Outer Austria, referring to earlier edicts of 1551 and 1573.

[199] Cf. Villingen's 16th-century ordinances, first restricting hawkers to markets and fairs, and latterly to fairs alone. StAVl, P 19 [no. 2939], pp. 12–13, n.d. (*circa* 1500); ibid. 27–28, 14 Jan. 1562; P 21 [no. 1527], 5 Mar. 1573.

As subsistence crises became more frequent on the Upper Rhine in the course of the sixteenth century, a litany of protests against 'foreign merchants', 'hawkers', and 'forestallers' who stockpiled goods, diverted them from local markets, and drove up prices rang out at regional assemblies on the Upper Rhine convened under the umbrella of the Rappen coinage league to regulate the supply of meat and grain to local markets. These assemblies will be examined in depth in Part III. For the moment, however, we need to ask whether more complex issues were concealed behind the clamorous denunciations of *welsche Krämer*. In the first place, not all foreign pedlars were 'foreign', in the sense of being seasonal or migrant hawkers from alpine valleys. They could just as well be craftsmen from neighbouring territories, selling their wares outside the chartered markets—for instance, the Palatine potters from Lauterbourg and Rheinzabern, who were accused of pinching the trade of urban potters in the margraviate of Baden-Baden by selling their wares beyond the regular markets.[200] In the second place, the concern of princes and magistrates to control marketing might collide with the sectional interests of the urban artisans themselves, whose protests at restraint of trade can be heard in both Austrian and Baden territories on the right bank of the Rhine. Artisans in Austrian towns—be they Freiburg's coppersmiths,[201] Breisach's cap- and trousermakers,[202] or Villingen's drapers[203]—at various times in the sixteenth century were all prohibited from hawking their wares outside market hours, or informally in the countryside and at church-ales.

Where crafts were organized on a territorial basis, as was generally the case in the margraviates of Baden, regulation might prove even harder to achieve, since the distinction between urban and rural crafts was correspondingly blurred. Thus the fraternity of haberdashers in Baden-Baden claimed in 1546 to have a long-established right to sell on Sundays, holidays, or at church-ales, which the margravial officials in Kuppenheim and Steinbach were disputing.[204] In 1567 the inhabitants of the district of Steinbach as a whole invoked a general right to buy and sell outside the chartered markets. In the town of Steinbach and its affiliated villages,

---

[200] GLA 74/10487, 12 Aug. 1582.    [201] AAEB, B 209/1, 29 July 1569.
[202] GLA 115/560, 8 Nov. 1597.
[203] StAVl, P 19 [no. 2939], pp. 16–17, n.d. (*circa* 1500).
[204] GLA 74/10501, n.d. (Apr. 1546).

they alleged, they had traditionally been allowed to buy meat, salt, grain, vegetables, and bread on Sundays and holidays; on such days, moreover, cobblers, and merchants passing through on their way to the Frankfurt fairs, had sold their wares in villages along the route. By avoiding the urban markets, they concluded, the evil of forestalling would be averted![205] That, of course, was nonsense, but confusion undoubtedly reigned, as the town of Baden lamented to margrave Philibert a few years earlier: why, it wailed, should the peasant visit an urban market when each weekday and holiday goods were delivered to his front door?[206]

The real problem, therefore, was not the presence of foreign pedlars, but the fact that the traditional autonomies of town and country, of primary and secondary economic sectors were disintegrating. If villagers would not come to urban markets, then urban craftsmen and traders must perforce go to the countryside, regardless of whatever prohibitions the civic authorities might seek to impose. There they had to compete for business alongside foreign hawkers, other local artisans—and, not least, the village craftsmen themselves.

# VIII

The proliferation of markets and of informal exchange was not peculiar to the right bank of the Rhine, if we can agree that the spate of urban foundations in Alsace before 1500 must have entailed market privileges as well. But only in the Breisgau, and to a lesser extent in the Ortenau, does their location and the ensuing overlap of market areas seem to have given rise to sustained and anguished competition. The establishment of salt-chests in the Austrian administrative districts of Upper Alsace, and the evidence of district or territorial guilds, leave no doubt that crafts and petty trading were commonplace in the Alsatian countryside, but we hear next to nothing of rival markets; only the salt-chests seem to have been a thorn in the flesh of the district capitals. The issue, therefore, is not whether the pattern of economic activity on either

---

[205] GLA 74/5114, 17 Nov. 1567. The submission stemmed from the five localities of the 'Heymerthumb'—Steinbach, Müllenbach, Gallenbach, Neuweier, and Weitenung. Another copy of the submission included the inhabitants of Beinheim, Baden's administrative district on the left bank of the Rhine in Alsace.

[206] GLA 74/6368, 2 Mar. 1563.

bank of the Rhine significantly diverged, but rather why essentially similar economic structures led to conflicts on the right bank but not on the left. If no obvious economic explanation springs to mind, perhaps the answer is to be found in differing political configurations. In this context consolidated and fragmented territorial landscapes must be considered separately. The block of Habsburg territory in Upper Alsace faced no immediate rivals, it appears, from within, with the exception of the city of Mulhouse, only the possibility of competition from beyond its borders. The division into *Ämter* was intended to reserve most commercial activity to the administrative seats where the markets were situated, a centrality impaired, but not seriously jeopardized, by salt-chests in the countryside. But as we have seen in an earlier chapter, Austrian Upper Alsace was by no means seigneurially homogeneous. Unlike the margraviates of Baden, all but bereft of a territorial nobility, a good deal of the Sundgau, especially at the fringes, was in the hands of local nobles, who resisted the absorption of their fiefs into a uniform Austrian territorial dependence. From this perspective they had good reason to promote economic activity, including markets, in their fiefs, if only to strengthen them against the threat of integration.

Moreover, many Austrian lordships in Alsace were (repeatedly) mortgaged,[207] giving the *Pfandherren* every incentive to maximize the returns from commercial sources as well as from the land itself, as happened elsewhere in the Austrian lands.[208] If Konrad Stürtzel, Hans Raphael von Reischach, and Lazarus von Schwendi could found markets in their Breisgau territories, why not *Pfandherren* in Alsace? Von Schwendi himself is a case in point. His principal pledged lordship was, after all, Hohlandsberg by Colmar, but although he is famous for his viticultural improvements there,[209] no new markets were established, perhaps because with the two small towns of Kientzheim and a third of Ammerschwihr the lordship had market outlets enough. Where lordships, by contrast, lay intermingled, the prospects for commercial rivalry were all the more enticing. In Lower Alsace, for instance, the bishop of Strasbourg could

---

[207] Cf. Stolz, *Geschichtliche Beschreibung*, 117 ff.

[208] Cf. Hermann Rebel, *Peasant classes: The bureaucratization of property and family relations under early Habsburg absolutism 1511–1636* (Princeton, NJ, 1983). Rebel describes the system of *Pfandherrschaften* as 'lien administration'.

[209] Though not for the introduction of the tokay (pinot gris) grape variety, which popular legend had it that von Schwendi had brought back from his victorious campaigns as Maximilian II's commander on the Hungarian front against the Turks.

readily have promoted markets in the various parts of his scattered territory to deflect trade and revenues from lesser imperial free cities such as Rosheim, or Obernai, yet the only instance appears to be the belated attempt to raise Châtenois to market status against the interests of Sélestat. The bishopric might have attempted something similar in the Upper Mundat in Upper Alsace, in order to loosen the stranglehold which Austria had upon the territory, but there is no sign of it. Political or territorial imperatives, therefore, cannot account for the discrepant incidence of commercial rivalry.

Three reasons for the absence of market conflict in Alsace may, however, be advanced. First, market provision was already adequate, so that rivalries (had they existed) would have revolved not around new market foundations but on competition between existing markets and the securing of unimpeded access to them. As far as food provisioning was concerned, there is no lack of evidence that Alsatian towns and cities, just as their counterparts on the right bank of the Rhine, felt that their markets were increasingly vulnerable to, and required protection against, evasion and forestalling by itinerant merchants and speculators, who distorted the natural buying and selling of produce. There are few indications, admittedly, that these anxieties extended to the production and distribution of craft goods. Second, Alsace was topographically and climatically more favoured than the Ortenau or the Breisgau. Its principal cash crop, wine, gave higher yields of greater quality—and hence value—than vineyards along the Black Forest foothills. Only Alsatian wine could command a premium in export markets beyond the adjacent upland areas of the Upper Rhine.[210] In short, Alsace was more prosperous. It is quite conceivable, therefore, that output could sustain a higher level of commercial activity, with communes able to make a decent living despite their shrunken hinterlands. The experience of the renowned wine-growing towns of Ammerschwihr, Kaysersberg, and Kientzheim, living in friendly rivalry while close enough to be within gunshot of each other, makes a telling contrast to those Baden and Austrian communes of the northern Breisgau, not all that much further apart, who were locked in a desperate struggle

---

[210] Some Breisgau wines, especially from the best vineyards of the Kaiserstuhl, were exported via Swabia as far as Bavaria, and to north-eastern Switzerland, in the 14th and 15th centuries. Hektor Ammann, 'Freiburg und der Breisgau in der mittelalterlichen Wirtschaft', in Hermann Eris Busse (ed.), 'Der Breisgau', *Oberrheinische Heimat*, 28 (1941), 251.

for market share. As fashion and consumption began to turn away from Alsace wines during the sixteenth century, this argument, however, becomes less compelling. Third, the promotion of new markets was a risky strategy, since conflict with existing markets was entirely predictable, and likely to lead to long and costly disputes over regalian rights. Since the lords' intervention was often to augment their revenues rather than to stimulate economic activity in any mercantilist sense, was it not better to resort to stratagems which would, though controversial, yield a quick return? Of these, tolls were a favoured device, particularly if important trade routes were at stake. In 1559, to cite only one example, barons Nikolaus and Johann von Bollweiler, lords of an Austrian fief to the west of Ensisheim (and who were significant mortgagee lords elsewhere in Alsace), imposed a turnpike-toll on the high road leading through their lordship from Burgundy to Strasbourg, from which the inhabitants of the Upper Mundat close by were quick to claim exemption.[211] And on a territorial level, toll disputes throughout the Upper Rhine, not least in Alsace, were to become more frequent as the authorities strove to safeguard supplies in the face of increasing dearth by erecting customs-barriers to prevent the export of vital foodstuffs.

The notion, therefore, of the Upper Rhine as a natural economic region—that is, contained within certain natural frontiers, and sustained by the interdependence of supply and demand between upland and plain—needs to be qualified. Economically, the region was not self-enclosed. Although the market disputes between Baden and Austria do indeed reveal exactly the kind of reciprocal exchange between upland districts of pastoralism, dairying, and forestry, and lowland areas of viticulture and cereals that one might expect, they also show that the right bank of the Rhine was closely linked to the economy of the Swabian plateau beyond the Black Forest. Moreover, while the Rhine itself constituted no sort of barrier, economic or political, the economy of Alsace was, in this period, clearly more resilient than that of territories on the right bank: it could sustain a greater density of population and settlement without unleashing conflict over economic resources within competing market areas. Economically, therefore, the two banks were not mirror images of each other. More generally, those who argue that the

---

[211] ADHR, 3 G 3/6, 22 Sept. 1559; 3 G 3/1, 9 Apr. 1561.

geographic region is the proper framework within which to understand secular economic transformation and development must recognize that, on the Upper Rhine, town and country—or central place and hinterland—were not always the mutually reinforcing and perfectly integrated economic agents which central-place theory might suggest, but were often economic and commercial competitors.

# PART III

*Economic Co-operation and Coexistence*

# 6

# The Rise and Decline of the Rappen
# Coinage League

## I

Part I sought to demonstrate that the political development of the Upper Rhine lends only modest support to the notion that it formed a natural region. The coherence of what at first sight appears to be a self-contained region was in fact the outcome of a late medieval contraction and concentration of political power, which had loosened the hitherto strong links between northern Switzerland and the Upper Rhine while at the same time leaving the Habsburgs as the dominant lords within a reduced area. Over that area, however, their authority was not absolute, and its limits coincided imperfectly with any perceived natural frontiers.

This chapter argues that an analogous, and indeed simultaneous, contraction can also be observed in the pattern of regional monetary co-operation. In the late fourteenth and early fifteenth centuries that co-operation had been vested in regional coinage associations, born of the necessity to achieve monetary stability as the precondition of economic and commercial prosperity in an age of weak or absent royal authority. Such associations sprang up across the length and breadth of Germany, uniting in particular the Wendish cities of the Baltic littoral in the north, the princes and cities of Franconia, the Rhineland, and Swabia in the centre and south, and the powers on the Upper Rhine, including all of germanophone western Switzerland.[1] Although their importance as agents of regional monetary policy needs no stressing, their significance in the longer term—at least on the Upper Rhine—lay in providing a framework for co-operation over fundamental issues of

---

[1] Joachim Schüttenhelm, *Der Geldumlauf im südwestdeutschen Raum vom Riedlinger Münzvertrag 1423 bis zur ersten Kipperzeit 1618: Eine statistische Münzfundanalyse unter Anwendung der elektronischen Datenverarbeitung* (Veröffentlichungen der Kommission für geschichtliche Landeskunde in Baden-Württemberg, B 108) (Stuttgart, 1987), 36.

'good police' and public welfare. As we shall see in the following two chapters, the coinage association of the southern Upper Rhine succeeded in retaining its indispensable role as a forum for the regulation of basic provisioning in meat and grain throughout the sixteenth century, even when its original function as the collective guarantor of sound money was being eroded by the intensifying 'early absolutist' power of the Habsburgs as territorial princes, as a result of which the coinage league itself was finally forced to disband. After its dissolution the erstwhile members continued to deliberate jointly—albeit under a different aegis—on matters of common economic concern; an awareness of a regional community of interests, in other words, managed to survive in a climate increasingly cool towards the communal-co-operative spirit which had informed its origins. As political (and confessional) lines became more sharply drawn during the sixteenth century, the coinage association of the southern Upper Rhine, in terms of its devolved responsibilities, remained a viable framework for, and the visible expression of, regional economic co-operation and solidarity.

Yet, as its initial membership makes clear, the Upper Rhenish coinage association was not, at the outset, identified with any self-defining region or sense of territoriality. Rather, it represented a banding together of lords and cities, whose interests might coincide or collide, and whose jurisdictions, in the case of the feudal nobility, were located in, but not necessarily bounded by, the area which it comprehended. The association, subsequently known as the Rappen coinage league, was originally designed to combat the profusion of minting regalities which had sprung up by default in an age of political entropy, across a relatively restricted area spanning the southern Upper Rhine, western Switzerland, and western Swabia around Lake Constance. To the east and north, similar efforts were undertaken to spur co-operation between lords and cities in the much larger, but equally fragmented, area of Swabia. On the Upper Rhine, much of the stimulus came from Basel, fearful for its mercantile pre-eminence if bad coin were to continue to circulate not only in its immediate hinterland but within its wider sphere of influence as well, which at that time—the late fourteenth century—stretched upriver to Lake Constance and took in the cities of the Swiss midlands north of the Alps. To begin with, however, Basel possessed no minting regality of its own. Only when the bishop of Basel ceded his minting rights to the city in 1373 was

the way open to press for the formation of a regional coinage association which would serve the city's interests. And that required,
first and foremost, an accommodation with the Habsburgs, whose
lands in northern Switzerland and on the Upper Rhine held the
city in a territorial clasp.[2]

But just how imprecise—or inchoate—a sense of common
regional economic interests was is evident not only from the political and jurisdictional imperatives which determined the association's membership but also from the failure of its members to agree
on a coinage valid throughout the region. The coinage agreement
reached in 1377 in Schaffhausen was intended to last fifteen years.
Its signatories included the Austrian dukes (duke Leopold III as
ruler of Tirol and the 'outer lands') for their mints in Switzerland (at
Schaffhausen and Zofingen) and on the Upper Rhine (at Freiburg
and Breisach in the Breisgau, and Bergheim in the north of Upper
Alsace); the counts of Kyburg (for their mint at Burgdorf near
Bern); countess Elisabeth of Neuenburg (for the mint and lordship
of Neuchâtel, which later reverted to the counts of Freiburg and
thence to the margraves of Baden); the lords of Krenkingen (for
their mint at Tiengen in the Klettgau); and the cities of Basel,
Zürich, Bern, and Solothurn.[3] What underlay this treaty was only
marginally a sense of geographical cohesiveness: the need to balance the Habsburgs' power against the cities' interests was paramount. Areally, the association was 'open' to the east—the frontier
towards the rest of Swabia, or eastern Switzerland, was defined by
the extent of Habsburg lordship, which impinged on the hinterland of Constance, a city subsequently at pains to establish itself
as the hub of an independent coinage association spanning Swabia
and northern Switzerland. Above all, the association made no initial effort to create a unitary currency. Instead, it delimited three
circles, each with its own coinage standard (*Münzfuß*). Broadly
speaking, it is true, these were distinguished geographically: the
Freiburg circle northernmost, then a circle around Basel, and finally
a third for the Swiss midlands. But in point of fact the Basel circle
embraced two northern Austrian mints, Bergheim in Alsace, and
Breisach (the latter logically assignable to the Freiburg circle as
part of the Breisgau).

[2] Julius Cahn, *Der Rappenmünzbund: Eine Studie zur Münz- und Geld-Geschichte des oberen Rheinthales* (Heidelberg, 1901), 22 ff.; Schüttenhelm, *Geldumlauf*, 287.
[3] Cahn, *Rappenmünzbund*, 25.

The treaty of 1377 did not run its full course. Continuing monetary instability was compounded by the political upheaval wrought by the Confederate victory over the Habsburgs and their allies at the battle of Sempach by Lucerne in 1386, one of the turning-points of Swiss history. To be sure, the new coinage treaty concluded the following year marked the greatest extent of a regional coinage association spanning both northern Switzerland and the Upper Rhine. It described a rough circle, on whose perimeter lay Bern to the south, Zürich and Schaffhausen to the east, Villingen in the eastern Black Forest, Bergheim in Alsace, and Neuchâtel in the southwest, comprising a total of seventeen mints and seventy-four towns.[4] But it quickly became obvious that the new treaty could not paper over the antagonism between the Habsburgs, by then in full retreat from inner Switzerland, and the Swiss cities of the north-west. The latter sheared away from the coinage league for political reasons, not because the economic fundamentals had changed. By the same token, Constance's links with Zürich came under increasing strain, as the city, far from forming a bridgehead on Lake Constance, was left high and dry between the 'cow-Swiss' (*Kuhschweizer*) and the 'sow-Swabians' (*Sauschwaben*).

How rapidly events unfolded in the closing decades of the fourteenth century is demonstrated by the quite different assumptions governing Basel's negotiations with Leopold IV of Austria in 1399. The Habsburgs, thrown back upon their lordships in Alsace and the Breisgau (though still in possession of the Thurgau), were keen to reach agreement with Basel on a new currency standard for the southern Upper Rhine alone, given the competition they faced from Strasbourg's strong silver penny coinage. Accordingly, they concluded a five-year bilateral treaty (to which Freiburg and Breisach as quasi-autonomous minting authorities within Outer Austria acceded), valid for the Upper Rhine and the territories of the city and bishopric of Basel. A new currency based on Stäbler pennies (of Basel's minting) and Austrian twopennies (*Zweilinge*) was agreed. On this basis a new and comprehensive treaty was signed in 1403. This used to be regarded as the foundation stone of the Rappen coinage league. Although we now know that its origins lay in the wider and looser agreements of the preceding decades, the 1403 treaty

⁴ Cahn, *Rappenmünzbund*, 31–32, and map, 33; Schüttenhelm, *Geldumlauf*, 287.

was indeed the first to mention the term Rappen,[5] the name henceforth given to the *Zweilinge* as Rappen league pennies, with the Stäbler effectively relegated to halfpennies. The treaty embraced the signatories of 1399, with the addition of the imperial free city of Colmar, each mint entitled to strike its allotted quota of bullion at an agreed weight and value. That applied also to Austria's mint at Thann in Alsace, established in 1387, which had no regalian rights of its own.[6]

The 1403 treaty is remarkable on two counts. First, its membership represented a considerable contraction over against the treaties of 1377 and 1387: effectively, the Swiss disappeared. Basel's decision to align itself with the Upper Rhine and Outer Austria—only a century later did it 'turn Swiss'—was entirely understandable. The Upper Rhine was a crucial provisioner of the city, supplying it with grain and wine, some for re-export to inner Switzerland; it was also the principal market area for the city's craft goods and the location of put-out textile manufacturing. The city's economic fortunes, in other words, were bound up with the Upper Rhine, where it functioned as a submetropolis within the wider orbit of the regional capital Strasbourg, with whom it vied for commercial advantage on the Rhine as a vital artery of trade. Indeed, Basel's interest in participating in a regional coinage association for the southern Upper Rhine may be seen as a conscious decision to avoid being commercially overwhelmed by its larger neighbour. The city's alliance with the Swiss Confederation in 1501 was taken against an utterly changed political backcloth, and did not alter its economic centrality as an Upper Rhenish city, even if it subsequently became a major centre of credit and finance for the Confederation as a whole.

Secondly, the provisions of the treaty for the first time described the limits of the coinage association in geographical terms, as did its renewal in 1425. Interestingly, however, the wording used to delineate the boundaries in 1403 did not altogether chime with that of 1425. In 1403 the membership was to comprise the area 'in these bounds and circumferences, namely from the Eckenbach this side, and the far side of the Rhine upriver as far as Rheinfelden [as far and

---

[5] On the origins and meaning of the name Rappen (which has nothing to do with *Rabe* (= raven)), cf. Cahn, *Rappenmünzbund*, 9–15.

[6] Ibid. 68; Schüttenhelm, *Geldumlauf*, 308.

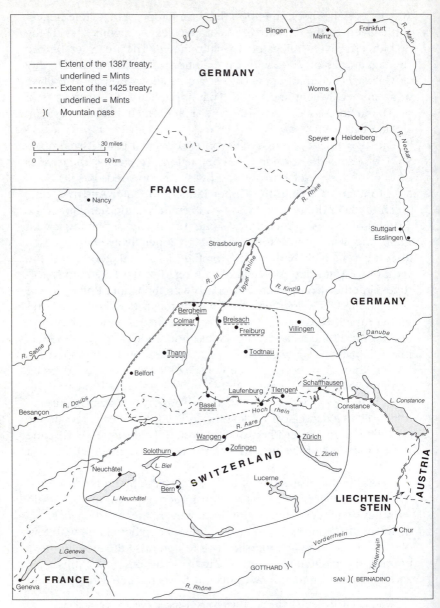

MAP 12. The development of the Rappen coinage league

wide as Austria's lower bailiwick extended, and in the towns and districts of Basel, Freiburg, Colmar, and Breisach]',[7] whereas twenty-two years later the diploma was if anything more geographically concrete and precise, applying 'in these bounds and circumferences, namely from the Eckenbach this side, and the far side of the Rhine upriver as far as [the] Hauenstein above Laufenburg, as far and wide as Alsace and the Sundgau [extend, and the towns and districts of Basel, Freiburg, Colmar, and Breisach lying between them]'.[8]

Over against the Schaffhausen treaty of 1377, whose unifying principle was seigneurial and regalian, the treaties of 1403 and 1425 spoke of (boundary) lines and circles, as if the area encompassed should primarily be comprehended areally or geographically. That is especially so in 1425, which supplemented the vague reference to districts flanking the Rhine as far as the Landgraben at the Eckenbach by specifying the *Landschaften* of Alsace and the Sundgau.

This shift may strike the reader as more apparent than real. After all, such delimitations only echo the wording of the numerous public peace agreements (*Landfrieden*) on the Upper Rhine during the preceding century, which were discussed in Part I. There the recourse to watersheds and rivers as marking the limits of their sphere of jurisdiction in turn reflected both existing diocesan boundaries and those of the relevant territorial bailiwicks. In any case, where such alliances were concluded between imperial cities, or between such cities and other feudal lords, the terminology of seigneurial jurisdictions was scarcely appropriate in defining boundaries. Moreover, the obvious discrepancy in setting the south-eastern frontier of the coinage area first at Rheinfelden and then further upstream at Laufenburg is less significant than it seems, for Austria's lower bailiwick, mentioned in the 1403 treaty, in fact extended as far as the rocky outcrop of the Hauenstein above Laufenburg, as well as taking in the Frick valley south of the Rhine. Nevertheless, it could be argued that the coinage treaties were belatedly adjusting themselves to an areal definition of political authority already manifest in the public peace accords.

---

[7] 'in disen zilen und kreissen, nemmlich von dem Eggembach hie disent und enent Rins haruff untz gen Rinfelden . . .' *Urkundenbuch der Stadt Basel*, v, ed. Rudolf Wackernagel (Basel, 1900), 319 (no. 302); Cahn, *Rappenmünzbund*, 49.

[8] 'in disen zylen und kreissen, nemlich von dem Egkenbach hie dise site und ennent Rins haruff uncz gen Houwenstein ob Loffemberg, als verre und wite Elsas und Suntgow . . .' *Urkundenbuch der Stadt Basel*, vi, ed. August Huber (Basel, 1902), 201–2 (no. 199); Cahn, *Rappenmünzbund*, 2.

At all events, by the later fifteenth century the geographical limits of the Rappen coinage league were so well established that the documents no longer refer to participating lordships but simply— as in duke Sigismund of Tirol's treaty with the four minting cities on the southern Upper Rhine in 1480—to the area 'in the district of the Rappen coinage' ('inn bezircke der rappenmùncze') or 'in this circle of the Rappen coinage' ('in disem kreysse der rappen- mùncze').⁹ Much more remarkable, however, was the manner in which the Rappen members came to define their association after 1500. In an edict against bad coin issued in 1522 they recalled that the league had originally been established 200 (!) years previously between Austria and 'those of the towns in the district of these Outer Austrian lands, namely from the Hauenstein down the Rhine as far as the Eckenbach, and through the Breisgau over the forest to Villingen and below it through Alsace as far as Montbéliard'.¹⁰ Here for the first time the area of the coinage league was described as lying within the district (*Bezirk*) of Outer Austria. But the signat- ories were self-evidently neither exclusively Austrian subjects, nor did the area of the coinage league equate to Outer Austria except in the most general terms. It was both larger and smaller: larger, in that the territory of the bishopric of Basel (without a mint of its own, after those rights had been transferred to the city) was always comprehended—thereby underscoring our earlier observation that the southern 'frontier' of Alsace cannot properly be marked off from the Ajoie, across the foothills of the Ferrette Jura; smaller, in that the Austrian outposts across the Black Forest, Villingen and Bräunlingen, although members of the Outer Austrian Estates, ceased to be regarded as part of the Rappen coinage association by the fifteenth century (even though Villingen had been a signat- ory in 1377 and 1387). This was to have repercussions in the assem- blies called to discuss meat and grain provisioning under the aegis of the Rappen league, for the Outer Austrian government could not forbear to invite Villingen, as an Outer Austrian subject, to attend,

---

⁹ *Urkundenbuch der Stadt Basel*, viii, ed. Rudolf Thommen (Basel, 1901), 462–63 (no. 594).

¹⁰ 'denen von stetten inn dem bezirckh diser vordern Osterreichischen Landen, namlich von dem Howensteyn, den Rẏn hẏnab bis an den Eckenbach vnd durch dz Breyßgow vber den waldt gen Villingen vnd vnden herauf durch das Elsass bys gon Mumpelgart'. GLA 79/1657, 14 Dec. 1522. This document is cited by Speck, *Landstände*, i. 495 without a date, but in a context which gives the impression that it belongs with the treaties of the early 15th century.

yet the latter riposted that it was not a member of the Rappen coinage league. Waldshut's position, too, was anomalous. As the one Forest Town lying east of the river Alb, that is, beyond Laufenburg, it would appear to be excluded from the orbit of the league, even though its political affiliation was to Outer Austria. It, like Villingen, was drawn into Constance's monetary circle, but the government in Ensisheim continued to regard it as bound by the Rappen convention.[11]

Since the area of the Rappen coinage league appeared to be increasingly defined by territoriality rather than political sovereignty —hence, perhaps, the rather curious wording of the treaty texts— scholars from Julius Cahn onwards have persisted in describing the league as contained within 'natural frontiers'—namely the Eckenbach (or Landgraben) to the north, and the watersheds of the Vosges and the Black Forest to the west and east.[12] Rather than mock them for an uncritical belief in natural frontiers, it would be more useful to recall than even Cahn acknowledged that these 'frontiers' seemed to vanish on the southern periphery of the league. The Hauenstein above Laufenburg was the traditional landmark at the south-eastern tip of the Breisgau, but it still vied with the line of the river Aare (the diocesan frontier) debouching into the Rhine further upstream at Koblenz opposite Waldshut as the generally recognized 'frontier' of the Upper Rhine in that area. To the south, it is true that the Rappen coinage league took in Basel's hinterland up to the lower and upper Hauenstein passes, which are in some measure a natural frontier, since they mark both a clear watershed and the present-day boundary between the cantons of Basel-Land and Solothurn, but the same cannot be said of the 'open' terrain of the Ajoie. Here no natural frontier was in play, and the bishopric of Basel's membership of the league was historically and politically, not territorially, determined. To the 'frontier' between Outer Austria and the county of Montbéliard we shall return; for the moment it is enough to recall that Outer Austria's western borders overrode or ignored any natural frontier or watershed. And even if it were conceded that the Vosges and the Black Forest indeed amounted to natural frontiers on the southern Upper Rhine, the

---

[11] See, for instance, the coinage mandate of 1501, denouncing base foreign coins and fixing new exchange rates, which referred to Alsace, Sundgau, and the Breisgau, 'ouch die *vier* stet am Rein' (my emphasis). StAFr, C 1 Münzsachen 1, 20 Oct. 1501.     [12] Cahn, *Rappenmünzbund*, 3; Schüttenhelm, *Geldumlauf*, 288.

Black Forest certainly did not represent one in the Ortenau, for the middle territories of the margraviate of Baden in the fifteenth century joined the Swabian coinage area constituted by the Ried-lingen treaty of 1423, and thereafter remained closely linked to Württemberg's coinage.[13]

Nevertheless, in comparison with the sprawling Swabian associ-ation, the Rappen coinage league operated within a much tighter compass, and its development took a different trajectory. The Swabian minting authorities—mostly cities—sought to embrace the widest possible area, but to restrict the number of mints: this was the guiding principle behind the Riedlingen treaty. The diffi-culties in holding such a vast area together, even discounting the political turbulence from Switzerland, were formidable, and it is no surprise that three smaller regional confederations of princes and cities emerged from it: Württemberg-Baden; Constance and environs; and Upper Swabia and the Allgäu, with the Swiss detach-ing themselves to form an association of their own.[14] By 1500 the Riedlingen treaty had effectively run its course. On the Upper Rhine, by contrast, mints had proliferated during the fourteenth century in a relatively circumscribed area.[15] But the Rappen coinage league, as we have seen, soon resolved itself into a much more compact association with only five mints. It lasted for the best part of 200 years, a feat all the more remarkable given the character of the Upper Rhine as a commercial crossroads, constantly prey to being inundated with foreign and inferior coin.

The character of the Rappen coinage league also presents an instructive contrast to its neighbour to the north, the circulation area of the Strasbourg penny. In the late fourteenth century Strasbourg had done its best to ensure that its coin dominated Lower Alsace,[16] but although its penny circulated on the right bank of the Rhine in the Ortenau (a treaty of 1393 had extended its currency area to include the secular territories of the bishopric of Strasbourg),[17] it

[13] Friedrich Wielandt, *Badische Münz- und Geldgeschichte* (Veröfftentlichungen des Badischen Landesmuseums, 5), 3rd edn. (Karlsruhe, 1979), 96; Schüttenhelm, *Geldumlauf*, 205.        [14] Ibid. 190.

[15] Bernhard Kirchgässner, 'Zur Neuordnung der Währungsräume Südwestdeut-schlands und der angrenzenden Eidgenossenschaft 1350–1500', in Hermann Aubin, Edith Ennen, Hermann Kellenbenz, Theodor Mayer, Friedrich Metz, Max Müller, and Josef Schmithüsen (eds.), *Beiträge zur Wirtschafts- und Stadtgeschichte: Festschrift für Hektor Ammann* (Wiesbaden, 1965), 326.        [16] Ibid. 323.

[17] Schulz, *Handwerksgesellen und Lohnarbeiter*, 318.

never managed to establish itself as the dominant, let alone the exclusive, currency, since it had to compete with the monetary policies of the margraves of Baden. In 1409 Baden had in fact sought to link itself to the Palatinate and the bishopric of Speyer (which had extensive right-bank possessions in the Kraichgau) in a currency union.[18] Thereafter, while the margravial territories in the Rhine plain remained open to the Strasbourg currency, the economic needs of the Black Forest rafting trade and Pforzheim's cloth industry nudged the margraves towards an alignment with Württemberg, which was formalized in the treaty of Leonberg in 1475.[19] Not only, therefore, was the circulation area of the Strasbourg penny less self-contained than that of the Rappen penny; it reflected a differing configuration of interests between the participating authorities as well. As landgrave of Lower Alsace, the bishop of Strasbourg assumed responsibility for convening regional monetary assemblies, which performed the same task of ensuring adequate provisioning and orderly marketing of foodstuffs as their counterparts on the southern Upper Rhine. But because the bishop's nominal authority was restricted to Lower Alsace, the regional assemblies summoned under his auspices never embraced the princes and cities of the Ortenau, which was only represented by virtue of Alsatian lords holding territories on the right bank of the Rhine, such as the city of Strasbourg, the counts of Hanau-Lichtenberg, or indeed the bishops themselves. None the less, the very profusion and fragmentation of lordships in Lower Alsace might be thought to have conduced to a much stronger sense of shared needs and reciprocal obligations than south of the Landgraben, where Austria's influence was so pronounced.

But the Strasbourg coinage area never reflected a balance of interests between potentially competing regalian authorities which was the hallmark of the Rappen league. As in the case of Basel, the bishops of Strasbourg had surrendered their minting rights to the city, but unlike Basel (whose bishops did nominally retain their regality) the former at various times continued to mint at Molsheim, particularly under bishop Johann IV von Manderscheid in the 1570s and 1580s.[20] Yet for much of the period under review the city of Strasbourg was the only minting authority in Lower Alsace. In that sense it was, unlike the city of Basel, accountable to no one but itself

---

[18] Schüttenhelm, *Geldumlauf,* 205.

[19] Wielandt, *Badische Münz- und Geldgeschichte,* 96; Schüttenhelm, *Geldumlauf,* 205.     [20] Ibid. 305.

—or rather, to its perception of its own commercial best interests, which ensured that the Strasbourg penny suffered little debasement.

Another reason for the different character of the two coinage areas lies in the availability of bullion to supply their mints. In Lower Alsace, neither the bishop nor the city of Strasbourg owned silver deposits (apart from the bishop's mine at Soultzmatt in the Upper Mundat in Upper Alsace, which was of little account).[21] Instead, the city was dependent upon its merchant houses to supply it with silver acquired on the open market, some of it from mines in the Val de Lièpvre, west of Sélestat. The main silver reserves on the Upper Rhine lay in Upper Alsace and the Breisgau, the majority on Austrian territory, rather than further north, so that the mints of the Rappen coinage league were almost self-sufficient in bullion throughout the period of its existence. Indeed, the league was able to enforce long-term delivery contracts on the mines to ensure continuity of supply. This enhanced the character of the league as a collective association sustained by a regionally self-subsistent economy, in a way that clearly did not hold good for Strasbourg and its coinage area.

The assured supply of local silver undoubtedly contributed to the cohesion of the Rappen league, but the productivity of the Upper Rhenish mines fluctuated throughout the 200 years of its existence. The Black Forest mines, which had earlier made Freiburg's fortune, were by no means worked out by the sixteenth century, but their running costs rose sharply as deeper shafts had to be sunk to compensate for the exhaustion of the shallower adits. The technology for pumping water out of the wet slopes of the Schauinsland above Freiburg was both expensive and rudimentary,[22] but some mines continued to give a good return. Although the general verdict is that the Black Forest mines lost ground to the richer seams in Alsace after 1500, one authority, at least, has argued that the mines at Todtnauberg and Schönau reached their greatest output after that date, and may even have rivalled Ste-Marie-aux-Mines, the leading mining community in the Val de Lièpvre.[23] At

---

[21] Otto Stolz, 'Zur Geschichte des Bergbaus im Elsaß im 15. und 16. Jahrhundert', *Elsaß-Lothringisches Jahrbuch*, 18 (1939), 40.

[22] Cf. Albrecht Schlageter, 'Der mittelalterliche Bergbau im Schauinslandrevier', pt. 1, *Schau-ins-Land*, 88 (1970), 157–61.

[23] Alfred Bissegger, *Die Silberversorgung der Basler Münzstätte bis zum Ausgang des 18. Jahrhunderts* (Basel, 1917), 41.

the beginning of the sixteenth century the principal silver-mining district in the Vosges stretched up the Val de Lièpvre from Ste-Croix-aux-Mines and Ste-Marie-aux-Mines over the watershed into Lorraine, where the dukes possessed an extensive regality in the higher side-valleys such as the Morte, around La-Croix-aux-Mines. In the main valley itself mining rights were shared between Austria, Lorraine, and the lords of Ribeaupierre.[24] Although the Ribeaupierre were progressively sucked into territorial dependence upon Austria in the course of the sixteenth century, their status as imperial vassals had required the Habsburgs the previous century to make terms with them in 1486, in order to ensure a steady flow of bullion from a district which was largely under the latter's control.[25] According to this agreement the Ribeaupierre were originally guaranteed one-third of the output of ore, but after Maximilian's accession that was increased to one-half, which yielded them a considerable profit. This arrangement worked well in the early decades of the sixteenth century, and indeed both Austria and the lords of Ribeaupierre entered into contracts with the Rappen mints to deliver bullion in regular quantities, which rendered the mints largely independent of outside procurement.[26] But the first signs of strain appeared shortly afterwards, as the price of silver on the European market rose, and demand from Swiss mints increased. In 1542 Ribeaupierre threatened to cancel its monopoly supply contract with Colmar unless the price were raised, or else it be allowed to sell on the open market.[27]

In these years the mines in the Val de Lièpvre were yielding around 6,500 marks of silver annually (equivalent to somewhat over 66,000 florins in value),[28] as well as further quantities of copper and lead, prompting one French observer to describe them as among the richest in all Germany.[29] That impression, however, was quite mistaken, for the Habsburgs' Tirolean mines in Schwaz alone

---

[24] Gisbert Roos, 'Die geschichtliche Entwicklung des Bergbaus, insbesondere des Bergrechts im Elsaß und in Lothringen' (Diss. ing. Technische Universität Clausthal, 1974), 15.     [25] Stolz, 'Bergbau', 134–36.

[26] Ibid. 156.

[27] Cahn, *Rappenmünzbund*, 160–61. Around mid-century Egenolph von Rappoltstein even considered minting his own coinage. Jordan, *Entre la Gloire et la Vertue*, 83.     [28] Schüttenhelm, *Geldumlauf*, 289–90.

[29] Cf. Augustin Calmet, *Histoire ecclésiastique et civile de Lorraine* (Nancy, 1728), ii. 1144–45. His account is drawn from the contemporary description by Paul-Émile [= Miles] Piguerre, a French Huguenot official, in his *Histoire de la France*, 1st edn. (Paris, 1550).

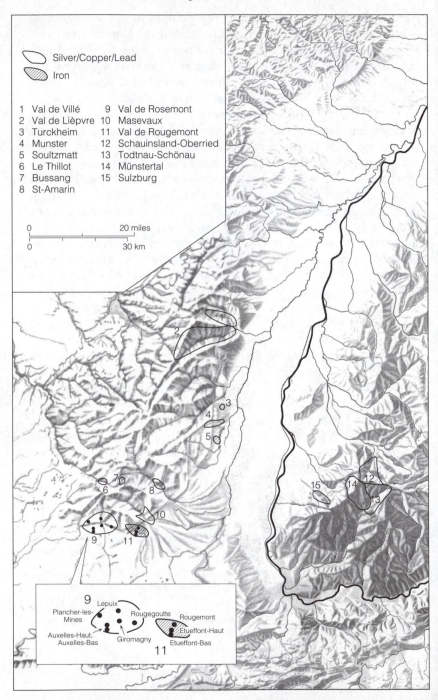

MAP 13. Minerals and mines on the Upper Rhine, 1400–1600

produced ten times the ore and six times the refined silver of the
Val de Lièpvre.[30] All the same, the output was anything but neg-
ligible, and even after they had passed their peak in mid-century,
the mines were still yielding up to 4,000 marks of silver annually;
Basel was receiving very nearly 3,000 marks each year from the
Val de Lièpvre alone well into the 1570s.[31]

By then the focus of attention had switched to the mines along
the foothills of the southern Vosges. These were strung out in an
arc from Steinbach by Cernay[32] and St-Amarin up the Thur valley
on Murbach territory,[33] to the Doller valley around Masevaux,[34] and
thence to the main district in the lordship of Rosemont above Belfort,
centred upon Lepuix, Auxelles, and Giromagny, with Plancher-les-
Mines as its western outlier.[35] These latter were still going strong
at the end of the sixteenth century, providing nearly 4,000 marks
of silver *per annum*, in addition to copper and lead.[36] Moreover,
the Murbach mines at St-Amarin discovered new lodes around 1550
which bore a good yield well into the next century.[37] Even so, the
Rappen mints from time to time did buy silver on the open market—in 1499, for instance, Colmar and Freiburg combined to purchase 300 marks' worth at Strasbourg (where did it come from?)[38]
—as far afield as Frankfurt.[39] On the other hand, since minting by
the authorities was never continuous—it might be suspended whenever debased coin threatened to drive out sound Rappen pence

---

[30] Stolz, 'Bergbau', 146.

[31] Schüttenhelm, *Geldumlauf*, 290; Bissegger, *Silberversorgung*, 174; Jordan, *Entre
la Gloire et la Vertue*, 82. It is possible that the slow decline of the Val de Lièpvre
mines had less to do with dwindling ore deposits than with difficulties in supplying the mines with sufficient timber for pit-props, housing, and, of course, smelt-
ing. R. Metz, 'Bergbau und Hüttenwesen', 161–62. Around 1200 new dwellings were
erected there in the 1520s. F. Metz, 'Die elsässischen Städte', 320.

[32] Stolz, 'Bergbau', 121.

[33] Bissegger, *Silberversorgung*, 38. Murbach, according to Cahn, *Rappenmünzbund*,
4, delivered all its bullion to the Rappen mints until it set up its own mint at
Guebwiller in 1544. What coin was issued is entirely obscure, and the mint seems
to have been abandoned.

[34] Bissegger, *Silberversorgung*, 38; Schüttenhelm, *Geldumlauf*, 290.

[35] Bissegger, *Silberversorgung*, 38; Stolz, 'Bergbau', 158; R. Metz, 'Bergbau und Hüttenwesen', 167–68. Lorraine also had mines just over the watershed at Bussang and
Le Tillot on the headwaters of the Moselle. Roos, 'Geschichtliche Entwicklung', 8.

[36] R. Metz, 'Bergbau und Hüttenwesen', 169.

[37] Bissegger, *Silberversorgung*, 38.

[38] Odile Kammerer, 'Colmar et Fribourg à la fin du Moyen Âge: Convergences
et divergences', *Annuaire de la Société d'Histoire et d'Archéologie de Colmar*, 37
(1990), 41.                                  [39] Schüttenhelm, *Geldumlauf*, 290.

—the mines had surpluses which they were able to market elsewhere. The difficulties which the league faced during the sixteenth
century, ultimately leading to its downfall, cannot be attributed to
bottlenecks in the supply of bullion. They were not even, at heart,
the result of the struggle to maintain the value of the currency in
the face of bad coin from Switzerland or Lorraine, constant pre-
occupation though that was, but rather the outcome of a changed
political environment which left little space for regional coinage
associations.

# II

Even at the outset the Rappen league had never been entirely
autonomous—that would have been inconceivable. As early as
1377 the value of its silver coinage was fixed against the Rhenish
gold florin,[40] originally at 240 pence Stäbler, or 10 shillings Rappen,
to one florin, a parity confirmed by the treaty of 1403 which marks
the true inception of the Rappen league. The rate was nominally
maintained until the mid-fifteenth century, but in the intervening
period it had already slipped to $11\frac{1}{2}$ shillings to the florin, and
by 1480 it was rebased at $12\frac{1}{2}$ shillings. In the sixteenth century it
weakened more rapidly, losing more than 50 per cent of its value
between 1520 and 1600, when it stood at almost 20 shillings to the
florin.[41] But more significant for economic life on the Upper Rhine,
perhaps, was its relation to the Strasbourg currency. Originally,
they had stood at par, for the Strasbourg penny had been fixed in
1391 at 10 shillings to the florin.[42] Although the fiction of parity
was maintained until the late fifteenth century,[43] in reality the value
of the Strasbourg coinage more or less kept pace with the Rhenish
florin; even in 1530 it was still being quoted at $11\frac{1}{2}$ shillings to the
florin. In Bergheim, just south of the Landgraben, where both cur-
rencies circulated freely, a wage tariff for the town's toll-collectors
early in the sixteenth century put the Strasbourg penny at a 25 per
cent premium to the Rappen penny, reckoning 8 Strasbourg shillings to 10 Rappen shillings.[44] Thereafter, it is true, the Strasbourg

---

[40] Schüttenhelm, *Geldumlauf,* 288.
[41] See the tabulation in Schulz, *Handwerksgesellen und Lohnarbeiter,* 320, 322.
These figures collate and correct the earlier data of Julius Cahn and Auguste Hanauer.
[42] Ibid. 318.        [43] Cf. StAFr, C 1 Münzsachen 1, n.d. (*circa* 1480).
[44] AMBg, FF 4/1, fo. 13ʳ. Cf. Auguste Hanauer, *Études économiques sur l'Alsace
ancienne et moderne,* i. *Les monnaies* (Paris/Strasbourg, 1876), 383 n. 2.

penny declined somewhat more rapidly, but by 1600 it was still set at 16 shillings to the florin, a premium of 20 per cent to the Rappen penny.[45] This discrepancy was to lead to friction between members of the respective currency areas, once the Rappen league sought to entice its neighbours north of the Landgraben to subscribe to a common price tariff, especially for grain.

After 1500 the alignment of the Rappen coinage to the florin exposed its members to increasing pressure to submit to imperial coinage ordinances, which took the florin as their anchor currency. In fact, already towards the end of the previous century Rappen members had felt Austria breathing down their necks. Archduke Sigismund of Tirol—contemptuously dubbed the 'coin-rich' (*der Münzreiche*) on account of his unrivalled ability to squander the output of his Tirolean mines—threatened to pull out of a new Rappen treaty in 1480 unless the other signatories accepted the Tirolean kreutzer at its face value.[46] This quarrel, though brought to a resolution, showed clearly enough who held the whip-hand in the league. After the turn of the century, some have argued, Basel's attachment to the Swiss Confederation weakened the solidarity of the league, especially among its four urban members confronted with Austrian assertiveness.[47] However true that may be, it cannot disguise that Basel was just as alarmed over the next decade at the threat to the integrity of the Rappen currency from inferior silver coin, the Rollebatzen, flooding in from Switzerland in the 1510s. The spread of the Rollebatzen also raised the delicate question of relations with the margraves of Baden, who were energetic in their denunciation of the league's attempts to suppress the new coin. In margrave Ernst of Hachberg's view, it was pointless to resist the onward march of the batzen, for they were minted in many parts of the Empire; for him, what mattered was that the batzen was quoted at fifteen to the florin (corresponding to 10*d*. Rappen) throughout Swabia and Württemberg, the districts 'with which these lands for the most part have their trade and commerce'.[48] He therefore brushed aside all blandishments to become a member of the Rappen league for his southern territories (Hachberg and the

[45] Schulz, *Handwerksgesellen und Lohnarbeiter*, 322.

[46] Cahn, *Rappenmünzbund*, 94–95.

[47] Schüttenhelm, *Geldumlauf*, 289; Kirchgässner, 'Neuordnung', 328.

[48] 'mit denen diße land mertheils ir gewerb und handtierung haben'. Wielandt, *Badische Münz- und Geldgeschichte*, 97.

Markgräflerland), even when archduke Ferdinand intervened personally to invite him to join in 1523,[49] because he considered that the league embraced too small an area to be able to stop the batzen on its own. Although his reference to commercial links with Swabia applied more to the Ortenau than to Baden's southern lordships, the three Forest Towns on the *Hochrhein* within the orbit of the league also affirmed their desire to retain the batzen as a recognized currency—not surprisingly, since their commercial ties were strongly with Switzerland.[50] These points underscore the relative 'openness' of the Black Forest mountain range discussed previously, with close economic contacts between the Rhine valley and the Swabian uplands, thereby rendering any identification of the area of the league with a supposed 'natural' economic region all the more hazardous.

In the end, margrave Ernst was proved right. Having at first been prepared with great reluctance to accept the Swabian batzen at no more than 9*d*. Rappen (and all other batzen at only 8*d*. Rappen), the league was obliged to halt its minting from 1523 to 1536; when it resumed, it bowed to the inevitable by minting its own batzen at 10*d*. Rappen.[51] The vulnerability of the league had been cruelly exposed, not only financially, but politically as well. Although for their southern territories the margraves of Baden accepted Basel's Stäbler and the other members' Rappen pennies as common coin, the fact that the most powerful dynasty on the right bank of the Rhine after the Habsburgs never formally joined the league was both a severe blow to its credibility and an indication that Baden did not regard its economic interests as adequately represented by a coinage association confined to the southern part of the Upper Rhine.

But these were minor blemishes compared with the much greater challenge posed by renewed efforts to establish a monetary ordinance for the Empire as a whole. After all, the regional coinage associations had sprung up to compensate for the lack of a strong central financial authority. Compared with an effective imperial monetary policy, therefore, they were destined to remain a *pis aller*. By the sixteenth century, when imperial and Austrian territorial policy began to converge, the Upper Rhine was quick to feel

[49] Wielandt, *Badische Münz- und Geldgeschichte*, 97; Cahn, *Rappenmünzbund*, 132–33.          [50] Cahn, *Rappenmünzbund*, 129, 132.
[51] Ibid. 136; Schüttenhelm, *Geldumlauf*, 294.

the impact of the Habsburgs' broader monetary policies. In 1535 king Ferdinand reached agreement with the elector Palatine and the Swabian cities on a new coinage convention valid for the inner Austrian lands and all of southern Germany (except Bavaria), whose main purpose was to stamp out the batzen.[52] When Ferdinand issued instructions for the convention to be promulgated in the Outer Austrian lands, the city members of the Rappen league found themselves impaled on the horns of a dilemma: to knuckle under politically to a seigneurial decree and so hasten the demise of their confederal association, or else accept gratefully the eclipse of the batzen (including by then, of course, their own belated mintings of that coin), which they had been unable to achieve on their own. It speaks volumes for the highly political character and self-perception of the Rappen league that its city members with regalian rights—two of whom, after all, were Austrian territorial towns—made the retention of monetary autonomy a higher priority than the prospect of monetary stability. The league's defiant stance cut no ice with Ferdinand, however, who threatened to block bullion supplies to the urban mints. By the end of the year the cities had capitulated, promising *inter alia* to surrender their dies for minting batzen.[53]

Although the common members of the Rappen league found the 1535 convention hard to swallow, there is little doubt that sheltering beneath a wider monetary umbrella helped to underpin the reputation of its coinage for the next half-century. At the imperial assembly in Nuremberg in 1551, for instance, which dealt with currency affairs, the Rappen coinage was declared sound; indeed, nine years before the league had been given a vote of confidence by Ferdinand in granting it the right to mint thalers of a very high standard.[54] What made the league's position increasingly precarious, however, was repeated interference by the Habsburgs, not as emperors, but as lords of Outer Austria. With the benefit of hindsight—looking backwards, that is, from the league's dissolution in 1584—it might appear that king Ferdinand and his successor, archduke Ferdinand of Tirol, were pursuing a deliberate policy of whittling away the regalian rights of the league's members. Doubtless in part they were; but the real reason for their intervention lay

---

[52] Cahn, *Rappenmünzbund*, 146.
[53] Ibid. 148; Schüttenhelm, *Geldumlauf*, 295.
[54] Cahn, *Rappenmünzbund*, 166, 155. The thalers were 891/1,000 fine. Ibid. 157.

elsewhere, in the search for guaranteed supplies of bullion in the first great age of European price inflation. That is why in 1549 king Ferdinand reserved one-third of the silver production within the area of the Rappen league to himself,[55] and shortly afterwards imposed a total blockade on sales of silver from the Val de Lièpvre to the league's mints, a shortfall which led to the virtual cessation of minting between 1552 and 1564.[56]

That Ferdinand's immediate goal was not the destruction of the Rappen league as such can be seen in the aftermath of the imperial coinage ordinance which was finally promulgated in 1559. For Ferdinand, by then emperor after the abdication of his brother Charles V, the ordinance represented the crowning achievement of his reign: by establishing a fixed standard for a common currency throughout the Empire it put an end to 200 years of monetary instability and made regional coinage associations in effect redundant, particularly since responsibility for supervising the new coinage was entrusted to the imperial circles (*Reichskreise*) which had been created as deliberative and juridical organs of imperial government at the beginning of the century.[57] In the peculiar constitution of the circles, however, lay perhaps the Rappen league's temporary salvation. The Upper Rhenish circle was an unwieldy monster stretching 'from the Hoher Meißner [in northern Hesse] to the Ligurian Sea', in the words of the recess of 1500.[58] But on the southern Upper Rhine the Outer Austrian lands were attached to the Austrian circle (which took in all the Habsburg possessions except Bohemia), so that any co-ordination of policy, let alone action, was most unlikely. Accordingly, the members of the Rappen league cherished hopes of retaining their ancient rights of silver procurement and independent fixing of their currency standard.

Tough negotiations ensued, in which Ferdinand considered reducing the number of the league's mints to one, to be placed under imperial or Austrian control, or else creating a separate Outer Austrian mint in Thann. As a compromise, he agreed that the two imperial free cities, Basel and Colmar, should be allowed to mint in accordance with the imperial ordinance of 1559, whereas Freiburg

[55] Cahn, *Rappenmünzbund*, 164.
[56] Schüttenhelm, *Geldumlauf*, 296; cf. Cahn, *Rappenmünzbund*, 172.
[57] Ibid. 174.
[58] Winfried Dotzauer, *Die deutschen Reichskreise in der Verfassung des Alten Reiches und ihr Eigenleben (1500–1806)* (Darmstadt, 1989), 236.

and Breisach were to be subjected to the Austrian territorial ordinance of the following year, whose terms were in fact identical with
those of the imperial edict. The anomaly of the latter towns' minting autonomy, in other words, was to end. These provisions were
finally enshrined in a new treaty in 1564, which brought the Rappen
currency fully into line with the imperial and Austrian ordinances,
except that the league was permitted to continue minting some
small Rappen coin of its own.[59] Thereafter the difficulties which
the league encountered in the remaining twenty years of its existence were essentially practical rather than political—how to secure
an adequate supply of bullion at a price which would enable its
members to mint at a profit.

But, of course, the practical question of bullion supply was at the
same time eminently political, given that Austria controlled most
of the mines (with the price of silver on the open market beyond
reach). And it was archduke Ferdinand of Tirol's decision in 1580
to suspend silver sales to league members as much as his declared
intention of setting up an Outer Austrian territorial mint which
sounded the death-knell of the Rappen coinage league. Even then,
matters did not move swiftly. Although the government in Ensisheim
presented the archduke's resolution as an ultimatum, not susceptible to negotiation, the flurry of correspondence which followed
held up its implementation for four years.[60] But in August 1584,
once the new Austrian mint had been opened in Ensisheim (Thann
was abandoned), the urban members of the Rappen league were
formally banned from minting independently,[61] and the final settlement of accounts took place in Colmar's town hall on 11 September. Thereafter Rappen coin was struck in the name of Austria,
though some minting continued at a low level in both Basel and
Freiburg.[62]

# III

At first sight, the collapse of the Rappen coinage league had the
ring of inevitability about it. The league had embodied a spirit of

---

[59] Cahn, *Rappenmünzbund*, 176–84; Schüttenhelm, *Geldumlauf*, 296.
[60] Cahn, *Rappenmünzbund*, 205–9; Schüttenhelm, *Geldumlauf*, 296.
[61] ADHR, 1 C 412/3, 31 Aug. 1584.
[62] Cahn, *Rappenmünzbund*, 211; Schüttenhelm, *Geldumlauf*, 296.

communal co-operation and solidarity for which there was no place
in the consolidating early modern territorial principality. That judgement, though ultimately correct, nevertheless overlooks the attraction which the Rappen league, even in its dying days, exerted upon
its territorial neighbour to the west, the Württemberg county of
Montbéliard in the Burgundian Gate. In 1577 its ruler, count Friedrich
of Württemberg, a minor under the guardianship of his brother duke
Ludwig, whom he was to succeed as prince of the reunited territory in 1593, applied to join the Rappen coinage league (or rather,
his councillors did on his behalf). His motive, according to Cahn
(who only briefly alludes to the *démarche*), was to establish a mint
for the Württemberg lordships in Alsace—Montbéliard, Horbourg,
and Riquewihr—whose coin would conform to the Rappen standard.[63] That is true as far as it goes, but it is by no means the full
story.

Montbéliard lay at the point of intersection of two currency
regions, the Rappen association, and the area of circulation of the
Besançon pound (*livre estevenante*).[64] Understandably, its rulers
had long cherished the notion of establishing their own coinage,
over which they would have full control. In 1554 and 1558 count
Georg had taken the first steps towards creating a separate mint
in Montbéliard.[65] Less obvious, however, is why the Württemberg
rulers sought alignment with the Rappen league rather than with
the Besançon currency area. In 1578 Friedrich's advisers made considerable play of Montbéliard's allegiance to the Empire:

> Que comme notre très illustre et redoubté prince et Seigneur, monseigneur
> le Comte Friderich, qui est ung prince du Sainct Empire, et ceste sa ville
> et comtez de Mombéliardt ressortissans aussi dudict St. Empire: Le meilleur
> et plus expédient seroit, de, au plus tost, reigler (aux mieux que possible
> sera) le prix et cours des monoyes selon la commune tauxe et ordon-
> nances dudict S. Empire . . .[66]

Such protestations of loyalty need not be taken at face value
(Friedrich's monetary plan coincided with the imposition of strict

---

[63] Cahn, *Rappenmünzbund*, 203–4.

[64] Jean-Marc Debard, *Les Monnaies de la principauté de Montbéliard du XVIe
au XVIIIe siècle: Essai de numismatique et d'histoire économique* (Annales
Littéraires de l'Université de Besançon, 220: Cahiers d'Études Comtoises, 26) (Paris,
1980), 22.                                                         [65] Ibid. 30.

[66] ADD, E 4942, 10/26 Feb. 1578. Cf. Debard, *Monnaies*, 32, 34.

Lutheran orthodoxy in his territories),[67] but political and diplomatic considerations were not entirely irrelevant. Montbéliard stood out on a limb, not only from Württemberg, but from the Empire as a whole, at a time when mounting military tensions between the Empire and France had already caused the Alsatian powers to band together in a defensive alliance (the *Schirmverein*) to patrol and defend the western frontier. The territory was peculiarly exposed, moreover, to bad coin circulating from Lorraine—indeed, the Ensisheim authorities as far back as 1534 had invited count Georg to attend joint deliberations on possible countermeasures[68]—so that the security of an alliance with the Rappen league's sound currency, especially when buttressed after 1564 by its acceptance within the imperial coinage ordinance, was attractive. But the fundamental reasons for looking eastwards rather than westwards for a monetary alliance were commercial. They emerge, for instance, in the grievances submitted by Montbéliard's merchants in 1557, who were obliged (they said) to change good money for bad in order to buy wine and cattle which they imported from Germany.[69] The idea that German (presumably Alsatian) wine might compete with Burgundian almost on its own doorstep, or that the Franche-Comté, traditional exporter of quality cattle, traded at the international mart at Cernay, might be unable to satisfy the demand of its immediate neighbourhood, runs contrary to all received wisdom. One might be tempted, therefore, to dismiss the merchants' plea as a gross distortion, were it not for the justification which count Friedrich himself gave for seeking to persevere in his efforts to join the Rappen league in 1578: 'Les fréquentations sont plus du ressor d'Allemaigne que de Bourgogne pour vin, bassine, et les tisserandz vendans en Allemaigne.'[70]

The county of Montbéliard's commercial orientation, by this reckoning, was more towards the Upper Rhine than to Burgundy, even though it lay west of the Belfort Gap. This seems to contradict other evidence which points to the significance of the Burgundian Gate as an important conduit of trade between France and southern Germany. In 1545, for instance, the customs-post

---

[67] Cf. Michel Billerey, 'Le Pays Montbéliard, carrefour historique entre l'Alsace, la Franche-Comté et la Suisse', in *Trois provinces de l'Est: Lorraine, Alsace, Franche-Comté* (Publications de la Société Savante d'Alsace et des Régions de l'Est: Grandes Publications, 6) (Strasbourg/Paris, 1967), 316.    [68] Debard, *Monnaies*, 30.
[69] Ibid. 31.    [70] Ibid. 36.

which count Georg set up on the Doubs crossing at Voujeancourt distinguished clearly between regional produce (grains and wine) and 'merchandise of Lyon', and, within the latter category, between goods destined for local consumption and others loaded on to special wagons for long-distance transport.[71] But the Belfort Gap was not necessarily the most convenient route for those merchants travelling directly to the fairs of Frankfurt or Cologne; they might prefer to continue up the Saône to Gray and then across into Germany from Lorraine. What trade passed through the Burgundian Gate was, with the exception of cattle on the hoof, largely local, or, to put it more precisely, between adjacent regions. That goes some way towards confirming André Gibert's lapidary judgement that France in general did not need Alsace's wine or textiles, and vice versa.[72] What sustained the commerce of Montbéliard, therefore, was principally its links with the Upper Rhine and with Württemberg itself.[73] Against that background, the pull of the Upper Rhenish coinage area upon Montbéliard's economy becomes altogether intelligible.

Nor was the attraction unrequited, for Montbéliard, in Jean-Marc Debard's words, lived in symbiosis with Basel as the metropolis of the southern Upper Rhine, bound in the sixteenth century by ties which were as much political and confessional as economic and commercial:

Le XVIe siècle est une sorte d'apothéose bâloise à Montbéliard, glacis de l'impérialisme helvétique. Bâle avait toutes sortes d'intérêts politiques et économiques dans la Porte de Bourgogne: dans les affaires minières du massif sud-vosgien, dans le contrôle plus ou moins avoué du passage vers la Franche-Comté, à Héricourt et jusqu'à l'Isle-sur-le-Doubs. Et puis, il y a la Réforme et son contexte social [the impact of the Peasants' War, and the preaching of Guillaume Farel].[74]

---

[71] Gibert, *Porte de Bourgogne*, 291.          [72] Ibid. 292.

[73] Although there were increasing commercial contacts from the end of the 16th century onwards between Strasbourg and the interior of France (with merchants from Lyon and elsewhere visiting Strasbourg's fairs), the commerce of both the Franche-Comté and Montbéliard never transcended the interregional level. Cf. François-Joseph Fuchs, 'Aspects du commerce de Strasbourg avec Montbéliard et la Franche-Comté au XVIIe siècle', in *Trois provinces de l'Est: Lorraine, Alsace, Franche-Comté* (Publications de la Société Savante d'Alsace et des Régions de l'Est: Grandes Publications, 6) (Strasbourg/Paris, 1967), 109, 111–12.

[74] Debard, *Monnaies*, 195; cf. Ehrensperger, 'Basels Stellung', 42. The phrase 'glacis de l'impérialisme helvétique' was originally Billerey's: cf. idem, 'Pays de Montbéliard', 315.

Montbéliard, he concludes, lay entirely within the orbit of Basel's currency area and was dominated by it: 'ses monnaies font poids sur le marché montbéliardais à un tel point que Frédéric a tout fait pour être intégré dans le système du "Rappenmünzbund".'[75] The issue therefore becomes, not why count Friedrich should have wished to join the Rappen league at all, but rather why his application was refused, even when his revised submission in February 1579 (after his initial rebuff) only sought permission to mint 3,000 florins' worth of small coin to the Rappen standard.[76] To this question the sources provide no direct answer, but two sticking-points spring to mind. In the first place, the establishment of a separate mint in Montbéliard was bound to put further strain on an already attenuated supply of silver;[77] then, and perhaps more ominously, the admission of another prince to the Rappen league would dilute, or indeed jeopardize, the regalian authority of the city members, who had had enough trouble from the Austrian rulers as it was. To admit Montbéliard might have sucked the Rappen coinage league into dependence upon Württemberg, with unpredictable consequences.

It may be unfair to accuse the Rappen league of short-sightedness in rejecting count Friedrich's overtures when its members must in any case have known that their days were numbered. Nevertheless, on attaining his majority in 1581, Friedrich looked afresh at plans to establish a Montbéliard currency. When they came to fruition, the Montbéliard mint, during its short existence from 1585 to 1591, struck coin not to the Rappen standard but to that prevailing in Besançon, Dôle, Savoy, and Lorraine, thereby signalling an apparent switch of economic orientation.[78] In fact, it proved harmful to Montbéliard's economy, because merchants from Alsace, the principal patrons of its markets and fairs, rejected the new coinage as inferior and stayed away.[79]

After 1584, the Austrian mint in Ensisheim concentrated on minting thalers, though it continued to strike those Rappen coins permitted under the terms of the imperial coinage ordinance.[80] To outward appearances, therefore, little had changed in economic

---

[75] Debard, *Monnaies*, 196.    [76] Ibid. 40.    [77] Cf. ibid. 41.
[78] Ibid. 42.
[79] Ibid. 52. Montbéliard's Catholic neighbours to the west were disinclined to come to its defence, since they took pleasure in the discomfiture of a Lutheran territory. Ibid. 53.    [80] Schüttenhelm, *Geldumlauf*, 309.

life, where the price of everyday goods was still quoted in Rappen pence (though complaints were heard that Ensisheim was failing to mint sufficient small coin).[81] What had altered was the political framework in which matters of monetary policy and the consequent regulation of prices and supplies of essential commodities were discussed and decided. Instead of assemblies of all the coinage league's members, these issues became the responsibility of the Austrian territorial diets. One consequence was that Villingen, Bräunlingen, and the abbey of St Blasien in the Black Forest, which had not been involved in the Rappen assemblies (or had claimed exemption), now found themselves as Outer Austrian subjects drawn into negotiations over exchange rates between Outer Austria and the county of Fürstenberg.[82] The decisions of Austrian diets could not, of course, bind the imperial Estates, which had hitherto participated in assemblies under the auspices of the Rappen league to regulate meat and grain provisioning, except by bilateral negotiation and agreement.[83] Political authority and economic co-operation on the southern Upper Rhine, in other words, no longer coincided. How far a sense of regional economic identity survived the collapse of the Rappen coinage league which, as the case of Montbéliard so tellingly illustrates, it helped in large measure to define, will be explored in the following two chapters.

[81] StAFr, C 1 Landstände 17, n.d. (1594).
[82] Speck, *Landstände*, i. 499.
[83] StAFr, C 1 Landstände 15, 23 Sept. 1586: negotiations over a new grain ordinance.

# 7

# The Regional Provisioning of Meat

## I

In Germany the sixteenth century ushered in the great age of what was known as 'good police' (*gute Polizei*), when governments for the first time began actively to intervene in economic and commercial affairs for reasons other than the purely fiscal (the raising of taxes). At imperial and territorial level the authorities began to tackle issues such as monopolies, price-rigging, and forestalling, as well as seeking to regulate and secure supplies of essential commodities. Issues of welfare, too, were part of good police, as princes and magistrates struggled to come to grips with the plague of the age—vagrancy and begging by the poor, the homeless, and unemployed or discharged mercenaries. In relatively self-contained territories such as Bavaria or Württemberg edicts to enforce good police flowed unimpeded from princely chanceries,[1] but on the Upper Rhine such policies required negotiation across territorial, geographical, linguistic, and ultimately confessional divides.

In Lower Alsace the extent of political fragmentation made co-operation essential, but the economic preponderance of Strasbourg and its coinage ensured that those lords and cities whom the bishop of Strasbourg (in his capacity as landgrave of Lower Alsace) convened to deliberate on *Polizei* took their cue from the region's most powerful city. South of the Landgraben, however, the situation was at once simpler and more complex. Territorial fragmentation gave way to the largely consolidated lands of Outer Austria in the southern half of Upper Alsace, and in the Breisgau. But the government in Ensisheim (without its own treasury until 1570) was very much

---

[1] For Bavaria cf. Volkmar Wittmütz, *Die Gravamina der bayrischen Stände im 16. und 17. Jahrhundert als Quelle für die wirtschaftliche Situation und Entwicklung in Bayern* (Miscellanea Bavarica Monacensia, 26) (Munich, 1970); for Württemberg cf. R. W. Scribner, 'Police and the state in sixteenth-century Württemberg', in Kouri and Scott, *Politics and Society*, 103–20. In general cf. Marc Raeff, *The well-ordered police state: Social and institutional change through law in the Germanies and Russia 1600–1800* (New Haven/London, 1983).

the country cousin of the administration in Innsbruck, which retained final responsibility for all the 'outer lands'. After the death
of Maximilian I in 1519 (or, at the very latest, with the peace of
Kaaden in 1534 which terminated the Austrian government of occupation in Stuttgart and restored duke Ulrich to his principality of
Württemberg) the Habsburgs no longer had any vital stake in the
fortunes of their Upper Rhenish possessions; economically and
financially they were peripheral to the crown lands in Austria itself,
with their extensive mineral resources and their commercial links
to central Europe and the Adriatic. Moreover, no one city (or its
coinage) dominated the southern Upper Rhine. Basel could not
call the tune in quite the way that Strasbourg did; by the sixteenth
century it was to some extent the victim of divided loyalties, pulled
southwards towards the rest of the Confederation both politically
and, increasingly, financially, but at the same time eager to maintain its economic *rayonnement* northwards through the hinterland
of the fertile river valley of the Upper Rhine and the mineral-rich
foothills of the Vosges.

This unusual balance between a powerful but remote dynasty
and a palpable but middle-ranking metropolis (and its satellites)
had already stamped the character of the Rappen coinage league,
which came to serve as the framework within which decisions on
economic regulation were hammered out. But the Rappen league
had no institutional identity of its own—no independent administration or constitutional authority: it existed at the will of its most
powerful members. Accordingly, the assemblies convened in its
name were summoned by the Outer Austrian government (the
Habsburgs were landgraves of Upper Alsace) and customarily met
in Ensisheim. But although the chancery of the Outer Austrian government acted as convenor, it had no power to compel those outwith its jurisdiction to accept the ordinances of 'police' diets; rather,
a flurry of correspondence both preceded and succeeded the diets,
as Austrian officials made bilateral overtures to other members of
the Rappen league or those within the area of its monetary circulation to secure agreement for the diets' resolutions. Of course,
the Outer Austrian Estates themselves—particularly the third Estate
of towns and districts—might debate questions of good police
within their own territorial assemblies. And it was not unusual for
decisions reached at diets of the Outer Austrian Estates (or at district assemblies of either bank of the Rhine) to form the basis of
discussions at subsequent diets convened for the area of the Rappen

league as a whole. But these two forums remained constitutionally distinct, and should not be confused.

The police assemblies of the Rappen league throughout the sixteenth century addressed two fundamental issues—the provisioning and price regulation of meat and grain—which were of existential importance in an age of rising population and gathering inflation. Yet behind the efforts to ensure continuity of supply to local markets at tolerable prices lay a much broader concern with the perceived principal economic evil of the day, the problem of *Fürkauf*, a term signifying not just forestalling in the narrow sense of pre-empting the market but commercial dealing in essential commodities *tout court*. The frequency of prohibitions on *Fürkauf* and the unavailing attempts to halt the upward march of prices testify to the difficulties facing the authorities in a region which, however abundant its natural resources, straddled major trade routes and could not isolate itself from the wider mercantile economy. But the pattern of supply and demand for meat and grain differed: the former was largely an import commodity from the fringes of the Upper Rhine in Swabia and Burgundy, whereas in good years the Upper Rhine produced surpluses of grain which it exported to its neighbours. Consequently, the sense of a regional community of economic interests varied according to the commodity in question. This chapter therefore explores the provisioning of meat, in order subsequently to contrast it with the somewhat differing considerations governing the marketing of grain, which will be discussed in the next chapter.

These preliminary remarks may inadvertently give the impression that co-operation over issues of good police between the authorities was unknown or unthinkable before the full-scale diets of the Rappen league in the sixteenth century. Yet without a tradition of bilateral consultations and agreements—especially between neighbouring cities—deliberations on the wider stage of the coinage league would have been much more likely to founder on the political and confessional antagonisms which scarred the Upper Rhine in the course of that century. The exchange of information on meat provisioning, price tariffs, and customs-rates can be traced to the last decades of the fifteenth century—we find, for instance, Basel corresponding with Colmar in 1488[2]—but only after the turn of the century does evidence of local co-operation flow more freely. Apart

[2] AMC, HH 58/78, 26 Mar. 1488.

from informal bilateral enquiries—such as that addressed to Colmar by Ribeauvillé in 1513[3]—what stands out (in Alsace, at least), are the attempts to forge binding agreements between immediate neighbours. In June 1515 the imperial city of Mulhouse, just 'turned Swiss', ascertained of its neighbours under three separate jurisdictions, Guebwiller (belonging to the abbey of Murbach),[4] Rouffach (the chief town of the bishop of Strasbourg's lordship of the Upper Mundat),[5] and the Austrian provincial capital Ensisheim,[6] whether they would be willing to align their meat tariffs with its own and, in the case of Guebwiller, received an assurance that it would do so. The following year four close neighbours in the north of Upper Alsace, Kaysersberg, Riquewihr, Kientzheim, and Ammerschwihr, a mixture of imperial and territorial towns, formally signed a joint meat ordinance, initially valid for one year,[7] but which was followed by similar agreements in 1518.[8]

Understandable though such local initiatives to combat rising prices and what were perceived as market distortions might be, they could not cope with issues which in the longer term could only be tackled on a regional or even supraregional basis. As early as 1502 it emerged from the submissions of the Outer Austrian Estates that the government in Ensisheim was seeking an agreement with interested parties to regulate the sale of meat, and that the Estates hoped that this precedent would be emulated at the next territorial diet.[9] In just what this agreement consisted is not known, but in the light of subsequent events we should be cautious of attributing to the Ensisheim authorities any great eagerness to act beyond their constitutional remit in the name of objective regional economic priorities. That is demonstrated by a short, but revealing, passage-of-arms between Freiburg and the government in 1515. After Ensisheim had issued a mandate in May, banning the purchase of cattle at Outer Austrian markets for commercial gain,[10] Freiburg urged that its provisions be enforced on the broadest possible canvas. The government's response at the beginning of July came as a cold douche, and deserves to be quoted at length:

[3] AMC, HH 59/76, 23 May 1513.        [4] AMMh, I 3207, 19 June 1515.
[5] AMMh, I 3208, 20 June 1515.        [6] AMMh, I 3209, 20 June 1515.
[7] AMKy, BB 9, fo. 166ʳ–167ᵛ, 20 Jan. 1516. They also agreed a joint fishing ordinance at the same time. Ibid. fo. 167ᵛ–168ᵛ.
[8] AMKy, BB 10, fo. 5ʳ, 12 Mar. 1518; ibid. fo. 12ʳ, 17 July 1518.
[9] StAFr, C 1 Landstände 1, n.d. (1502), § 12.
[10] ADHR, C 179/1, 12 May 1515.

for many reasons we regard it as neither necessary nor good to negotiate [on the matter] with anyone outside our government's jurisdiction other than . . . the margrave on behalf of the lordships of Rötteln, Badenweiler, and Hachberg, count Wilhelm of Fürstenberg, and lord Conrat von Schellenberg alone, for it is not our intention to extend [the remit of] the ordinance and forestalling [provisions] any further than our government's jurisdiction, just as we do not do so here on this account in the two districts of Alsace and the Sundgau.[11]

The government's stance requires some elucidation. The southern territories of the margraves of Baden lay within the circulation area of the Rappen coinage league, and for that reason the margraves were regularly invited to participate in police diets. Though they rarely attended, they were usually content to fall into line with the ordinances which were subsequently published. But the Fürstenberg and Schellenberg territories, on the other hand, lay beyond the area of the league on the Swabian uplands. Up to a point, the decision to include them in consultations had both an economic and a political rationale: their territories surrounded or abutted the Outer Austrian outposts of Villingen and Bräunlingen; and the commercial links between the Upper Rhine valley and the Swabian uplands in the cattle trade have been traced in an earlier chapter. But the government in Ensisheim was not being consistent. If Swabian lordships, why not extend discussions to those territories engaged in the much more intensive cattle trade from Burgundy through the Franche-Comté to the fulcrum of the international cattle mart on the Ochsenfeld at Cernay on Austrian territory? For the government to be willing to overstep its jurisdictional bounds in the Black Forest, but to draw in its horns at the Belfort Gap made little sense for the Upper Rhine in economic terms. The altercation in 1515 is significant because it sets the scene for what were to be abiding features of the struggle to secure regional supplies of basic foodstuffs for the rest of the century: namely, the conflict between political responsibilities and economic needs, encapsulated in an

---

[11] GLA 79/1644, 7 July 1515: '. . . vnnd will vnns vss allerleÿ vrsachen nit not oder gůt bedunckhen, daruon mit yemanden anndernn, der vsserthalb vnnser Regÿments verwaltigung gesessen, dann alleÿn mit . . . dem marggrauen der herrschafften Roteln, Badenwile vnd hochberg halber, derglichenn mit graff wilhelmen von furstenberg vnd herr Conratten von Schellenberg zu handln, dann vnnser meynung nit ist, die ordnung vnd furkoff witer zuerstrecken dann vnnser Regyments verwaltigung geet, als wir och hie dÿßhalb inn den beiden lannden Ellsasz vnd Sungkow ouch nicht anders handlen'.

undercurrent of tension between the government in Ensisheim, which remained sensible of the constitutional and jurisdictional niceties, and the urban members of the territorial Estates (and of the Rappen coinage league as a whole), who were, in their capacity as direct economic actors, alert to economic imperatives which might transcend political frontiers.

In the initial stages of good police assemblies the surviving record (admittedly patchy) indeed suggests that the initiative lay more with the towns themselves than with the Outer Austrian administration. A hitherto overlooked meat ordinance for Alsace in 1503 speaks of an agreement reached by the 'common Estate' (that is, towns and districts) of 'these lands' as well as certain of the 'lower towns' such as Colmar, Sélestat, Kaysersberg, Ammerschwihr, and others.[12] Its wording is remarkable in two respects. The distinction between 'these lands' of the Sundgau and the 'lower towns' of Upper Alsace proper, lying north of the river Thur, has already been noted in an earlier context, but among these 'lower towns' was included Sélestat, even though it lay beyond the Landgraben in Lower Alsace and was a member of the Strasbourg currency area.[13] Efforts by its close neighbours to bring Sélestat within the orbit of the Upper Rhenish police assemblies of the Rappen coinage league in the face of the Ensisheim government's avowed reluctance only bore fruit much later in the century, but the first signs of an awareness of bonds of regional solidarity defined by economic and commercial interests are unmistakable. Moreover, although the meat ordinance was to be referred back for approval, it was proposed, if general assent were forthcoming, to draw up similar ordinances to regulate an entire spectrum of crafts and trades on a regional basis, from bakers, millers, taverners, haberdashers, spicemongers, goldsmiths, joiners, and smiths to carpenters, by inviting each town to submit its domestic ordinances to the government in Ensisheim, which would act as their collator. Whether anything came of this proposal—a bold initiative quite distinct from the regional journeymen's ordinances of the preceding century—is unknown, but it does indicate a widespread eagerness on the part of the Alsatian towns to co-operate on economic affairs with little regard for traditional geographical or political demarcations.

---

[12] AMTh, HH 4/1, 3 Jan. 1503.
[13] Cf. AMSé, HH 33 (1520); AMS, AA 2037, fo. 13ʳ, 29 Feb. 1520.

On the right bank of the Rhine the political map offered less scope for a display of urban solidarity across territorial frontiers, since there were no imperial cities to range against the numerous towns of the Austrian Breisgau, while the few towns of the Markgräflerland had to take their cue from the margrave of Baden's administrative officials. But that did not prevent Freiburg from seizing the initiative independently of any summons from Ensisheim, as in February 1520, when it called together Breisach, Neuenburg, Endingen, Kenzingen, Waldkirch, and the administrator of the lordship of Staufen to discuss a common ordinance for the Austrian Breisgau,[14] a full five weeks before it received a summons from the authorities to attend a general police diet in Ensisheim on the issue.[15] Freiburg was instructed to invite margrave Ernst of Baden to attend, but the despatch of the letter a mere twenty-four hours before the assembly was due to meet strongly suggests an afterthought by the government.[16] Nevertheless, the meat ordinance issued on 20 April 1520 for the Outer Austrian territories of (Upper) Alsace, the Sundgau, and the Breisgau was the first comprehensive attempt at policy-making for the southern Upper Rhine on both banks of the river,[17] and thus paved the way for all subsequent assemblies embracing both Outer Austria and the members of the Rappen coinage league.

## II

The need to regulate meat provisioning, apart from demographic pressure on supplies and prices, stemmed from the changing character of the international cattle trade in western Europe in the century after 1470. From that date the marketing of cattle in north-western Europe was transformed as regional markets collapsed in the face of burgeoning long-distance cattle-droving overland from Denmark, Poland, and above all Hungary.[18] The cities of western and southern

---

[14] StAFr, B 5 XI x, fo. 250$^v$, 29 Feb. 1520; cf. A I VI e ε 26, 29 Feb. 1520; Speck, *Landstände*, ii. 812.

[15] StAFr, B 5 XI x, fo. 260$^r$, 9 Apr. 1520. The instruction to Freiburg to extend the summons to the Outer Austrian Breisgau towns is incomprehensibly listed by Speck, *Landstände*, ii. 813, as a separate diet of the Austrian right bank of the Rhine.

[16] StAFr, B 5 XI x, fo. 261$^r$, 18 Apr. 1520.

[17] StAFr, A I VI e ε, 27, 20 Apr. 1520.

[18] Blanchard, 'European cattle trades', 433, 436. Cf. also Franz Lerner, 'Die Bedeutung des internationalen Ochsenhandels für die Fleischversorgung deutscher Städte im Spätmittelalter und der frühen Neuzeit', in Ekkehard Westermann (ed.), *Internationaler Ochsenhandel (1350–1750): Akten des 7th International Economic History Congress Edinburgh 1978* (Beiträge zur Wirtschaftsgeschichte, 9) (Stuttgart, 1979), 197–217.

Germany ceased to rely chiefly on local stock-rearing and instead bought cattle which were sold at major new cattle markets established in Poland (at Brzeg), Saxony (at Buttstädt near Weimar), or on the Austro-Hungarian border (at Győr, and Bruck an der Leitha).[19] In Ian Blanchard's words: 'As the pastoral base of western European marketing systems retreated before an expanding system of arable cultivation, the international trades . . . became the mainstay of the west-central European system of metropolitan meat-provisioning.'[20]

Heavier oxen from the Hungarian steppes were traded throughout Swabia and as far as Strasbourg which, with its population of over 20,000, is reckoned to have consumed 4,000 head a year, not to mention the 1,000 sheep or more which were slaughtered each evening.[21] Because Strasbourg was the terminus for this international cattle trade, however, the regional cattle trade on the Upper Rhine, centred on the mart at Cernay, continued to do good business as the point of exchange between the pastures of Burgundy, the Franche-Comté, and the Franches Montagnes in the Swiss Jura, and urban consumers in the Upper Rhenish cities. In normal times Cernay was no more than a market of the second rank, essentially linking adjacent regions, but whenever shortages or disruptions of supply arose it could rapidly become the target of a much wider circle of consumers, as in the mid-1570s, when a severe shortfall in the supply of Polish and Hungarian cattle caused buyers from the south German cities to descend on Cernay *en masse*, with the upshot that stock-rearers from as far afield as Savoy and Lorraine began to patronize it.[22] Cernay, in other words, was never exclusively a market for the southern Upper Rhine, supplying only the needs of Outer Austria and the members of the Rappen coinage league. Cattle brought to market there were regularly sold to butchers from Strasbourg and other cities in Lower Alsace. Moreover, the Württemberg government made frequent requests to be allowed to drive cattle from its territory of Montbéliard through Outer Austria via Cernay to supply the needs of the court in Stuttgart.

As a consequence, decisions on meat provisioning had to strike a fine balance between satisfying domestic demand on the southern

---

[19] Othmar Pickl, 'Routen, Umfang und Organisation des innereuropäischen Handels mit Schlachtvieh im 16. Jahrhundert', in Alexander Novotny and Othmar Pickl (eds.), *Festschrift Hermann Wiesflecker zum sechzigsten Geburtstag* (Graz, 1973), 147.

[20] Blanchard, 'European cattle trades', 441.        [21] Fuchs, 'Foires', 300.

[22] Vogt, 'Grandeur et décadence', 133; Blanchard, 'European cattle trades', 443.

Upper Rhine and not damaging the commercial importance which Cernay enjoyed. That was a difficult trick to pull off, and as the century wore on the authorities found themselves ever more torn between the desire to stamp out *Fürkauf* and the recognition that within the area of the Rappen league lay districts whose economy was in fact dependent on commercial cattle-rearing. These difficulties were exacerbated, moreover, by the spread of Protestantism to cities and territories on the southern Upper Rhine, who no longer had any cause to observe the prohibitions on meat consumption during Lent and on other fast-days which the solidly Catholic Outer Austrian government was committed to uphold.

That concerns of this kind were uppermost in the mind of the authorities from early in the sixteenth century is evident from the summons which the government in Ensisheim sent early in March 1527 not only to the territorial towns of Outer Austria but to the cities within the radius of the Rappen league as well to discuss difficulties in meat provisioning.[23] The diet, which was held at Ensisheim at the end of the month, is the first which can unequivocally be identified as a 'police' assembly of the Rappen league convened under Austrian auspices, rather than as a territorial diet of the Outer Austrian Estates.[24] The government invoked explicitly the Turkish invasion of Hungary the previous year (which had led to the crushing defeat of the Hungarian forces at the battle of Mohács) and to the increased consumption of meat by adherents of the new faith as the reasons for the sudden shortage of beef.[25] In fact, at that time the only major city on the Upper Rhine to have embraced Protestantism was Strasbourg, though within the area of the Rappen league Mulhouse had introduced the Reform in 1523, while in Basel evangelical preaching was in full swing from 1525 onwards, even though the formal adoption of the new doctrines was delayed until 1529. It is doubtless significant, therefore, that although invitations were sent to the imperial cities of Upper Alsace and to other non-Austrian subjects[26] Basel and Mulhouse received none: they were,

---

[23] StAFr, A I VI e ε 29, 13 Mar. 1527–11 Sept. 1528 (summons to Freiburg, 13 Mar. 1527); AMC, HH 59/20 (summons to Colmar).

[24] The entries in Speck, *Landstände*, ii. 843, are in this regard at best misleading.

[25] As n. 23.

[26] Colmar and Kaysersberg (imperial cities); Ammerschwihr (divided between three overlords, the lords of Hohlandsberg, of Ribeaupierre, and the city of Kaysersberg); Riquewihr (Württemberg); Guebwiller (prince-abbacy of Murbach); Ribeauvillé (lordship of Ribeaupierre); Kientzheim (lordship of Hohlandsberg): cf. ADHR, C 179/4, 8 Apr. 1527.

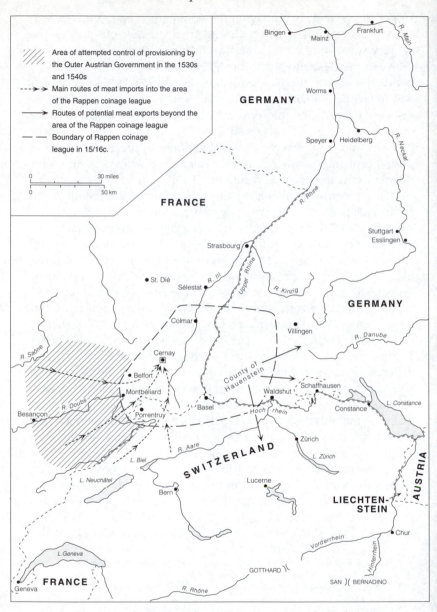

Map 14. Regional meat provisioning

of course, by that time both Swiss, the one a full, the other an associate, member of the Confederation.

The recess of the diet was published as a printed proclamation on 8 April, and circulated widely, not simply to those who had attended the deliberations in Ensisheim.[27] In it the Outer Austrian government bewailed the spread of regrating and profiteering on the part of those, both native and foreign, who bought up locally reared fatstock ('vff Merschatz vnd gewiñ bestelt fürkaufft') from the peasantry in advance of the due market day (thereby depriving the peasants of the proceeds of an open sale), and who then either shunned the local market and drove the cattle away from the area of the Rappen coinage league, or else offered the cattle for sale at prices which no local butcher could afford. Such actions should be reported to the authorities, and the culprits (especially foreigners) severely fined. Those unable to reach a convenient market should, however, be entitled to sell to local butchers direct, so long as the latter undertook not to forestall. Whoever purchased cattle with the intention of driving it 'below Ensisheim' (that is, into Lower Alsace) must obtain a passport from the chancery in Ensisheim certifying that they were not buying for commercial gain. The mandate concluded by setting the highest price at which fat cattle should be sold ($2\frac{1}{4}d$. Rappen per lb.).[28]

At first sight these provisions appear to be self-explanatory. Both Austria and the urban magistrates closed ranks to oppose any commercial traffic in cattle, as if opposition to *Fürkauf* were regarded as a litmus test of regional solidarity within the Rappen coinage league. But on the southern Upper Rhine, where Cernay functioned as an interregional and at times international cattle market, matters could never be reduced to a seemingly simple commitment to autarky and protectionism. Even the government in Ensisheim, which had no commercial interest in the cattle trade, did not dispute that commerce in livestock should be allowed—provided that meat supplies were not endangered. Indeed, within the month it had intervened in support of three Freiburg butchers whom the town had prevented from driving old cattle, no longer fit for prime butchering,

---

[27] Cf. TLA, Pestarchiv, Akten XXIX, no. 25; AMKy, FF 39; AMMu, HH 3; SABs, Missiven A 28, fo. 133$^{r-v}$.

[28] StAFr, A I VI e ε 29, 13 Mar. 1527–11 Sept. 1528: 8 Apr. 1527. Cf. Eberhard Gothein, *Wirtschaftsgeschichte des Schwarzwaldes und der angrenzenden Landschaften*, i. *Städte- und Gewerbegeschichte* (Strasbourg, 1892), 500–1.

to the fair at Villingen[29] (a journey described by the three men, *nota bene*, as 'exporting', thereby acknowledging that the Outer Austrian outpost in the Baar lay beyond the area of the Rappen coinage league).[30]

We therefore need to ask what exactly the members of the Rappen league meant in setting their faces against *Fürkauf.* But the answer to that question rests, in turn, on how contemporaries perceived commercial transactions, or, indeed, whether they had any concept of the 'market' at all. This is a contentious issue. Certainly, both urban magistrates and merchants and craftsmen within towns were concerned first and foremost with protecting their own interests, whether collectively as corporations charged with furthering the commonweal or individually as producers and suppliers. In that sense, they were anything but free marketeers, and what they regarded as a 'true market' or 'just prices' was what guaranteed their livelihood and economic privileges. But that is not the same thing as hostility to commerce or markets as such, or a pervasive espousal of protectionism, the 'closed urban economy' (*geschlossene Stadtwirtschaft*) which liberal historians of the nineteenth century saw as the besetting sin of medieval guildsmen. What informed merchants and craftsmen in our period (if not always the civic authorities or princely bureaucrats) was a desire to control commerce and access to markets, in other words, a hostility to competition, especially from foreigners, not an aversion to profit as such.[31] Too much has been made of the tag of *auskömmliche Nahrung* (which we might freely translate as an 'elegant sufficiency') as part of the pre-industrial mentality, as if such a goal did not all too often conceal under a cloak of communality what were brazenly sectional interests. From that perspective it would be unwise to attribute a general rejection of commerce, or of profit, to the participants in the 'police' diets; rather, they shared an anxiety that the market in essential commodities such as foodstuffs might slip out of their control. Indeed, the wording of the 1527 mandate lends much support to such an interpretation. What alarmed the participants—notwithstanding loud asseverations of the vileness of profit (*Gewinn*) —was the fact that the chartered markets of the towns which they represented were being evaded (here we see another dimension

---

[29] StAFr, A I VI e ε 29, 13 Mar. 1527–11 Sept. 1528: 28 Apr. 1527.
[30] Ibid. n.d. (Apr. 1527).          [31] Cf. Scott, *Freiburg and the Breisgau*, 138–41.

to the threat of market competition previously analysed) and that profits were going to foreigners, or else being realized outside the area of the coinage league.

It therefore made sense to seek acceptance of the mandate by as many neighbouring lords and cities as possible. Without Basel's participation, for instance, it would have remained a dead letter, and within a few days the Outer Austrian government had sent a copy to the city council,[32] which promptly consulted Basel's butchers, who signalled their willingness to comply. The magistrates pointed out, however, that the mandate would not be effective unless embraced by those lords in whose territories the leading cattle-dealers operated. Basel therefore recommended sounding out the bishop of Basel, the city of Constance, and the lords of 'Warre im Trybelberg', promising to help matters by interceding itself.[33] The Ensisheim government responded with a mixture of enthusiasm and caution. It made no overtures to Constance, an imperial free city beyond the Rappen coinage area and indeed the centre of its own monetary region, but it did approach bishop Philipp of Basel as well as the mysterious lords in the Trybelberg,[34] who were none other than the margraves of Varembon, counts de la Roche, lords of a strategically significant area between Alsace and north-western Franche-Comté, with their seat in St-Hippolyte-sur-Doubs.[35] They controlled territories in the Jura mountains abutting the bishop of Basel's secular territory on the western fringes of the circulation area of the Rappen coinage.

The reluctance of the Austrian authorities to act beyond the remit of the Rappen league did not deter Basel, however, from invoking the solidarity of its Swiss fellow-Confederates in a string of appeals to combat forestalling directed at Bern,[36] Solothurn,[37] and

[32] StAFr, A I VI e ε 29, 13 Mar. 1527–11 Sept. 1528: 12 Apr. 1527.

[33] Ibid. 29 Apr. 1527; cf. SABs, Missiven A 28, fo. 133[r–v], 134[v]–135[r]; AMC, HH 59/23.

[34] StAFr, A I VI e ε 29, 13 Mar. 1527–11 Sept. 1528: 2 May 1527; ADHR, C 179/4.

[35] I am indebted to Dr Leo Neuhaus, former Director of the Archives de l'Ancien Évêché de Bâle in Porrentruy for this information. The Ensisheim government was clearly unsure who they were, for its letter to the margraves in the name of the Rappen league was initially addressed to the 'herren' and subsequently improved to the 'Grafen zu ware vnd zu wareben'. The 'Trybelberg' can have nothing to do with the Mont Terrible, a name for the otherwise innocuous Mont Terri, south of Delémont, which was only coined in the French Revolution.

[36] SABs, Missiven A 28, fo. 135[v]–136[r], 1 May 1527; ibid. fo. 145[v]–146[r], 6 June 1527.

[37] Ibid. fo. 135[v]–136[r], 145[v]–146[r].

Zürich,[38] as well as its own subjects in the Baselbiet.[39] It also alerted Ensisheim to the danger of Säckingen, Laufenburg, and Rheinfelden on the *Hochrhein* being pulled towards the Constance currency area, thereby putting upward pressure on meat prices.[40] The situation worsened after Easter, once grazing cattle began to come on to the market, that is, cattle which had not been fattened over winter and which had not yet been put out to summer pastures. Some cattle-dealers, it transpired, were claiming (quite spuriously) that the April mandate did not cover grazing cattle, but only fatstock.[41] Accordingly, Ensisheim decided to convene a second meat assembly in July, but this time, in an important shift of policy, Basel was included from the outset;[42] from then on for the rest of the century Basel remained a linchpin of the Rappen league's efforts to control meat provisioning.

What was agreed at Ensisheim on 5 July (and eventually promulgated in a printed mandate a month later) echoed the concerns of the April assembly, but differed appreciably in substance. The new meat ordinance, to apply 'in the area of the Rappen coinage' ('im btzirck der Rappenmuntz'), sought namely to outlaw forestalling in the pastoral districts west of the Rhine outside the area of the Rappen league, upon which the latter largely depended for supplies. Of course, the authorities could not directly prevent commercial cattle-dealing beyond their own jurisdictions; instead, they threatened a trade embargo against any city outside the Rappen area which defied the mandate. Anyone entering the Rappen area who had purchased cattle by *Fürkauf* as far as the river Saône, that is, in the heartlands of Burgundy and up into Lorraine, would have their cattle confiscated. At the same time, renewed efforts were to be made to get the bishop of Basel and the counts of Württemberg (given the key position of Montbéliard) to comply. Those who bought cattle beyond the proscribed area, however, could import them freely on payment of a transit toll; if the cattle were then sold within the Rappen area, it must be on the terms of the ordinance. The earlier price tariff, meanwhile, was confirmed.[43] The

---

[38] SABs, Missiven A 28, fo. 146ʳ–147ᵛ, 6 June 1527.

[39] Ibid. fo. 136ᵛ–137ʳ, 1 May 1527 (to the bailiffs of Farnsburg, Waldenburg, Homburg, and Ramstein); ibid. fo. 147ʳ⁻ᵛ, 6 June 1527 (to its customs-officers in Liestal, Sissach, and Waldenburg).        [40] Ibid. fo. 144ᵛ–145ᵛ, 6 June 1527.

[41] Ibid.; SABs, Fleisch K 2, 10 June 1527.        [42] Ibid. 30 June 1527.

[43] StAFr, A I VI e ε 29, 13 Mar. 1527–11 Sept. 1528: 5 July 1527; cf. ADHR, C 179/4.

gravitational pull westwards of the Rappen league's economic concerns is unmistakable, all the more so if we contrast the boundary of the supply area in the west—up to the Saône—with its delimitation in the east, which stretched no further than Laufenburg!

Strictly speaking, the dire penalties contained in the mandate were only enforceable within Outer Austria itself in the first instance; it was up to the other Rappen league members to give their assent for their own jurisdictions. But if the latter's subjects contravened the mandate, as the government was quick to point out to those sovereign princes with territories lying within the Rappen area, they would duly be barred from Outer Austrian markets—not an idle threat, given that the principal cattle mart lay on Austrian territory at Cernay.[44] The question of passports—or rather, their cost—exercised some Rappen members,[45] but trouble was in fact less likely to come from those within the area of the league (who had a clearly articulated awareness of the need for mutual support)[46] than from those in neighbouring territories accustomed to trade at Cernay. Already in May, in response to count Georg of Württemberg's protest at the imposition of higher tolls and the requirement to obtain passports for the transit of livestock,[47] the Ensisheim authorities had conceded that Montbéliard cattle-dealers were being placed at a disadvantage and promised to rescind the higher toll-rates imposed upon them,[48] though it was not prepared to suspend passports.[49] But when the Austrian officials sent out the printed ordinance in August, with its generous reclamation of all land to the Saône, count Georg replied—with some justice!—that it constituted a complete innovation for his territories and so refused to commit himself.[50] Indeed, he appealed to emperor Charles V in person, who ordered the Outer Austrian government to explain itself to the imperial governing council at Speyer.[51] And though Württemberg subsequently acceded to the meat ordinances for its lordships within Upper Alsace (Horbourg and Riquewihr) it never subscribed to them on behalf of the county of Montbéliard—though late in the century

---

[44] Ibid. 10 Aug. 1527: to the bishops of Basel and Strasbourg, the abbot of Murbach, and margrave Ernst of Baden-Hachberg; cf. AMC, HH 59/27.

[45] ADHR, C 179/4, 18 May 1527 (Kaysersberg); 25 July 1527 (bishop of Strasbourg).

[46] e.g. the bishop of Strasbourg on behalf of the Upper Mundat: ADHR, C 179/4, 4 Sept., 13 Oct. 1527. [47] Ibid. 29 Apr. 1527.

[48] AMS, IV 37/30, 22 May 1527. [49] ADHR, C 179/4, 8 June 1527.

[50] AN, K 2208/I, 4, 10 Aug. 1527; I, 5, 29 Aug. 1527; cf. SABs, Fleisch K 2, 4 Sept. 1527. [51] ADHR, C 179/4, 23 Sept. 1527.

things might well have turned out differently if Montbéliard had joined the Rappen league, as count Friedrich hoped.

Yet even if the sovereign authorities agreed to co-operate within the framework of the Rappen league, stamping out commercial cattle-dealing on the ground was quite another matter. In the spring of 1527 Basel had forwarded to bishop Philipp of Basel a list of suspected forestallers under his jurisdiction, operating around the convent of Bellelay, Montfauçon, Porrentruy, and in the St-Imier valley, but without result.[52] By the summer Basel had managed to identify six ringleaders from the Franches Montagnes in the south of the bishopric, as well as a particularly persistent offender, Hans Heinrich von Garten, from Levoncourt by Pfetterhouse in the north, together with others from Porrentruy and across the border in Montbéliard.[53] When challenged by Basel's own butchers at various cattle markets, they had cocked a snook at the Rappen meat ordinance, and threatened to descend quite openly on Cernay each Tuesday.[54] That turned out to be an injudicious piece of braggadocio, however, for the Austrian authorities, now furnished with their identities, promptly arrested them. When brought to court in Ensisheim, the forestallers claimed that the ordinance permitted them to fatten their cattle on pasture or in byres for six weeks within the area of the Rappen league before selling them.[55] That was indeed the case, but, as Basel tartly informed the government, Hans Heinrich von Garten was buying up cattle in such quantity in the Franches Montagnes that his pastureland in Levoncourt must be grazed bare; moreover, as soon as he returned home, he was overrun by eager purchasers who seemed disinclined to wait six weeks for delivery.[56] The outcome of the trial is not known, but from the absence of complaints about *Fürkauf* over the next few years we may assume that the Jura cattle-dealers had been punished severely enough to deter them.[57]

Compared with these difficulties in the west, the disaffection of the towns on the *Hochrhein* at the terms of the ordinance was a bagatelle, but it neatly illustrates the truth that perceptions of regional economic identity and interest might override purely formal

---

[52] SABs, Missiven A 28, fo. 134ᵛ–135ʳ, 30 Apr. 1527; Missiven A 29, fo. 88ʳ, 14 May 1527.     [53] SABs, Missiven, A 28, fo. 151ʳ⁻ᵛ, n.d. (14 Aug. 1527).
[54] ADHR, C 179/4, 14 Aug. 1527; SABs, Missiven A 28, fo. 151ʳ⁻ᵛ, n.d. (14 Aug. 1527).     [55] SABs, Fleisch K 2, 16 Sept. 1527; ADHR, C 179/4, 11 Sept. 1527.
[56] SABs, Missiven A 29, fo. 102ʳ, 14 Sept. 1527.
[57] They demanded the return of their cattle seized at Altkirch, but it is most unlikely that their request was granted. ADHR, C 179/4, 14 Sept. 1527.

considerations such as membership of a coinage league. Throughout the summer of 1527, as Basel complained, Rheinfelden's butchers
had been selling their best beef at one kreutzer per lb. (equival-
ent to $2\frac{1}{2}d$. Rappen) instead of $2\frac{1}{4}d$. Rappen, as the ordinance laid
down.[58] Rheinfelden regretted the transgression but replied that its
butchers were beholden to sell at the same price as their competitors in Schaffhausen, Constance, Bern, and Radolfzell, that is,
broadly speaking within the Constance monetary area.[59] If they did
not, they would be left without meat. When at the end of the year
Laufenburg made the same point, it added that by then Basel's
butchers were themselves selling at one kreutzer, whilst those outside the Rappen area had gone up as far as $3d$. Rappen per lb.[60]
Here, at least, the remedy was simple: to agree a common price
rise, binding on all members, which would not place the Rappen
league at a disadvantage over against its neighbours. That was duly
accomplished in a revision to the 1527 ordinance concluded on
24 March 1528, which confirmed the price of fattened beef at one
kreutzer per lb., as well as extending the scope of the provisions
to cover mutton, pork, and innards as well.[61] Faced with a choice
between holding prices and losing supplies, or raising prices to
remain competitive, the Rappen members could only fall in line
with neighbouring districts, since they relied upon imports from
those neighbours—or else on cattle-dealers within their coinage
area (such as those in the Franches Montagnes) refraining from the
export of cattle *grosso modo*. Nevertheless, Rheinfelden only accepted
the new tariff on condition that its neighbours did likewise.[62] Some,
on the other hand, asked to be allowed to sell at lower prices if
their markets would bear it: Colmar for all meats,[63] and Belfort for
some innards.[64]

A quite different objection came from Freiburg im Breisgau,
which had to contend with truculence from Baden—this was the
decade in which the margraves were refusing to co-operate with

[58] SABs, Missiven A 29, fo. 95$^{r-v}$, 31 July 1527; ibid. fo. 102$^r$, 14 Sept. 1527.

[59] SABs, Fleisch K 2, 16 Sept. 1527.

[60] GLA 81/53, 22 Dec. 1527. In a later undated instruction for its delegates to a
meat diet in Ensisheim Basel sought to excuse its unilateral price rise by pointing
out that its butchers had to pay an excise not levied anywhere else, and that they
were not allowed to sell their meat with its tripe. SABs, Fleisch K 2, n.d. (1528):
'Instructionn des fleisch kouffs halber gon Enssheim.'

[61] StAFr, A I VI e ε 29, 13 Mar. 1527–11 Sept. 1528: 24 Mar. 1528; cf. SABs, Fleisch
K 2; Gothein, *Wirtschaftsgeschichte des Schwarzwaldes*, 501.

[62] ADHR, C 179/4, 6 Apr. 1528.  [63] AMC, HH 59/29, 30 Mar. 1528.

[64] ADHR, C 179/4, n.d. (after 24 Mar. 1528).

the Rappen league in denouncing the batzen. The previous year margrave Ernst, the ruler of Hachberg and the Markgräflerland, had refused to accept the April meat ordinance on the grounds that it was purely an Outer Austrian document, and that he preferred to issue his own[65]—thereby running the risk that his subjects would be treated as foreigners.[66] But now Freiburg had decided to hold back from the new ordinance unless the margraves signed up for the two southern Baden territories lying within the geographical area of the Rappen league, that is to say, Hachberg and the Margräflerland, with which it could not avoid having commercial dealings.[67] To combat the shortage of meat the town opposed any further price increase—which, it declared, would only put more money into the peasants' pockets![68]—and claimed that its butchers would shortly be in a position to supply grazing cattle from their own meadows every bit as good as cattle fattened over winter. Yet by the summer of 1528 the failure of other communities in the Breisgau to observe the tariff[69] was putting upward pressure on prices, which Freiburg found it impossible to ignore.[70]

In Alsace, too, all was not plain sailing. Mulhouse declared its willingness to observe the March ordinance (despite reservations),[71] but by the summer could put its hands on only two butchers actually prepared to sell at the published tariff, and therefore faced the prospect of being denied access to the Cernay market.[72] In the

[65] GLA 81/53, 18 May 1527. In its reply (ibid. 19 May 1527), the Outer Austrian government declared that other sovereign lords within the Rappen coinage league had already accepted the ordinance, including the lordship of Montot on the Haute-Marne! That is the only reference to this territory, lying north of the headwaters of the Saône. It was presumably approached as being adjacent to the Saône, but it was certainly not a Rappen member.

[66] See the difficulties over passports experienced by margravial butchers from Auggen and Ehrenstetten bringing back cattle from Cernay via the Austrian toll-station at Bantzenheim; their Austrian companions were allowed to pass freely, but the margravial cattle were seized. GLA 67/209, fo. 529ʳ–530ʳ.

[67] StAFr, B 5 XI xiii, fo. 94ᵛ–95ʳ, 3 Apr. 1528.

[68] Austrian subjects in the Black Forest, on the fringes of the Rappen league, complained in July 1528 at a ban on selling their cattle beyond the Rappen area, where they could presumably achieve higher prices, just as the cattle-dealers in the Franches Montagnes. HSA, B 17 1*, fo. 126ᵛ, 30 July 1528.

[69] Neuenburg was identified as one of the culprits. StAFr, A I III f 67, 19 Aug. 1528.

[70] StAFr, B 5 XI xiii, fo. 113ᵛ–114ʳ, 24 Aug. 1528; cf. GLA 81/53. Freiburg's new tariff, issued on 11 Sept. 1528, in fact confirmed the March tariff, but it was shortly to be superseded by a general tariff for the Rappen area the same month. StAFr, A I VI e ε 29, 13 Mar. 1527–11 Sept. 1528.

[71] AMMh, XIII A 2, pp. 12–13, 26 Mar. 1528.     [72] Ibid. p. 15, 26 Aug. 1528

Upper Mundat the bishop of Strasbourg's subjects objected to the detour via Ensisheim in order to obtain passports (for which, moreover, they had to pay),[73] and by the autumn they, too, had been banned from the market at Cernay.[74] Given such disarray, the Outer Austrian government had no option but to convene another assembly in September to seek agreement on the necessary price adjustments.[75] The revised ordinance, issued on 22 September, appears to have restored some calm to the cattle market, for the next we hear is Basel reporting to Ensisheim a year later that there was by then such a glut of meat in Switzerland, especially in Bern and Solothurn, that the tariff might be reduced.[76]

In fact, prices continued to hold steady and were confirmed in a new ordinance in 1532, which sought to rectify the deficiencies which had emerged since 1527.[77] Thereafter the issue became essentially one of political will: whether meat provisioning was to be determined by the interests of Outer Austria or by the wider concerns of the Rappen league as a whole—or, not to put too fine a point on it, how access to the market at Cernay was to be regulated. In 1530 the Ensisheim government had already responded at some length to an enquiry from Colmar by stating that all cattle driven 'between the mountains down the Rhine' to the weekly market at Cernay must be offered for sale by 1 p.m. and not exported beyond Outer Austria or the Rappen coinage area. If any cattle remained unsold, they could afterwards be driven on to Colmar's market, but there offered only to Rappen members, whereupon, if still unsold, they should be returned and not sent downriver (that is, into Lower Alsace)! Only cattle from beyond the Saône could be traded freely, on production of the requisite passports.[78] This bureaucratic nightmare was obviously intended to create commercial conditions so restrictive that they amounted in effect to an assertion of Cernay's monopoly: no wonder that Colmar hesitated to accept the 1532 ordinance.[79] But its footdragging only led to the

---

[73] ADHR, C 179/4, 7 Apr. 1528.     [74] Ibid. 4 Sept. 1528.
[75] Cf. SABs, Fleisch K 2, 9 Sept. 1528.
[76] SABs, Missiven A 29, fo. 164ᵛ, 20 Nov. 1529. In January that year, however, Basel had reprimanded its magistrate in Liestal for allowing the butchers there to sell at prices higher than in its own ordinance. Ibid. fo. 149ᵛ, 23 Jan. 1529.
[77] StAFr, AI VI e ε 31, 20 Mar. 1532. It was preceded by a territorial ordinance (for the Breisgau alone?) on 18 Mar. 1532: StAFr, A I VI e ε 30; cf. Speck, Landstände, ii. 857.     [78] AMC, HH 59/112, 14 Sept. 1530.
[79] AMC, HH 59/34, 13 June 1532.

city's butchers being prevented from 'exporting' cattle bought at Cernay to Colmar;[80] only when they agreed to abide by the ordinance were their beasts released.[81] But then they discovered that the ordinance was being flouted in Outer Austria itself, both at Ensisheim and at Cernay.[82] The government denied the charge,[83] and so did the Ensisheim town council, though the latter admitted that its butchers were restive.[84] The Colmar magistrates therefore deemed that the best course of action would be to stick to the terms of the ordinance for meat bought at Cernay—the principal provisioner—but to tolerate slightly higher prices elsewhere.[85]

The desire to impose strict conditions on access to the Cernay market was not, of course, necessarily incompatible with attempts to widen the catchment area of those subscribing to the meat ordinances. For in one sense the more lords and cities who could be brought into the net, the greater the likelihood that Outer Austrian subjects would be spared shortages of meat supplies or abrupt price rises, even if that meant in another sense easing access to Cernay. But the Ensisheim officials remained as chary of overstepping the traditional boundaries of their competence as in 1515. Their treatment of the imperial free city of Sélestat on the river Ill well illustrates the point. Sélestat, with close commercial ties to its neighbours south of the Landgraben as well as northwards into Lower Alsace, was keen to take part in the Rappen meat diets in order to gain privileged access to the Cernay mart, and to that end had enlisted Colmar's assistance in 1528, in the wake of the first comprehensive Rappen ordinance the previous year.[86] For its part, Colmar was happy to support Sélestat's application as a fellow-member of the Decapolis (and doubtless in order to provide a counterweight to the Austrian government as well). The latter, however, rejected its overture as inappropriate, 'since it [Sélestat] lies outside the area of the Rappen coinage'.[87] But Sélestat did not give up so easily, and turned to archduke Ferdinand for help, pointing out that it was being excluded from the meat marts at Cernay, Thann, and Ensisheim because it lay across the Landgraben, unlike its imperial city neighbours immediately to the south.[88] Ferdinand

[80] AMC, HH 59/35, 17 Apr. 1533.      [81] AMC, HH 59/37, 19 Apr. 1533.
[82] AMC, HH 59/38, 4 July 1533.      [83] AMC, HH 59/39, 5 July 1533.
[84] AMC, HH 59/54, n.d. (July 1533).      [85] AMC, HH 58/24, 8 July 1533.
[86] AMC, HH 59/87, 28 Apr. 1528.      [87] AMC, HH 59/30, 30 Apr. 1528.
[88] ADHR, C 179/4, n.d. (before 6 Apr. 1529).

thereupon instructed the government in Ensisheim to discuss the possibility seriously with Colmar, given that Sélestat maintained friendly relations with Austria (it had resisted the blandishments of the Reform) and that it might have been 'inadvertently' excluded from the Rappen meat agreements.[89] The detail of these negotiations has not survived, but by 1533 it looks as if Sélestat, having already agreed to conform to the Rappen league police ordinances despite belonging to the Strasbourg coinage area,[90] was admitted as an exceptional case.[91] From then on its name regularly appears among the list of signatories to the Rappen league meat ordinances.

# III

For the rest of the 1530s meat supplies on the southern Upper Rhine ran smoothly, but by the end of the decade forestalling was again becoming a problem. At a diet in Baden (Aargau) in 1539 the Swiss Confederates decided that the best tactic was to prosecute forestalling vigorously in the countryside but to allow unrestricted purchases at the chartered markets, a solution which Basel recommended to the authorities in Ensisheim.[92] To have accepted this, however, would have meant the latter abandoning their highly protectionist policy. Instead, the government eventually issued a new proclamation against *Fürkauf* in 1541, which was little more than a rehash of the 1527 provisions.[93] The recrudescence of forestalling signalled fresh pressure on prices, and by 1543 Colmar, for instance, was allowing best beef to be sold at $\frac{1}{2}d$. dearer than the tariff stipulated, that is, at $3d$. Rappen per lb.[94]

The Outer Austrian administration prevaricated (as was its wont), so missing the chance of getting a new agreement in place in time for Easter 1544 (the traditional switch-over after Lent from winter fatstock to spring grazing cattle), with the upshot that it wrote around hurriedly trying to glean information in advance of a consultative

---

[89] Ibid. 10 Apr. 1529; AMC, HH 59/32, 11 Apr. 1529.
[90] Cf. AMC, HH 59/89, 29 Mar. 1533.
[91] Cf. AMSé, HH 42/4, 21 Apr. 1533. A copy of the 1532 ordinance, significantly, is also preserved in the Sélestat archives. AMSé, HH 36/7, 20 Mar. 1532.
[92] SABs, Missiven B 2, fo. 263ʳ–264ʳ, 13 Sept. 1539.
[93] StAFr, A I VI e ε 33, 12 Mar. 1541; cf. ADHR, C 180/1.
[94] AMRf, BB 3, fo. 171ᵛ–172ʳ, 4 Mar. 1543. As early as 1540 the city was struggling to prevent its butchers from raising their prices. AMC, HH 58/30, 13 Mar. 1540.

assembly set down for 28 April, two weeks after Easter.[95] Basel instructed its delegate, the councillor Melchior Rys, to raise the activities of certain village nobles who had installed butchers in their localities with no limit on the prices they charged[96]—a rare insight into what was happening at grass-roots level, which suggests that the authorities had more to contend with than simply commercial cattle-dealing. While the diet did not recommend any concessions on meat tariffs, it strongly urged that the bishop of Basel and duke Christoph of Württemberg be brought into the agreement, as well as the abbot of Murbach and the bishop of Strasbourg, all of whom were to be encouraged to send delegates to the conclusive diet a month later.[97] Basel was particularly keen to include these sovereign princes as signatories, and told Melchior Rys to use his best offices if they looked like refusing.[98] But the only such names to appear on the printed mandate issued on 28 May were those of the bishop of Strasbourg (for the Upper Mundat) and margrave Ernst of Baden (for his southern territories in the Breisgau).[99]

The chances of duke Christoph agreeing to enforce the new Rappen ordinance in his territory of Montbéliard were certainly not improved by the Austrian officials in Thann's seizure a month earlier of a large number of cattle bought at the Cernay market by three merchants from the town of Montbéliard, who had refused to pay a transit toll of 4 fl. per beast,[100] or by Ensisheim's rejection of their claim that they were not engaged in cattle-dealing.[101] With this dispute still unresolved,[102] it is perhaps surprising that duke

---

[95] AMC, HH 59/41, 21 Mar. 1544 (to Colmar); SABs, Fleisch K 2, 21 Mar. 1544 (to Basel); ibid. 24 Mar. 1544 (Basel's reply). The government responded to Basel's suggestion of a new assembly by inviting it to attend (ibid. 28 Mar. 1544), but in fact it had already invited Colmar on its own initiative ten days earlier (AMC, HH 59/40, 18 Mar. 1544).          [96] SABs, Fleisch K 2, n.d. (before 28 Apr. 1544).

[97] StAFr, A I VI e ε 36, 28 Apr. 1544; cf. SABs, Fleisch K 2. The bishop had in fact instructed his bailiff in Rouffach, Wilhelm Böcklin von Böcklinsau, to attend the April meeting, but he never turned up. To the May diet the bishop then sent his Licenciat, and called the elders of the Upper Mundat communes together to discuss tactics a few days beforehand, on the basis of the April proposals referred back for approval. ADHR, 3 G 3/1, 28 Mar. 1544; 3/2, 23 Apr. 1544; 3/3, 28 Apr. 1544; 3/4, n.d. (May 1544); 3/5, 18 May 1544; AMRf, BB 3, fo. 235ᵛ–239ʳ, 25 May 1544.

[98] SABs, Fleisch K 2, 24 May 1544.

[99] StAFr, A I VI e ε 37, 28 May 1544; cf. SABs, Fleisch K 2; AMMh, I 4332.

[100] AN, K 2208/I, 2, 19 Apr. 1544; cf. I, 8; I, 9, n.d. (Apr. 1544).

[101] Ibid. I, 10, 22 Apr. 1544; I, 11, 27 Apr. 1544. The Austrian authorities conceded, however, that they had recently let some cattle pass toll-free for duke Christoph's own household.          [102] Cf. ibid. I, 14, 8 May 1544; I, 15, 17 May 1544.

Christoph should have replied positively to the despatch of the provisional ordinance of 28 April, though he proposed to take no immediate action since his father, duke Ulrich, had earlier promulgated his own mandates.[103] Suitably encouraged, the government in Ensisheim sent copies of the final mandate of 28 May to both duke Christoph[104] and count Georg (who had promised to combat forestalling in his lordship of Horbourg),[105] as well as to the bishop of Basel.[106]

It was obvious within a year that, whatever success in curtailing *Fürkauf* may have been brought by the ban on access to Outer Austrian markets looming over transgressors, the price regime imposed by the 1544 ordinance within the Rappen coinage area could not be sustained. In Lower Alsace, Strasbourg was already allowing its butchers to sell fatstock beef at $3d.$ per lb.—in effect more than a 30 per cent premium to the $2\frac{1}{2}d.$ per lb. permitted under the Rappen tariff, given the greater strength of the Strasbourg currency.[107] Mulhouse, too, which objected to its butchers being forbidden to buy at Cernay because they bid prices above the tariff, complained that Austrian subjects themselves were offering more.[108] Cracks began to appear in the wall of solidarity which members of the Rappen league presented to the outside world, beginning with a plea by the butchers of the Val de Lièpvre in April 1545 to be allowed to exceed the price ceiling. Their argument, backed up by the Ribeaupierre mining supervisor and territorial judge, was that, since the mining communities in the valley raised no cattle, no butcher could afford to supply the miners' considerable appetite for meat by purchasing stock at the stated prices at distant markets.[109] Dissatisfaction with the outcome of a further assembly called by the Ensisheim administration in late September[110] finally

---

[103] Ibid. I, 19, n.d. (May 1544).   [104] Ibid. I, 16 and I, 17, 28 May 1544.

[105] Ibid. I, 18, 28 May 1544.

[106] SABs, Fleisch K 2, 28 May 1544. Ensisheim sent covering copies of these letters to Basel in order to demonstrate that it was responding to the city's urgings. Ibid. 6 June 1544.   [107] ADHR, C 180/3, n.d. (Mar 1545).

[108] Ibid. 1 Apr. 1545; AMMh, I 4353, 2 Apr. 1545.

[109] ADHR, C 180/3, 18 Apr. 1545.

[110] Cf. SABs, Fleisch K 2, 13 Aug. 1545; ibid. 14 Aug. 1545; AMC, HH 59/44, 14 Aug. 1545. Basel had set its face against any increase in Rappen meat prices. SABs, Fleisch K 2, 19 Sept. 1545 (instructions for its delegates). The government invited Villingen to attend this diet, which elicited the tart response that the town had ignored the 1544 mandate since it was not a member of the Rappen coinage league; its butchers purchased their meat in Württemberg and around Rottweil. It did, however, promise to combat forestalling. GLA 81/54, 17 Sept. 1545.

prompted Wilhelm von Rappoltstein, the lord of Ribeaupierre and seigneur of the Val de Lièpvre, to summon his neighbours to a local meeting for the north of Upper Alsace, who turned out to share the same grievances.[111]

One after the other, Colmar, Munster, Kaysersberg, Ammerschwihr, Turckheim, and Kientzheim, as well as Wilhelm von Rappoltstein himself, confronted the Outer Austrian government with the unpalatable fact that it had always been harder to keep to the meat ordinances in the north of Upper Alsace, where meat was never plentiful and stock-rearing (of beef, at least) a negligible quantity, compared with the extensive pasturelands of the Sundgau.[112] Even Colmar, despite complaining that its butchers, too, could find no meat to buy at Cernay, was alleged by its neighbours to be better placed than Ammerschwihr or the territory of Ribeaupierre nearby.[113] Wilhelm von Rappoltstein therefore proposed strict adherence to the meat ordinance within the area of the Rappen league itself, but meat bought elsewhere should be allowed to be traded freely and sold at higher prices.[114] This, of course, would have driven a coach-and-horses through Ensisheim's ambition to control the commercial cattle trade as far as the Saône. In spite of these difficulties, several communes declared that they would do their best to enforce the meat mandate, but first Kaysersberg threw in the towel by employing foreign butchers at a higher tariff,[115] and then Kientzheim announced that it was abandoning Cernay for markets in other coinage areas (presumably Lower Alsace).[116] It is a sign of the helplessness and incompetence of the Outer Austrian government that its first reaction was to send copies of this entire correspondence to Basel with a plea for advice,[117] and to moan to Freiburg that another diet would soon be necessary.[118] But no action ensued until February 1546, four months later.[119]

[111] AMC, HH 59/93, 26 Sept. 1545.

[112] StAFr, A I VI e ε 38, 25 Sept. 1545–*circa* 1550: 26 Sept. 1545 (Colmar); 5 Oct. 1545 (Wilhelm von Rappoltstein); 3 Oct. 1545 (Munster, Kaysersberg); 5 Oct. 1545 (Turckheim); 7 Oct. 1545 (Kientzheim). Cf. AMC, HH 59/46, 26 Sept. 1545; ADHR, C 180/5, 5 Oct. 1545.

[113] Ibid.; StAFr, A I VI e ε 38, 25 Sept. 1545–*circa* 1550: 4 Oct. 1545.

[114] Ibid. 5 Oct. 1545.        [115] Ibid. 3 Oct. 1545.        [116] Ibid. 7 Oct. 1545.

[117] SABs, Fleisch K 2, 24 Oct. 1545.

[118] StAFr, A I VI e ε 38, 25 Sept. 1545–*circa* 1550: 24 Oct. 1545.

[119] Cf. ADHR, E-dépôt 4: AMAm, AA 25, 10 Feb. 1546; AMC, HH 59/47, 10 Feb. 1546; SABs, Fleisch K 2, 10 Feb. 1546.

When the Rappen delegates finally assembled on 2 March, a clear rift was discernible between north and south on the left bank of the Rhine. The northern members, squeezed between Outer Austria and Strasbourg, were desperate for a price increase in the face of continuing shortages, but Basel (which had no reason to provide Ensisheim with flanking fire) was firmly opposed to any increase, arguing that it would be preferable to impose a territorial levy (*Landschatzung*), though quite how that would have alleviated the situation is unclear.[120] Yet Basel did have a point when it claimed that all previous increases had merely left the Rappen members chasing their tails in a spiral of price rises. An increase to 3 *d.* per lb. until 25 July was proposed,[121] and after referral that was accepted at a conclusive diet on 29 March. For the first time, however, the difficulties facing Ribeauvillé, Bergheim, Kaysersberg, Ammerschwihr, and Kientzheim were publicly acknowledged, so that their willingness to sign the mandate, on condition that they be allowed to sell their best meat at 3 *d.* per lb. throughout the whole year, was gratefully accepted.[122] Although there was subsequently some grumbling, particularly from Basel, at leaner cattle and calves being sold at the same price as fatstock,[123] the 1546 ordinance seems to have held, presumably because meat became once again in plentiful supply. But the negotiations leading up to the new mandate had ruthlessly exposed the fissures within the Rappen league and the fundamental dilemma of whom the meat ordinances were supposed to benefit—the Rappen league as a whole or merely Outer Austria.

Modern economic analysis might suggest that the remedy for periodic meat shortages and the problem of forestalling would have been to let the law of supply and demand take its course and throw the Outer Austrian cattle marts open to all-comers. Basel, as a commercial metropolis, could afford to take that view (though it was just as keen as its fellow-members of the Rappen league to stamp out informal marketing in the countryside by *Winkelmetzger*). But this approach ran counter to sixteenth-century perceptions

---

[120] Ibid. n.d. (before 1 Mar. 1546).
[121] StAFr, A I VI e ε 38, 25 Sept. 1545–*circa* 1550: 2 Mar. 1546.
[122] ADHR, C 180/6, 29 Mar. 1546; cf. SABs, Fleisch K 2.
[123] StAFr, A I VI e ε 39, 26 July 1546. Its enquiries to Freiburg and Breisach elicited the response that no price rises were on the horizon in those two towns. SABs, Fleisch K 2, 28 July 1546; ibid. 29 July 1546.

of 'good police'. Not only was it anathema to the authorities in Ensisheim; it was not shared by the northern communes of the Rappen league in Upper Alsace either, who were caught in a cleft stick between the virtual absence of local meat supplies and in-sufficient economic clout to dominate the inconveniently distant markets of the Sundgau. By mid-century the prevailing belief was that more protection and exclusion were the answer.

In 1551 there were already indications that the mandate pub-lished five years earlier was no longer being universally obeyed,[124] and by 1554 several Rappen members were pressing for another general convention, including Freiburg, which advocated at the very least a territorial diet for the Austrian Breisgau.[125] The pro-visional ordinance duly issued on 12 March 1555 contained some radical innovations. In the first place, it was agreed that no meat whatever should be sold within the area of the Rappen league to non-members, and that no beasts should be exported for sale at foreign markets—regardless of whether the dealers were forestall-ing or merely supplying domestic needs. Moreover, in order to reduce the consumption of meat, the (Catholic) fasting provisions were to be strictly observed, and the size of weddings curtailed, as well as limiting the amount of meat to be served at other fest-ivities such as church-ales or baptisms. Before the delegates recon-vened to commit themselves to a binding mandate, the government in Ensisheim was instructed to make the usual approach to import-ant neighbours such as the bishop of Basel or the princes of Baden and Württemberg, as well as to Sélestat (its special status now accepted and acknowledged) and—an extraordinary departure!—to the city of Strasbourg itself.[126]

These provisions represented both a relaxation and a tighten-ing of the policies hitherto embraced, most clearly spelt out in the Outer Austrian government's response to Colmar's enquiry in 1530. Gone were any restrictions on foreign cattle traded at the Outer Austrian markets: the curious attempt to dictate the pattern of cattle-dealing as far as the river Saône was quietly abandoned. In their place stood the harshest penalties for those seeking to corner the market in local cattle raised within the area of the league. The

---

[124] SABs, Missiven A 34, p. 22, 20 Apr. 1551; SABs, Fleisch A 1, 21 Apr. 1551.

[125] SABs, Fleisch K 2, 2 Mar. 1554; GLA 81/54, 14 Jan. 1555.

[126] SABs, Fleisch K 2, 12 Mar. 1555. A copy of the provisional mandate is located in AMSé, HH 36/6, 12 Mar. 1555. Another copy is in AMGb, HH 3, wrongly dated to 1515.

overture to the city of Strasbourg should be seen as an attempt to placate a powerful neighbour, whose butchers had been major purchasers of cattle at Cernay, by inviting it to subscribe to the Rappen provisions and thus benefit from 'most favoured nation' status. Although the Cernay market could, in times of general shortage, become a magnet for cattle-dealers from Burgundy to Swabia, its principal function remained the provisioning of the southern Upper Rhine, that is, the members of the Rappen league: as Colmar reminded its delegate to the conclusive diet at the end of March 1555, a shortage of grazing cattle from the Franches Montagnes and Montbéliard must inevitably put pressure on the prices charged by the league.[127] That the desire to safeguard local supplies was paramount (rather than any conscious attempt to suppress commercial dealing as such) is underscored by the wording of the final mandate. The delegates had clearly used the intervening fortnight to reflect on how the Rappen area's meat provisioning might best be protected, for they agreed to outlaw any means of subverting exchange at local market-places. Specifically, they banned contracts between foreigners and local peasants to raise cattle on the former's behalf (a sort of *Verlag*, which brought the additional evil of credit dependency with it), and all joint enterprises whereby foreigners might reserve pastures and buy up local cattle without being identified as non-league subjects.

Furthermore, the fasting provisions, mooted earlier in the month, were confirmed, and anyone rejecting the ordinance was to be debarred from purchasing cattle.[128] Since the Rappen league included several Protestant members, it may seem astonishing that they were willing to be bound by what were effectively Catholic rules—but, then, perhaps they were early disciples of Bertold Brecht: *Polizei* before principle. Basel, however, the leading Protestant city member, was not at all happy, and initially refused to accept the mandate.[129] By mid-April it had agreed to sign on condition that it ignore the ban on meat sales and butchering during Lent.[130] Margrave Karl

---

[127] AMC, HH 59/53, n.d. (before 27 Mar. 1555).
[128] StAFr, A I VI e ε 46, 27 Mar. 1555–18 June 1597: 27 Mar. 1555; cf. SABs, Fleisch K 2; AAEB, B 209/6.          [129] SABs, Fleisch K 2, 8 Apr. 1555.
[130] SABs, Missiven A 34, pp. 783–85, 13 Apr. 1555. Mulhouse, on the other hand, accepted the ordinance without demur; its only worry was continuity of supply. It reported to Ensisheim that it might have to instruct its butchers to alternate between slaughtering cattle for one week and other livestock the next fortnight. AMMh, II A 1/1, fo. 249ᵛ, 4 Apr. 1555; II A 1/2, fo. 13ʳ, 18 Mar. 1556.

II of Baden, a declared Protestant sympathizer, was also minded to accept the ordinance—but he was still six months away from the security of the Religious Peace of Augsburg, under whose protection he completed the confessional switch for his territory of Baden-Durlach.[131] In the end, his signature was added by hand to the printed ordinance—which, remarkably enough, included count Georg of Württemberg, an avowed Lutheran.[132]

Count Georg had in fact first consulted his officials in Riquewihr, who reported that the town's butchers would only accept the ordinance if their counterparts in Kaysersberg did so as well.[133] At first, the Kaysersberg butchers rehearsed the grievances which had dogged negotiations ten years earlier in the autumn of 1545, and only gave way to the town council's entreaties when granted a rent easement.[134] With that, count Georg fell into line, but insisted on issuing the ordinance under his own name, so as not to give the impression that he was acquiescing in an Outer Austrian decree,[135] but there was still no question of extending its scope to take in Montbéliard. Ensisheim brushed aside pleas from the remoter parts of the Rappen coinage area—such as the Val de Lièpvre—to be allowed to exceed the stipulated tariff,[136] and reiterated that access to Cernay would only be permitted to those who accepted the ordinance in full.[137] Yet this stance did not even have the merit of consistency, since the government sought to impose the ordinance on the one Austrian community in Alsace which lay north of the Landgraben, namely the Val de Villé. This was clearly a political-territorial, rather than an economic, decision, for the Val de Villé lay foursquare within the Strasbourg currency area. Not surprisingly, the valley announced in the summer of 1555 that its butchers,

    [131] SABs, Fleisch K 2, 8 Apr. 1555. Cf. Volker Press, 'Baden und die badischen Kondominate', in Anton Schindling and Walter Ziegler (eds.), *Die Territorien des Reichs im Zeitalter der Reformation und Konfessionsbildung. Land und Konfession 1500–1650*, v. *Der Südwesten* (Katholisches Leben und Kirchenreform im Zeitalter der Glaubensspaltung, 53) (Münster, 1993), 132–33.

    [132] Cf. the copy of the mandate in StAFr, A I VI e ε 46, 27 Mar. 1555–18 June 1597: 27 Mar. 1555.

    [133] AN, K 2208/I, 20, 12 Mar. 1555; I, 21 and I, 22, 14 Mar. 1555; I, 23, 27 Mar. 1555.        [134] Ibid. I, 25, 11 Apr. 1555.

    [135] Ibid. I, 24, 16 Apr. 1555; I, 26, 29 Apr. 1555. The Outer Austrian government pointed out that if the Württemberg butchers equipped themselves with passports they could then export cattle not only from Outer Austria but from the entire area of the Rappen league. Ibid. I, 28, 2 May 1555.

    [136] ADHR, C 180/7, 8 Apr. 1555; 10 May 1555. Cf. also Bergheim's protests that autumn, ibid. 6 Oct. 1555.        [137] Cf. AMC, HH 59/49, 13 Apr. 1555.

accustomed to the higher Strasbourg prices, had simply gone on strike.[138]

The rigid attitude of the Outer Austrian administration did little to advance the Cernay market as a supplier of local needs. As its official, the deputy marshal Benedikt Urban (sent to observe business at Cernay) reported in April, five Strasbourg butchers had succeeded in acquiring eighty head of cattle from a grazier in Angeot in the western Sundgau (though Strasbourg, despite its invitation, had not subscribed to the ordinance); moreover, he was suspicious of the intentions of dealers from Porrentruy and Belfort. Rightly, it transpired, for the next year Urban discovered that Strasbourg butchers had been buying direct from Porrentruy, while the Württemberg authorities had instructed their dealers in Montbéliard to patronize their own local market. Butchers from Colmar and Sélestat, he continued, had been able to buy cattle at Cernay, but since they failed to obtain the necessary passports he had intervened to cancel the sale.[139]

Whether the sharp distinction in the treatment of local and foreign cattle would have alleviated the difficulties of meat provisioning for the Rappen league in the long run is a moot point. But in any case the Ensisheim government shot itself in the foot two years later by imposing a new transit toll on cattle exports. As it tried to reassure Colmar, the toll only applied to cattle bought outwith the Cernay market (and other Outer Austrian markets, too, one assumes) but driven through Outer Austrian territory.[140] Then Porrentruy claimed the same exemption from transit tolls as Colmar:

For the aforesaid town of Porrentry lies in an exposed spot in the hills (bordering on several foreign lands and lordships), in which place we have very little sustenance or livelihood except by raising beef cattle, which we have lang syne driven through the . . . emperor's Outer Austrian lands, from which we have hitherto . . . rendered a large toll in Cernay or Ensisheim.[141]

Despite Porrentruy's assertion that it had paid tolls in the past, it does seem that a new impost was being demanded, for the Confederate diet in Baden (Aargau) on 5 April 1557 added its voice in

---

[138] ADHR, C 180/7, 13 July 1555.   [139] ADHR, 1 C 180/8, 1555–56.
[140] AMC, HH 59/51, 20 Apr. 1557; cf. HH 59/50, 2 Apr. 1557.
[141] ABP, I/IV, 54, n.d. (1557).

protest that non-members of the Rappen league were being prevented from buying cattle in the Black Forest or elsewhere in Outer
Austria, a ban which contravened the long-established 'hereditary
agreement' (*Erbeinigung*) of 1511 between Austria and the Swiss,
which had guaranteed free trade and outlawed new customs duties.[142]
At this time the butchers of Strasbourg also petitioned their city
council to have the restrictions on their purchases both at Cernay
and—beyond Outer Austria—in the Upper Mundat lifted.[143] Matters
seemed to have reached an impasse.

# IV

Exclusion could not be the answer to a problem which was insol-
uble in the terms presented: a desire to guarantee local supplies,
principally by promoting a market—Cernay—which would flourish only if allowed to develop as an international entrepôt for livestock. Moreover, the Ensisheim administration could not make up
its mind whether it was legislating for Outer Austria as a whole or
for the economic area defined by membership of the Rappen coinage league. At the end of the 1550s the Austrian communes in the
eastern Black Forest were still receiving summons to attend 'police'
diets of the Rappen league, of which they were not members.
Fuelled by complaints that the Black Forest peasants were selling
cattle to foreign butchers,[144] Ensisheim tried to impose the Rappen
meat mandate on Villingen (which foretold the demise of its butchers,
were it to comply),[145] even though the town was an established
participant in Swabian meat assemblies alongside its neighbours,
the counts of Fürstenberg and the lords of Schellenberg, under the
aegis of the duchy of Württemberg.[146] Waldshut showed itself a
little more conciliatory. It did agree to send an emissary—strictly
as an observer—to a meat diet in Ensisheim, but only to protest
that it was constrained by its adherence to the Constance coinage

---

[142] SABe, A IV 38, OO, pp. 36–37. For the provisions of the *Erbeinigung* cf.
*Amtliche Sammlung der älteren Eidgenössischen Abschiede*, iii. 2, ed. Anton Philipp
Segesser (Lucerne, 1869), 1344.

[143] AMS, V 2/12, 6 Mar. 1557. In the same year Ensisheim also had a brush with
the lord of Ribeaupierre, whose butchers in Ribeauvillé raised the same objections
to observing the price tariff that had been advanced in 1545. ADHR, E 707.

[144] Cf. StAFr, A I VI e ε 46, 27. Mar. 1555–18 June 1597: 1 Mar. 1559.

[145] GLA 81/55, 13 Mar. 1559.

[146] Baumann and Tumbült, *Mitteilungen aus dem f. fürstenbergischen Archive*,
ii. 32 (nos. 48, 48a).

area to follow the lead of its fellow-members there. Were it to introduce the proposed Outer Austrian tariff, based on Rappen coinage, butchers from the districts of Fürstenberg, Sulz, and Baden (Aargau), as well as from Schaffhausen, would simply sweep the market clean of meat and leave Waldshut empty-handed.[147]

Between 1559 and 1560, however, the Outer Austrian government gave some inkling that it at last understood that meat provisioning within the Rappen area could only be satisfactorily regulated by acknowledging the disparities between different parts of the league, and, by extension, ensuring the co-operation of neighbouring authorities in order to prevent a free-for-all throughout the Upper Rhine. A diet on 17 March 1559 had ended without firm agreement precisely because the participants—especially those near the border with Lower Alsace—could not accept the proposed tariff (appreciably lower than elsewhere) without being starved of meat.[148] In calling a fresh assembly at the end of that year,[149] the authorities adopted an entirely different strategy. The interests of Strasbourg (fleetingly acknowledged in 1555), as the largest consumer of meat on the Upper Rhine, were at last to be taken properly into account: because it had hitherto been excluded from Outer Austrian markets, it was now invited to attend the deliberations in order to help resolve an intractable situation. The result was that, for the first time since police diets of the Rappen league had been convened, a two-tier price structure was agreed in December 1559. The cities and lordships of northern Upper Alsace (including the Austrian lordship of Hohlandsberg) were to be allowed to sell fatstock at 4*d.* Rappen per lb. (given that in Lower Alsace 3*d.* Strasbourg was the going rate), whereas throughout Outer Austria as a whole a maximum of $3\frac{1}{2}d.$ Rappen up to mid-summer and 3*d.* Rappen thereafter was fixed.[150] This tariff was to be valid for two years, provided that the other parties held to their somewhat higher prices. By logical extension, the category of those prohibited as foreigners from buying cattle within Outer Austria was revised to exclude

---

[147] GLA 81/55, 13 Dec. 1559. It does seem, however, that the Outer Austrian government continued to issue local meat ordinances for the four Forest Towns and the 'upper quarter', i.e. the southern Black Forest. Cf. StARf, 127, 15 Aug. 1576. But, as in this instance, Waldshut expressed itself dissatisfied with their provisions.

[148] ADHR, C 181/1, 21 Mar. 1559. (Colmar); ibid. 25 Mar. 1559 (Hohlandsberg, and for Riquewihr and Kaysersberg); ibid. 28 Mar. 1559 (Ammerschwihr).

[149] Cf. SABs, Fleisch K 2, 22 Nov. 1559.

[150] ADHR, C 181/3, 19 Dec. 1559; cf. ADHR, E 707; AAEB, B 209/6.

Strasbourg and, it seems, members of its coinage area as well. Over
the next six weeks, the participants in the diet all signalled their
assent to these new arrangements, including Strasbourg, though it
gave notice that it had been obliged to agree a top price of $3\frac{1}{4}d$.
Strasbourg with its butchers for the best beef.[151]

In its new-found alertness to the special difficulties of the northern members of the Rappen league in Upper Alsace, and in its
belated recognition that Strasbourg was economically too powerful
a city simply to be brushed aside (as if the stroke of a clerk's pen in
the Ensisheim chancery could prevent the meat-hungry butchers
of Strasbourg from descending on Cernay), the Outer Austrian government had, alas, overlooked its major counterpart to the south.
Basel—which had attended the diet—sharply reminded Ensisheim
that no provisions had been agreed for its own territory of the
Baselbiet (though it did indicate its general willingness to accept
the new ordinance).[152] In fact, the government conceded that both
Basel and Strasbourg deserved special consideration on account of
the size and movement of their populations.[153] By March 1560 the
government was able to announce that the bishop of Basel, the
abbot of Murbach, margrave Karl II of Baden, and the guardians
of count Georg of Württemberg (the heir to the Alsatian territories)
had accepted the new package.[154]

The principle of differential price tariffs was precisely what some
members of the Rappen league had long struggled to avert. Freiburg, for instance, on the right bank of the Rhine and not exposed
to the same pressures which affected the north of Upper Alsace,
had instructed its emissaries in the spring of 1559 to resist any such
proposal,[155] and continued to argue during the following decade
that, if unitary pricing could not be enforced in Alsace and the
Sundgau, then at least it should be maintained in the Breisgau and

---

[151] ADHR, C 181/3, 2 Jan. 1560. The city council objected, moreover, that the
communes allowed to sell their best meat at 4d. Rappen weighed innards together
with the meat, a practice strictly forbidden in Strasbourg.

[152] SABs, Missiven B 8, fo. 109ʳ⁻ᵛ, 8 Jan. 1560.

[153] Cf. AAEB, B 209/6, 12 Jan. 1560; AN, K 2208/I, 33, 20 Jan. 1560.

[154] AMC, HH 59/57, 16 Mar. 1560. On the same day it wrote to Sélestat to do likewise. AMSé, HH 36/8. Württemberg's acceptance was, as always, for the lordship
of Riquewihr (and Horbourg), not for Montbéliard. AN, K 1851/I, 24 Apr. 1560; cf.
ADHR, C 181/3. Its officials in Riquewihr showed markedly less enthusiasm for
the new regulations than did their administrative superiors in Montbéliard. Cf. AN,
K 2208/I, 31, 1 Dec. 1559; I, 33, 20 Jan. 1560; I, 34, 30 Jan. 1560; I, 35, 16 Mar. 1560.

[155] StAFr, A I VI e ε 46, 27 Mar. 1555–18 June 1597: 15 Mar. 1559.

Black Forest.[156] But, because of its location, it was Alsace that mattered when it came to meat supplies: as the French saying has it, *chacun son métier, les vâches seront bien garder.* And it is beyond dispute that the crucial change of course adopted by the Outer Austrian government brought relative tranquillity to the meat market for the next fifteen years. Of course, whenever meat was scarce, there was the danger that Strasbourg's butchers could use their greater financial muscle to outbid their counterparts within the Rappen league.[157] But, in general, the opening up of Cernay to butchers from Lower Alsace created a demand which in turn stimulated a regular supply of livestock to Cernay. In the later 1570s, as a subsequent report observed,

Each week a large number of cattle from Burgundy, Lorraine, Savoy, the Franches Montagnes, the county of Montbéliard, Porrentruy, and other places . . . are offered at market . . . Whenever a cattle mart was held in Burgundy, [it was agreed between butchers and cattle-dealers] to drive the cattle bought there, as many as a hundred or 150 head, [straight] to Cernay where butchers [from Lower Alsace] were waiting for them, striking a deal without wasting words, paying [up front] in cash or at an agreed date, in such a way that both cattle-dealers . . . and butchers . . . reposed trust in each other.[158]

At the same time, this liberalization of the meat market revealed how contingent and precarious the concept of a regional economic identity might be. Certainly the members of the Rappen league had interests in common which they did not share with outsiders: the circulation area of a particular coinage, as the disputes with the Black Forest communes well illustrate, did go a long way towards marking the boundaries of a perceived economic region. But the Rappen league, in a region as commercially open as the Upper Rhine, could never circumscribe a self-contained economic community. Its interests were overlaid by, and had to adjust to, the commercial imperatives of a much wider transregional and on occasion international market in meat, in which Strasbourg was the dominant player.

In any case, meat provisioning came to be overshadowed as the century drew to a close by the more urgent necessity of obtaining

---

[156] StAFr, B 5 XI xix, fo. 341$^{r-v}$, 13 Sept. 1563; cf. GLA 81/55; StAFr, B 5 XI xix, fo. 377$^{v}$–379$^{r}$, 14 Jan. 1564; ibid. fo. 391$^{v}$, 20 Mar. 1564; ibid. fo. 392$^{v}$–393$^{r}$, 20 Mar. 1564; ibid. fo. 468$^{r}$–469$^{v}$, 19 Jan. 1565.       [157] Vogt, 'Grandeur et décadence', 132.
[158] Ibid. 133.

adequate stocks of grain to feed a population hard hit by a string of bad harvests, and consequent dearth and famine. Whereas the Rappen league found itself discussing grain provisioning repeatedly in the early 1570s and again in the mid-1580s,[159] the supply of meat was rarely a contentious issue until the very end of the century. Only a meat shortage in 1574/5 led to a brief flurry of activity to stem the rise in prices. This was set in motion by complaints initially voiced by the third Estate of Outer Austria before archduke Ferdinand of Tirol in person at a territorial diet in May 1574,[160] though it was not until February the following year that a meat diet of the Rappen league as a whole was finally convened.[161] The delegates were unanimous that forestalling must be stopped, but less sure about how best to do so; the problem was worst, they noted, in the county of Montbéliard, where local forestallers and others from Porrentruy and the Franches Montagnes were active, just as they had been earlier in the century.[162] That made it all the more regrettable that Montbéliard was the only Württemberg territory in Alsace to which the provisions of the Rappen meat ordinances had never applied. As a consequence, the Montbéliard authorities complained that their butchers and cattle-dealers were being treated as foreigners and excluded from the Outer Austrian markets—an old accusation now reheated.[163] Indeed, on one occasion the Ensisheim government was only prepared to allow a consignment of cattle to pass through on its way to Strasbourg on condition that the city's butchers must in future produce certificates to show that their cattle had been bought in France, Burgundy, Savoy, or Switzerland—anywhere as long as it was not Montbéliard.[164] The latter's cattle-dealers were instead driven to using secret tracks through the mountains to Lorraine in order to get their beasts to northern outlets.[165]

[159] Although the Rappen league itself was formally dissolved in 1584, police diets continued to be convened by the Outer Austrian government for the circulation area of the Rappen coinage.

[160] StAFr, B 5 IXa iii, fo. 273[r], 13 May 1574; B 5 XI xxiv, fo. 6[r]–8[r], 10 Jan. 1575.

[161] Cf. ADHR, E-dépôt 4: AMAm, AA 25, 31 Jan. 1575; AMC, HH 59/58; SABs, Fleisch K 2; AAEB, B 209/6.          [162] ADHR, C 182/1, 21 Feb. 1575.

[163] ADHR, 1 C 879/9, 4 Apr. 1575; 1 C 182/1, 11 Apr. 1575.

[164] Jean Lebeau and Jean-Marie Valentin (eds.), *L'Alsace au siècle de la Réforme 1482–1621: Textes et Documents* (Nancy, 1985), 42–43.

[165] AAEB, B 209/6, 14 May 1575. For attempts to suppress forestalling in the bishopric of Basel cf. ADHR, C 182/1, n.d. (before 3 Mar. 1575); AAEB, B 342, fo. 106[v]–107[r], 17 Aug. 1575; B 209/6, 30 Aug. 1575.

The delegates were far from unanimous, however, on the suspension of meat sales during Lent. The Baden-Durlach representatives were under instructions to withhold assent; the Württemberg emissaries were only prepared to suspend meat sales on Saturdays and Sundays; Basel, though not in principle opposed, observed that one should eat what the Lord had provided.[166] These responses by the leading Protestant associates and members of the Rappen league were much less emollient than they had been twenty years earlier. Nor was there any consensus on pricing, Strasbourg, as usual, advocating a higher tariff than anyone else.[167] On 23 February 1575 a new ordinance was finally agreed, subject to referral. It suggested that the unitary price structure, abandoned in 1560, should be readopted, with the best beef to be sold throughout the Rappen area at $4\frac{1}{2}d$. Rappen per lb. till late July, and thereafter pasture cattle at $4d$. Rappen per lb.[168] But in its response Basel disclosed that it had already conceded slightly higher rates to its butchers, and took up its old refrain that the best policy would be to stamp out unlicensed village butchers and reserve the trade exclusively to the towns.[169] When the city received a copy of the printed mandate a month later, it took exception to certain clauses which, it claimed, were prejudicial to the Swiss Confederation (although unspecified, these undoubtedly referred to the free passage of goods guaranteed by the 1511 treaty). Indeed, the council demanded that its name be deleted from the list of signatories.[170] This all sounds rather more dramatic than it was, for Basel also promised to observe the mandate as far as lay in its powers. Sélestat, too, signalled its agreement, with the proviso that its location within the Strasbourg coinage area entailed some adjustments to the published price tariff.[171]

Whether the towns and lordships of northern Upper Alsace were in fact willing to adhere to a unitary tariff, after the concessions of 1560, is altogether doubtful. In August 1575 the Ensisheim authorities accused Egenolph von Rappoltstein of exceeding the permitted price ceiling in his lordship of Ribeaupierre: his excuse was

---

[166] ADHR, C 182/1, 21 Feb. 1575.
[167] Ibid. This confirms Strasbourg's participation in the deliberations, although the city does not appear as a signatory on the published mandate.
[168] SABs, Fleisch K 2, 23 Feb. 1575; cf. AAEB, B 209/6.
[169] ADHR, C 182/1, 16 Mar. 1575; cf. SABs, Fleisch K 2.
[170] Ibid. 30 Mar. 1575.
[171] ADHR, C 182/1, 28 Mar. 1575; cf. AMSé, HH 36/9, 18 Mar. 1575.

that all his neighbours were doing likewise.[172] In what then appears to be a significant climb-down, the government informed him that he should promulgate a meat tariff for Ribeaupierre sufficient to ensure continuity of supplies throughout the year—in effect, an open invitation to raise prices to an appropriate level.[173] Scattered evidence indicates that meat prices in Alsace fluctuated over the next decade, but could in general be pegged at $4\frac{1}{2}d.$ or at most $5d.$ Rappen per lb.[174]

In the Breisgau, Freiburg struggled hard to hold the price of pasture cattle at $4d.$ Rappen,[175] but it had to concede that not all its Austrian neighbours owned such extensive pastures (both Breisach[176] and Endingen[177] registered protests), while margravial subjects in Hachberg villages were already selling at $4\frac{1}{2}d.$ Rappen. Confronted with these uncomfortable facts, the Outer Austrian government capitulated, and in 1576 reverted to the spirit of the 1560 negotiations. But this time it proposed that each 'region' should draw up its own price tariff. What it meant by 'region' is unclear, but it seems that Ensisheim was not thinking in terms of the districts of Outer Austria flanking the Rhine (*breisgauisches* and *sundgauisches Gestade*), but of the two halves of the Rappen coinage area bisected by the river. That, at least, is what can be deduced from Freiburg's rather half-hearted shouldering of the responsibility for summoning the totality of Breisgau lords and towns, whether Austrian vassals or not, to an assembly to decide on meat pricing for the coming year.[178]

How far this decision—which all but acknowledged that the Rappen area no longer constituted (if it ever had) a coherent economic region in terms of meat provisioning—served as a precedent in the succeeding years is hard to determine. Certainly, local consultations continued in the Breisgau: in 1578, at a time when

[172] ADHR, E 707, 26 Aug. 1575.    [173] Ibid. 29 Feb. 1576.

[174] Cf. ibid. 11 Apr. 1576; ibid. 29 Aug. 1580; AMRb, BB 1, fo. 47ʳ, 25 Apr. 1579; fo. 66ʳ, 8 Aug. 1579; fo. 181ᵛ, 20 Apr. 1585. For comparison, prices in Rouffach in the Upper Mundat varied between $4\frac{1}{2}d.$ and $5d.$ Rappen from the late 1570s until the end of the century. AMRf, HH 3.

[175] StAFr, B 5 XI xxiv, fo. 116ᵛ–117ʳ, 8 Aug. 1575.

[176] Cf. ibid. fo. 121ᵛ–123ʳ, 16 Aug. 1575.    [177] GLA 81/56, 17 Sept. 1575.

[178] StAFr, B 5 XI xxiv, fo. 213ʳ–216ʳ, 16 Mar. 1576. Freiburg wrote to the commander of the Knights of St John in Heitersheim; the margravial officials of Hachberg and Badenweiler; the count of Tübingen's officials in Lichteneck; the lords of Staufen; the administrator of the *Kirchspiel* Kirchhofen; the senior bailiff of the St Gallen lordship of Ebringen; as well as to Breisach, Neuenburg, Kenzingen, Endingen, Waldkirch, and Burkheim.

Freiburg was agonizing over a glut of meat and trying (without success) to persuade Ensisheim to call a diet to discuss price *reductions*,[179] it suggested another meeting to the margravial official in Badenweiler, whose task should be to reach an agreement for the Breisgau, and disregard Alsace.[180] But a new ordinance for the entire area of the Rappen league, issued in June 1579, which in most respects simply reiterated the terms of the 1555 and 1575 edicts, made no mention of 'regional' variations or differential pricing.[181]

The last meat diets of the sixteenth century were not summoned until 1597, nearly twenty years after the preceding ordinance had been published, and a good thirteen years after the Rappen coinage league had formally been dissolved. Yet the principle of co-operation across territorial, political, and indeed confessional, boundaries remained intact. No longer were assemblies convened in the name of the Rappen league; instead, Outer Austria and its neighbouring princes, cities, and Estates were described as belonging to the *Verein*, or association of those lying within the circulation area of the Rappen penny (which continued to be minted),[182] a neutral term designed to gloss over the upheavals which had led to the demise of the league itself. The long elapse from the previous ordinance of 1575 demonstrates that price stability in the mean time had made further deliberations unnecessary. But the two diets of 1597, together with a revising assembly the following year, were held in circumstances which boded ill for the future of regional economic co-operation on the southern Upper Rhine. Indeed, they contributed to a crisis in meat provisioning which saw the mart at Cernay wither from a major regional entrepôt to no more than a local market centre supplying those able to reach it in a day's journey. The root cause of this sudden reversal of fortune lay in renewed attempts, well-intentioned but ill-conceived, to prevent forestalling and to protect the Cernay market. An ordinance drawn up on 20 March 1597 for 'these lands above the Landgraben', as Colmar phrased it,[183] failed to find acceptance because it had set prices too low,[184] so that a fresh assembly was set down for 17 June.

---

[179] Ibid. fo. 474ᵛ–475ʳ, 1 Mar. 1578.    [180] Ibid. fo. 502ʳ–504ᵛ, 9 May 1578.
[181] StAFr, A I VI e ε 52, 1579–12 Sept. 1597: 18 June 1579.
[182] Cf. AAEB, B 209/6, pp. 126–28, 20 Mar. 1597.
[183] AMC, HH 103/17, 10 Apr. 1597.
[184] Cf. AMRf, HH 3, 20 Apr. 1597; ibid. 17 May 1597; AMC, HH 103/12, 17 May 1597; ADHR, 1 C 104/3, 14 May 1597 (Sélestat).

But trouble was already brewing elsewhere. At the end of March three Porrentruy butchers complained that two of their Ensisheim counterparts, claiming to act on their lords' (that is, the town council's) behalf, had sought to foreclose on cattle which the former had bought from peasants in the Doller valley above Masevaux and left with the vendors for fattening until Easter.[185] A petition submitted by two of the Porrentruy butchers makes it clear that they had also been prevented from buying cattle direct throughout the territory of the bishop of Basel, even though there was no shortage of beasts at the time.[186] This incident gives an inkling of what the Outer Austrian government was up to. For it tabled proposals for discussion at the July assembly which, if adopted, would once again have curtailed the free market in meat, required all transactions to take place at Cernay, and banned foreigners from its market.[187] These proposals amounted to a regression to the principles which had so clearly failed earlier in the century, and they provoked a predictably hostile response.

Those on the margins of the Rappen coinage area were quick to react. The town of Delémont, in the centre of the bishopric of Basel, declared that it would have great difficulty in denying market access to 'foreign' neighbouring lordships on Bernese or Solothurn territory, whose inhabitants lived principally from pastoralism, and with whom cattle constituted the sole commodity of exchange. It also objected to a ban on 'forestalling', since the town lay distant from any cattle mart and depended on passing merchants for the sale of its cattle. Moreover, to demand certificates of origin for all the cattle passing through Delémont would be both impractical and costly, since far more cattle were re-exported than slaughtered there.[188] These objections were laid before the diet by the bishop's emissary, Heinrich Dochtermann,[189] but the final mandate took little account of them. Instead, it introduced a fresh distinction between fatstock and lean stock. The former could only be sold to Rappen members at market, and was on no account to

[185] ADHR, 1 C 183/17(a), 27 Mar. 1597; cf. AAEB, B 351, fo. 42ʳ⁻ᵛ.

[186] ADHR, 1 C 187/17(b), n.d. (Mar. 1597).

[187] The proposals do not survive as such, but their contents can be inferred from the protests which they elicited.

[188] AAEB, B 209/6, 12 June 1597; cf. the milder objections of St-Ursanne, ibid. 10 June 1597.

[189] Cf. AAEB, B 351, fo. 72ᵛ, 15 June 1597. A protocol of the negotiations is in AMRf, HH 3, 17 June 1597.

be exported, whereas lean cattle could be bought freely by members throughout the countryside for fattening and eventual resale. The prohibition on meat sales during fasts was also renewed.[190] Although the bishop of Basel agreed to accept the new mandate, he pointed out that his subjects were deeply unhappy about it.[191] Basel and Strasbourg, too, expressed reservations. The latter held off replying to the ordinance until it had a chance to consult both Colmar[192] and Basel.[193] When it did, the city was concerned above all that the terms of the mandate were designed to protect Austrian subjects first and foremost, and would, in effect, exclude Strasbourg from the meat markets of Upper Alsace.[194] In particular, the imposition of tolls, from which Austrian subjects were exempt, would disadvantage Strasbourg's butchers, since they were only to be levied on routes leading northwards from Cernay. The city council also claimed (somewhat disingenuously) that its butchers should not have to pay the Rappen price tariff in their own coin, since the Rappen and (stronger) Strasbourg penny, it insinuated, were commonly exchanged at par,[195] thereby causing them to lose money (to which the Outer Austrian government tartly riposted that prices could readily be rebased in kreutzers or other imperial coin).[196] For its part, Basel refused to reply to the government at all.[197]

The publication of the ordinance went ahead, therefore, without the explicit consent of several key players. Not surprisingly, the government in Ensisheim found it necessary to convene a new assembly in April 1598 to review its shortcomings.[198] It transpired that not only subjects of the bishop of Basel but those of the abbey of Murbach and peasants from the county of Hauenstein in the Black Forest as well were adamant that the ordinance placed them at a grievous disadvantage, on account of their geographical location and the nature of their agricultural economy. All depended largely on pastoralism for their livelihood and, lying on the fringes

---

[190] StAFr, A I VI e ε 52, 1579–12 Sept. 1597: 18 June 1597; cf. AAEB, B 209/6.

[191] Ibid. 27 June 1597.      [192] AMC, HH 103/16, 21 June 1597.

[193] SABs, Fleisch K 2, 21 June 1597.

[194] Ibid. 11 July 1597 (Strasbourg to Basel).

[195] ADHR, 1 C 104/3, 53, 2 July 1597; cf. SABs, Fleisch K 2, 11 July 1597; AMC, HH 103/4, 11 July 1597.

[196] ADHR, 1 C 104/3, 54, 24 July 1597 (draft). If this were to happen, it stated, 'gibt es ein guets conveniencz vnd glichmeßige proportion'.

[197] Cf. SABs, Fleisch K 2, 15 July 1597. Its reservations can partly be inferred from its correspondence with Strasbourg.

[198] Cf. ibid. 31 Mar. 1598; AAEB, B 209/6, 31 Mar. 1598.

of the Rappen coinage area, were at once remote from the main
cattle markets and beholden to trade with their immediate neighbours beyond the coinage area. The government and the other
Rappen associates therefore agreed to allow the Hauensteiners to
sell their lean meat freely to Switzerland and Swabia, provided that
they reserved their fatstock for consumers within the Rappen area.
Similarly, butchers and cattle-traders from Porrentruy, the Franches
Montagnes, Delémont, and St-Ursanne should be permitted to trade
with La Neuveville (on Lake Biel), Biel, Moutier, and the Aargau,
so long as fat cattle from those districts found their way to markets
in the Rappen area. A further concession was made to Strasbourg
(and to Sélestat), in view of the greater value of the Strasbourg penny,
that their butchers could buy the best beef at $4\frac{1}{2}d$. Strasbourg, a
halfpenny less than the $5d$. Rappen on the published tariff.[199]

But these measures, however much they might bring relief to particular areas, did nothing to revive the Cernay market in the longer
term. Foreigners remained excluded from it, and that only encouraged greater recourse to forestalling, as informal deals outside the
market were struck between peasants and foreign cattle-dealers to
export livestock illegally, thus denuding Cernay of supplies.[200] In
its place, new markets sprang up. The mart at Montbéliard, hitherto in Cernay's shadow, began to flourish after 1600, attracting
trade from France and the Franche-Comté, which soon became the
preferred outlet for cattle raised in the Franches Montagnes and
around Porrentruy. Even cattle from Outer Austria itself were driven
to Montbéliard for sale. Strasbourg and other buyers from Lower
Alsace and Swabia now had recourse to Montbéliard, and drove
their cattle home through Lorraine and down the *Zaberner Steige*,
thereby avoiding the area of Rappen circulation and Outer Austria.[201]
Around the same time, a new cattle mart was established at St-Dié,
on the western flanks of the Vosges in Lorraine,[202] which not only
drew cattle away from Cernay, but stimulated a secondary market
at Villé, which experienced a sudden boom.[203] As a result (as the

---

[199] ADHR, 1 C 104/4, 5, 22 Apr. 1598; cf. AMC, HH 103/20; AMMh, IV A 44/2.

[200] Vogt, 'Grandeur et décadence', 134–35.

[201] Ibid. 137–38. They also drove cattle through the Val de Villé to Scherwiller,
thereby passing through Austrian territory, but the Val de Villé, lying north of the
Landgraben, had never been included in the Rappen coinage area. ADHR, 1 C
104/3, 50, 15 July 1597; ibid. 52, 16 July 1597.

[202] ADHR, 1 C 104/5, 5, 27 Mar. 1600.

[203] ADHR, 1 C 104/3, 55, 24 July 1597.

toll-collector and town clerk of Cernay lamented in 1601), often only two or three cattle-dealers from Belfort visited the market there, whereas twenty years previously it had been flourishing. The only remedy, the two officials argued, was to lift all restrictions on access to, and trade at, the Cernay market.[204]

The Rappen area authorities were both alarmed and perplexed at this turn of events. Sélestat—by now a long-standing associate, though not a member, of the Rappen coinage area—complained to the government in Ensisheim in the spring of 1603 that Swabian cattle-dealers, in defiance of the ban, were buying up cattle at Cernay for resale at higher prices in Montbéliard.[205] Discussions on how to remedy the situation proved abortive. The administration in Ensisheim introduced passports for its own subjects, to prevent cattle being exported illegally,[206] a measure which could only stifle the market still further. Another suggestion was to blockade the mountain passes in the Vosges, though even Ensisheim could divine that this was not the way forward![207] The Rappen delegates finally pinned their hopes on the peace negotiations in Hungary and Poland, which would allow those who had traditionally bought cattle there, Swabians and Bavarians to the fore, to resume business and stop descending on the Cernay market.[208] These bizarre proposals testify to an extraordinary blindness on the part of the authorities in the Rappen area, when the obvious solution was staring them in the face—restore a free market in cattle and lift all restrictions on trade, as their own butchers and the Cernay officials kept telling them.[209]

Finally the Outer Austrian authorities yielded to pressure and changed tack, but in such a way as almost to vitiate their new policy. Both to combat forestalling (market evasion) and to stimulate the flagging Cernay market, trading restrictions were indeed suspended, but simultaneously tolls on cattle driven away from Cernay were not only raised sharply but applied differentially to boot, with foreigners being required to pay double the rate for Rappen members.[210] Two years later, moreover, the provisions were tightened again to bar foreigners from the market unless they could produce

---

[204] ADHR, 1 C 104/5, 9, 12 Aug. 1601.
[205] AMSé, AA 167/3, 16 Apr. 1603; HH 42/3, 25 May 1603.
[206] AMSé, HH 42/2, 20 Mar. 1604.      [207] AMSé, AA 167/6, 6 Aug. 1604.
[208] AMSé, HH 36/3, 9/19 Aug. 1604.      [209] Vogt, 'Grandeur et décadence', 136.
[210] ADHR, 1 C 105/1, 5, 17 Nov. 1603.

a certificate indicating that they were exporting cattle for domestic use alone.[211] It comes as no surprise that these half-hearted concessions failed to give a lasting boost to commerce at the Cernay cattle market, which subsided into merely local significance alongside its rivals in Burgundy and Lorraine.

The decline of the Cernay market stands as a symptom of the failure of the Rappen coinage authorities to devise a system of meat provisioning which would reconcile their perception of common regional economic interests and the reality of the Upper Rhine as an international transit route for cattle. In the course of the sixteenth century they had shown a growing awareness that their economic interests could not simply be defined by membership of the Rappen league alone. First Sélestat, because of its close economic ties to its neighbours south of the Landgraben, and then Strasbourg (by *force majeure*, as it were) were brought into the circle of participants. The Ensisheim government had come to a similar recognition over the status of Outer Austria's frontiers. The towns of the eastern Black Forest were allowed to go their own way, since it was finally accepted that they belonged to adjacent coinage areas, whatever their political affiliation to Outer Austria. Villingen, in fact, had turned the tables in 1597 by suggesting to count Albrecht of Fürstenberg, when calling for a Swabian meat diet to be convened, that among its other neighbours it would be appropriate to invite Freiburg im Breisgau to take part.[212]

Regional co-operation over meat provisioning on the basis of the circulation area of the Rappen coinage continued after the formal collapse of the Rappen league itself in 1584: that in itself is a testimony to the existence of a perceived regional solidarity driven directly by economic needs rather than being defined by political or territorial categories. But the Rappen authorities found it almost impossible to accept that the meat market at Cernay could be the object of legitimate interest to those well beyond their frontiers, or that free trade was more likely to secure adequate provisioning than a welter of restrictions and prohibitions, all of which were constantly evaded or subverted. In this regard it was particularly damaging that Montbéliard's relations with the Rappen league were never satisfactorily resolved. Had count Friedrich's overtures after

[211] ADHR, 1 C 105/2, 16, 28 Mar. 1605.
[212] Baumann and Tumbült, *Mitteilungen aus dem f. fürstenbergischen Archive*, ii. 691 (no. 936).

1577 succeeded, the county would have become integrated into the web of commercial and financial interests which bound the Rappen league together. The economic pull of the Rappen area towards Burgundy in terms of meat provisioning would have acquired institutional expression, as the limits of the southern Upper Rhine as an economic region shifted visibly south-westwards. Instead, Montbéliard stayed outside the Rappen area; its merchants were treated as foreigners, so that their commercial activity remained a constant irritation to the Rappen authorities, to the point where Montbéliard's market began to supplant Cernay's.

After that, attempts to supervise the meat trade on the southern Upper Rhine were largely abandoned. In the midst of the chaos of the monetary inflation of the early 1600s (the *Kipper- und Wipperzeit*) and the onset of hostilities in the Thirty Years War, a last flicker of regulatory activity was discernible in 1625. Had the struggle been in vain? Eberhard Gothein's verdict is pithy enough: 'This [meat provisioning] policy is remarkable, all the same, because it shows how political and religious animosities and particularist jealousies could be repressed and overcome for the sake of achieving a cherished socio-political goal. It is only regrettable that these uniting forces addressed themselves to a task incapable of solution.'[213]

Yet what drove the authorities on the southern Upper Rhine was not, I would suggest, so much a commitment to an unrealistic objective of 'good police', but an awareness of common economic needs within a regional framework. That perception, however, was bound to create tensions between regional identity and solidarity couched in terms of self-sufficiency, and the commercial reality of the Upper Rhine as an artery of trade reaching out beyond its regional frontiers.

[213] Gothein, *Wirtschaftsgeschichte des Schwarzwaldes*, 505.

# 8

# The Regional Provisioning of Grain

## I

Unlike the constant struggle to regulate the meat market on the southern Upper Rhine, the provisioning of grain rarely presented the authorities with a serious challenge until the last third of the sixteenth century, when a series of harvest failures, possibly exacerbated by demographic pressure, led to repeated bouts of dearth and famine. Not only was the Upper Rhine self-sufficient in all types of grain, with rye and spelt the predominant crops, it commonly exported surpluses to its neighbours, principally the Swiss. Alsace, and especially its southernmost part, the Sundgau, was more of a bread basket than the Breisgau, on account of its warmer climate and lower rainfall, but even on the right bank of the Rhine peasants from the Markgräflerland habitually sold their produce at the Basel market. Even the Ajoie, the territory of the bishops of Basel, although better-known for its upland cattle-pastures, grew vines and corn on the lower lands around Porrentruy.[1]

Hence the Upper Rhine was an 'open' region in terms of grain supplies, that is to say, the authorities were under no compulsion—except in times of dearth—to control access to markets, to restrict exports, or to strive for self-sufficiency within a defined area. Their only concern was to prevent *Fürkauf*, understood in this context not as a general hostility to commerce or towards foreigners, but in the exact sense of forestalling, pre-empting the workings of a

---

[1] Anne-Marie Dubler, 'Das Fruchtwesen der Stadt Basel von der Reformation bis 1700', *Jahresbericht des Staatsarchivs Basel-Stadt*, 1968, Beilage, 28. Cf. the council of Porrentruy's declaration in 1585 that the majority of its population lived from tillage and viticulture, as justification for its plea to be allowed to export grain from the Ajoie. ABP, I/IV, 54, 3/27 June 1585. This statement, however, should be set alongside Porrentruy's submission earlier in the century, quoted in Chapter 7, which argued that the district lived from cattle-rearing alone! This serves to underline the point that all such submissions *pro bono suo* must be read against the grain. Porrentruy served both as an entrepôt for cattle-dealers from the upland fringes of the bishopric of Basel and as the distribution centre for local arable produce and wine.

free market by buying corn on the ear direct from the peasantry or at unlicensed markets in the countryside. Only when shortages beckoned did speculation in grain—buying cheap, hoarding, selling dear (known as *Fürkauf auf Mehrschatz*, or forestalling for profit)—become the target of public prohibitions;[2] then, too, the desire to conserve dwindling stocks of grain within a given territory prompted bans on exports, though these (as we shall see) were subject to innumerable exceptions.

Whereas with meat the Rappen league had depended on supplies brought into its area either from its fringes or from abroad, with grain its members traded freely throughout the Upper Rhine. Freiburg, for instance, regularly bought grain at Strasbourg,[3] whose famous granary, the largest in the region, doled out sacks of corn in times of dearth to needy customers from both near and far. Again, the close commercial ties across the Landgraben between Colmar and Sélestat, which had led to the latter's inclusion in the Rappen league's meat ordinances, were reflected in a lively trade in grain between the two communes.[4] Cities and lordships had their own corn markets and often granaries as well. No one market dominated the region's supplies, in contrast to Cernay's pivotal role in the cattle trade, though Basel's geographical location and political affiliation (after 1501) made it a centre for exports to the Confederation.

Such exports are documented from the early fifteenth century, though they are likely to have occurred much earlier,[5] given the

[2] On the various types of *Fürkauf* see Hans-Gerd von Rundstedt, *Die Regelung des Getreidehandels in den Städten Südwestdeutschlands und der deutschen Schweiz im späteren Mittelalter und im Beginn der Neuzeit* (*Vierteljahrschrift für Sozial- und Wirtschaftsgeschichte*, suppl. 10) (Stuttgart, 1930), 101–33.

[3] Karl Friedrich Müller, *Geschichte der Getreidehandelspolitik, des Bäcker- und Müllergewerbes der Stadt Freiburg i. Breisgau im 14., 15. und 16. Jahrhundert* (*Zeitschrift der Gesellschaft für Beförderung der Geschichts-, Altertums- und Volkskunde von Freiburg, dem Breisgau und den angrenzenden Landschaften*, suppl. 3) (Freiburg im Breisgau, 1926), 29.

[4] von Rundstedt, *Regelung des Getreidehandels*, 44. In this respect the corn trade on the Upper Rhine corresponded to the general pattern in south German towns, which dealt multilaterally with each other, unlike the Hanseatic cities, which controlled their own areas of production and consumption. Cf. Wolfgang Habermann and Heinz Schlotmann, 'Der Getreidehandel in Deutschland im 14. und 15. Jahrhundert: Ein Literaturbericht', pt. 1, *Scripta Mercaturae*, 11:2 (1977), 31.

[5] von Rundstedt, *Regelung des Getreidehandels*, 33. Hektor Ammann, 'Elsässisch-schweizerische Wirtschaftsbeziehungen im Mittelalter', *Elsaß-Lothringisches Jahrbuch*, 7 (1928), 45–46; Ehrensperger, 'Basels Stellung', 32–33.

dependence of the inner cantons in particular on large-scale pastoralism. Around one-third of Switzerland's annual consumption, it
has been reckoned, needed to be imported, with Alsace, Swabia,
and Lombardy the principal suppliers. In the Forest cantons hardly
any grain was grown; in the mountainous districts of the Jura in
the west and in much of eastern Switzerland there was rarely
sufficient corn; only in the Swiss midlands, the belt of lowland
stretching from below Lake Geneva to the Thurgau, could the
population expect to satisfy its needs locally in normal years: here
Bern, Solothurn, and the Aargau were occasionally able to send
small surpluses to their neighbours.[6]

For most of northern Switzerland Basel acted as the conduit of
grain supplies from the Upper Rhine, and it became a commonplace to refer to the Sundgau as the granary and wine-cellar of
the Swiss. Despite periodic hostilities between the city and Austria
during the fifteenth century, the mutual need to ensure the free
passage of goods to the Basel market had always been recognized, as in the Breisach Accord of 1449 ('the capstone to the well-
nigh hundred-year struggle between Austria and Basel', in Rudolf
Wackernagel's words), which put an end to the Old Zürich War
and restored customs exemption, safe conduct, and free trade
between the hitherto warring parties.[7] Its role was most evident in
times of dearth, when the city's imposition of export restrictions
elicited hefty protests from its fellow-Confederates. Basel's mandate of 1556, for example, banning grain purchases by foreigners
was denounced as contravening good neighbourly relations at a
Confederate diet in Baden (Aargau) in 1560.[8] One result of the pressure put on Basel to display Helvetic solidarity was that the city
was obliged to grant large consignments of grain to a variety of
Swiss cantons in 1557 and 1560, as well as in subsequent years of
dearth,[9] though where and how it acquired the extra grain is uncertain. What we do know is that even Basel was driven to make

---

[6] Frank Göttmann, *Getreidemarkt am Bodensee: Raum—Wirtschaft—Politik—
Gesellschaft (1650–1810)* (Beiträge zur südwestdeutschen Wirtschafts- und Sozialge-
schichte, 13) (St Katherinen, 1991), 174; Reinhold Bosch, 'Der Kornhandel der Nord-,
Ost-, Innerschweiz und der ennetbirgischen Vogteien im 15. und 16. Jahrhundert'
(Diss. phil. Zürich, 1913), 2.

[7] *Urkundenbuch der Stadt Basel*, vii, ed. Johannes Haller (Basel, 1899), 336;
Rudolf Wackernagel, *Geschichte der Stadt Basel*, i (Basel, 1907), 599–600; Dubler,
'Fruchtwesen', 35.                                                [8] Ibid. 33–34.

[9] Ibid. 34 n. 29.

purchases in Strasbourg in years of extreme scarcity such as 1538, 1571, and 1586.[10]

Of course, it was not only Basel among the cities of the Upper Rhine which enjoyed close economic relations with the Swiss. Mulhouse's status as an associate member after 1515 ensured regular contacts, especially with the Protestant cantons. But perhaps the most striking example is Strasbourg itself, whose conclusion of a defensive alliance (*Burgrecht*) with its Zwinglian neighbours Zürich, Bern, and Basel in 1530 guaranteed the Swiss cities, *inter alia*, unimpeded access to Strasbourg's corn market, provided that they were only covering their own domestic requirements.[11] So intense, in fact, were the commercial links in grain provisioning between Switzerland and Alsace that proposals had already been put forward to regulate the corn trade on a regional basis at the end of the fifteenth century. During efforts to resurrect the Lower Union in 1491, a draft document for a renewed alliance with the Confederates proposed the abolition of any customs barriers and new tolls between the two parties, provided that free trade did not lead to forestalling.[12] By its terms the Swiss would in effect have been granted unrestricted access to the grain stocks of Alsace, thus foreshadowing the *Erbeinigung* concluded in 1511. While grain purchases were customarily for cash, less attention has been paid to the exchange of primary produce between Switzerland and Alsace, but a mandate issued by Lucerne in 1592 indicates that merchants from Basel and Strasbourg were accustomed to buy up butter and cheese in the inner cantons for resale on the Upper Rhine,[13] a practice that must surely date from well before the later sixteenth century.

[10] Bernard Vogler, 'Une alliance manquée: Strasbourg et les XIII cantons (1555–1789)', in *Cinq siècles des relations franco-suisses: Hommage à Louis-Edouard Roulet* (Neuchâtel, 1984), 114.

[11] Bosch, 'Kornhandel', 8; the text of the *Burgrecht* ibid. 114–15. On Strasbourg's economic links to Bern and Zürich cf. Vogler, 'Une alliance manquée', 113. Strasbourg had already been recorded as a grain exporter in the 14th century, though the evidence relates to Swabia, not Switzerland. Habermann and Schlotmann, 'Getreidehandel', 41. On the famous journey on the part of Zürich councillors by river to Strasbourg in 1576 with a cauldron of hot millet gruel cf. Rodolphe Reuss, *Die Hirsebreifahrt der Zürcher nach Straßburg 1576* (Zürich, 1976); Ammann, 'Elsässische-schweizerische Wirtschaftsbeziehungen', 37.

[12] von Rundstedt, *Regelung des Getreidehandels*, 33 n. 10; *Urkundenbuch der Stadt Basel*, ix, ed. Rudolf Thommen (Basel, 1905), 118 (no. 134).

[13] SALu, A 1 F 1, 910, 4 Nov. 1592; cf. Ammann, 'Elsässisch-schweizerische Wirtschaftsbeziehungen', 45.

## II

Against this background it is perhaps not surprising that the mandates which were periodically issued throughout the fifteenth and sixteenth centuries to prevent forestalling and the export of grain in times of dearth should frequently have failed to observe the boundaries within which meat provisioning was regulated, that is, largely (though not entirely) coterminous with the areas of coinage circulation, which in turn reflected ancient human and political divisions on the Upper Rhine. Regional corn ordinances often cast their net wider than meat ordinances, oblivious to such otherwise significant lines of demarcation as the Landgraben. That can be seen from ordinances issued in the name of the bishop of Strasbourg after 1400. In 1438—a year of great dearth—the bishop drew up a mandate to prohibit corn exports from a district which, to judge by its other signatories, embraced both Lower Alsace (the lords of Fleckenstein and Andlau, and the cities of Strasbourg and Sélestat) and a territory in Upper Alsace, namely the lordship of Ribeaupierre, together with Kenzingen in the northern Breisgau, which at that time was pawned to the city of Strasbourg.[14] Almost one hundred years later, in 1530, a mandate against corn forestalling was issued for the entirety of the bishopric's secular territories in Alsace 'in our lordship on this side of the Rhine from Haguenau as far as our lordship of the Upper Mundat, including the same', in other words, taking in the one part of the episcopal lands lying in Upper Alsace and within the orbit of the Rappen coinage league and its police ordinances.[15] Even when six weeks previously the bishop in his capacity as landgrave of Lower Alsace had called the latter's Estates to a diet at Molsheim to discuss the prevailing shortage of grain north of the Landgraben, summons to attend were sent to three members of the Decapolis situated in Upper Alsace (Colmar, Kaysersberg, and Turckheim), though none of them in fact turned up.[16]

[14] von Rundstedt, *Regelung des Getreidehandels*, 62; Karl Albrecht (ed.), *Rappoltsteinisches Urkundenbuch*, iii (Colmar, 1904), 505–9 (no. 1061). The treaty referred to exports from our 'bishopric and territories', suggesting that it was circumscribed by the boundaries of the Strasbourg diocese and/or the bishopric's secular territories. But even though the diocese included the northern tip of the lordship of Ribeaupierre, around Ste-Marie-aux-Mines, Kenzingen lay in the diocese of Constance.        [15] AMS, R 4, fo. 94ʳ–98ʳ, 2 Dec. 1530, here at fo. 94ʳ.
[16] ADBR, G 217, fo. 8ʳ–11ʳ, 25 Oct. 1530. No invitation was extended on this occasion to Munster (whose interests were often represented by Colmar).

This might be thought to be an aberration, for the following year another mandate against forestalling was promulgated for the traditional confines of Lower Alsace, namely the district between the Forest of Haguenau and the Eckenbach (Landgraben),[17] and that applied to subsequent ordinances in 1533 and 1545 as well.[18] But in 1552 the same thing occurred again, only this time in even more confusing circumstances. On 29 January that year two separate ordinances were proclaimed. The first was a general police ordinance for Alsace as a whole, issued in accordance with the terms of the 1551 statute for the Upper Rhenish Circle, which had divided the sprawling area of the Circle into four, with the bishop of Strasbourg as convenor of the Alsatian quarter.[19] In this context it was quite proper for the imperial Estates within Alsace as a whole to be summoned: alongside the Upper Alsatian cities of Colmar, Kaysersberg, Turckheim, and Munster there appeared as signatory the abbot of Munster.[20] But the second ordinance, which referred specifically to forestalling, agreed by the same parties (with the addition of the Mark of Marmoutier)[21] contains clauses virtually identical with a subsequent corn mandate issued by the bishop five months later for Lower Alsace alone, after a diet at which no Upper Alsatian lords or cities were present.[22]

The most likely explanation for this discrepancy is that the May 1552 ordinance for Lower Alsace, in addition to repeating earlier bans on forestalling, also contains a price tariff which was denominated in Strasbourg pence: mandates without tariffs were clearly not bound in the same way to the circulation area of a particular coinage. But this accounts neither for the odd 1530 ordinance, nor for the fact that subsequent ordinances for Lower Alsace alone —such as that in 1562—expressly invoked the precedent of the wider mandate of January 1552.[23] The point has been made earlier, of course, that ordinances for Lower Alsace never delimited

---

[17] ADBR, G 217, fo. 7ʳ–7(a)ᵛ, 31 Oct. 1531; cf. ibid. fo. 22ʳ–25ʳ, 211ʳ; AMS, R 3, fo. 198ʳ⁻ᵛ.

[18] ADBR, G 217, fo. 36ʳ–37ᵛ, 14 Oct. 1533; cf. AMS, X 267, 22 Oct. 1533 (and other copies in AMS, R 3, fo. 220ʳ–221ᵛ, 222ʳ–223ᵛ); ADBR, G 217, fo. 184ʳ, 10 Dec. 1545; cf. AMS, R 4, fo. 204ʳ.      [19] Dotzauer, *Reichskreise*, 250.

[20] AMS, R 5, fo. 8ʳ–26ʳ. Note that the abbot of Murbach and the lord of Ribeaupierre (both sucked into dependence upon Austria) were not party to the ordinance, despite being listed among the imperial Estates of the Upper Rhenish Circle. Cf. Dotzauer, *Reichskreise*, 238–39.

[21] ADBR, G 217, fo. 185ʳ; cf. AMS, R 5, fo. 81ʳ–82ʳ; AMO, AA 61/8.

[22] ADBR, G 217, fo. 197ʳ–198ʳ, 31 May 1552.      [23] Cf. SADa, D 21 A, 38/1.

their sphere of jurisdiction as tightly as those for Upper Alsace. Despite the apparent unambiguity of the formula 'from the Forest of Haguenau to the Eckenbach', the circulation of Strasbourg's coinage in the Ortenau and the presence in the latter of dependencies in the hands of lords whose primary holdings lay on the left bank of the Rhine—the counts of Hanau-Lichtenberg in the Hanauer Land,[24] or the bishops of Strasbourg themselves—ensured that Lower Alsatian mandates were enforced on parts of the right bank as well.

Because the free market in grain reduced the need to reach regional agreements except in times of real scarcity, it was largely left to individual territories and cities to issue their own mandates whenever necessary. Outer Austria imposed bans on grain exports, for instance, in 1482[25] and 1502,[26] though the latter provoked a hostile reaction from Basel. Once the Perpetual Accord (*Erbeinigung*) had been concluded between Austria and the Swiss in 1511, however, the legal basis for prohibiting exports from Outer Austrian territory to Basel and the Swiss interior was destroyed, though that did not prevent Outer Austrian third Estate members in Alsace clamouring for a renewed ban in 1516,[27] or further (temporary) injunctions being proclaimed in the decades that followed. *Per contram*, Basel was hardly in a position to complain too vociferously about the behaviour of the authorities in Ensisheim, given that it imposed export restrictions itself on its subjects in the Baselbiet at various times during the sixteenth century (as did the city of Strasbourg for its own dependent territory).[28]

Yet the flow of correspondence between Basel and Ensisheim shows that the authorities were aware of the need to avoid mutually crippling injunctions, and that a sense of regional economic cohesiveness and identity evident in the negotiations over meat provisioning was by no means lacking when shortages in the grain

---

[24] The counts of Hanau-Lichtenberg were regular signatories to Lower Alsatian corn ordinances throughout the sixteenth century. Cf. SADa, D 21 A, 38/1.

[25] TLA, Kopialbücher, ältere Reihe, Lit. C Embieten, fo. 373ᵛ, 24 May 1482.

[26] SABs, Missiven A 22, p. 22, 13 Aug. 1502; ibid. pp. 25–27, 23 Aug. 1502. In 1499 at a diet in Neuenburg the Estates of Outer Austria in a wide-ranging set of reform proposals—*ordnung und anschlag*—had urged the setting-up of granaries on both banks of the Rhine, to store wheat in particular. Johann Heinrich Schreiber (ed.), *Urkundenbuch der Stadt Freiburg im Breisgau*, ii (Freiburg im Breisgau, 1829), 675; Bischoff, *Gouvernés et gouvernants*, 104.

[27] ADHR, C 7, pp. 280–82, 5 Nov. 1516.

[28] Cf. AMS, X 264, 25 Sept. 1529; ibid. 13 Sept. 1539.

supply threatened. That emerges from the precautions taken by both Basel and Outer Austria to safeguard their grain stocks at the time of the first serious dearth on the southern Upper Rhine at the end of the 1520s. Already in late 1527—the year of the first regional meat ordinance of the Rappen league—Basel had instructed its bailiffs in the Baselbiet to stop corn being exported over the Hauenstein passes (to inner Switzerland) or beyond the Schachenmatt (into Alsace).[29] Early the following year, in what appears at first sight to be a tit-for-tat reprisal, the Outer Austrian government banned sales effected by forestalling on exports to those it termed 'the enemies of Austria' and their soldiery, though exactly who these enemies were was not specified.[30] That they did not include Basel, at any rate, is clear from an exchange of letters which reveals that the edict had been issued partly in response to Basel's own prompting.[31] An aggressive form of words, it seems, masked tentative attempts at co-ordination, if not full collaboration.

In the next two years on the Upper Rhine the grain harvest turned out poorly; the government in Ensisheim responded to calls from the Outer Austrian Estates to take steps against forestalling by issuing a territorial mandate in August 1529,[32] but it appears to have had little effect. By late 1530 the situation was so desperate that the Ensisheim administration was at last persuaded to summon a diet of all the powers of the region to discuss remedies. From the wording of the summons it is quite clear that this was to be an assembly of Rappen league delegates,[33] and the edict against forestalling which was duly agreed was signed by many of the powers who had earlier subscribed to the first comprehensive meat ordinance.[34] But, just as in this instance, there were significant omissions as well as inclusions. No mention was made of the lordships of Murbach, Ribeaupierre, or Hohlandsberg, or of the Württemberg territories in Alsace; of the imperial free cities, both Mulhouse and Turckheim were missing. But Basel—given its pivotal role in the grain trade with the Swiss—was a signatory from the outset (in marked contrast to Ensisheim's reluctance to include it in deliberations over the first meat ordinance), as were the bishop of Basel

---

[29] SABs, Missiven A 29, fo. 108^{r-v}, 20 Nov. 1527; ibid. fo. 109^r, 23 Nov. 1527. The precise location of the Schachenmatt is unclear.

[30] SABs, Frucht und Brot, M 1, 1, 28 Jan. 1528.     [31] Ibid. 1 Feb. 1528.

[32] StARf, 622, 3. Aug. 1529 (2 copies).     [33] Cf. AMC, HH 95/15, 9 Nov. 1530.

[34] AAEB, B 209/6, 2 Dec. 1530.

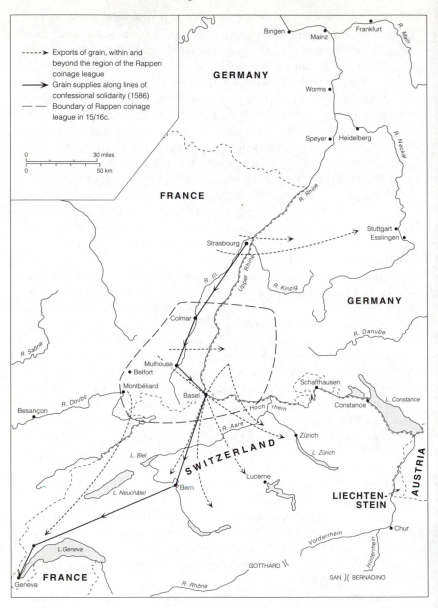

MAP 15. Regional grain provisioning

and (despite his coolness towards the Rappen league) margrave Ernst of Baden. The four Forest Towns on the *Hochrhein,* along with Villingen and Bräunlingen, also consented to adopt the grain ordinance—a telling sign of their dependence on grain supplies from the Rhine valley, whereas with meat they could afford to cock a snook at Ensisheim's attempts to command their attendance as Outer Austrian subjects.

But unlike the meat diets, this grain assembly of Rappen members in 1530 was superimposed on, and subsequent to, quite separate efforts to reach agreement on grain provisioning for the whole of Alsace, culminating in a general diet in Haguenau on 7 November 1530, to which the imperial cities of Upper Alsace had been invited.[35] Indeed, Kaysersberg claimed that the Outer Austrian government had subsequently accepted its provisions.[36] If that is so, it may help to explain the scope of the bishop of Strasbourg's mandate against forestalling previously mentioned, which bore the same date as that of the Rappen league's ordinance but was to be valid for all his territories, both north and south of the Landgraben, inasmuch as he could claim to be acting upon decisions reached at Haguenau a month earlier.

Two distinct strands of regional regulation of the grain trade can therefore be discerned. One took in Alsace as a whole (but ignored the right bank of the Rhine); the other dealt with the area of the Rappen league, or else of Lower Alsace (that is, the Strasbourg coinage area, which did spread across the river): but there is no clear indication how, or indeed whether, they were co-ordinated. One Austrian official, it is true, treated the Rappen league mandate of 1530 as if it applied merely to Outer Austria, for the bailiff of Delle in February 1531 tried to stop a burgher of Basel exporting grain bought in the Sundgau. But, as the city riposted, its burgher Wolfgang Heberling was not buying for profit or for resale beyond the area of the Rappen coinage league.[37] This should have been an open-and-shut case, but, astonishingly, the parties were

---

[35] Cf. AMC, HH 95/10, 5 Oct. 1530. The diet was summoned by the bailiff of Lower Alsace, Hans Jakob von Mörsberg. The fact that it was called by the imperial bailiff of Alsace (or Haguenau), rather than by the bishop of Strasbourg (the landgrave of Lower Alsace), underscores its application to (the imperial Estates of) Alsace as a whole. Von Mörsberg's invitation to the bishop of Strasbourg to attend is in ADBR, G 217, fo. 12ʳ, 12 Oct. 1530.          [36] AMC, HH 95/6, 10 Dec. 1530.

[37] SABs, Missiven A 28, fo. 328ᵛ, 4 Feb. 1531; ibid. fo. 329ᵛ–330ʳ, 23 Apr. 1531; ibid. fo. 333ᵛ, 4 Mar. 1531.

still haggling two years later over compensation which Heberling was demanding from the bailiff, who seemed unwilling to recognize the remit of the Rappen league.[38]

By then, the immediate crisis over grain supplies had given way to some good harvests. But that only confronted Basel with new difficulties, since itinerant petty grain-dealers (*Hodler*) from the interior of Switzerland, doubtless to make good the shortfall of recent harvests, began to descend on the Basel market to buy up corn in large quantities, with the result that prices remained unacceptably high. To alleviate the situation the city council approached the government in Ensisheim in the autumn to convene another grain diet of Rappen league members.[39] To assist its deliberations, Basel undertook to gather the latest information on the state of the grain market from places such as Zürich, Aarau, and Zofingen. But Ensisheim failed to react immediately[40]—probably because it regarded the problem as peculiar to Basel, rather than as an issue for the Rappen league as a whole.[41] Only in December 1533 is there any sign of a joint initiative, but this seems to have consisted of co-ordinating separate ordinances, such as the mandate which Basel had already put out in October, and promising to enforce them in each other's territory.[42] Out of Confederate solidarity Basel allowed the Swiss to purchase grain for household consumption, but that was not enough to placate the inner cantons, who used a Confederate diet at Baden (Aargau) to accuse Basel of discrimination.[43] What they really objected to, it transpired, was the high transport costs incurred by individual merchants, who were only permitted to buy and ship small consignments. Here Basel was willing to show some

---

[38] SABs, Missiven A 30, fo. 137ʳ–138ʳ, 15 July 1533.

[39] Ibid. fo. 120ᵛ–121ʳ, 17 Sept. 1533.

[40] Cf. Basel's reminder, ibid. fo. 126ʳ⁻ᵛ, 15 Oct. 1533.

[41] In its letter to Lucerne of 13 Dec. 1533 Basel referred to a 'renewed' ordinance issued in the name of the city, the Outer Austrian government, and the margrave of Baden, but it is probable that this refers to the first collective ordinance in 1530, since no other reference to a mandate in 1533 survives. Ibid. fo. 140ʳ–141ᵛ.

[42] Ibid. fo. 127ʳ–128ᵛ, 20 Oct. 1533; cf. ibid. fo. 135ʳ–136ᵛ, 19 Nov. 1533. At a diet in Lucerne on 16 December Basel claimed that the previous mandate agreed between the city, Outer Austria, and Baden had been so successful that they had now renewed their mandates, and that their collective character meant that Basel could not unilaterally derogate therefrom. Whether that statement refers to one mandate for the entire Rappen area, or to separate but co-ordinated ones for each territory is unfortunately not clear. Cf. *Amtliche Sammlung der älteren Eidgenössischen Abschiede*, iv. 1c, ed. Karl Deschwanden (Lucerne, 1878), 228–29 (no. 119).

[43] SABs, Missiven, A 30, fo. 129ᵛ–130ʳ, 28 Oct. 1533.

flexibility, for it allowed those without their own transport to band together into companies to share a joint load.[44]

When the same problem recurred at the end of the 1530s, Basel rather changed its tune. The forestallers, the city now claimed, were buying corn on the ear direct from the peasantry—as much as 20,000 sackfuls—and coarse cloth (*Zwilch*) to boot, which they planned to send to Italy or Romania![45] Since Basel had had to suffer accusations of hostility to free trade in the past (a pointed reference to the unpleasantness of 1533), the council now proposed that corn in any quantity should henceforth be freely available for purchase at the chartered markets, provided that forestalling in the countryside be rigorously prosecuted,[46] a policy in line with Basel's attitude towards meat provisioning. This was the view which it vouchsafed when approached for information by the Ensisheim government, apparently keen to draw up a mandate of its own against *Fürkauf* and the export of grain. Although the wording of this mandate,[47] and of a further one in 1543,[48] gives the impression of applying to Outer Austria alone, a subsequent passage-of-arms between Basel and Zürich in 1551 concerning the activities of 'an old *Hodler*', Felix Eygermann, who was buying grain at Basel's market in order to store it in the Sundgau for later resale, caused Basel to denounce his dealings as contravening the Outer Austrian ordinance on forestalling, by which clearly only a mandate intended to encompass the area of the Rappen league as a whole could have been meant.[49]

Certainly the Outer Austrian ordinance against forestalling in 1559, issued at a time of real, though not acute, shortage, despite its injunction to 'those residing within our jurisdiction', took the Rappen area as its wider framework of reference[50]—the bishop of

[44] Ibid. fo. 140ʳ–141ᵛ, 13 Dec. 1533; cf. SABs, Missiven B 1, pp. 219–21, 9 Mar. 1534.

[45] SABs, Missiven B 2, fo. 252ᵛ–253ʳ, 9 Aug. 1539; cf. Bosch, 'Kornhandel', 42.

[46] SABs, Missiven B 2, fo. 263ʳ–264ʳ, 13 Sept. 1539. The council had sent instructions to this effect to all its *Ämter* in August. SABs, Missiven A 31, fo. 20ᵛ, 9 Aug. 1539; cf. ibid. fo. 25ʳ, 13 Sept. 1539; Missiven B 2, fo. 200ʳ, n.d. (*circa* 1 Sept. 1539).

[47] ADHR, C 177/1, 12 Sept. 1539.

[48] Cf. Bosch, 'Kornhandel', 13–14. The mandate applied 'in dem bezirk unsers regiments verwaltigung', according to the extract printed in *Amtliche Sammlung der Älteren Eidgenössischen Abschiede*, iv. 1d, ed. Karl Deschwanden (Lucerne, 1882), 315.    [49] SABs, Missiven, A 33, pp. 49–50, 18 Feb. 1551.

[50] SAZh, A 55/1, 21 Oct. 1559; 'Das ouch niemanden . . . dheiner Commun oder gmeindt mith sonder personen in stetten, flecken, dörffern, oder gerichten in dem bezirckh vnser verwaltigung *vnd der Rappenmüntz* [my emphasis] gelegen gesessen

Basel, for instance, subsequently requested a copy to proclaim in his own territory.[51] Although the ordinance gave a nod towards Basel's view that corn should be freely available at chartered markets, it still drew the wrath of the Confederates on account of the limit on the quantity purchasable; as Zürich complained, it was simply not convenient or practicable for individuals to travel to markets on the Upper Rhine to satisfy their household requirements.[52] Despite the Swiss contention that the provisions contravened the *Erbeinigung*, the Ensisheim authorities showed no inclination to relax them so as to permit purchases outside the chartered markets or in commercial quantities. All they conceded was that, should insufficient corn be available at market, merchants might then have recourse to corn-staples or granaries (*Kästen*), provided that they had no intention of forestalling.[53]

Nevertheless, there were signs of a creeping rigidity in Ensisheim's attitude towards grain-dealing within the boundaries of Outer Austria as well. In 1563 merchants who had bought corn in Alsace and the Sundgau for resale in the Breisgau had been punished, though, as Freiburg protested, the practice was not only commonplace but necessary, since on the right bank of the Rhine grain was less plentiful than on the left. The town also reminded its superiors in Ensisheim that peasants from the Black Forest were accustomed to exchange their butter and cheese for grain at the Freiburg market. Not only would they suffer, therefore, but the Freiburg market would itself decline, all the more so (it alleged in tones reminiscent of Basel's) since rich reeves in the villages were buying corn on the ear from the peasantry and hoarding it for later speculative sale at market.[54] The government had, in fact, already toyed with a *dirigiste* policy ten years earlier when, faced with preparations for war on the Upper Rhine, it had ordered corn to be stockpiled in Breisach and Ensisheim (though without much success, as it later admitted).[55]

einich getreytt . . . ze kouffen nit zugelassen noch vergöndt werden . . .' Cf. Bosch, 'Kornhandel', 17.

[51] AAEB, B 335, fo. 76ʳ, n.d. (early Nov. 1559); cf. ibid. fo. 81ᵛ, 18 Nov. 1559. The mandate appears to have gone astray or been mislaid, for four years later Ensisheim sent the bishop another copy in response to his request for information about grain provisioning. AAEB, B 198/1, 4 June 1563.          [52] SAZh, A 55/1a, 11 Jan. 1560.

[53] Bosch, 'Kornhandel', 17–18.

[54] StAFr, B 5 XI xix, fo. 377ᵛ–379ʳ, 14 Jan. 1564.

[55] AAEB, B 198/1, 4 June 1563.

After mid-century harvest failures and consequent crises in grain provisioning became more frequent, so that not only the administration in Ensisheim but several Austrian district towns in Alsace as well resorted to precautionary measures against dearth, either by issuing their own local mandates against forestalling (as with Cernay and Thann) or by constructing their own granaries (as did Delle).[56] Then, in 1570, the Ensisheim government, in addition to renewing its restrictions on Swiss access to the markets of the southern Upper Rhine, set up three new Austrian corn-staples, to which its subjects were henceforth obliged to deliver their grain.[57] Sales at the Basel market were denied them: at the customs-posts officials unhitched horses from their carts, leaving the loads of grain stranded.[58] Free trade began to yield to protectionism and confessional solidarity to override the ties of reciprocal support which had bound the members of the Rappen league together.

# III

The subsistence crises of the last third of the sixteenth century, especially those in the early 1570s and mid-1580s, which affected many parts of western Europe, not just the Upper Rhine, are well-known in the historical literature, but there is no consensus about their underlying cause. Certainly, demographic growth during the century must have put pressure on food supplies and given farmers every incentive to turn land back from animal husbandry to tillage. But it is well-nigh impossible to suggest an accurate figure for the rate of population growth on the Upper Rhine in this period or to gauge what proportion of the land was returned to cereal cultivation. For neighbouring Switzerland a population increase of one-third between 1500 and 1600 has been posited,[59] but whether the tempo of growth remained steady, or accelerated palpably towards the end of the century, leading to more frequent acute food shortages, is uncertain. Moreover, even if more land was given over to

---

[56] ADTB, E-Dépôt 33: ACD, HH 1/1, 20 Mar. 1568.

[57] Seidel, *Oberelsaß*, 143; cf. SABe, A IV 41, RR, p. 244, 10 Feb. 1570. The Bernese protest mentions four staples, but this may include the recently established granary in Delle.

[58] *Amtliche Sammlung der älteren Eidgenössischen Abschiede*, iv. 2, ed. Joseph Karl Krütli (Bern, 1861), 489 (diet of 10 Feb. 1572); Bosch, 'Kornhandel', 22.

[59] Christian Pfister, *Bevölkerung, Klima und Agrarmodernisierung 1525–1860: Das Klima der Schweiz von 1525–1860 und seine Bedeutung in der Geschichte von Bevölkerung und Landschaft*, ii (Bern, 1984), 82.

tillage, on the recognition that cereals could feed more mouths per hectare than stock-rearing, the consequent reduction in the area of pasture and meadow brought problems of its own, namely a shortfall of manure, of draught capacity, and of animal protein. The population became trapped in a vicious circle of deteriorating nutrition, both in terms of quality and of quantity, and hence of greater mortality. As a consequence of what Christian Pfister has termed the 'manure gap', the productivity of grain tillage in western Europe stagnated for centuries.[60] In fact, all the agricultural ecotypes which he investigated for Switzerland—tillage, stock-rearing, and viticulture—were what he designates as 'systems of zero growth' (*Nullwachstumssysteme*), from which the peasantry could not break free, and which, with their marginal returns, were peculiarly susceptible to variations in climate.[61]

And it is in a climatic shift, rather than in population pressure, that Pfister would have us locate the fundamental reason for the late sixteenth-century subsistence crises. After a warm phase between 1530 and 1564, in which there were no shortages of fodder and very few poor vintages,[62] a colder, wetter period ensued. Cool springs followed by high rainfall in the high and late summer marked the successive periods of dearth in 1569–74, 1586–9, and 1593–7, all accompanied by flooding.[63] Whether these Swiss findings can be applied wholesale to the altogether warmer and drier Rhine valley is arguable, though the chronology of crisis years is largely identical. What can be ventured is that real famine beckoned if there were harvest failures several years in a row, when the population had no chance to replenish stocks; a single year of dearth could quickly be overcome. That seems indeed to have been the case on the Upper Rhine, where the cries of desperation—most audible in an unending litany of supplications to Strasbourg by communes in the Ortenau for rations from its capacious granary—rang out the loudest in 1573 and 1574, rather than at the beginning of the decade.[64]

The subsistence crises of the later sixteenth century did not destroy the sense of reciprocal responsibility between neighbours (in an area as fragmented as the Upper Rhine the maxim of 'every lordship for itself' would have spelt economic suicide), but they wrought

---

[60] Pfister, *Bevölkerung*, 127.    [61] Ibid. 60–61.
[62] Ibid. 81.    [63] Ibid. 63.
[64] See the extensive correspondence in AMS, IV 17/31–17/68; V 18/58.

a perceptible change in the way that mutual obligations were conceived. Economic co-operation between Rappen members across territorial boundaries was eroded by political imperatives in the first instance, and then increasingly by the pull of confessional solidarity. As the century progressed, grain provisioning came to be regulated more by co-ordination between the constituent members of the Rappen league rather than by collective ordinances agreed at assemblies of the league as a whole. The Ensisheim government recognized, for instance, that its 1570 mandate, issued in the name of archduke Ferdinand of Tirol, would remain a dead letter unless neighbouring authorities whose markets were patronized by Outer Austrian subjects followed suit.[65] But a blockade of the Basel market was hardly calculated to encourage such co-operation![66] In its protest to the Austrian bailiffs of Altkirch and Landser, however, Basel no longer claimed—as it had done to their counterpart in Delle in 1531—that as a member of the Rappen league it should not be treated as foreign territory, but rather that the Austrian embargo contravened the *Erbeinigung* of 1511.[67] The ground had shifted significantly: in Basel's argument, political allegiance to the Confederation now took precedence over membership of the Rappen league. Such an altered angle of vision could, in a different context, result in a discernible narrowing of focus. The committee of the Outer Austrian Estates, beset by the worsening situation over grain supplies, in 1574 urged a renewed territorial ordinance upon archduke Ferdinand, whose terms would prevent 'forestallers' exporting to markets in the margraviate of Baden. The southern lands of the margraviate, it seems, were now to be regarded as foreign territory rather than as lying within the Rappen coinage area.[68] An interesting sidelight on the potential disruption to trade within the region which territorially restrictive ordinances could cause is cast by a petition in the summer of that same year, 1574, by Franz Perenot, the ensign (*Bannerherr*) of the Ajoie, who expressed the fear that the bishop of Basel might prevent the impending export of corn from his territory in exchange for several casks of 'good

---

[65] SABs, Frucht und Brot, M 1, 1, 20 Sept. 1571.

[66] Even in 1502, Basel riposted, Austria had never resorted to such a drastic measure. SABs, Missiven A 38, pp. 539–41, 28 Nov. 1571.

[67] SABs, Missiven B 12, pp. 428–32, 27 Oct. 1571.

[68] StAFr, B 5 IXa iii, fo. 269ᵛ–270ᵛ, 13 May 1574.

old wine' which Perenot had secured in Ammerschwihr on condition that he deliver corn to equal value in return.[69]

But what really sapped the willingness of the powers on the
southern Upper Rhine to sustain co-operation over 'good police'
within a regional economic framework were the ever more vociferous appeals by confessional allies for grain supplies *in extremis*.
Here the contrast with meat provisioning is at its starkest. The necessity of importing meat into a region which was not self-sufficient
sharpened Rappen league members' perception that if they did not
hang together they would assuredly hang separately—even to the
point where Basel, a Protestant bastion, for the sake of the common good was willing to swallow some of the Catholic decrees
on fasting. When it came to grain, however, which several areas
on the Upper Rhine grew in sufficient abundance to produce surpluses for export, the need to cling together was less compelling.
As a matter of course the region was attuned to the requirements
of the Swiss market, with its permanent grain deficit, but a genuine
symbiosis of adjacent areas of complementary production and consumption never developed in this period, not least because the lines
of supply were increasingly shaped by confessional solidarity.

The threat of cutting off supplies to confessional opponents,
often coupled with explicit promises of aid to co-religionists, was
not new. On the eve of hostilities between Zürich and its Zwinglian
allies, and the Catholic inner cantons in the late 1520s, king Ferdin-
and had offered a compact to the latter, whereby they would be
guaranteed free trade with Austria in wine, grain, salt, and the like
in the event of war, even if Protestant Basel were placed under
an embargo.[70] Half a century later, by the same token, the five inner

---

[69] In an access of economic liberalism Perenot argued that it was not forbidden
to exchange goods of equal value—'die Commercia, do wahr vmb wahr geben
vnd genomen würdt'. AAEB, B 198/1, 7 July 1574. Some years later suspicion fell
on Perenot that he was in reality a grain speculator who was exporting corn from
the Ajoie on a large scale. Ibid. 29 Jan. 1583. However that may be, thirty years earlier Perenot had acted as a perfectly open and legitimate buying agent for Bern. Cf.
SABe, A III 37, KK, pp. 792–93, 5 Apr. 1533. He was still doing so in 1586. SABe,
A III 39, MM, pp. 222–23, 13 Sept. 1586.

[70] *Amtliche Sammlung der älteren Eidgenössischen Abschiede*, iv. 1b, ed. Johannes
Strickler (Zürich, 1876), 16; cf. Bosch, 'Kornhandel', 12. A codicil to the first peace
of Kappel in 1529 allowed the evangelical cities to impose a grain embargo on the
five inner cantons if the latter broke the terms of the peace, but several Protestant
magistracies, including Basel (and Strasbourg), had grave reservations about the
wisdom of such a step. Ibid. 109.

cantons held out the prospect of military support for Outer Austria if Alsace were overrun by foreign (French) troops, in return for a guarantee of grain deliveries.[71] Explicit invocations of confessional loyalty by the Catholic powers were, in fact, not all that frequent—Fribourg's appeal for corn supplies from the bishopric of Basel in 1591 being a rare instance[72]—but an undercurrent of religious solidarity can reasonably be inferred in the case of similar appeals by both the five inner cantons,[73] and the seven self-styled 'Catholic cantons' (the previous five, together with Fribourg and Solothurn) in 1590/91, to which the bishop responded favourably.[74]

Rather, it was the sense of beleaguered solidarity among the Protestants—above all between the Reformed cities of Switzerland and on the Upper Rhine—which led to far-flung appeals for grain supplies. Often these were relayed between cities strung out like pearls along attenuated lines of communication stretching, say, from Geneva to Strasbourg or beyond. Isolated pleas for help can, of course, be found before the 1570s. In 1543, for instance, Mulhouse allowed Geneva to purchase 4,000 sacks of corn, prompting Basel to complain that exports on such a scale would provoke uproar in town and country.[75] Nothing could be more revealing than this protest by Mulhouse's immediate neighbour and fellow-member of the Rappen coinage league: although both a political and a confessional ally of Mulhouse, Basel sensed that domestic needs were being sacrificed to the interests of a distant city which, despite its shared faith, lay well beyond the compass of the Upper Rhine as an economic region.[76]

By the last third of the sixteenth century, however, the pull of confessional solidarity grew visibly stronger, as dearths became commonplace. Sometimes the evidence is indirect, but none the less compelling for that. Why, for instance, should Zürich have striven to obtain grain supplies from Mulhouse in 1571, when the latter

---

[71] Ibid. 23. Bosch shrewdly observes that this was a pretext for military intervention on the Upper Rhine. [72] AAEB, B 198/1, 3 Jan. 1591.

[73] Ibid. 4 Jan. 1591; cf. B 349, fo. 1$^{r-v}$; B 198/1, 30 Nov. 1591.

[74] Ibid. 4 Jan. 1591; ibid. 17 Dec. 1591; cf. B 349, fo. 197$^v$–198$^r$.

[75] AMMh, I 4321, 10 Oct. 1543.

[76] The following year, however, Geneva approached Basel, whom it described significantly as its 'alliée et creancière', for grain, and also instructed two large city merchants to open negotiations with Strasbourg. Whether these overtures were successful is unclear. Jean-François Bergier, 'Commerce et politique du blé à Genève aux XV et XVIe siècles', *Schweizerische Zeitschrift für Geschichte*, 14 (1964), 546.

was neither a major entrepôt for grain (unlike Basel), nor the ruler of an extensive rural territory, if not in the hope that confessional ties would help it to evade Catholic Outer Austria's embargo on exports?[77] Its efforts that autumn to secure stocks of grain, Mulhouse complained, had actually driven prices up.[78] Schaffhausen and St Gallen, too, as Protestant cities, made purchases in Mulhouse, though they had to run the gauntlet of the Outer Austrian customs officials in Habsheim.[79]

The most remarkable example of co-operation between Protestant cities, however, began in the dying days of 1585, when Geneva, the victim of an embargo imposed during renewed hostilities with Savoy, turned to Strasbourg 'de nous assister de l'abondance que dieu vous a donné à quelques prix tollerables'.[80] Strasbourg was willing to help Geneva, but at a price which the latter did not regard as 'tolerable'.[81] Geneva held off until the spring, 'd'esperans que dieu par sa misericorde adonciroit sa main dessus nous et soulageroit nostre peuple', but was finally forced to accept Strasbourg's offer, though it asked 'si faite se peult nous atermoier le payement'.[82] By the summer, however, its supplies of grain were once again reaching the point of exhaustion, but this time Geneva enlisted Zürich[83] and Bern[84] to put in a good word for it. Bern explained that it had no grain to spare;[85] indeed, the city was itself engaged in trying to buy grain from Mulhouse and Colmar (Protestant since 1575), as well as Strasbourg.[86] Instead, Bern suggested that, if Strasbourg were to buy up what grain it could and store it on Geneva's behalf, it would cover both the cost of purchase and the expense of storage. This generous offer by Bern was accompanied a month later by the despatch of troops to help guard Geneva, though that only pitched the latter into even graver difficulties of provisioning, as it now reiterated its plea to Strasbourg for further supplies to help feed 'oultre trois compagnies de noz tres chers allies de Zurich et de Berne que nous avons reccu ces

[77] AMMh, I 4884, 22 Mar. 1571 (cf. I 4867, 1 Sept. 1570).
[78] AMMh, I 4897, 26 Sept. 1571; I 4898, 3 Nov. 1571; XIII A 8, fo. 185$^r$–187$^v$, 29 Oct. 1571.        [79] Ibid. fo. 127$^{r-v}$, 21 May 1571; ibid. fo. 159$^{r-v}$, n.d. (May 1571).
[80] AMS, AA 1820, fo. 1$^r$, 29 Dec. 1585; cf. Bosch, 'Kornhandel', 25–26.
[81] AMS, AA 1820, fo. 6$^{r-v}$, 9 Mar. 1586.
[82] Ibid. fo. 8$^r$, 19 Mar. 1586; ibid. fo. 11$^r$, 27 Apr. 1586.
[83] Ibid. fo. 18$^{r-v}$, 27 July 1586.        [84] Ibid. fo. 16$^{r-v}$, 19 July 1586.
[85] Ibid. fo. 23$^r$–24$^r$, 29 Aug. 1586; cf. SABe, A III 39, MM, pp. 199–200.
[86] Ibid. pp. 220–21, 11 Sept. 1586; ibid. pp. 222–23, 13 Sept. 1586.

jours pour la garde'.[87] It was only appropriate, therefore, that Bern and Zürich should lend their weight to this request.[88]

The question was how to get the grain transported to Geneva. Mulhouse, playing the role of co-ordinator, disclosed that a citizen of Colmar had ample stocks of grain in store at Strasbourg, which he was prepared to sell, albeit at a stiff price.[89] But then Colmar imposed its own ban on large-scale exports, and only relented when Mulhouse intervened. Once the grain had reached Mulhouse, Bern was to send payment thither for Colmar to collect. But permission still had to be sought for passage through Outer Austria, a task entrusted to Bern's diplomacy.[90] All this, Mulhouse assured Bern, it had undertaken for Geneva out of Confederate loyalty ('uß Eÿdtgnossischer trüwe').[91] All these efforts failed to alleviate Geneva's continuing plight, for in December it again approached Strasbourg for supplies to tide it over until it received an expected delivery from the (Protestant) Palatinate.[92] The following year brought further appeals, to which Strasbourg acceded wherever possible.[93]

At no point in these arrangements, it should be stressed, did any of the cities expressly invoke bonds of confessional loyalty: the most one discerns is Mulhouse's allusion to Confederate solidarity. But the Confederation was deeply riven by confessional divisions, and the cities engaged in this long-distance grain provisioning were without exception adherents of the Reformation (though not necessarily of the same profession of faith), willing to come to each other's defence in an emergency, as Zürich and Bern's intervention in Geneva showed, and even prepared to offer some financial subsidy. In this context, therefore, Confederate loyalty meant standing shoulder-to-shoulder with co-religionists; the categories were not interchangeable, to be sure, but for each side of the confessional divide they certainly overlapped. Of course, it can be objected that appeals were directed to Strasbourg because of the considerable

---

[87] AMS, AA 1820, fo. 25$^{r-v}$, 7 Oct. 1586.

[88] Ibid. fo. 29$^{r-v}$, 13 Oct. 1586; ibid. fo. 31$^{r}$–32$^{r}$, 17 Oct. 1586.

[89] SABe, A V 742, pp. 429–30, 8 Sept. 1586.

[90] SABe, A III 39, MM, pp. 262–63, 10 Oct. 1586; ibid. pp. 265–66, 13 Oct. 1586. Bern pointed out that the grain had not been bought on Outer Austrian territory.

[91] SABe, A V 742, pp. 433–37, 7 Oct. 1586.

[92] AMS, AA 1820, fo. 33$^{r-v}$, 15 Dec. 1586.

[93] Cf. ibid. fo. 37$^{r}$, 8 May 1587; SABe, A III 40, NN, pp. 1002–4, 21 July 1590; and several instances in 1591 (AMS, AA 1823).

stocks of grain held in its granary, rather than for reasons of religious solidarity. One only has to cast a glance at the strings of appeals to the city from Baden and Swabia, regardless of confession, to take the point.[94] That is scarcely a convincing argument in the case of Geneva, however, which would much rather have foregone the tribulations and expense of transport from the Upper Rhine, had it been able to meet its needs closer at hand in Burgundy or the Franche-Comté, but these were areas under Catholic control. Geneva may have been, in Hugh Trevor-Roper's words, the 'Protestant Internationale', but geographically it was a vulnerable outpost on the southern edge of the Swiss Reformation. For Bern, given its proximity to the Upper Rhine, the same argument is admittedly less compelling, but the city declined to petition the Outer Austrian government 'for permission to purchase or export' stocks of grain, 'well knowing that such would be in vain and bring in nothing':[95] in vain—Bern made no bones about it—because Austria had imposed an embargo.[96] But would the embargo have been so strictly upheld if Bern had been Catholic? We are dealing here, admittedly, with evidence which is indirect and circumstantial.

In any case, the argument should not be pressed too far. During the subsistence crises of the 1570s and 1580s Protestant lords and cities might approach their Catholic neighbours for supplies, and vice versa. The Catholic inner cantons occasionally bought grain in Basel, though, as the Lucerne records show, most of their trade was focussed on the south towards the transalpine bailiwicks (*ennetbirgische Vogteien*) and Lombardy.[97] Uri on its own had recourse to Mulhouse in both 1566 and 1571,[98] and Zug to Strasbourg in the latter year, though its request for 300 quarters of wheat was turned down.[99] In the late 1580s the bishop of Basel approached Strasbourg and Colmar in addition to more likely sources of support in the Basel cathedral chapter (resident in Freiburg im Breisgau) and the Knights of St John at Heitersheim in the Breisgau.[100] By contrast, Zürich sent its corn-dealers to both banks of the Upper

[94] Cf. the enumeration in Fuchs, 'Foires', 326–28.

[95] SABe, A III 39, MM, pp. 222–23, 13 Sept. 1586.

[96] Ibid. pp. 271–73, 15 Oct. 1586. Bern instead sent its territorial bailiffs in Wangen, Aarwangen, Aarburg, Lenzburg, and Schenkenberg 1,000 fl. to purchase grain.

[97] Bosch, 'Kornhandel', 44. A review of the relevant *Akten* in SALu reveals virtually no correspondence over grain provisioning with Basel or the Upper Rhine, though a little with Zürich.        [98] AMMh, I 4922, 30 Oct. 1573.

[99] Fuchs, 'Foires', 327–28.        [100] AAEB, B 198/1, 16 Jan. 1597.

Rhine in 1571 to obtain supplies wherever possible—be it from Protestant Mulhouse or Catholic lords such as the Knights of St John, the counts of Sulz, or even the Outer Austrian government itself.[101] Ensisheim turned Zürich down, but then so did Mulhouse, pointing to the large consignments which it had already despatched to St Gallen and Schaffhausen.[102] Even the little commune of Hallau, under Schaffhausen's jurisdiction, tried to buy grain in April 1571 from the arch-Catholic Freiburg im Breisgau, with the blessing of the city council.[103] The bishopric of Basel, too, was the target of corn-dealers from Protestant cities. Bern, while eschewing any approach to Ensisheim, used Franz Perenot (whom we have encountered above) to scour the Ajoie on its behalf.[104] And even Geneva was driven in 1585 to search for stocks both in Montbéliard (a Protestant territory, albeit Lutheran rather than Calvinist), and in the Ajoie, though it had to petition the bishop for an exemption from tolls, which was granted on the grounds that the corn was destined for the inmates of its city hospital.[105]

But these are the exceptions which prove the rule: in times of dearth grain provisioning was organized along increasingly (though never exclusively) confessional lines. While easy enough to demonstrate for the Protestant cities, it is harder to do so for the Catholic powers, though here we must bear in mind the strained relations between the Outer Austrian government and the great Counter-Reformation bishop of Basel, Jakob Christoph Blarer von Wartensee, as the two bastions of Catholicism on the Upper Rhine. In 1586, for instance, Ensisheim's request to deliver stocks of corn to the nearest Austrian markets was greeted with a promise to send a mere 150 quarters at most to the market at Porrentruy to await collection, whereupon, the government, giving thanks through clenched teeth, reminded the bishop that it was 1,000 quarters, not 100, that it had asked for.[106] Very occasionally, however, the veil was lifted to reveal that the implications of confessional divisions were never far from the minds of those grappling with apparently mundane and yet in reality existential issues such as grain provisioning. Amidst the welter of supplications to Strasbourg from the Ortenau in 1573, Oberndorf by Rastatt expressed the hope that the recent

---

[101] Bosch, 'Kornhandel', 19.    [102] Ibid. 20; cf. above n. 79.
[103] Müller, *Getreidehandelspolitik*, 36.    [104] Cf. above, n. 69.
[105] AAEB, B 198/1, n.d. (before 25 May 1585); ibid. 25 May 1585.
[106] Ibid. 31 May 1586; ibid. 18 June 1586; ibid. 19 June 1586.

'alteration of religion' (the re-Catholicization of the margraviate of Baden-Baden) would not be held against it in its request for 50 quarters of rye.[107]

The conclusion seems inescapable that grain provisioning in the course of the sixteenth century lost whatever dimension of regional co-operation it had once possessed: agreements to combat forestalling or to prevent the export of corn in times of dearth were concluded bilaterally, rather than within the framework of the Rappen coinage league or, after 1584, by the *Verein* of those within its circulation area. One can point, for instance, to local negotiations between the administration in Ensisheim and the city of Mulhouse in the 1560s,[108] or to the edict against grain forestalling drawn up in 1587 by the four neighbours Kaysersberg, Colmar, Kientzheim, and Ammerschwihr (strangely reminiscent of the 1516 meat ordinance between three of them and Riquewihr, which had predated the wider assemblies of the Rappen league).[109] But the sense of a common regional identity had not been entirely obliterated. In October 1573, for instance, the non-Austrian lords and cities of Upper Alsace met in Colmar to prepare an agreed submission to a forthcoming corn diet in Ensisheim, which implies that co-operation within the Rappen league had not ceased. Among the signatories to the 'instruction' handed over to the bishop of Strasbourg's official was Württemberg, the only instance I can discover of its inclusion in grain negotiations on the southern Upper Rhine. Sélestat, too, was listed as a signatory, though the assembly was far less comprehensive than its predecessor in 1551, which had comprised all the members of the Alsatian quarter of the Upper Rhenish circle.[110]

But this is not the whole picture. Even after the collapse of the Rappen league, the Outer Austrian administration—perhaps chastened by the backlash which its unilateral bans of the early 1570s had provoked—remained aware that negotiations with its immediate neighbours were the only sure means of supervising the

---

[107] AMS, IV 17/57, 12 May 1573.

[108] Cf. AMMh, I 4728, 12 Dec. 1565; I 4867, 1 Sept. 1570.

[109] AMKy, FF 39, 30 Dec. 1587.

[110] AMC, HH 95/26, 1 Oct. 1573. The wording and scope of the 'instruction' are far from clear. Nevertheless, the preparatory character of the meeting is clear from the decision 'vmb vff nechstkünfftige zusammen kommung sollichs alles . . . widerumb zu referieren haben'. The signatories were the lords of Württemberg, Ribeaupierre, von Schwendi (Hohlandsberg), and the cities of Sélestat, Colmar, Kaysersberg, Munster, Turckheim, and Ammerschwihr.

grain market on the Upper Rhine. And in the crisis year of 1586 these negotiations once again took a collective, not bilateral, form. In May the Ensisheim authorities issued a mandate ordering the immediate delivery of all available stocks to market and fixing price ceilings,[111] and, fearing the likelihood of a 'dangerous uprising' throughout the land, ordered an inventory of corn reserves the following month.[112] To underscore its earnest, the government imposed swingeing tolls on exports, though it hastened to reassure Basel that access to its market (and to those of Colmar and Mulhouse) would remain unimpeded, as was the custom![113] Given Austria's previous behaviour, their apprehensions were understandably not allayed, so that by September the administration had agreed to summon an assembly to Ensisheim to discuss grain provisioning[114] within what it termed (in extraordinarily convoluted language) 'the district of the immediately adjacent neighbourhood and this [i.e. Outer Austrian] land'.[115]

Attendance and proceedings can be gleaned from the memorandum subsequently presented to the Outer Austrian Estates. The government had not cast its net quite as widely as for the meat assemblies—no emissaries from lordships in the north of Upper Alsace were present—but the main cereal districts were all represented (the Upper Mundat, the southern Baden territories, Murbach's secular territory), along with the main market centres (Basel, Mulhouse, and Colmar).[116] All were agreed in principle on the need to combat forestalling and on the desirability of a common grain tariff, but there the unanimity ceased. The government's counterparts insisted that an embargo on exports was no way to overcome dearth; instead, they took up the old refrain that the chartered corn markets in the three cities (and in Murbach's commune of Guebwiller) should be open to all-comers, while stamping out informal marketing and sales direct from corn-chests in the countryside. Colmar took the lead in opposing any attempt to discriminate between foreigners and locals at market, contending that it would be better to demand certificates from the former that they

---

[111] StAFr, C 1 Landstände 15, 17 May 1586.
[112] Ibid. 28 June 1586. Cf. the list of corn stocks in the Breisgau, ibid. n.d. (1586).
[113] Speck, *Landstände*, i. 502–3. His reference to GLA 79/2569 cannot be traced.
[114] Cf. AMMh, I 5421, 27 Aug. 1586; I 5422, 2 Sept. 1586; I 5423, 6 Sept. 1586.
[115] StAFr, C 1 Landstände 15, 6 Sept. 1586, in a letter to Freiburg inviting its comments: 'Bezürckh der negstanrainenden benachbarschafft und dis Lanndts'.
[116] Ibid. 23 Sept. 1586. This assembly is listed erroneously in Speck, *Landstände*, ii. 949 as a diet of the committee of the Outer Austrian Estates.

were only buying for their own consumption. Basel then chipped in to recall the dire consequences which boycotting 'foreigners' had produced during the Kappel wars, when the Catholic cantons had been threatened with an embargo. The Ensisheim administration was forcefully reminded that any unilateral export ban would entail reprisals (as well as contravening the *Erbeinigung*), and that in turn would lead to the exclusion of Austria's Black Forest subjects and the four Forest Towns from the Basel corn market. Any unitary price tariff, moreover, should if possible be extended to other neighbouring lords, including Württemberg.[117] Despite protracted discussions, no common ground could be found. Only Baden broke ranks by declaring that it would reach its own agreement with Outer Austria, provided that Basel was party to it.[118]

Confronted with this impasse, the Ensisheim government decided to call a diet of the committee of the three Estates in late October, at which it emerged that the Estates had at last abandoned the advocacy of a purely territorial policy, which had led to their hostile stance towards Baden twelve years earlier. Not only did the Estates leap to the defence of Austrian subjects in Alsace who had been brought to justice by the procurator-fiscal for selling grain at 'foreign' markets in Rouffach, Soultz, Guebwiller, and Colmar;[119] in the Breisgau, too, Freiburg's instructions to its delegates left no doubt that a territorial approach was doomed to failure. It would only encourage foreigners to buy corn at Outer Austrian markets (where prices were capped), but not to supply them. Freiburg repeated its view that its market depended on the free exchange of goods and produce between the Black Forest and the Rhine valley: subjects of the lords of Fürstenberg, Reischach, Landeck, and the abbot of St Peter, as well as Austrian cameral subjects in Schönau, Todtnau, and the county of Hauenstein, were accustomed to deliver butter, cheese, and timber weekly to the Freiburg market in return for grain. But since Austrian subjects were so backward in supplying grain to the market, 'one cannot do without the margravial subjects', and consequently no grain ordinance and

---

[117] The participants suggested the bishop of Strasbourg (who had failed to send an official, despite being invited) and the count of Württemberg (i.e. the ruler of the Alsatian territories) in particular, as those who had faithfully supplied 'this land, especially Colmar' in the past.

[118] Cf. the protocol of these discussions in StAFr, B 5 IXa v, fo. 416ᵛ–425ʳ; vi, fo. 124ʳ–131ʳ.        [119] StAFr, C 1 Landstände 15, 30 Sept. 1586.

tariff could be concluded 'unless the margraviate of Hachberg and Badenweiler reaches a neighbourly agreement with the towns of Freiburg, Breisach, Endingen, Kenzingen, and Waldkirch'.[120]

These reservations were shared by the Estates' committee as a whole, which advanced a barrage of reasons for rejecting a unilateral territorial ordinance. Some were patently threadbare—the risk of grain being admixed with tares, the different weights and measures used throughout Outer Austria—and others were plainly scaremongering—the likely reaction of the Swiss who, denied access to Austrian markets in contravention of the *Erbeinigung*, might simply seize stocks of grain by force! But there was substance to the charge that civic markets would be swept clean of grain (Freiburg had already indicated as much), and to the concerns of the Breisgau Estates in general that the extensive rents and renders which they received from their estates on Baden territory would be blocked. A hostile attitude towards Baden, moreover, would force the Forest Towns to resort to Basel, Aarau, or Brugg for supplies, where as foreigners, however, they would be excluded from the market. Basel had already banned its millers from selling flour to Austrian subjects, and Mulhouse had done likewise. The only answer, the Estates' committee insisted, was a free market in grain coupled with a ban on forestalling and speculative dealing.[121] In other words, when faced with acute dearth, the Estates finally realized that the situation required deregulation, rather than protection, just as had more commonly been the case with meat provisioning. There was nothing like scarcity for focussing their minds on regional economic interests and the necessity of upholding a common regional policy.

The positions of the Outer Austrian government and the Estates appeared irreconcilable, and a minor constitutional crisis blew up over the winter and into the following spring, with the Estates appealing over Ensisheim's head to Innsbruck, and the second Estate of nobles calling a diet off its own bat to denounce the proposed ordinance.[122] Despite this fracas, the government remained in contact with the Baden authorities, who for their part were keen

---

[120] Ibid. n.d. (before 29 Oct. 1586).
[121] StAFr, B 5 IXa v, fo. 428ᵛ–434ᵛ; vi, fo. 135ʳ–141ᵛ, 30 Oct. 1586; cf. C 1 Landstände 15.
[122] StAFr, B 5 IXa v, fo. 435ʳ–436ʳ, 6 Jan. 1587; cf. vi, fo. 143ʳ–145ʳ; Speck, *Landstände*, i. 503–4.

to reach an accommodation which would prevent their subjects being branded as foreigners in the Austrian Breisgau.[123] How the differences between the Ensisheim authorities and the Estates were resolved is uncertain. The latter seem to have backed down from open defiance of the government, and there are still some instances of Austrian territorial bans on exports to neighbours in the 1590s.[124] But as soon as the dearth passed, free trade was resumed. Amidst the fevered atmosphere of the 1586 negotiations, nevertheless, several features stand out.

The Outer Austrian government was prepared—with some reluctance—to consult its neighbours on the Upper Rhine, but how etiolated the old spirit of collective decision-making had become is evident from the fact that the September negotiations did not include the Outer Austrian Estates (who were summoned separately a month later). Certainly the government sought the opinion of powerful towns such as Freiburg, but a place at the negotiating table was denied both it and Breisach, whereas once they would have had every right to attend as constituent members of the Rappen coinage league. The Estates, by contrast, having overcome their brief flirtation with a protectionist policy on grain provisioning, retained a sense of regional economic co-operation which the Rappen league (however imperfectly) had embodied. Freiburg's submissions to Ensisheim reveal how well it grasped that autarky on a political-territorial footing was a mirage. Yet the Estates' enthusiasm for a free market in grain sprang from distinctly mixed motives. In times of dearth they had come to realize that it was the only way to ensure supplies, or else each territory would adopt a beggar-my-neighbour policy of embargoes. But when grain was plentiful, they were just as concerned to uphold free trade for a quite different reason, namely that their prosperity depended on sustaining their export market with Switzerland.[125] The one motive was calculated to reinforce the solidarity of those who perceived themselves bound together in an economic region; the other motive could only attenuate that solidarity. The former conduced to collective action and identity, the latter to the pursuit of individual interests and gain. But even when collective economic interests prevailed, the perception of what constituted collectivity underwent a shift as

---

[123] StAFr, C 1 Landstände 15, 8 Dec. 1586; ibid. 2 Jan. 1587.
[124] Cf. AAEB, B 350, fo. 133$^{r-v}$, 21 Nov. 1592; B 351, fo. 27$^{r-v}$, 5 Mar. 1596.
[125] Cf. Speck, *Landstände*, i. 504.

confessional ties linking cities arterially began to overlay the bonds between lords and cities forged by mutual economic interests within the radius of the southern Upper Rhine.

Only at the margins was the creation of the imperial Circles able to buttress a sense of regional economic co-operation, for the Upper Rhine was caught between two Circles, the Upper Rhenish and the Austrian, the latter embracing all the Habsburg patrimonial lands from Austria to Alsace. Ordinances concerning grain provisioning issued for the Alsatian quarter of the Upper Rhenish Circle had no validity in Outer Austria. Here a comparison with the Swabian Circle is most revealing, for this Circle encompassed an area which was also heavily involved in grain exports to Switzerland, yet had no jurisdiction over the Austrian lordships scattered across the map of Swabia. From 1572 the Swabian Circle began to issue mandates enjoining the use of chartered markets, and banning forestalling and loans to pre-empt the harvest,[126] as the Upper Rhenish Circle was never able to do on so comprehensive a scale. At the same time, the Swabian Circle had to tread the same fine line between safeguarding local supplies and maintaining the profitable trade with the Swiss as did the powers on the Upper Rhine.[127] More and more, however, in the seventeenth century and beyond, the Swabian economy adapted to the demands of the Swiss market. Swabia became, if not an area of monoculture, then a region specializing in cereal agriculture in order to supply the needs of the northern Swiss cantons, whose own economy was increasingly dominated by village crafts and cottage industries. Such a symbiosis reflected what Frank Göttmann terms '*eine raumwirtschaftliche Eigendynamik*',[128] that is, the stimulus to an independent economic dynamism based on the given resources and potential of a spatially defined region.

Nothing comparable occurred on the Upper Rhine, either in the sixteenth century or later, even though the preconditions may appear to have been remarkably similar. The reasons for this failed 'transition' will be examined in the concluding chapter. For the present, what the comparison of meat and grain provisioning on the Upper Rhine up to the end of the sixteenth century has shown is that the sense of regional economic identity and interests was not

---

[126] Göttmann, *Getreidemarkt*, 84. However, the Swabian Circle only resorted to grain embargoes much later.
[127] Cf. ibid. 107 (with reference to the 18th century).     [128] Ibid. 57.

fixed but mutable. It shifted according to the commodity traded. Meat provisioning extended the commercial catchment area of the Upper Rhine south-westwards; grain provisioning drew the Upper Rhine into close commercial relations with Switzerland. It shifted, too, according to the balance between exports and imports. Meat provisioning encouraged the authorities on the southern Upper Rhine to huddle together within the framework of the Rappen league, pre-occupied with securing supplies for their own membership; grain provisioning allowed them to look outwards, eager to uphold free trade and open markets, and less concerned to define a regional economic identity in terms of exclusiveness or protectionism.

In that sense, economic co-operation on the southern Upper Rhine led not to the crystallization of a single regional identity, shaped by natural frontiers and political alliances (the Rappen league), but rather to the simultaneous coexistence of overlapping regional identities superimposed upon one another,[129] predicated upon varying economic needs and opportunities and structured by principles of both centrality and arterial networks. Cartographically, these can be imagined as a succession of overhead-projector sheets laid on top of one another, all covering a core area, but each describing the varying outlines of a particular regional configuration stretching beyond it. The core area, however, must on no account be equated with any 'true' or 'natural' or 'essential' region: quite the opposite. In *economic* terms—this is the conclusion of our exhaustive ana-lysis—there was no such thing.

---

[129] Göttmann, Rabe, and Sieglerschmidt, 'Regionale Transformation', 128, use a similar term, 'Überlagerung unterschiedlich dimensionierter Regionen', but they have in mind the varying market hinterlands of the Swabian cities, rather than the fluidity of the boundaries of an economic region as such.

# PART IV

*The Region and its Economy in Decline*

# 9
## The Fracturing of a Regional Identity

## I

From 1300 onwards the shifting balance of political and military fortunes on the Upper Rhine had fostered the growth of regional solidarity. The requirements of public peace on the western frontiers of the Empire found their expression in the many defensive treaties which bound local lords and cities together. These requirements were compounded in the fifteenth century by the increasing assertiveness of the Swiss and the rising star of Burgundy as a new political force with expansionist designs. From the Burgundian *débâcle* emerged the Lower Union, which brought the Swiss, the Habsburgs, and the Upper Rhenish imperial Estates together in an uneasy alliance, so that, for Georges Bischoff, the 'épisode bourguignon agit comme un rélevateur en restaurant l'idée d'une solidarité régionale'.[1] But this was essentially a negative solidarity, born of defensive necessity; once the danger had passed old antagonisms and suspicions resurfaced, as Maximilian discovered in attempting to revive the Lower Union in 1493.

Yet a sense of positive solidarity, grounded in the perception of enduring common interests, in other words, structural rather than functional, had also emerged in the two centuries before 1500. Its most obvious manifestation was the transformation of the Rappen coinage league from a loose association stretching well into Switzerland to a coinage area restricted to the southern Upper Rhine, whose boundaries were defined more by geography and commerce than by ties of lordship, so that it became clearly marked off from neighbouring coinage areas to the north and south. Friedrich Wielandt, indeed, the past master of numismatics in south-west Germany, once described the Rappen coinage league as the economic complement

---

[1] Bischoff, *Gouvernés et gouvernants*, 159.

to the Lower Union.[2] Although that judgement is neither chronologically nor geographically accurate, it does at least draw attention
to the way the composition and orbit of the Rappen league reflect
an awareness of common regional economic interests, precisely
because it rested upon a compact between powerful territorial
princes—the Habsburgs—and independent cities, quite unlike the
Strasbourg coinage area which reflected the *rayonnement* of the
regional metropolis. Within that framework, moreover, the dictates
of 'good police', as one of the constant preoccupations of magistracies in the sixteenth century, came to be elaborated in a series
of assemblies specifically convened to regulate the provisioning of
meat and grain. From a coinage association the Rappen league
developed some of the characteristics of an economic *Zweckverband*,
an association dedicated to a particular economic end, even though
the administrative co-operation which it embodied lacked formal
institutional expression.

Any verdict on the effectiveness of the Rappen coinage league,
however, must be tempered by a cold eye for its obvious limita-
tions. The apparent equipoise between prince and cities upon which
it rested, and which made it so distinctive, could easily be upset.
One does not need to share Georges Bischoff's view that the
Rappen coinage area simply marked the extent of the Outer Austrian
government's concern for good police—'pourquoi ne pas étendre
à l'ensemble de l'Alsace et des régions voisines ce qui a été jugé
bon pour les Vorlande?'[3]—to concede that Ensisheim's organiza-
tional role in convening the police diets (quite apart from Austria's
political preponderance on the southern Upper Rhine) lent it a
weight in the Rappen league's affairs which tipped the balance
away from communal-regional towards autarchic-territorial policies
as the economy of the Upper Rhine came under increasing strain
in the later sixteenth century.

The collapse of the Rappen league in 1584—in effect, its super-
session by an Outer Austrian coinage area based on the minting
of thalers—may be seen as a cruel but deserved stroke of fate for
an association which was so blinkered by its own immediate interests that it failed to perceive the opportunity for reinvigoration contained in count Friedrich of Württemberg's overtures a few years

---

[2] Friedrich Wielandt, 'Münzgeschichtliche Beziehungen zwischen Baden und
dem Elsaß', *Elsaß-Lothringisches Jahrbuch*, 16 (1937), 62.
[3] Bischoff, *Gouvernés et gouvernants*, 209.

earlier by extending its remit to include Montbéliard, and thereby strengthening its members' commercial ties with Burgundy, the source of much of the Upper Rhine's meat. At that time, to be sure, Cernay's market was still flourishing; twenty years on the argument might have been very different. A sense of regional economic solidarity remained, in any case, contingent: where *demand* within the area of the league took precedence (as with meat provisioning), a common purpose survived the eclipse of the Rappen league, as the Ensisheim government continued to consult former Rappen members within the *Verein*; but where *supply* was paramount (as with grain exports to Switzerland), the willingness to subordinate individual to collective interests was predictably weaker. In the face of intensifying subsistence crises in the last third of the sixteenth century the fear of unilateral embargoes on grain exports ensured that temporary co-operation supervened, though more and more by means of bilateral negotiations rather than through regional assemblies. Furthermore, it needs to be recalled that, however much it embodied a sense of *regional* solidarity, the Rappen league was incapable (being bereft of the necessary administrative or legal powers) of preventing *local* conflicts between its members over market competition and commercial rivalry, though here, at least, the more emollient attitude of the Outer Austrian (particularly the Breisgau) Estates towards Baden in the 1580s suggests that they had learnt some lessons from the ultimately self-defeating conflict over village markets and country crafts which had soured relations during the 1570s.

# II

None the less, the structural deficiencies of the Rappen coinage league itself cannot disguise that its cohesion as a regional economic *Zweckverband* was undermined in the course of the sixteenth century by a political climate whose chill winds began to blow away the web of collective ties which had once existed across political, territorial, and confessional frontiers. The primacy of economic and commercial interests, the lifeblood of the urban communes, yielded to the imperatives of administrative rationalization, territorial consolidation, and, not infrequently, religious uniformity. From these pressures even Outer Austria, the stepchild of Habsburg dynasticism after the death of Maximilian, was not spared, especially once archduke Ferdinand II of Tirol assumed the reins of power over the 'outer lands' in 1563. His long rule of over thirty years witnessed substantial changes both in the government of Outer Austria itself and in its diplomacy towards its neighbours on the Upper Rhine.

At the beginning of his reign archduke Ferdinand showed himself determined to redeem territories long mortgaged to important officials or creditors. In 1566 he bought back the most extensive pawn in Alsace, the lordship of Ferrette, from Hans Jakob Fugger, at the same time undertaking to shoulder whatever debts Fugger might have.[4] This was not the generous gesture it might appear, for Ferdinand immediately set about raising the required sum from the Outer Austrian Estates.[5] Although several other pawns—notably those held by the von Schwendi and von Bollweiler—were not redeemed, the archduke had given an earnest of his intention to take in hand the somewhat ramshackle administration of the lands on the Upper Rhine, so remote from the purview of the authorities in Innsbruck. That same year he despatched a commission to investigate whether to establish a separate treasury for Outer Austria; but when its recommendations became reality four years later, the rules setting out the procedures of the new treasury (*Kammer*) significantly enough made it closely dependent on decisions in Innsbruck, with the Outer Austrian governor being excluded from any say in its running. Although the limits of its competence over against the government proper (*Regiment*) were left imprecise, it was given what Seidel regards as explicitly cameralistic duties: to search for new sources of revenue; to administer the cameral estates; to oversee leases and their potential revenue; to effect savings in administrative costs; and, not least, to supervise the mines.[6] Part and parcel of this policy was the concern to protect stocks of foodstuffs in an age of recurrent dearth, hence the initiative mentioned in Chapter 8 to establish granaries in three cameral *Ämter*, Rheinfelden, Ensisheim, and Altkirch.[7]

The decision to commence minting a separate Outer Austrian coinage fits seamlessly into this programme of territorial consolidation. Archduke Ferdinand, it will be recalled, had issued a minting ordinance in 1564, which subjected Freiburg's and Breisach's mints to Austrian territorial control and aligned the Rappen coinage to

---

[4] Cf. StAFr, C 1 Landstände 9, 24 June 1566.     [5] Seidel, *Oberelsaß*, 102.
[6] Ibid. 141–43.     [7] Ibid. 143.

the imperial edict of 1559. Although the end was postponed for another twenty years, the writing was on the wall for the Rappen league; by then it had outlasted all similar coinage associations of late medieval provenance in southern Germany. That it survived for so long is attributable in part to the benign neglect bestowed upon Outer Austria until the energetic advent of archduke Ferdinand. But it is also a tribute to the resolve of its urban members—Basel, above all—in sustaining a collective monetary policy, and that, in turn, was bolstered by the recognition that, whatever the merits of an imperial coinage, the economy of the southern Upper Rhine was more likely to thrive if it could rely on a sound regional currency of everyday exchange, rather than capitulate to the influx of bad coin from parts of Switzerland and Lorraine. That Austria continued to mint Rappen pence alongside imperially recognized coin after 1584 speaks for itself.

Efforts towards greater effectiveness in the conduct of the Outer Austrian administration were matched towards the end of the century by a distinctly more aggressive stance towards its neighbours. Relations between Ensisheim and the bishopric of Basel had never been entirely smooth, since the bishop remained the feudal superior of the lordship of Ferrette, the cornerstone of Austrian territorial power in Alsace. Throughout the century, moreover, the activities of the ecclesiastical court, with its seat in Altkirch after 1529, had been a source of constant irritation.[8] But that was a ripple of discontent compared with the furious row which erupted when the Counter-Reformation prelate, Jakob Christoph Blarer von Wartensee, attempted to launch a visitation in his diocese in 1601, after complaining at constant Austrian interference in his jurisdictions, both temporal and ecclesiastical, since his inauguration a quarter of a century earlier. Austria promptly invoked the right to send a secular official to accompany the visitation, by virtue of its stewardship over the see.[9] The ensuing conflict, which lasted more than two decades, was simply a pretext for both sides to rehearse a litany of long-standing grievances. We may safely ignore who was principally to blame; what matters is that the Outer Austrian government has been accused, in the ringing verdict of one historian (a Basel

---

[8] Ibid. 76–77.
[9] Joseph Schmidlin, 'Der Visitationsstreit der Bischöfe von Basel mit der österreichischen Regierung um das Ober-Elsaß vor dem Dreißigjährigen Krieg', *Archiv für elsässische Kirchengeschichte*, 3 (1928), 120–21; Seidel, *Oberelsaß*, 77–79.

apologist, *bien sûr*) of Caesaropapalism reminiscent of the darkest days of the Investiture Contest![10] However preposterous the charge, it does at least indicate that Austria's lack of compunction in meddling in the bishopric's affairs had soured relations to breaking-point.

Nor was this an isolated incident of interference in episcopal jurisdiction. After a century's quiescence the Ensisheim government once again sought to extend its influence over the bishop of Strasbourg's lordship of the Upper Mundat in the early years of the seventeenth century by claiming (as with the lords of Ribeaupierre fifty years earlier) that the district was a 'vacated Estate' of the landgraviate of Upper Alsace. Accordingly, Austria affirmed sovereignty over two of the convents there (St Valentin in Rouffach, and Lautenbach), as well as over the landed estates of Austrian nobles lying within the Upper Mundat.[11] It is worth adding in this regard that Austria had also sought to make capital out of the disputed inheritance of the lords of Hattstatt by sequestering half the village of Zimmerbach in the Fecht valley above Turckheim, but the court case dragged on for nearly fifty years without Austria's territorial sovereignty being recognized.[12] In short, around 1600 the Ensisheim government gave every appearance of wishing to revive the plans to establish, if not a unitary territory, then at least an impregnable power-block on the Upper Rhine, which had marked Maximilian's rule at the turn of the fifteenth century.

What had changed in the intervening period was the rise of confessional divisions, which gave an added twist to the intricacies of dynastic politics. No confessional barrier separated the Outer Austrian government from the bishops of Basel and Strasbourg, of course, but with the imperial city of Mulhouse, a Swiss and Protestant enclave in the heart of the Sundgau, the situation was quite different. Any attempt to mediatize the city, however, whether by invasion or subversion, was fraught with risk, since it would constitute a flagrant breach of the Perpetual Accord of 1511 between Austria and the Confederation, and was likely to call forth military reprisals by the Protestant cantons, if not the Confederation as a whole. But that did not deter emperor Rudolf II from trying to capitalize upon the factionalism which from the 1580s had rent Mulhouse. The internal upheavals—known as the Finninger affair

[10]  Schmidlin, 'Visitationsstreit', 115.        [11]  Seidel, *Oberelsaß*, 79.
[12]  Ibid. 73–74; Bischoff, *Gouvernés et gouvernants*, 160.

—revolved around a *parvenu* family which had flirted with Catholicism in order to gain power. An attempted intervention by the Catholic cantons backfired, with the result that they had renounced their treaty of protection with the city in 1586.[13] Eleven years later Rudolf (with the clandestine support of the Catholic Swiss) declared Mulhouse's associate membership of the Confederation null and void. Not only did he thereupon insist that it submit anew to his suzerainty as emperor; he also advanced jurisdictional claims over the city in his capacity as landgrave of Upper Alsace. When these came to nought, he turned instead in 1601 to exerting pressure on the Swiss to exclude Mulhouse from any renewal of their alliance with king Henri IV of France.[14] That, too, proved a blind alley, but at the end of the 1620s the Outer Austrian chancellor Isaac Volmar could still be found composing an elaborate memorandum on how best to annex or mediatize the city.[15]

Confessionalism, moreover, might have direct economic repercussions. Entry to guilds or fraternities was on occasion restricted to those of a particular faith. When the Outer Austrian government issued a territorial ordinance for beret- and trouser-makers in 1596, for instance, it required all such craftsmen under its jurisdiction to be Catholic. Naturally Basel and Strasbourg as Protestant cities refused to subscribe to the ordinance, though they took care to issue regulations of their own which were similar enough in content to permit a common policy throughout the Upper Rhine.[16] No such tacit co-operation informed relations between the two margraviates of Baden. Once Baden-Baden had finally plumped for Catholicism (and began energetically to prosecute the work of Catholic reform), it declared Protestant Baden-Durlach to be foreign territory and forbade its subjects from visiting the latter's markets, despite their protests that Durlach's was both convenient and essential to their livelihood.[17] Territorial craft ordinances spanning both territories do seem to have remained in place, however, as the example of the potters with their annual convention for Baden and Durlach discussed in Chapter 4 demonstrates.

---

[13] Georges Livet and Raymond Oberlé, *Histoire de Mulhouse des origines à nos jours* (*Collection Histoire des Villes d'Alsace*) (Strasbourg, 1977), 79–80.

[14] Ibid. 81. [15] Seidel, *Oberelsaß*, 80, 157–58.

[16] Schulz, *Handwerksgesellen und Lohnarbeiter*, 9, 269–70.

[17] Eberhard Gothein, *Die badischen Markgrafschaften im 16. Jahrhundert* (Neujahrsblätter der Badischen Historischen Kommission, NS 13) (Heidelberg, 1910), 19.

Just as confessional imperatives might cut across natural economic links between lordships on the Upper Rhine, so, by contrast, could religious solidarity forge new bonds of economic co-operation which were linear rather than radial, following urban networks rather than conforming to patterns of centrality. That was the case, it was suggested in the previous chapter, with the Protestant cities on the Upper Rhine and in Switzerland, who in the mid-1580s established a veritable relay of command to ensure that supplies of grain reached their languishing co-religionists in Geneva. In both these ways, therefore, a sense of regional economic identity and cohesion was fracturing as the sixteenth century drew to a close. Increasingly, economic policy was conceived in territorial or exclusive terms, although autarky was never a realistic option.

It is not necessary to ascribe this development to the spread of mercantilist or cameralist doctrines, whose golden age in Germany in any case came after the Thirty Years War; rather, it was immanent in the logic of territorial consolidation from the outset. The foundation of new markets and the imposition of restrictions on access to foreign ones, as the analysis of the conflicts between Baden and Austria has shown, can be traced to the early fifteenth century. But as the economy of the Upper Rhine began to falter— a theme which will be explored in the final chapter—the desire to retain all available resources and revenues within a territory grew palpably stronger. In this respect it is no coincidence that the fiercest and most protracted rivalry between Austrian and Baden communes over craft and market competition occurred after the mid-sixteenth century. In the running battle between the franchised markets of Catholic Outer Austria and the village markets of Protestant Baden-Durlach in the 1570s and 1580s, moreover, confessional polarities were never far below the surface, witness the protests of the Austrian communes that margravial markets were gaining an unfair advantage by selling meat on fast-days.

# III

The territorial and confessional antagonisms which scarred the Upper Rhine in the later sixteenth century did not, however, prevent the princes and cities of the region from closing ranks in the face of external military emergencies, just as they had done in early centuries. Although the Upper Rhine was largely spared direct invasion, or political *Fremdbestimmung*, as had occurred during the Burgundian mortgage, the constant threat from France kept the authorities on the alert. Either they might fall victim to an escalation of the Habsburg–Valois struggle (or, more precisely, to France's skilful manipulation of the confessional divisions within the Empire), or else the religious wars raging through France might spill over into Alsace. The century was filled with schemes of local defence, known as *Landsrettungen*, a telling phrase which implies that the Upper Rhine was conceived as a *Land* or *pays*, in short, a landscape with a distinct identity of its own. In that sense the *Landsrettungen* were the natural successors of the many defensive territorial alliances (*Landfriedensbündnisse*) of the fourteenth and fifteenth centuries.[18]

Although the earliest demands for such preparations emanated from the Outer Austrian Estates,[19] military logic dictated that, to be effective, any *Landsrettung* must be mounted along the entire line of the Vosges, thereby ignoring the division between Upper and Lower Alsace. The Estates had indeed recognized as much by entering negotiations with the imperial bailiwick of Haguenau to that end in 1515.[20] But the first defensive treaty to embrace Alsace as a whole was concluded in 1537, after the duke of Guise had overrun the village of Saales in the Val de Villé.[21] The shock of this incursion brought Outer Austria—whose only possession north of the Landgraben was the Val de Villé—into a proposed alliance with the bishop of Strasbourg, the counts of Hanau-Lichtenberg and Bitche-Zweibrücken, the commune of the Val de Villé itself, and the cities of Strasbourg, Haguenau, Sélestat, and Colmar in a defensive pact (*Schirmverein*) which went beyond the bounds of previous *Landsrettungen* which had been territorially circumscribed.[22] But such *Schirmvereine* regularly threatened to break asunder on account of the political and confessional animosities

---

[18] Cf. Stolz, 'Landsrettungen', 181.

[19] StAFr, C 1 Landstände 1, 22 July 1515; Bischoff, *Gouvernés et gouvernants*, 192.

[20] Ibid. 193 and 198 n. 72.     [21] Speck, *Landstände*, i. 428.

[22] StAFr, C 1 Landstände 2, 21 Mar. 1537. The alliance was concluded in Sélestat 'auf Hintersichbringen', i.e. for confirmation after referral to the signatory powers. Strasbourg, however, demurred at joining any alliance with the Outer Austrian government, lest it compromise the commercial interests of its merchants in France. Thomas A. Brady, Jr., *Protestant politics: Jakob Sturm (1489–1553) and the German Reformation* (Atlantic Highlands, NJ, 1995), 155.

between the contracting parties. In 1552 king Henri II of France's German campaign once again threw Alsace into a panic, but exhaustive negotiations to prolong the *Schirmverein* were finally abandoned.[23] Within five years, nevertheless, a new defensive alliance had been concluded, which was regularly renewed until formally renegotiated in 1572.[24] Over time, however, the scope and character of such alliances changed. The Strasbourg *Schirmverein* of 1580 (with the highest profile of all the century's alliances) included —under the rubric of convents in Lower Alsace!—four abbeys on the right bank of the Rhine in the Ortenau which lay within the diocese of Strasbourg, namely Ettenheimmünster, Gengenbach, Schüttern, and Schwarzach.[25] The advantages of extending defensive alliances across the Rhine to encompass lordships in the Ortenau and Breisgau became ever more apparent as the military danger was seen to lie not merely in a direct attack by France but from the passage of pillaging mercenaries throughout the Upper Rhine as well.[26] The Protestant imperial Estates, for their part, were keen to see the *Schirmverein* expanded to include not only Baden-Durlach but the elector Palatine and the city of Speyer, too,[27] not least as a counterweight to Austria's dominant influence under archduke Ferdinand of Tirol. Fear of Austrian hegemony was as responsible as Protestant distrust of Catholics for the *Schirmvereine* failing to acquire a permanent identity in the form of a standing army or a common arsenal.[28]

But while a sense of regional identity on the Upper Rhine never quite succeeded in overcoming territorial or confessional divisions, the perceived threat from France ensured that in the course of the sixteenth century the crest of the Vosges became firmly fixed as the frontier between France and the Empire.[29] This is evident from two Outer Austrian *Landsrettungen* in mid-century which were specifically designed to block and guard the seven major passes over

---

[23] Speck, *Landstände*, i. 428. For Strasbourg's attempts, guided by Jakob Sturm, to construct a regional defensive pact see Brady, *Protestant Politics*, 360–62.

[24] Speck, *Landstände*, i. 428–29.     [25] StAFr, C 1 Landstände 14, 14 Feb. 1580.

[26] Speck, *Landstände*, i. 432–33.     [27] Ibid. 432.

[28] Cf. Seidel, *Oberelsaß*, 84.

[29] Bischoff, 'Markante Züge', 280. For the dukes of Lorraine, too, the crest of the Vosges seems to have become the *de facto* frontier, for the dairy-farmers of the Munster valley suddenly found themselves expelled around 1600 from the high pastures on the western slopes of the Vosges where they had grazed their cattle for centuries. Fischer, 'Verdrängung', 11–48.

the Vosges into Upper Alsace.[30] What was striking about these ordinances, moreover, the first in 1543 and the second ten years later, was that they pushed the line of defence westwards in a salient to embrace the town and abbey of Lure in Lorraine (the convent being the sister-house of Murbach).[31] The purpose was to forestall a French advance, not to lay claim to territory beyond the Vosges, for the same ordinances clearly identified Belfort, described as holding the key to the Burgundian Gate, as the western limit of Outer Austria;[32] and its castle was explicitly named by archduke Ferdinand in 1578 as marking the frontier-post towards Burgundy.[33]

# IV

A sense of regional identity on the southern Upper Rhine, we may conclude, had by 1600 neither collapsed nor disappeared—but it had become progressively fractured in the face of territorial and confessional politics. These were not indifferent to regional considerations: the survival of the Rappen coinage circulation area, the continued summoning of regional meat assemblies, and the search for a common defence all bear witness that certain fundamental issues, both political and economic, could only satisfactorily be addressed on a regional basis. Yet the tendency to seek solutions through bilateral negotiations, rather than within the framework of a regional association (which the Rappen league had once constituted) cannot be overlooked. This was, to adopt Tom Brady's phraseology, the 'princely' way, the way of the early modern territorial state (often loosely termed early absolutism), rather than the 'communal' way, the way of the late medieval cities, which pursued regional co-operation as the means of resolving common economic and political problems.[34] But in an area as territorially fragmented as the Upper Rhine, the princely way could never obliterate the

---

[30] Speck, *Landstände*, i. 434–35.

[31] Stolz, 'Landsrettungen', 195–96. Bischoff points out that Lure had already served as an Austrian outpost in the later 15th century. Idem, *Gouvernés et gouvernants*, 195.     [32] Stolz, 'Landsrettungen', 198: 'Beffort ein Ortschlüsseel dieser Landen'.

[33] Georges Bischoff, 'Un symbole de l'Alsace Autrichienne: Belfort du début du XVIe siècle à la Guerre de Trente Ans', in Yvette Baradel, Georges Bischoff, André Larger, Yves Pagnot, and Michel Rilliot, *Histoire de Belfort* (Roanne/Le Coteau, 1985), 108.

[34] Cf. Brady, *Turning Swiss*, especially his conclusion, 222–30, though his argument and mine serve somewhat different purposes.

communal way, all the more so since the pursuit of territorial consolidation—state-building at local level—ran up against the awkwardness of seemingly natural frontiers, which on the Upper Rhine were in fact always too permeable and too vague to permit an easy equation between 'territory' and 'region'.

What stamped a sense of regional identity on the Upper Rhine, as our analysis has traced, was precisely its fluidity and contingency: borders were perceived to follow, and spheres of interest to match, in part, given natural frontiers; in part, political and territorial configurations; and in part, economic and commercial ties. None of these elements—not even the allegedly natural frontiers —was immutable. On the contrary, we have sought to demonstrate how the balance between these variables shifted over time, especially as territorialization began to influence economic and commercial policy. It will be the task of the concluding chapter, therefore, to investigate whether the decline in the economic vitality of the Upper Rhine during the sixteenth century can be attributed to a waning sense of regional economic solidarity.

# 10

# The Faltering of a Regional Economy

## I

The picture of the Upper Rhine as a land flowing with milk and honey, painted in such vivid colours by the Revolutionary of the Upper Rhine around 1500, was the work, not of a realist, but of a landscape impressionist. The rich natural endowment of the Upper Rhine had allowed it to develop throughout the later Middle Ages into one of the most densely urbanized and commercialized areas of Germany, its fortunes underpinned by a flourishing export trade in wine and the exploitation of precious metals, which in turn helped stimulate a lively demand for goods within the region itself. Yet even before the dawn of the seventeenth century and the ravages of the Thirty Years War, the signs of economic sclerosis could not be overlooked. Indeed, the faltering of the regional economy was part of a wider *malaise* affecting the major trading and manufacturing cities of Upper Germany as a whole, including northern Switzerland.

The regional metropolis of the Upper Rhine, Strasbourg, was severely shaken by the collapse in 1559 of the French financial consortium, the Grand Parti, in which its merchants had invested heavily. In its wake many of Strasbourg's merchant families tumbled into bankruptcy in a domino effect over the next two decades, at a time when the city's wine trade was also being exposed to the winds of competition.[1] In the case of Switzerland, the downturn can be measured by the fall in toll receipts from the 1560s in places such as Schaffhausen, Lucerne, or Olten, with textile manufacturing languishing at the same time in major centres such as Zürich and St Gallen, or, as in Fribourg, even earlier.[2] On the Upper Rhine, for the regional submetropolis Basel, however, as Knut

[1] Fuchs, 'Richesse et faillite', 210–11, 215–16; idem, 'Foires', 331–33.
[2] Körner, *Solidarités financières suisses*, 436.

Schulz has argued, the decline should be sought much earlier, back in the opening decades of the fifteenth century. There he instances the perceptible slump in toll revenues levied on the Rhine at Kleinkembs: between 1420 and 1470 they had dropped by more than 50 per cent.[3]

The situation of the leading craft towns on the Upper Rhine was scarcely any better, and their difficulties, too, can be traced to well before 1500. Both Freiburg and Colmar struggled to retrench in the face of demographic wasting and the lack of consumer demand. In the 1450s Freiburg had reduced the number of its guilds from eighteen to twelve,[4] and in 1521 Colmar followed suit by halving the guilds represented on the city council from twenty to ten.[5] Though political and administrative measures should not be taken as a reliable guide to underlying economic circumstances, the evidence of village crafts and market competition, though patchy and uneven before the sixteenth century, suggests that the traditional function and autonomy of local urban centres of manufacturing and distribution was being eroded.

Of course, the picture was not altogether one of unrelieved gloom. Basel's leading role in the Swiss capital market has already been mentioned, and the trickle of wealthy refugees from Catholic lands admitted by the city during the sixteenth century laid the foundations for a revived textile industry, no longer in woollen cloth, but in the luxury stuffs of lace, velvet, and silk.[6] Freiburg im Breisgau's promotion of cutting and polishing semi-precious stones, initially unfettered by guild regulations, represented a unique regional specialization on the Upper Rhine, with a thriving export market (although the trade succumbed to restrictions on production and on new techniques after 1544).[7]

Nevertheless, what once had been a prosperous region with a diversified economy, driven by the interaction of agriculture and manufacturing, was relegated by the late sixteenth century, together

---

[3] Knut Schulz, 'Rheinschiffahrt und städtische Wirtschaftspolitik am Oberrhein im Spätmittelalter', in Erich Maschke and Jürgen Sydow (eds.), *Die Stadt am Fluß: 14. Arbeitstagung in Kehl 14.–16. 11. 1975* (Stadt in der Geschichte: Veröffentlichungen des Südwestdeutschen Arbeitskreises für Stadtgeschichtsforschung, 4) (Sigmaringen, 1978), 175 (table).

[4] Scott, *Freiburg and the Breisgau*, 58. The smallest guilds, no longer capable of sustaining an independent political existence, were merged with larger ones.

[5] Sittler, 'Corporations', 50.        [6] Guggisberg, *Basel*, 39–40.

[7] Gothein, *Wirtschaftsgeschichte des Schwarzwaldes*, 570 ff.

with the whole of southern Germany, to what Immanuel Wallerstein has termed the 'semi-periphery' of an emerging capitalist world-economy, sidelined between strong core economies in northern Europe and their colonial exploited peripheries in eastern Europe and overseas. Though Wallerstein's analysis is highly deterministic, in accepting Perry Anderson's epithet of a 'thwarted Rhenish economy' by the seventeenth century he does acknowledge that the potential to overcome its undoubted difficulties existed within the region, even if it was strangled from outside.[8] What, therefore, were the underlying causes of economic decline on the Upper Rhine, and to what extent should they be regarded as insuperable?

A long list of likely suspects, structural, functional, ecological, has traditionally been paraded. The hidebound policies of the urban craft guilds have frequently been identified as the chief culprit, ever since the writings of liberal economic historians in the nineteenth century. Instinctively hostile towards competition, distrustful of outsiders, and suspicious of technological innovation, the guilds sought to restrict access to membership and to place ceilings on employment and output by individual masters, in order to prevent the accumulation of wealth and therewith economic clout in the hands of a few at the expense of the many artisans, who were thus dragged down into wage-working dependence and social degradation. It is on this general charge that even a modern historian such as Knut Schulz can still indict the guilds of all the Upper Rhenish cities, especially in the last third of the sixteenth century,[9] though he also arraigns Basel's guild of boatmen on the same count in the fifteenth century. It was they who abandoned the city's 'open waters' policy of the preceding century by curtailing admission to the guild (which lost over half its membership by 1500, dropping from over thirty to a mere fifteen), while at the same time enforcing a haulage monopoly downriver as far as Strasbourg. This victory was not achieved without damaging conflicts both with Strasbourg itself, and with the Austrian towns on the *Hochrhein* and Upper Rhine, not least with Breisach, which sought to impose pilotage on all craft passing downriver from Basel on the stretch below the town to Strasbourg. Shipping on the

[8] Immanual Wallerstein, *The modern world-system*, ii. *Mercantilism and the consolidation of the European world-economy, 1600–1750* (New York/London/Toronto/Sydney/San Francisco, 1980), 197.

[9] Schulz, *Handwerksgesellen und Lohnarbeiter*, 453.

Upper Rhine was severely disrupted as a consequence, as the dwindling toll revenues at Kleinkembs testify.[10] Strasbourg, by contrast, which boasted around 150 boatmen in its Anchor guild around 1600, upheld unrestricted navigation at least until the mid-seventeenth century.[11] Increasingly, Schulz argues, merchants were forced to take the slower and more expensive land route through Alsace, thereby adding to their transaction costs. This evidence, taken together with the fateful consequences of the weavers' triumph over the merchant drapers, capped by the protectionist legislation in 1526, bears out with undeniable starkness the dismal judgement on Basel's artisans passed by Traugott Geering over a century ago. As the sixteenth century progressed there would be no room in the city for another buccaneering entrepreneur in the mould of Ulrich Meltinger.

This damning verdict on the craft guilds has been returned elsewhere on the Upper Rhine, notably in Freiburg, where Hermann Flamm, writing at the beginning of this century, believed that it was the predeterminate intention of the craft guilds, once they had acquired power in the later fourteenth century, to introduce a policy of a *geschlossene Stadtwirtschaft*, that is, a closed urban economy, geared to self-sufficiency, hostile to profit, and socially egalitarian.[12] And Lucien Sittler, writing more recently, argued that in Colmar, too, the guilds' natural instincts when faced with adversity were to cling to what they already held: 'D'une façon générale, les corporations devinrent de plus en plus conservatrices.'[13] While the evidence furnished by the guilds' actions is not in doubt, the interpretation of their motives is open to question. In the case of Freiburg, as I have argued elsewhere, an innate predisposition towards exclusion and protectionism cannot always be assumed: these may rather have been the natural and understandable reaction to adversity—to a deterioration in the terms of trade, to market competition, to the exhaustion of resources, to demographic retreat, or to external political upheavals—of which the guilds were the victims, not the culprits.[14] The willingness of the Freiburg council

---

[10] Schulz, *Handwerksgesellen und Lohnarbeiter*, 'Rheinschiffahrt', 170–79.

[11] Ibid. 168.

[12] Hermann Flamm, *Der wirtschaftliche Niedergang Freiburgs i. Br. und die Lage des städtischen Grundeigentums im 14. und 15. Jahrhundert: Ein Beitrag zur Geschichte der geschlossenen Stadtwirtschaft* (Volkswirtschaftliche Abhandlungen der badischen Hochschulen, 8, suppl. vol. 3) (Karlsruhe, 1905).

[13] Sittler, 'Corporations', 50.      [14] Scott, *Freiburg and the Breisgau*, 128–41.

—the very embodiment of artisan aspirations after 1450, according to Flamm—to tolerate deregulation of cloth production from the 1470s, or to promote cutting and polishing as a competitive industry (whatever constraints were subsequently imposed), or, again, the encouragement given to luxury manufactures in Basel and its remarkable rise as the chief financial and credit centre of the Swiss Confederation under the governance of a council whose composition and mentality reflected the dominance achieved by the artisans in the 1520s, give the lie to any supposedly inherent characteristics of craft guilds, a point which has recently been underscored for western Europe as a whole.[15]

Those who have written most authoritatively on the economy of the Upper Rhine have not confined their criticism to the craft guilds alone. Guilds, merchants, and councils have collectively been accused of a failure of nerve, of putting up the shutters, rather than allowing restrictive practices to be blown away by the winds of competition. That was true even in Strasbourg, it has been suggested, where the spate of bankruptcies stretching into the 1570s made the merchant-dominated council increasingly averse to risk at a time when subsistence crises were recurring with alarming frequency. The laudable desire to ensure adequate supplies of grain for its inhabitants also prompted the council to introduce a compulsory staple on wine, which varied according to the size and quality of the vintage. In 1574 the city's wine merchants were obliged to offer every third cask for domestic sale at a fixed price, and foreigners every sixth; in 1577, by contrast, each had to staple every fourth barrel, amidst repeated complaints that local purchasers could not be found.[16] By resorting to a staple policy, the council deterred exports and so contributed in the long run to the decline of the Alsace wine trade, on which the city's fortunes had principally been made, and therewith to the toppling of Alsatian viticulture from the pinnacle among German wine-growing regions.

The example of Strasbourg shows that even the élite of a commercial metropolis could be caught in the dilemma of either satisfying immediate needs or else safeguarding its longer-term interests. How much smaller, therefore, may we presume the ability of ordinary craftsmen to have been, with a generally poor level of knowledge

---

[15] John Langton and Göran Hoppe, *Town and country in the development of early modern western Europe* (Historical Geography Research Series, 11) (Norwich, 1983), 39. [16] Barth, *Rebbau des Elsaß*, i. 414, 417–20.

about resources and markets, supply and demand, to grasp complex economic linkages and to act on them once in office. Instead, we need to ask whether the general economic climate on the Upper Rhine from the fifteenth to the late sixteenth century afforded towns and cities opportunities which they squandered, or obstacles which could not readily be surmounted. We shall need briefly to consider the volume and pattern of commercial activity, the continuing availability of natural resources, and the balance between population and land, though the surviving sources and state of research rarely allow us to draw definite conclusions.

# II

From a European perspective it is a commonplace that the hub of commerce was shifting from its medieval heartland in the Mediterranean to northern Europe and the Atlantic seaboard in particular by the sixteenth century, as a result of the search for a direct passage to the East Indies and the 'discovery' and colonization of the Americas. The old trade routes from Italy to northern Europe overland across the Alps or by inland waterway up the valley of the Rhône yielded to maritime transport along the coasts or overseas. However accurate that may be as a general statement, it cannot by chronology account for the etiolation of water-borne commerce on the Rhine during the fifteenth century, particularly since trade between Italy and the south German cities was still flourishing in this period, as the burgeoning fairs of Geneva, Zurzach, and Frankfurt am Main testify.[17] The Basel boatmen, so excoriated by Schulz, were not in other words understandably but misguidedly seeking to shore up an already dwindling trade, but rather, by their blinkered self-interest, diverting what was still a sizeable volume of commerce from water on to land. Yet, by 1500, receipts in Basel's Exchange had once again reached the levels of the 1420s and 1430s, which suggests that the city's commerce at large had recovered, even if Basel's conflict with Strasbourg over their share of water-borne trade had deflected trade away from the Rhine and so weakened that integrative element in the regional economy.[18]

---

[17] Schulz, 'Rheinschiffahrt', 178.
[18] Ulf Dirlmeier, 'Mittelalterliche Zoll- und Stapelrechte als Handelshemmnisse', in Hans Pohl (ed.), *Die Auswirkungen von Zöllen und anderen Handelshemmnissen auf Wirtschaft und Gesellschaft vom Mittelalter bis zur Gegenwart: Referate*

To focus on the Rhine alone in any case narrows one's angle of vision to no more than the north–south artery of trade. While commerce between France and Germany along a south–west axis through the Burgundian Gate rarely achieved more than local significance (with the exception of livestock), the routes over the Vosges saw bustling traffic between Alsace and Lorraine at least until 1520. After that date, it is true, a depression set in, notwithstanding the opening up of new silver-mines in the southern ranges of the Vosges. This manifested itself in the decline of St-Nicolas-de-Port near Nancy in Lorraine, where routes over the Vosges came together in what Odile Kammerer has termed 'a European crossroads', its merchants fanning outwards to do business in France, Switzerland, and Germany.[19] The mountains, once a spinal cord whose vertebrae had linked Alsace with Lorraine, now became a barrier, a true political frontier. The power-struggle between the Empire and France must bear much of the blame—witness the *Landsrettungen* which were ready to guard and block the major passes—aside from any epochal shift to an Atlantic economy.

But another culprit has commonly been identified as sapping commercial vitality: the profusion of imposts, be they turnpike tolls (*Wegegelder*) or customs duties (*Zölle*). The succession of tollstations down the Rhine—from Strasbourg to the Dutch border thirty-one survived from the Middle Ages to the Napoleonic era, mostly concentrated between Mainz and Cologne—has invariably been invoked as a grotesque example of the Empire's parlous division into a welter of duodecimo principalities, each jealously asserting its diminutive independence. Surely, it is often argued, the inevitable inflation of transaction costs must have crippled commerce. This view has recently been challenged by Ulf Dirlmeier, who points out that until the mercantilist era tolls were essentially transit dues rather than protectionist imposts, and that a toll levied for fiscal purposes at a rate so high that it blocks the flow of goods must lead logically *ad absurdum*. Moreover, goods shipped on the Rhine often paid a flat-rate considerably lower than the sum of individual tolls, and the weights and measures used to calculate toll-charges were frequently much less than those applied to the

---

*der 11. Arbeitstagung der Gesellschaft für Sozial- und Wirtschaftsgeschichte vom 9. bis 13. April 1985 in Hohenheim* (*Vierteljahrschrift für Sozial- und Wirtschaftsgeschichte*, suppl. 80) (Stuttgart, 1987), 36, 38.

[19] Kammerer, 'Carrefour alsacien-lorrain', 94.

goods themselves.[20] Confirmation of this line of argument may be found in the fact that, until the sixteenth century, the most sought-after wines from Germany in overseas markets were those from Alsace, precisely the wines which had to pass the greatest number of customs-posts on their journey downriver. There is no evidence that the burden of toll-charges on the Rhine below Strasbourg increased disproportionately to the point where they might be held responsible for a decline in wine exports.

That was not necessarily true of the river Ill, however, the Rhine's flanking tributary in Alsace, along whose banks was strung out a network of wine-trading cities, with Colmar and Sélestat the most prominent. Right at the end of the sixteenth century, in 1595, the Outer Austrian government increased the toll-rates on water-borne goods, and in 1611 actually doubled the new tariff, thereby hitting Colmar's exports as they passed the customs-post at Illhaeusern. In a petition to archduke Maximilian four years later, the city lamented that its wine exports to Holland, once amounting to several thousand barrels annually, had shrunk to little over one hundred, with Dutch merchants transferring their attention to Lower Alsace and the Palatinate.[21] Austria's need to raise revenue in the face of constant campaigns against the Ottomans on its eastern frontier had already led in the mid-sixteenth century to a wide-ranging enquiry throughout the length and breadth of its scattered possessions into the prospects of raising toll-rates on the principal highways.[22] One of the recommendations was to add a sixth toll-stage on the Rhine itself between Basel and Strasbourg at Biesheim, which the Upper Austrian government in Innsbruck believed would do least damage to trade on the river or overland.[23] (Austria already had eleven toll-posts on land routes through Upper Alsace, though only one on the right bank, at Breisach.)[24]

That was a mere pin-prick in comparison with the new customs duties levied throughout Outer Austria in 1560 on all imported and

---

[20] Dirlmeier, 'Mittelalterliche Zoll- und Stapelrechte', 20, 26–29.

[21] Barth, *Rebbau des Elsaß*, i. 429.

[22] Otto Stolz, 'Die Verkehrsverbindungen des oberen Rhein- und Donaugebiets um die Mitte des 16. Jahrhunderts', *Zeitschrift für die Geschichte des Oberrheins*, 77 (NS 38) (1923), 61.

[23] Ibid. 74. The other five toll-stages were at Neuenburg, Breisach, Burkheim, Limburg, and Rhinau.

[24] Toll-posts in Alsace were situated at Cernay, Thann, Masevaux, Habsheim, Ottmarsheim, Battenheim, Staffelfelden, Ensisheim, Dessenheim, Illhaeusern, and Bergheim. Seidel, *Oberelsaß*, 186.

exported goods except foodstuffs, which so provoked the wrath of the territorial Estates. The Innsbruck authorities, while sceptical that the clamour bore much relation to the actual harm inflicted, were willing to alter the provisions so that they applied solely to goods from beyond Outer Austria, though, as we have seen, the other powers on the Upper Rhine—the imperial cities, the Upper Mundat, or the Württemberg lordships—were treated in this regard as foreign territory despite lying within the area of the Rappen coinage league. The political fragmentation of the Upper Rhine offered ample scope for commercial extortion by those who controlled strategic routes and vantage-points, as the disputes between the lords of Bollweiler and the inhabitants of the Upper Mundat alluded to earlier, or—with the boot on the other foot—the complaints by Murbach subjects in Guebwiller in 1525 at double tolls demanded of them when they traversed the Upper Mundat, testify.[25]

By the same token, it lay in the logic of territorial fragmentation on the Upper Rhine that tolls as a means of raising revenue —whether quantitatively in terms of tariffs or qualitatively by the discriminatory treatment of foreigners—were at best a blunt instrument, for, if pressed too far, they merely elicited the threat of retaliation, evasion, or boycott. The officials caught up in the long-running conflict between Austrian and Baden markets and customs-posts in the Breisgau, were, as we have noted, prone to reflect on the futility of a policy of territorial autarky *à l'outrance*. Yet the path to territorial consolidation, as it passed through the lengthening shadows of inflation and dearth, led ineluctably towards policies which put territorial before regional interests, as Austria's imposition of tolls on grain exported even to fellow-members of the Rappen coinage league indicates. Though suspended whenever plenty returned, restrictions on free trade in foodstuffs (including wine) by whatever means, however prudent as a precaution against food riots, reflected a mercantilist mentality which in the narrow confines of the Upper Rhine was more likely to enervate than to stimulate the regional economy.

When we turn to reserves of minerals and precious metals and their extraction, a chronological divergence between both banks of the Rhine is immediately apparent. Although the sixteenth century witnessed something of a mining boom in Alsace, the heyday of silver-mining in the Breisgau had long passed. The fortunes

---

[25] Bischoff, *Recherches*, 147.

which Freiburg's patrician families had derived from their stake in
the mines of the southern Black Forest mountains enabled the town
to outgrow its original limits, as the population swelled to perhaps
10,000 by the mid-fourteenth century, engaged both in craft production and in a flourishing woollen textile industry. Yet Freiburg's
rapid decline after 1350 (which had several causes) shows just how
precarious the foundations of an urban economy driven by the exploitation of mineral resources might be. Technological difficulties
(essentially how to pump out water from the deeper shafts) rather
than exhaustion of the lodes were chiefly to blame, and once better
pumping equipment had been devised the mines on the Schauinsland and environs (particularly the Münster valley, and the Zastler
valley above Oberried)[26] enjoyed a modest revival in the sixteenth
century, though the few mining speculators who risked their capital in new ventures never, it seems, recouped their investment.[27]

In Alsace, by contrast, no city was as heavily dependent on
mining as Freiburg had been, so that when production in the Val
de Villé and the Val de Lièpvre passed its peak after 1550 the yields
(which dwindled only gradually until the end of the century) made
far less severe an impact on the local urban economy. In any case,
new mines in the foothills of the southern Vosges began to come
on stream, so that the quantity of silver which Basel, for instance,
was able to draw from Giromagny and Haut-Auxelles quickly out-
stripped the Val de Lièpvre after 1560.[28] But how far these new
mines attracted investment from urban entrepreneurs is another
matter. Towards the end of the century, their shareholders seem
largely to have been drawn from the ranks of Outer Austrian nobles
and officials;[29] indeed, a leading member of the second Estate,
Hans Ulrich von Stadion, emerged in 1590 as the controlling member of a joint-stock company which was granted the right to smelt
ore from mines on Austrian territory throughout the Upper Rhine.[30]
The mines of the Vosges also yielded some lead and copper (as
one would expect in the proximity of argentiferous rock), but in
the lordship of Rosemont in the southern Vosges iron-ore was discovered as well, though whether its extraction ever achieved more

[26] Bissegger, *Silberversorgung*, 42.
[27] Schlageter, 'Der mittelalterliche Bergbau', 157–61; Scott, *Freiburg and the
Breisgau*, 114.          [28] Bissegger, *Silberversorgung*, 174.
[29] Speck, *Landstände*, i. 497–98.
[30] Stolz, 'Geschichte des Bergbaus', 155–56; Speck, *Landstände*, i. 498.

than local significance is uncertain: an iron-mining concession granted on Murbach territory in the Thur valley in 1479 had never come to much.[31]

Nevertheless, the availability of silver had sustained the viability of a regional coinage system long after similar endeavours had foundered elsewhere, so that the termination of the Rappen league in 1584, although *au fond* a political act by archduke Ferdinand of Tirol, reflects also the growing difficulties which the league faced in procuring adequate supplies of bullion at a tolerable price. A comparison with the quite differently organized Strasbourg coinage area should counsel us against becoming too dewy-eyed at the demise of the Rappen league; rather, it is the impetus which it gave to regional economic co-operation on a wider scale which counts, for the erosion of that solidarity by territorial and confessional imperatives was but another aspect of the impediments to trade which new tolls and staples might cause.

The hardest of the issues to address is the balance between population and land. If one accepts the argument that the demographic growth rate provides a *rough* index of economic performance (taking Malthus's view that pre-industrial populations would eventually expand if the resources to sustain them were available),[32] then a recovery from the economic and demographic trough of the fifteenth century can be posited for the Upper Rhine (as for most other parts of Europe) from approximately 1470 until the middle decades of the sixteenth century. After 1560, however, it appears that the population was once again knocking at the limits of what existing agricultural productivity could support. The ensuing subsistence crises of the latter part of the century would, over time, have doubtless restored the homeostatic balance between people and land (following the classic Malthusian pattern), but the campaigns of the Thirty Years War, when armies vied for control of the strategic artery of the Upper Rhine, devastated the region and left it emasculated for much of the seventeenth century. If Christian Pfister's findings for Switzerland can be applied to the Upper Rhine, with some adjustment for the generally warmer climate, then the region may have suffered the double blow after 1560 of a deteriorating climate, both cooler and wetter, with correspondingly lower

---

[31] Bischoff, *Recherches*, 149.
[32] Cf. Epstein, 'Cities, regions, and the late medieval crisis', 16.

crop yields, in the context of a zero-growth agrarian system which was incapable of sustaining an increase in output to feed a swelling population.

One assumption commonly made on the basis of evidence from other parts of Europe is that in response to this dilemma pastoral land was turned back to tillage in a desperate attempt to grow more bread grain. But the impoverishment of the population at large and the retreat from a hitherto diversified and specialized agricultural regime only dampened consumer demand and so contributed to a spiral of economic decline. We have no statistical information to say whether recourse to cereal agriculture (*Vergetreidung*, as it is called in German) was widespread on the Upper Rhine, though in 1571, at the onset of the first prolonged dearth, the Strasbourg council considered reducing the cultivation of hemp in its rural territories to make more land available for cereals.[33] Some general observations, however, can be put forward. By comparison with its neighbours, the Upper Rhine continued to be regarded as a breadbasket (and as a wine-barrel, for that matter) well into the seventeenth century. That may have deterred the authorities from importing grain on a large scale, on the grounds that the crises were periodic, not systemic. Pastoralism was never so prevalent on the Upper Rhine—as the agonizings of the Rappen league over meat provisioning so abundantly document—that it encouraged (or necessitated) the kind of solution to a structural deficit of cereals adopted most famously in the Low Countries, which began to import grain on a vast scale after 1500. For Alsace, and to a lesser extent the Breisgau, the issue in any case was not so much pastoralism as viticulture. And here the arguments in favour of a switch from wine-growing to arable husbandry were much less compelling. Since viticulture could employ eight times the manpower of cereal agriculture, it was far more capable than tillage of absorbing a swelling band of landless labourers in what was an area of thoroughgoing partible inheritance at a time of presumed population growth. An increase in land under grain cultivation would have made the problem of idle hands far more acute; moreover, the best viticultural sites, on account of their steep elevation and exposure, were quite unsuited to arable farming.

To assess the balance of economic advantage on the Upper Rhine—how far an export-geared viticulture was able to keep the

---

[33] Fuchs, 'Foires', 327–28.

rural population's head above water—we would need to know what percentage of Alsatian, and Breisgau or Ortenau, wine was in fact exported; what proportion of land under vines was ranged along the well-situated slopes or located in the less well-drained lowlands of the valley floor; and what rate of return viticulture was yielding as the century progressed. Certainly vines were in retreat from the rolling downs of the Sundgau (where cereals may very well have replaced them), and from the northernmost districts of Lower Alsace,[34] but the true calamity occurred (as logic would dictate), not in a period of population pressure, but when the population had been decimated by warfare in the early 1600s, thereby stripping viticulture of its labour force. The real problem for viticulture in the sixteenth century seems indeed to have been a fall in exports. Reliable figures for either bank of the Upper Rhine are well-nigh impossible to compute (for the Breisgau more so than Alsace), quite apart from the allowances which must be made for wide fluctuations in the quantity and quality of each vintage. The statistics for Strasbourg, for instance, contained in various chronicle sources from the 1570s onwards are so discrepant as to be, in Médard Barth's view, all but worthless. But, taken in the round, they do seem to show an unmistakable deterioration in the volume of exports after the mid-1580s.[35] In part, Alsace may have been the victim of fashion, for we know that plantings of red varietals increased in the sixteenth century to meet the competition from heavier wines grown in France and the Mediterranean, while the Palatinate and the Rheingau had already begun to challenge the supremacy of Alsace wines towards the close of the fifteenth century.[36] And the increased consumption of beer (much cheaper than wine), not only in many north German cities but, after 1500, in parts of southern Germany as well, notably Bavaria, caused the market for the premium Alsatian wines to shrink further.[37] But Alsace was also the victim of its own success. In Switzerland, a major export market for Alsatian wines in the Middle Ages, first Zürich in the fifteenth century, and then Bern, after its conquest of the

[34] Barth, *Rebbau des Elsaß*, i. 39.     [35] Ibid. 427–28.

[36] Ibid. 407; Wolff, 'Le Vignoble', 449, 455. Cf. also Klaus Militzer, 'Handel und Vertrieb rheinischer und elsässischer Weine über Köln im Spätmittelalter', in Alois Gerlach (ed.), *Weinbau, Weinhandel und Weinkultur: Sechstes Alzeyer Kolloquium* (Geschichtliche Landeskunde, 40) (Stuttgart, 1993), 165–85.

[37] Cf. Scott, 'Economic landscapes', 13; Dirlmeier, 'Mittelalterliche Zoll- und Stapelrechte', 35, argues that the switch to ale can be dated to the 15th century, thereby helping to account for the decline in Rhine shipping before 1500.

wine-growing district of the Vaud on Lake Geneva in 1536, imposed discriminatory tolls or even import bans to protect their own fledgling wine industry,[38] though exports to other parts of the Confederation still flourished.[39] As far as profitability is concerned, the most that can be said is that the presumed cooler and wetter climate after 1560 would have brought a greater frequency of poorer vintages and therewith smaller returns in its train, but the sources do not allow us to put any statistical flesh on the bare bones of this hypothesis. We should remember at the same time, however, that any abandonment of lesser vineyards in favour of those which produced better-quality wines may have created a scarcity which could only bolster prices.

The setbacks which viticulture, the bell-wether of the agrarian economy, encountered on the Upper Rhine in the course of the sixteenth century place a question-mark over the resilience of the rural economy as a whole. Clearly the subsistence crises after 1570 hit some areas harder than others. The pleas for doles of corn from its capacious granary which reached the city fathers of Strasbourg in such numbers were chiefly submitted by communities on the right bank of the Rhine in the Ortenau and the Black Forest—or even beyond into Swabia—rather than from Alsace itself.[40] No doubt such appeals were expressed with calculated plangency, but they were widespread and frequent none the less. It would be useful to know how many villages were able to pay promptly and in full for any stocks received, though the fact that such requests were reiterated (and acceded to) year after year suggests that no large debts were run up;[41] only a few remote Black Forest communes asked for corn on tick.[42] The problems of rural debt and credit, and

---

[38] Ammann, 'Wirtschaftsgeltung', 112; idem, 'Elsässisch-schweizerische Wirtschaftsbeziehungen', 51–52; Barth, *Rebbau des Elsaß*, i. 425–26.

[39] Lucien Sittler, 'Le Commerce du vin de Colmar jusqu'en 1789', *Revue d'Alsace*, 89 (1949), 50–51; Barth, *Rebbau des Elsaß*, i. 424–25.

[40] Fuchs, 'Foires', 326–27.

[41] To take one example: in March 1573 the magistrate of Rotenfels by Rastatt requested 60 quarters of corn, with the villagers to stand surety for the debt, which was to be discharged between Martinmas and Christmas (i.e. after the next wine harvest); in a codicil, the Baden-Baden administrator in Kuppenheim promised to use his office to ensure that the money was paid. AMS, IV 17/35, 16 Mar. 1573.

[42] Cf. the request by Völkersbach, Burbach, and Metzlinschwanderhof (in or near the Alb valley) (AMS, IV 17/51, 14 Apr. 1573); Ersingen and Bilfingen (north-west of Pforzheim) (AMS, IV 17/55, 27 May 1573); and Grünwettersbach by Durlach (AMS, IV 17/65(a), 1 June 1573).

the vulnerability of peasant smallholders locked into petty commodity production for the market, have barely been explored for
the Upper Rhine, but, if the tenor of the grievances voiced during
the market disputes between Baden and Austria in the Breisgau is
any guide, then the struggle over access to markets concealed a
deeper dysfunction in a rural economy which was still bound by
rigidities of production and distribution, and yet whose dependency on the market left it peculiarly exposed to any general economic depression.

A provisional balance-sheet, therefore, having taken into account
the increasing institutional handicaps to commerce, the shrinkage
of natural resources, and the discrepancy between mouths to feed
and the land available to grow food, might conclude that the economy of the Upper Rhine experienced structural difficulties which
even the most enlightened officials in princely chanceries or urban
council chambers, charged with weighing political, territorial, and
social priorities against economic advantage, would have been
hard put to overcome. To test this verdict, we must now set these
empirical findings for the Upper Rhine in the context of recent
theoretical approaches to the transformation of the European economy between late medieval and early modern times.

# III

In his study of the Dutch rural economy in the sixteenth and seventeenth centuries, Jan de Vries begins by postulating two models
of rural development, which he terms the 'peasant' and the 'specialization' models. Each presumes an initial balance between population and resources, which is disrupted by demographic growth,
and not readily rectified given the limited opportunities for trade.[43]
But the response of each model to this imbalance could not be
more different. In the 'peasant' model, holdings are subdivided, and
the demand for foodstuffs requires more intensive cultivation of
the land, with a concomitant increase in labour input. Farm incomes
decline, so that peasants seek a variety of by-employments. At the
same time, peasants cannot produce enough grain for themselves
and are forced to buy elsewhere, but because grain prices therefore rise peasants have less cash surplus to buy other goods, and

[43] Jan de Vries, *The Dutch rural economy in the Golden Age, 1500–1700* (New
Haven/London, 1974), 4.

so they shun the urban markets. They revert to what is effectively a subsistence economy, succumb to debt and a deterioration in their tenancy rights at the hands of institutional landowners, such as the Church or noble dynasties, who alone can benefit from the crisis because their estates are not subject to parcellization. Differences of wealth and status open up among the peasantry, notably with the rise of a cottar class, whose wage-rates are squeezed. Above all, the attenuation of commercial ties between town and country inhibits urban growth and so puts a brake on wider economic development.[44]

In the 'specialization' model, by contrast, peasants adopt an entirely different strategy. Not only are farms kept intact and not subdivided, peasants abandon non-agricultural by-employments and concentrate on raising agricultural output in order to sell their surplus on the open market to townsfolk, buying craft goods in exchange. The upward pressure on agrarian prices bestows a measure of prosperity on peasants, which acts as a barrier against predatory urban capitalists. Any surplus rural population either emigrates to the towns or else finds new rural full-time employment in building roads or canals, in ironmongery or petty trading. The interaction of town and country stimulates local or regional trade (rather than long-distance commerce) as a decisive precondition for urban growth. The countryside becomes peopled with specialized producers, no longer the peasantry as 'the' rural class, but as 'a' class of farmers alongside another group who are artisans living and working in quasi-urban settlements, communities distinct from purely agricultural villages (known as *vlekken* in the area of the northern Netherlands studied by de Vries).[45]

This is the path followed by the Dutch economy from the sixteenth century onwards in certain parts of the Low Countries—in essence, the maritime provinces of the north-west and centre, rather than the provinces further east or south. Here the population of farmers remained steady, while the output from pastoralism and dairying improved markedly; instead, it was the non-farming population which grew, independently of any urban investment or the spread of the putting-out system, engaging in activities directly supportive of an intensified, market-integrated agriculture (shipbuilding

---

[44] de Vries, *Dutch rural economy*, 4–7.     [45] Ibid. 7–11, 102, 120.

for transport, petty trading to supply consumer goods to farmers).[46] New village markets in *vlekken* and elsewhere sprang up, in the teeth of opposition from the towns in what was already a densely urbanized landscape, as outlets for more frequent and convenient marketing of agrarian produce. These markets, however, did not undermine the older urban centres (despite the latter's vociferous protests), which maintained their general dominance of the commodity markets.[47]

The contrasting outcomes of the 'peasant' and the 'specialization' models are highly suggestive in the context of the Upper Rhine, for many of the features which seem to stamp its economy in our period—the diversification and commercialization of its agriculture, the spread of rural crafts (and guilds) and village markets, the mutual stimulus given by differing yet adjacent ecologies and topographies to the development of an integrated regional economy—turn out, in the light of de Vries' findings, to be rather less significant than they first appear. No one, not even Robert Brenner, doubts that the traditional peasant economy of medieval Europe contained the capacity to innovate and to develop. The spread of industrial crops such as hemp, flax, woad, and madder, or the concentration of production in certain areas on viticulture, dairying, or horticulture speak for themselves. But these improvements were achieved, as Brenner reminds us, by means of greater labour intensity to the point of peasant 'self-exploitation', not by greater efficiency on the part of the labour deployed. Any talk of 'development', therefore, is highly misleading; these changes could be wrought without any transformation in the mode of production.[48]

This is particularly clear in the case of viticulture on the Upper Rhine. It is beyond question that the spread of wine-growing underpinned the remarkable flowering of its regional economy in the later Middle Ages. Without the profits from wine exports beyond the region to northern Germany and internationally to countries overseas, the commercialization of the rural economy, on the one hand, and the profusion of urban centres as entrepôts and relay-points for distribution, on the other—in short, the integration of town and

---

[46] Ibid. 125–27, 137.     [47] Ibid. 155–57.

[48] Robert Brenner, 'Agrarian class structure and economic development in pre-industrial Europe', in T. H. Aston and C. H. E. Philpin (eds.), *The Brenner debate: Agrarian class structure and economic development in pre-industrial Europe* (Cambridge, 1985), 50.

country in a regional economic system of reciprocal supply and demand between central places and their complementary hinterlands to which its rich natural endowment already predisposed it would have been much less intense. Yet, however commercially successful viticulture may have been (and that was always truer of Alsace than of the vineyards on the right bank of the river), it left the structure of social relations untouched. Communal village institutions, tenurial rights, inheritance customs (this was an area of partible inheritance, with the inherent danger of parcellization!), never mind the web of seigneurial ties which bound peasants to their feudal overlords, were neither altered nor eroded. Above all, the peasantry itself, or rather, the peasant household economy based on family or kin-group labour, remained intact. Viticulture may have brought prosperity but, as Barrington Moore once sardonically replied to those who attributed the backwardness of the *ancien-régime* economy in France to a depression in the wine trade, 'while it is pleasant to contemplate wine-drinking as at least a potential cure for economic backwardness', the prospect was not realistic— though he admitted that his remarks applied to *vin ordinaire*, 'and not to a luxury product from which it was possible to make a fortune and put a shoulder to the economy'.[49]

Within the 'peasant' model, commercial agriculture supplying regional or international markets proved itself incapable of overcoming a homeostatic imbalance between population and resources. That has been clearly demonstrated in the sixteenth century for the fertile Île de France, whose output was geared to the consumer demand of the Parisian market. After production had peaked at the start of the century, a rise in the rural population encouraged peasants to parcel out their smallholdings and to turn more land over to meeting their immediate subsistence needs. Flax and hemp, which had been grown as commercial crops, declined, as did stock-rearing, in favour of tillage. By 1540, less grain, not more, was being sent to the Parisian market. Brenner concludes that 'the peasant grip on production was clearly responsible for shifting the growth of output'.[50] That commercial agriculture in the Low Countries

[49] Barrington Moore, Jr., *Social origins of dictatorship and democracy: Lord and peasant in the making of the modern world* (Harmondsworth, 1969), 46–47. I am indebted to Jan de Vries for this reference.

[50] Robert Brenner, 'The agrarian roots of European capitalism', in Aston and Philpin, *Brenner debate*, 307.

failed to succumb to this Malthusian crisis, Brenner ascribes (true to the primacy which he accords class analysis) to a fundamentally differing set of social relations. The absence of a powerful landlord class able to resort to extra-economic coercion, indeed, the virtual disappearance of serfdom itself (if it had ever existed in the northern Netherlands), the lack of an entrenched 'patriarchal' and 'possessing' peasantry, and the early development of leasehold tenancies (the key to the rise of capitalist agriculture) all played their part.[51] Here Brenner is content to follow de Vries's own arguments,[52] though he is willing to concede de Vries's further point that the nature of agricultural production itself—specialization in dairying and pastoralism for exchange, and a concomitant need to buy grain on the open market—was also significant, over and above the pattern of class relations.[53] In more general terms, regions within Europe which produced only food or raw materials for the international market, on whatever scale, failed to impart a stimulus to the specialization of their domestic economies. That was true, for instance, of the Scandinavian timber trade, which flourished alongside a traditional peasant household economy; and a similar point has been made for ore-mining in Russia.[54] Even luxury wines, therefore, despite Barrington Moore's concession, may in fact have been incapable of invigorating the wider economy of their region.

A convenient way of assessing which set of conditions, 'peasant' or 'specialization', obtained on the Upper Rhine is to examine the grievances voiced by the rural population during the Peasants' War of 1524–26. These make it abundantly clear how irksome the restrictions on freedom of person, property, and movement weighed upon the subjects of feudal lords. Even the one treaty of pacification which offered some easement of the peasants' burdens, that concluded at the end of May 1525 between the princes and imperial knights of the Ortenau and their subjects, which held out the prospect of the abolition of serfdom, seems thereafter to have been quietly allowed to lapse.[55] But what is so striking about the peasants' demands on the Upper Rhine (and throughout Upper

---

[51] Ibid. 319–20.
[52] de Vries, *Dutch rural economy*, 233; idem, 'On the modernity of the Dutch republic', *Journal of Economic History*, 33 (1973), 194–95.
[53] Brenner, 'Agrarian roots', 320.     [54] Prak, 'Regioni', 26.
[55] Cf. Scott and Scribner, *German Peasants' War*, 284–88 (no. 136).

Germany in general) is that they nowhere reflect the significant growth within the agrarian economy of rural crafts and village markets. To take the grievances of 1525 at face value, one would be led to believe that a single undifferentiated class of smallholding tenants was in revolt, with scarcely a word wasted on cottars, landless labourers, or artisans. Yet, given that these groups undoubtedly existed, do they confirm or contradict the 'peasant' model put forward by de Vries?

An unequivocal answer is hard to give because the waters have been somewhat muddied by the debate over proto-industrialization.[56] Wilfried Reininghaus singles out south-west Germany and northern Switzerland, we may recall, as the areas with the greatest concentration of crafts and the highest population density, yet with relatively little rural immiseration.[57] His argument is based on several local studies, but these are essentially confined to Switzerland, and present evidence which chronologically does not stretch back before the mid-sixteenth century.[58] These studies identify a vast proliferation of crafts in the *seventeenth* century—precisely the period when the population of northern Switzerland was growing rapidly (quite unlike most of Germany, of course, because Switzerland largely escaped the depredations of the Thirty Years War) and diversifying into domestic industries to the point where the countryside became a true proto-industrial *Gewerbelandschaft*, dependent on grain imports from neighbouring Swabia,[59] a process more akin to the 'specialization' model elaborated for the northern Low Countries than the phenomenon of rural by-employment. Those whom one might term 'traditional' rural craftsmen—tailors, cobblers, cabinetmakers, coopers, tanners, tinsmiths, potters, rope-makers, saddlers, cartwrights—alongside textile workers, who may in some cases have been put-out by urban employers, can certainly be found before 1600,[60] but they were neither all that numerous nor

---

[56] Cf. most recently Sheilagh Ogilvie, 'Institutions and economic development in early modern central Europe', *Transactions of the Royal Historical Society*, 6th series, 5 (1995), 221–50.     [57] Reininghaus, *Gewerbe in der frühen Neuzeit*, 70.

[58] Cf. esp. Jean Jacques Siegrist, 'Beiträge zur Verfassungs- und Wirtschaftsgeschichte der Herrschaft Hallwil', *Argovia*, 64 (1952), 5–533; Anne-Marie Dubler and Jean Jacques Siegrist, 'Wohlen: Geschichte von Recht, Wirtschaft und Bevölkerung einer frühindustrialisierten Gemeinde im Aargau', ibid. 86 (1974), 5–709; Jean Jacques Siegrist, 'Muri in den Freien Ämtern', i. 'Geschichte des Raumes der nachmaligen Gemeinde Muri vor 1798', ibid. 95 (1983), pp. i–xii, 1–292.

[59] Göttmann, *Getreidemarkt*, 14 and *passim*.

[60] Siegrist, 'Hallwil', 426; Dubler and Siegrist, 'Wohlen', 506–7; Siegrist, 'Muri', 235–36.

did they destroy the fabric of rural society: they were 'specialists in a world of fairly balanced self-subsistence'.[61] Moreover, a recent study of the Zürich lowlands, a traditional area of tillage, for the *eighteenth* century has concluded that the traditional rural crafts-men (known as *Professionisten*) were completely integrated into rural society, which they helped to shape and sustain, quite unlike the impact of proto-industrialization on the countryside, as in the contrasting hill country of the Zürich Oberland.[62] The traditional craftsmen were as socially differentiated as the rest of the rural population, and their status corresponded very closely to the size of their *agrarian* holdings. Even the richer craftsmen, those who possessed an operating franchise and often owned their own plant or machinery (the *Ehaftenbesitzer*, as they were termed), while constituting a sort of craft aristocracy, were not much different from the larger peasants.[63] No need to focus on landless labour or by-employment, therefore—these independent craftsmen with monopoly privileges and an urban masterpiece behind them were also part and parcel of the peasant economy and society.

These findings help to put the situation on the Upper Rhine into perspective. Even if it can be shown that the ranks of rural artisans in the Breisgau, Ortenau, and in Alsace had in some cases detached themselves entirely from the primary sector and were indeed full-time master craftsmen (with apprentices) or petty dealers, and not simply peasants eking out their existence through by-employments, as the patchy evidence considered earlier suggests, that does not in itself prove that the specialization model was replacing a disintegrating peasant model. By the same token, the emergence of rural guilds in the later sixteenth century (for which the evidence is much less ambiguous) cannot be taken as a sign of decisive social and economic transformation, for their origins in most cases can be traced either to a reflex on the part of rural arti-sans to seek safety in numbers, or to pressure to form confessional groupings, at a time of economic depression (as Dubler has argued

---

[61] Dubler and Siegrist, 'Wohlen', 521.

[62] Thomas Meier, *Handwerk, Hauswerk, Heimarbeit: Nicht-agrarische Tätigkeiten und Erwerbsformen in einem traditionellen Ackerbaugebiet des 18. Jahrhunderts (Zürcher Unterland)* (Zürich, 1986), 267. For the contrasting situation in the Zürich Oberland, see the classic study by Rudolf Braun, *Industrialisierung und Volksleben: Die Veränderungen der Lebensformen in einem ländlichen Industriegebiet vor 1800*, 2nd edn. (Göttingen, 1979).

[63] Meier, *Handwerk, Hauswerk, Heimarbeit*, 266.

for Lucerne),[64] or to the administrative desire of princes and urban magistracies to territorialize guilds, that is, to bring urban and rural craftsmen under one roof for the sake of better supervision, in order to check or suppress the spread of rural crafts, which had for so long been the bane of urban guildsfolk.

Nevertheless, the existence of rural guilds is a crucial indication (in the absence of reliable quantitative evidence) that artisanal by-employment was entrenched on the Upper Rhine. But what our earlier arguments have suggested is that the spread of rural crafts can be observed well before the demographic revival of the sixteenth century. If the complaints of a town such as Freiburg im Breisgau can be believed, the secondary sector was flourishing in the countryside in the fifteenth century, when the economy was generally still flat. Add to that the relative insignificance of a rural landless proletariat (where viticulture's labour needs may have provided a demographic safety valve), and Helga Schultz's contention acquires some force, namely that the peculiarly intensive exchange between town and country evident in Baden (and Württemberg), by giving a powerful boost to both agrarian and artisanal simple commodity production, contributed to a commercial vitality within the regional economy which in the long term was more significant in creating and sustaining employment (and prosperity) than long-distance trade.[65] What can be said, however, is that the characteristic division within the specialization model between true agricultural villages dedicated to commercial production, on the one hand, and quasi-urban rural settlements such as the *vlekken*, on the other, subsisting in economic symbiosis with their farming neighbours, never gained a foothold on the Upper Rhine in the early modern period. Even in eighteenth-century Baden, where as many as 30 per cent of village households comprised craftsmen, the latter remained part of their existing communities, not hived off into separate settlements.[66]

In this context the proliferation of markets in the countryside needs to be interpreted with caution. While it is true that on the

[64] Dubler, *Handwerk, Gewerbe und Zunft*, 193.

[65] Schultz, *Landhandwerk im Übergang*, 76–77.

[66] Cf. Albrecht Strobel, *Agrarverfassung im Übergang: Studien zur Agrargeschichte des badischen Breisgaus vom Beginn des 16. bis zum Ausgang des 18. Jahrhunderts* (Forschungen zur oberrheinischen Landesgeschichte, 23) (Freiburg im Breisgau/Munich, 1972), 183, 205 (app. 2).

Upper Rhine complementary zones of production—dairy produce, hides, timber, honey in the hills; cereals, fruits, wine, industrial crops in the plain—gave an automatic stimulus to commercial exchange, that in itself tells us little about the background to particular market foundations. During the later Middle Ages the welter of urban charters and market franchises can be taken to reflect, however obliquely or belatedly, the needs of a growing population and volume of consumer demand. But given that market foundations were dependent on regalian authority, economic motives were always heavily laced with seigneurial and territorial designs. By the sixteenth century, however, the latter often outweighed any commercial rationale (or, put more precisely, became indistinguishable from the latter under the sign of autarky): hence the spate of what Meinrad Schaab called 'mutually paralysing' little central places. Baden's conflict with Austria over markets was as much a political as an economic trial of strength. Had the margraves' primary intention been to assist the general economic development of their territories, one might well have expected the deliberate promotion of certain towns as commercial centres and the encouragement of (territorial) manufactures there. Instead, Baden remained a land of few towns (or, in the Lower Margraviate, of too many petty ones with insufficient hinterlands),[67] and margravial policy became increasingly concerned to territorialize the craft guilds, thereby stripping urban artisans of most of the privileges which had once distinguished them from their rural competitors. The foundation of markets in the margraviate of Hachberg at Malterdingen and Emmendingen was an act of state, clearly designed to embarrass and incommode the Austrian territorial towns which for centuries had dominated the local trade of the Breisgau; it was not the outflow of an agricultural specialization which required more and better outlets, as in the northern Netherlands. Far from facilitating regional trade, the new markets in the Breisgau, because they were invariably accompanied by injunctions to shun foreign markets, put up new institutional barriers to economic integration and progress. Only in Switzerland, and then somewhat later in the seventeenth century, does one find echoes of the Dutch specialization model of rural markets. These new foundations complemented the existing market network, for they grew up in landscapes, such as

---

[67] Leiser, 'Zentralorte', 6.

the alpine foothills, which were not densely urbanized or populated, but which were being given over to a genuinely specialized
export trade in cattle and latterly in cheese.[68]

Measured against de Vries's Dutch findings, therefore, the rural
economy of the Upper Rhine in the fifteenth and sixteenth century
never escaped the constraints of the peasant model. Once demographic pressure upset the homeostatic balance, the peasantry failed
to overcome adversity by specializing in production. Partible inheritance, structurally, may have predestined the rural population to
a strategy which militated against the consolidation of holdings,
while cereal agriculture, functionally, may have encouraged a retreat
into self-sufficiency. At this point, however, doubts begin to surface. Whatever the consequences of partible inheritance elsewhere,
in areas of commercial viticulture peasants may have been able to
tolerate a much greater degree of parcellization of their holdings
without undue hardship. Moreover, the early references to country crafts, and the lack of any obvious signs of widespread rural
immiseration or of a switch to cereal agriculture on the Upper Rhine,
may reflect an economy somewhat more resilient and adaptable
than the peasant model allows for. Certainly, before 1600 the Upper
Rhine never embraced anything resembling the Dutch specialization model, but were there not other strategies which the peasantry might have adopted? To answer this question, we need to
broaden the scope of the argument to consider whether the economy of the southern Upper Rhine as a whole can be regarded
as a regional system.

# IV

In their analysis of economic change in early modern Europe, John
Langton and Göran Hoppe have argued that all existing accounts
are deeply flawed. To search for the mainsprings of a secular
transition from feudalism to capitalism in either town or country
perpetuates an artificial antithesis which ignores the increasing specialization and interdependence of the rural and urban sectors. In
reality, 'town' and 'country' are constructs in need of explanation,
rather than explanatory devices in their own right. The only proper
framework within which to comprehend secular economic change,

[68] Peyer, 'Märkte der Schweiz', 33. Peyer recognizes the parallels with the Low
Countries. Ibid. 37.

they insist, is the geographical region which embraces both cities and their hinterlands as complementary dimensions of an integrated economic system.[69] For historians of modern economic history a regional approach has proved remarkably fruitful in analysing the spread of industrialization throughout Europe, and the location of proto-industries. But those who have championed this approach have cautioned, in turn, against reifying the 'region', just as others have stylized 'town' or 'country'. For Sidney Pollard, 'the region must have an operative as well as a descriptive meaning'[70] (indeed, he would be inclined to doubt whether any landscape before the onset of industrialization deserves the epithet of an *economic* region); while for Pat Hudson, 'the region has too often been used merely as a convenient box into which masses of descriptive material is stuffed'.[71]

Our analysis of the pre-industrial economy of the Upper Rhine entirely bears out these words of warning by historians of the industrial age. Neither geographical (natural) nor political-territorial boundaries are sufficient in themselves to describe the arena of economic activity; rather, the perception of a regional economic identity varied according to the shifting balance of supply and demand. Nevertheless, in any pre-industrial economy, as Stephan Epstein has recently affirmed in his study of late medieval Sicily, economic activity was so heavily influenced by institutional constraints that he has no hesitation in declaring 'my definition of the economic region is straightforwardly political'.[72] Though accepting that 'economic influences and relations clearly did not stop at political frontiers', the relative ease with which such institutional constraints—tolls, tariffs, taxation—could be altered or abolished within rather than between territories meant that, in his view, 'late medieval specialization was mainly the outcome not of long-distance trade in predominantly high-value commodities, but of the operation and interaction of differences in natural and social endowments within regions themselves'.[73] From that starting-point he

---

[69] Langton and Hoppe, *Town and country*, 31, 38, 40.

[70] Sidney Pollard, *Peaceful conquest: The industrialization of Europe 1760–1970* (Oxford, 1981), 32.

[71] Pat Hudson, *Regions and industries: A perspective on the Industrial Revolution in Britain* (Cambridge, 1989), 21.

[72] Stephan R. Epstein, *An island for itself: Economic development and social change in late medieval Sicily* (Cambridge, 1992), 82.

[73] Ibid. 83–84; idem, 'Cities, regions, and the late medieval crisis', 10.

goes on to argue that the key to regional economic growth lay in the dispersion of economic activity among a multiplicity of centres or markets, rather than in the concentration of commercial (and institutional) power in the hands of a dominant metropolis or its mercantile élite.[74]

No attempt will be made here to emulate the range and sophistication of Epstein's analysis of Sicily for conditions on the Upper Rhine: the frequent absence of reliable—or even any—quantitative data on output, consumption, trade, or even population makes such a task otiose. But we can use his insights to point to some general shortcomings in the presumed dynamic of a regionally integrated economy on the Upper Rhine. Much is rightly made of the commercialized and diversified character of its agrarian economy, abetted by topographical and ecological advantages. But the Upper Rhine had nothing to compare with the rise of the Sicilian silk industry, which transformed the latter's rural economy. From the mid-fifteenth century, at a time when the population was still stagnant, silk cultivation developed in response to overseas demand, first in western Sicily but thereafter more rapidly in the east of the island, particularly in the eastern Val Demone, where a 'distinctive constellation' of ecological, social, and institutional features aided its growth. Here the requisite technical knowledge was to hand; here also access to international markets was assured through Messina, but, above all, strong tenurial rights encouraged peasants, who in any case lacked good arable land to farm, to risk embarking on a new industrial venture, given that they could rely on a sufficient outside supply of foodstuffs.[75] Towards 1500, Epstein concludes,

A peculiar agricultural system had begun to develop, which combined into an integrated whole the individual seasonal rotations of the production and transformation of flax (in the high summer and winter), silk (between May and August), wine (in the spring and autumn) and also, by the end of the century, oil (in the early spring and mid-winter).[76]

The hallmark of this rural economy was not so much the fact of its specialization and diversity, as that its specialization was *season-*

---

[74] Epstein, *An island for itself*, 133, 150 ff., 158; idem, 'Cities, regions, and the late medieval crisis', 19, 40 ff., extending the analysis to Florence and its *contado*.
[75] Idem, *An island for itself*, 208–9.
[76] Ibid. 207; cf. idem, 'Cities, regions, and the late medieval crisis', 36, where he adds to the equation seasonal employment in the sugar industry.

*ally* dovetailed. Peasants could switch between various employments —and differing market opportunities—as the year progressed. This, then, was quite different from the specialization model in the sense of the rise of monocultures (dairying and pastoralism), put forward for the Low Countries, though both areas did come to depend on the import of grain. If anything, it was a variant of the peasant model, but one with much greater adaptability and flexibility, predicated in the final analysis on the assumption (which I share) that, *ceteris paribus*, peasants will voluntarily engage in the market when they discern an obvious benefit and limited risk[77]—and that such an economic system is capable of sustaining and absorbing population growth without tumbling into homoeostatic imbalance.

On the Upper Rhine, however, not only did the rural economy never attain the *degree* of specialization evident in eastern Sicily, its diversity remained *zonal*, not seasonal. Wine-growing peasants along the slopes of the Vosges, for instance, may have pursued some artisanal by-employments, but when they were not busy in their vineyards they did not suddenly turn to flax-growing in high summer or oil-pressing in midwinter. The climate and ecology of the Upper Rhine, it is true, are sometimes loosely described as 'Mediterranean', but a Sicilian peasant would have searched in vain for olive trees (or orange groves, or sugar cane) on the Upper Rhine in the height of summer, never mind in the dead of winter.[78] The zones of agricultural production certainly stimulated the circulation of goods and services within the region and thereby contributed to economic growth, but the opportunities to achieve surpluses which would feed further consumption and investment were clearly fewer than in a system of *seasonal* specialization. Furthermore, the economic potential of viticulture was itself ultimately limited. Wine-growing may have absorbed otherwise surplus labour (as well as giving employment to coopers, cartwrights, and dealers), but it

[77] Cf. idem, *An island for itself*, 209; idem, 'Cities, regions, and the late medieval crisis', 8.
[78] Though the occasional mulberry tree can be found! Metz, *Oberrheinlande*, 54. In general, however, Metz, writing from a nationalist stance, was quick to rebut any suggestion that the Upper Rhine's climate, flora, and fauna resembled those of France. Ibid. 49–50. This point should not be confused with the quite separate observation that, in terms of settlement patterns and landholding systems, the Upper Rhine was more Mediterranean than Germanic. Étienne Juillard, 'Paysans d'Alsace, paysans rhénans', in *Paysans d'Alsace* (Publications de la Société Savante d'Alsace et des Régions de l'Est: Grandes Publications, 7) (Strasbourg, 1959), 624.

can scarcely be said to have created added value in the way that manufacturing processes did.

None the less, the Upper Rhine remained one of the most diversified and prosperous areas of late medieval Germany, able to support a profusion of smaller market centres. It is pertinent to enquire, therefore, how far the resilience of its economy should be attributed to the *dispersion* of commercial activity among a multiplicity of central places, rather than its concentration in a regional metropolis. From the perspective of central-place theory, as we have seen, the distribution of the larger cities on the Upper Rhine corresponds reasonably well to a ranking system which combines the marketing and traffic principles. Strasbourg, the unquestioned regional capital, with a population in excess of 20,000, did not so far outstrip its nearest rivals that it can be described as a primate city breaking the mould of a regular central-place dispersion,[79] unlike both Palermo and Messina (to take Epstein's Sicilian examples), each in the late thirteenth century with a population three or four times the size of the next largest town (at 50,000 and 30,000 respectively),[80] which 'were typical primate centres which monopolized and concentrated the resources of their tributary areas, leaving the latter relatively poorly endowed and serviced'.[81] That would apply, though on a lesser scale, to the leading Flemish cities, the *drie steden* of Bruges, Ghent, and Ypres in the fourteenth century.[82] Strasbourg, it is true, controlled its own currency area, but that was a far cry from attempting to monopolize the resources of its hinterland, and in any case it may have taken second place behind Basel in the actual volume of trade passing through its quays and warehouses in the later Middle Ages.[83] Here the contrast with another flourishing region within Germany at the end of the fifteenth century is most enlightening. Eastern Swabia, Prak's chosen instance of a micro-region, driven by the vigour of its textile industry in town and country, experienced an intensification of urban growth which in turn promoted agricultural specialization. But here the outcome was to reinforce a hierarchy of relations

---

[79] Cf. Carol A. Smith, 'Regional economic systems: Linking geographical models and socioeconomic problems', in idem (ed.), *Regional analysis*, i. *Economic systems*, 30–32.          [80] Epstein, *An island for itself*, 55.

[81] Ibid. 152.

[82] David M. Nicholas, 'Town and countryside: Social and economic tensions in fourteenth-century Flanders', *Comparative Studies in Society and History*, 10 (1968), 462–65.          [83] Ehrensperger, 'Basels Stellung', 53.

between the various ranked urban centres which led to Augsburg emerging as the regional metropolis, sucking other towns into dependence upon its market. This process was perhaps most visible in the city's efforts to extend its privileged market precinct (*Bannmeile*) at the expense of its neighbours.[84] Because Augsburg came to monopolize access to the network of international trade beyond the region, the towns and cities of eastern Swabia in the long run found their economic vitality stunted in the shade of Augsburg's commercial upas-tree, a contradictory result of market integration which, as Maarten Prak observes, seems to reflect a general pattern in the early modern European economy.[85]

Of course, economic domination cannot be separated from political or territorial suzerainty, which conferred upon city magistracies the institutional powers to control their hinterlands, and that included economic exploitation. Throughout Germany, many imperial and free cities took advantage of their immediate dependence on the emperor to acquire rural territories, and Strasbourg and Basel were no exception. Yet a glance at the map suffices to show that neither city sought to construct a *contado* along the lines of the more powerful merchant communes of Lombardy or Tuscany. Strasbourg's territory remained highly disjointed, relatively modest in size,[86] and, in so far as it was intended to bolster the urban economy at all, essentially provided feudal incomes for the city's patrician families and ecclesiastical corporations.[87] In the case of Basel, commercial interests certainly informed the acquisition of the Baselbiet, which controlled the trade routes over the Jura passes, but the city never extended (or was able to extend) its territory westwards into the rich agricultural lands of the Sundgau.[88] Strategic and defensive motives were always paramount, and that applies equally to the few territorial towns on the Upper Rhine which managed to construct a rural territory in the later Middle Ages, Freiburg im Breisgau being the most obvious example.[89] Here again, the

---

[84] Cf. Kießling, *Die Stadt und ihr Land*, 261–62, 624–25, 714–41.

[85] Prak, 'Regioni', 21.

[86] Wunder, *Straßburger Gebiet*, 115–17 (maps); idem, *Straßburger Landgebiet*.

[87] Thomas A. Brady, Jr., *Ruling class, regime and Reformation at Strasbourg, 1520–1550* (Studies in Medieval and Renaissance Thought, 22) (Leiden, 1978), 147–62; on the family holdings of Jakob Sturm, which were conservatively administered, with no thought to commercial exploitation, cf. idem, *Protestant politics*, 18.

[88] Rippmann, *Bauern und Städter*, 144–54.

[89] Scott, 'Territorialpolitik', 7–24; idem, *Freiburg and the Breisgau*, 39–46.

leading Upper Rhenish cities were a world apart from the Flemish communes (though the latter never succeeded in establishing themselves as independent city-states),[90] or, in the case of Italy, from Florence, the city which *par excellence* in the course of building up a vast *contado* had by the sixteenth century subordinated not only the countryside but other powerful mercantile cities in the vicinity as well—Pisa is the most notorious instance—to its political and commercial will.[91]

That leaves the issue of bourgeois landholding in the countryside—often regarded as the key to economic relations between town and country,[92] and, in later centuries in particular, to the introduction of 'improved' agriculture—still to be considered. On the Upper Rhine it was certainly widespread in the case of the larger cities, being well-documented for both Strasbourg and Basel, but was of much less account elsewhere. To take a specific but telling example: even as late as the eighteenth century in the margraviate of Hachberg, as Albrecht Strobel's meticulous researches have revealed, the landlords were overwhelmingly ecclesiastical institutions—convents, charitable foundations, parishes—with some nobles, and only a smattering of burghers (often, in fact, professional men); the margraves of Baden themselves held remarkably little land.[93] Here a note of caution must in any case be struck. Even if bourgeois landownership had been more extensive, it is far from certain that urban proprietors were moved, in this period at least, by the prospect of maximizing their returns from estate investments. In Flanders, for instance, with its commercialized agriculture and rural manufacturing from the thirteenth century onwards, bourgeois land purchases were commonplace. On such estates, emphyteutic (that is, improving) leases, crop specification, or land reclamation, dyking, and road-building can all be found, but most urban landlords were absentees who sublet to tenants. Although they appear to have made a good return on their investment, such landlords were equally content to act as usurers, buying annuities from peasants

[90] Nicholas, 'Town and countryside', 471 ff., 484.

[91] Epstein, 'Cities, regions, and the late medieval crisis', 38; cf. ibid. 42–43.

[92] Cf. Rolf Kießling, 'Bürgerlicher Besitz auf dem Land—ein Schlüssel zu den Stadt-Land-Beziehungen im Spätmittelalter, aufgezeigt am Beispiel Augsburgs und anderer ostschwäbischer Städte', in Pankraz Fried (ed.), *Bayerisch-schwäbische Landesgeschichte an der Universität Augsburg 1975–1977: Vorträge, Aufsätze, Berichte* (Augsburger Beiträge zur Landesgeschichte Bayerisch-Schwabens, 1) (Sigmaringen, 1979), 121–40.        [93] Strobel, *Agrarverfassung*, 189–204 (app. 1).

and confiscating their land if they defaulted: they did not bestride the Flemish countryside as capitalist farmers.[94]

By buying land, burghers were above all buying status and security; they were therefore willing in most instances to behave as rentiers rather than as entrepreneurs, who treated land as a 'substitute bank'.[95] For France it has even been argued in this regard that the rentier mentality of bourgeois landowners was responsible for stifling the 'entrepreneurial attitudes of the middle peasantry': ruthless exploitation of their estates was 'always tempered by a desire to bolster the seigneurial system and become true seigneurs themselves'.[96] This is a verdict which it is barely possible to test in detail for the Upper Rhine, but the wider point underlying it, that urban landholders chose to align themselves with the aristocracy, certainly holds good. Many patricians of Freiburg im Breisgau, for instance, who had grown rich on their investment in silver-mining, gradually withdrew to their country estates after the town's submission to Austria in 1368, and within a generation or so had become indistinguishable from the rural nobility.[97] The pattern was repeated elsewhere: some of the most illustrious Strasbourg families, who in the sixteenth century still had a foot in both camps, that is to say, they were both merchants and feudal landlords, by the seventeenth had reappeared on the bench of nobles as members of Outer Austria's second Estate.[98]

But even in their heyday as entrepreneurs there is little sign of merchants from the Upper Rhenish cities investing in the countryside or actively engaging in the land market in order to promote commercial crops or rural industries. The Upper Rhine valley, as we have observed, was never a classic area of textile production based on rural outwork of spinning and weaving in the smaller towns and villages, the one exception being the group of Lower Alsatian textile centres between Strasbourg and Haguenau (though

[94] Nicholas, 'Town and countryside', 475–80.

[95] Cf. Kießling, *Die Stadt und ihr Land*, 154; Konrad Fritze, 'Probleme der Stadt-Land-Beziehungen im Bereich der wendischen Hansestädte nach 1370', *Hansische Geschichtsblätter*, 85 (1967), 38–57, esp. 52 ff.

[96] Patricia Croot and David Parker, 'Agrarian class structure and the development of capitalism: France and England compared', in Aston and Philpin, *Brenner Debate*, 88.

[97] Scott, *Freiburg and the Breisgau*, 31; cf. Hermann Nehlsen, *Die Freiburger Familie Snewlin: Rechts- und sozialgeschichtliche Studien zur Entwicklung des mittelalterlichen Bürgertums* (Veröffentlichungen aus dem Archiv der Stadt Freiburg im Breisgau, 9) (Freiburg im Breisgau, 1967).

[98] e.g. the von Kageneck, and Röder von Diersburg.

even in Swabia, the prime area in Germany of rural textile manufacturing organized by the putting-out system, the connection
between the acquisition of landed property and the spread of flax
or textile production can seldom be proved).[99] In assessing the balance of advantage in town–country relations on the Upper Rhine
we would in any case be blind in one eye to focus on production
alone. As Stephan Epstein has again stressed, seigneurial power may
have dominated peasant *production*, but urban power was generally concentrated on *distribution*, with cities bent on controlling
factor and product *markets*.[100] The struggle to suppress village markets, particularly on the right bank of the Upper Rhine, shows that
the middling craft towns lacked the economic and legal clout
to prevail, but such problems do not seem to have arisen for the
larger regional centres, namely Strasbourg and Basel. The former's
decision to tighten its grip on Alsatian wine distribution towards
the end of the sixteenth century, however, was perhaps an omin-
ous sign of a more *dirigiste* approach.

This brings us neatly back to our starting-point. Was the perceptible faltering of the Upper Rhenish economy after the mid-sixteenth
century—on which all the scholarly authorities are agreed[101]—part
of a deterioration in the wider economy of southern Germany,
or was it rather local and self-inflicted? Or, to put matters in their
true light, why did the integration and diversity of the economy
up to the mid-1500s prove insufficiently resilient to withstand the
vicissitudes of the latter part of the century? If the economic vigour
of the Upper Rhine stemmed in the first instance from exchange
within the region (with the rise of a long-distance export trade the
result, not the cause, of that vigour), as Odile Kammerer has argued,
echoing the general observations of Schultz and Epstein,[102] to what
extent is the subsequent economic sclerosis attributable to the
erosion of regional integration and, more broadly, of a sense of
regional economic solidarity?

To speak of regional economic integration at all in an area as
politically fragmented as the Upper Rhine may appear a contradic-

---

[99] Kießling, *Die Stadt und ihr Land*, 420.

[100] Epstein, 'Cities, regions, and the late medieval crisis', 15.

[101] Cf. Fuchs, 'Foires', 330; Kammerer, 'Carrefour alsacien-lorrain', 90; Rapp, 'Routes
et voies', 207; Körner, *Solidarités financières suisses*, 436.

[102] Cf. Odile Kammerer, 'Échange et marchands à la fin du Moyen Âge dans
l'Oberrhein', in *Le Marchand au Moyen Âge* (Société des Historiens Médiévistes de
l'Enseignement Supérieur Public, 19e Congrès, Reims 1988) (Nantes, 1992), 139.

tion in terms: surely the institutional barriers must have blighted intra- and inner-regional exchange? Quite apart from the fundamental significance of the Perpetual Accord (*Erbeinigung*) of 1511 between Switzerland and Austria, we have seen that over questions of essential provisioning the authorities in the southern part of the region could co-operate across political and judicial boundaries to reach agreement on common price tariffs, tolls, and import and export regulations. Obviously, the supply of meat and grain constituted only one part, albeit a crucial one, of the economy of what was already a rich agricultural area. That co-operation rested in turn upon a perception of common regional economic interests, of which the Rappen league—in its narrower configuration after 1400—was the most tangible expression. What the Rappen league could not do was to prevent *bilateral* conflicts between its members or associates over markets and market access. Indeed, Odile Kammerer goes on to contend that the profusion of market centres in the Rhine valley upset the balance between town and country and was therefore detrimental to the economy at large,[103] a sentiment which would have been music in the ears of the burghers of the Austrian Breisgau towns, and will delight the more rigid adherents of central-place theory *à la* Walter Christaller. But were these conflicts as harmful as the aggrieved parties alleged? If we accept that dispersion, not concentration, of economic activity was ultimately beneficial to the growth of a regional economy (as Epstein has argued for Sicily, and as the counter-example of eastern Swabia increasingly under the sway of Augsburg seems to indicate), then the contention may seem askew. But the dispersion of centrality was in the end more imagined than real, with the traditional urban market centres of the Breisgau able to reassert their predominance over the upstart margravial markets.

Here the question of marginal advantage comes into its own, for the problems of the Breisgau towns were not replicated on the left bank of the Rhine in the more densely urbanized landscape of Alsace. Without rehearsing again the possible reasons for this slippage (*Gefälle*), what it suggests is that the Upper Rhenish economy, despite its commercialization and diversification, was weaker than it appeared, or rather, that some parts of the region were more resilient than others. In the long run, however, the region as a whole

---

[103] Ibid. 144.

was seized by an economic downturn. May it have become the
victim of its own success? Commenting on the crisis of the Sicilian
silk industry after 1650, in the wake of three centuries of prosperity, with a buoyant population and constant trade surpluses, Epstein
wonders whether that success made it hard for Sicilians to adapt
to rapidly deteriorating conditions: '[T]heir economy had specialized
too far to submit to rapid structural transformation.'[104] What may
have made such a transformation all the more difficult was the fact
that Sicily was mainly an agricultural exporter, and it is harder as
a rule to convert agricultural investment than to restructure industry, since the former ties up capital for longer and is constrained
by the immobility of land and often the labour tied to it.[105] That
in turn raises the question of market opportunities. The generally
low level of labour productivity in most of continental Europe (in
marked contrast to its rapid increase in early modern England and
the Low Countries) suggests that even areas which were stamped
in large measure by regional specialization could not of themselves
achieve a fundamental economic transition unless they had access
to, and were willing to exploit, new market outlets.[106]

It is tempting to apply this diagnosis to the viticulture of the
Upper Rhine, which dominated Germany's export markets until
fashion and jealous neighbours turned against Alsatian wine in the
sixteenth century. Did the very success of viticulture for so long dis-
courage alternative investment and offer no stimulus to enhanced
productivity? Strasbourg, which has rightly been castigated for imposing a wine staple to protect its share of the market,[107] did at
least make fitful efforts to promote fustian manufacturing towards
the end of the century, though they were vitiated by the onset of
the Bishops' War, the conflict between Catholic and Protestant
parties over the election of a new bishop to the Strasbourg see,
which raged from 1583 to 1604. But these were responses to, not
the causes of, a deteriorating economic situation. Without denying
the devastating blow that the French crown's default dealt to Strasbourg's financial houses, Odile Kammerer detects an earlier and
more general failure of energy and will on the part of the region's

---

[104] Epstein, *An island for itself*, 409.          [105] Ibid. 408.
[106] Prak, 'Regioni', 30.
[107] Dirlmeier points out that staples harmed not only trade on the Rhine, but
on the Elbe as well, where Hamburg enforced a staple in this period. Idem,
'Mittelalterliche Zoll- und Stapelrechte', 37.

mercantile class as a whole. As well as clinging to rudimentary bookkeeping systems, merchants never created sufficient active wealth: too much was tied up in rentier, as opposed to commercial, capital, and there was too little investment in new commercial ventures (she notes the relative absence of putting-out).[108]

Peasants, craftsmen, merchants—no doubt all must share some of the blame for a failing to rise to the challenge of worsening economic conditions. But they were also by the sixteenth century the victims of circumstance. The consolidation of territorial authority and the pull of confessional allegiance undermined the foundations of a specifically regional economic identity which had rested on a balance of interests between the cities and the princes of the southern Upper Rhine. That balance was never completely destroyed, but the institutional impediments to economic co-operation across territorial boundaries increased. For the regional economy, the 'communal' way yielded to the 'princely' way; and nowhere is that better illustrated than in the career of the one outstanding entrepreneur of the region at the end of our period. The rafting company of the Murg valley, once the most powerful and successful collective association of timber shippers and factors in the Black Forest, faced a recession at the end of the sixteenth century to the point where the territorial ruler of the Murg valley, margrave Philipp of Baden-Baden, toyed with the idea of taking over the business as a state enterprise. Instead, he chose to set up a territorial monopoly, installing Jakob Kast, one of the leading rafting shareholders, as manager, with an agreement to split the profits down the middle. Under Kast's energetic direction the business once again prospered—principally to his own benefit. By exploiting his monopoly franchise he became virtually the sole employer in the Murg valley, relying upon put-out labour, and shone forth as a beacon of early capitalist enterprise on the Upper Rhine. Known derisively as the 'little Murg valley Fugger' (*Murgtäler Fuggerle*), Kast amassed a fortune which on his death in 1615 amounted to just short of half a million florins, a staggering sum.[109]

---

[108] Kammerer, 'Échange et marchands', 150.

[109] Max Scheifele, 'Flößerei und Holzhandel im Murgtal unter besonderer Berücksichtigung der Murgschifferfahrt: Ein Beitrag zur Wirtschaftsgeschichte des Nordschwarzwaldes', in idem (ed.), *Die Murgschifferschaft: Geschichte des Floßhandels, des Waldes und der Holzindustrie im Murgtal* (Schriftenreihe der Landesforstverwaltung Baden-Württemberg, 66) (Stuttgart, 1988), 182–90; Holbach, *Frühformen von Verlag und Großbetrieb*, 497–99.

Kast's achievement would have been inconceivable without the backing of Baden-Baden, and it stands in strong contrast to the mercantile activities of the patricians of the proud independent cities of the Upper Rhine. Strasbourg's élite gambled and lost on lending to the French crown; Basel's élite cannily became bankers to the Swiss Confederation. But whether failure or success, neither investment was directly calculated to stimulate the *regional* economy of the Upper Rhine, since they created neither employment nor manufacturing output. The transition from commercialized agriculture and rural manufacturing to early capitalist industrial ventures never occurred on the Upper Rhine. To the economic recession of the later sixteenth century were soon to be added the calamities of the Thirty Years War, whose outcome handed the left bank of the Rhine to France and relegated Alsace to a peripheral province of the French monarchy. Although the customs frontier remained the Vosges until the French Revolution, the Upper Rhine had been shorn of whatever integrity and coherence as an economic region it had once possessed. To restore its regional economic identity today across three national frontiers will be a true measure of the unifying capacity of the European Union.

# Bibliography

## I. Unpublished Sources

A. *Archives in Austria*

1. Innsbruck, Tiroler Landesarchiv (TLA)
   Pestarchiv, Akten XXIX
   Maximiliana XIV
   Kanzleibücher, ältere Reihe, Lit. C; Lit. D
   Kopialbücher:
   An die königl. Majestät oder fürstl. Durchlaucht
   Embieten und Befelch
   Gemeine Missiven
   Geschäft vom Hof
   Gutachten an Hof
   Missiven an Hof
   Von der königl. Majestät
2. Vienna, Haus-, Hof- und Staatsarchiv (HHSA)
   Maximiliana 23; 33

B. *Archives in France*

1. Belfort, Archives Départementales du Territoire de Belfort (ADTB)
   E-Dépôt 33: Archives Communales de Delle (ACD)
   EE 1
   HH 1
   E-Dépôt 46: Archives Communales de Florimont (ACF)
   AA 3
2. Bergheim, Archives Municipales (AMBg)
   AA 3
   FF 4
3. Besançon, Archives Départementales du Doubs (ADD)
   E 4942; 5067; 5094
4. Colmar, Archives Départementales du Haut-Rhin (ADHR)
   C 7; 177; 179; 180; 181; 182; 188; 406; 588; 674
   1 C 104; 105; 149; 180; 183; 187; 412; 879; 929
   E 707
   3 G 3
   10 G 8; 10
   H 67
   1 H 19

16 J 175
17 J 19
E-Dépôt 4: Archives Municipales d'Ammerschwihr (AMAm)
AA 25
5. Colmar, Archives Municipales (AMC)
HH 58; 59; 95; 103
6. Guebwiller, Archives Municipales (AMGb)
HH 3
7. Kaysersberg, Archives Municipales (AMKy)
BB 9; 10
FF 39
8. Masevaux, Archives Municipales (AMMx)
BB 5
HH 1; 3
9. Mulhouse, Archives Municipales (AMMh)
I 3207; 3208; 3209; 4321; 4332; 4353; 4728; 4867; 4884; 4897; 4898; 4922;
5421; 5422; 5423
II A 1
IV A 44
XIII A 8
10. Munster, Archives Municipales (AMMu)
HH 3
11. Nancy, Archives Départementales de Meurthe-et-Moselle (ADMM)
B 9648
12. Obernai, Archives Municipales (AMO)
AA 61
13. Paris, Archives Nationales (AN)
K 1851; 1901; 2017; 2208
14. Ribeauvillé, Archives Municipales (AMRb)
BB 1
15. Rouffach, Archives Municipales (AMRf)
BB 3
HH 3
16. Sélestat, Archives Municipales (AMSé)
AA 167
HH 33; 36; 42; 128
17. Strasbourg, Archives Départementales du Bas-Rhin (ADBR)
C 38
E 2926
8 E 481
G 217
18. Strasbourg, Archives Municipales (AMS)
AA 1820; 1823; 2037
R 3; 4; 5

X 264; 267
IV 17; 37
V 2; 18
19. Strasbourg, Bibliothèque Nationale et Universitaire de Strasbourg (BNUS)
MS. 845
20. Thann, Archives Municipales (AMTh)
HH 4
21. Turckheim, Archives Municipales (AMT)
AA 19 bis

## C. Archives in Germany

1. Darmstadt, Hessisches Staatsarchiv (SADa)
D 21 A
2. Donaueschingen, Fürstlich Fürstenbergisches Archiv (FFA)
Jurisdictionalia C
3. Emmendingen, Gemeindearchiv (GAEm)
Akten V, 2
4. Freiburg im Breisgau, Stadtarchiv (StAFr)
A 1 I d
A 1 III f
A 1 VI e ε
A 1 VII b
B 5 III c 10
B 5 IXa
B 5 XI
C 1 Fremde Orte: Kirchhofen; Neuenburg; Triberg; Waldkirch
C 1 Landstände 1; 3; 7; 9; 11; 14; 15; 17
C 1 Münzsachen 1
F A 15/1
F B 27/21
L Deposita 1: Stadtarchiv Breisach (StABr)
Akten 916
5. Karlsruhe, Badisches Generallandesarchiv (GLA)
D 79; 477; 613; 619; 1052
21/2; 223; 427
36/286
67/209; 215
74/2872; 5114; 6368; 9615; 9618; 9619; 9620; 10487; 10497; 10501; 10579
79/1644; 1657; 1702; 2569
81/47; 53; 54; 55; 56
115/560; 613
122/84; 85; 307
138/97

184/478; 479
198/203
208/425
220/792
229/8577; 24537; 51503; 56506; 56808; 60778; 64261; 64262; 64263; 100736;
    100737; 103818; 103819; 103820

6. Kenzingen, Stadtarchiv (StAKz)
   Urkunden 70; 71; 97
7. Neuenburg, Stadtarchiv (StANb)
   AA A 77; 92; 97; 108; 109
8. Stuttgart, Württembergisches Hauptstaatsarchiv (HSA)
   B 17
9. Villingen, Stadtarchiv (StAVl)
   AAAb/1
   E 7; 13a; 18
   G 20
   H 36; 37
   N 13; 17; 18
   P 19; 21
   QQ 1; 2
   W 2

D. *Archives in Switzerland*

1. Basel, Staatsarchiv des Kantons Basel-Stadt (SABs)
   Fleisch A 1
   Fleisch K 2
   Frucht und Brot M 1
   Missiven A 22; 28; 29; 30; 31; 33; 34; 38
   Missiven B 1; 2; 8; 12
2. Bern, Staatsarchiv des Kantons Bern (SABe)
   A III 37; 39; 40
   A IV 38; 41
   A V 742
3. Lucerne, Staatsarchiv des Kantons Luzern (SALu)
   A 1 F 1
4. Porrentruy, Archives de l'Ancien Évêché de Bâle (AAEB)
   B 198; 209; 335; 342; 349; 350; 351
5. Porrentruy, Archives de la Bourgeoisie de Porrentruy (ABP)
   I/IV
6. Rheinfelden, Stadtarchiv (StARf)
   127
   622
7. Zürich, Staatsarchiv des Kantons Zürich (SAZh)
   A 55

## II: Atlases

Wolfram, Georg, and Ernst Gley (eds.), *Elsaß-Lothringischer Atlas: Landeskunde, Geschichte, Kultur und Wirtschaft Elsaß-Lothringens* (Schriften des Wissenschaftlichen Instituts der Elsaß-Lothringer im Reich) (Frankfurt am Main, 1936), with accompanying *Erläuterungsband.*

*Historischer Atlas von Baden-Württemberg,* ed. Kommission für geschichtliche Landeskunde. in Baden-Württemberg (Stuttgart, 1972–88), with *Beiworte.*

## III: Printed Primary Sources

Albrecht, Karl (ed.), *Rappoltsteinisches Urkundenbuch,* iii (Colmar, 1904).

*Amtliche Sammlung der älteren Eidgenössischen Abschiede,* iii, 2, ed. Anton Philipp Segesser (Lucerne, 1869).

—— iv. 1b, ed. Johannes Strickler (Zürich, 1876).

—— iv. 1c, ed. Karl Deschwanden (Lucerne, 1878).

—— iv. 1d, ed. Karl Deschwanden (Lucerne, 1882).

—— iv. 2, ed. Joseph Karl Krütli (Bern, 1861).

Baumann, Franz Ludwig, and Georg Tumbült (eds.), *Mitteilungen aus dem f. fürstenbergischen Archive,* 2 vols. (Tübingen, 1894–1902).

*Deutsche Reichstagsakten, middle series,* v. *Wormser Reichstag 1495,* i. 2, ed. Heinz Angermeier (Göttingen, 1981).

Franke, Annelore, and Gerhard Zschäbitz (eds.), *Das Buch der hundert Kapitel und der vierzig Statuten des sogenannten Oberrheinischen Revolutionärs* (Leipziger Übersetzungen und Abhandlungen zum Mittelalter, A 4) (Berlin, 1967).

Franz, Günther (ed.), *Der deutsche Bauernkrieg: Aktenband,* 2nd edn. (Darmstadt, 1968).

Lebeau, Jean, and Jean-Marie Valentin (eds.), *L'Alsace au siècle de la Réforme 1482–1621: Textes et Documents* (Nancy, 1985).

Meyer, Friedrich, and Elisabeth Landolt (eds.), 'Andreas Ryff (1550–1603), Reisebüchlein', *Basler Zeitschrift für Geschichte und Altertumskunde,* 72 (1972), 5–135.

Ministerium für Elsaß-Lothringen, Statistisches Bureau (ed.), *Das Reichsland Elsaß-Lothringen: Landes- und Ortsbeschreibung,* i; iii (Strasbourg, 1898; 1903).

Mossmann, Xavier (ed.), *Cartulaire de Mulhouse,* i (Strasbourg, 1886).

*Regesten der Markgrafen von Baden und Hachberg 1050–1515,* iv, ed. Albert Krieger (Innsbruck, 1915).

Riezler, Siegmund (ed.), *Fürstenbergisches Urkundenbuch,* iv (Tübingen, 1879).

Ruser, Konrad (ed.), *Die Urkunden und Akten der oberdeutschen Städte-bunde vom 13. Jahrhundert bis 1549*, 2 vols. (Göttingen, 1979–88).

Schreiber, Johann Heinrich (ed.), *Urkundenbuch der Stadt Freiburg im Breisgau*, ii (Freiburg im Breisgau, 1829).

Scott, Tom (ed.), *Die Freiburger Enquete von 1476: Quellen zur Wirtschafts- und Verwaltungsgeschichte der Stadt Freiburg im Breisgau im fünf-zehnten Jahrhundert* (Veröffentlichungen aus dem Archiv der Stadt Freiburg im Breisgau, 20) (Freiburg im Breisgau, 1986).

—— and Bob Scribner (eds.), *The German Peasants' War: A history in documents* (Atlantic Highlands, NJ/London, 1991).

*Urkundenbuch der Stadt Basel*, v, ed. Rudolf Wackernagel (Basel, 1900).

—— vi, ed. August Huber (Basel, 1902).

—— vii, ed. Johannes Haller (Basel, 1899).

—— viii, ed. Rudolf Thommen (Basel, 1901).

—— ix, ed. Rudolf Thommen (Basel, 1905).

## IV: Printed Secondary Works

Ammann, Hektor, 'Die deutschen und schweizerischen Messen des Mittelalters', in *La Foire* (Recueils de la Société Jean Bodin, 5) (Brussels, 1953), 149–73.

—— 'Elsässisch-schweizerische Wirtschaftsbeziehungen im Mittelalter', *Elsaß-Lothringisches Jahrbuch*, 7 (1928), 36–61.

—— 'Freiburg und der Breisgau in der mittelalterlichen Wirtschaft', in Hermann Eris Busse (ed.), 'Der Breisgau', *Oberrheinische Heimat*, 28 (1941), 248–59.

—— 'La Place de l'Alsace dans l'industrie textile du Moyen Âge', in *La Bourgeoisie alsacienne*, 71–102.

—— 'Das Städtewesen des Mittelalters', in Wolfram and Gley, *Erläuter-ungsband zum Elsaß-Lothringischen Atlas*, Erläuterungen zu Karte 34.

—— *Wirtschaft und Lebensraum der mittelalterlichen Kleinstadt*, i. *Rheinfelden*, n.p., n.d. [Aarau, 1947].

—— 'Von der Wirtschaftsgeltung des Elsaß im Mittelalter', *Alemannisches Jahrbuch*, 1953, 95–202.

*Artisans et Ouvriers d'Alsace* (Publications de la Société Savante d'Alsace et des Régions de l'Est: Grandes Publications, 9) (Strasbourg, 1965).

Aston, T. H., and C. H. E. Philpin (eds.), *The Brenner debate: Agrarian class structure and economic development in pre-industrial Europe* (Cambridge, 1985).

Baradel, Yvette, Georges Bischoff, André Larger, Yves Pagnot, and Michel Rilliot, *Histoire de Belfort* (Roanne/Le Coteau, 1985).

Barth, Médard, *Der Rebbau des Elsaß und die Absatzgebiete seiner Weine: Ein geschichtlicher Durchblick*, i (Strasbourg/Paris, 1958).

Bauer, Wilhelm, *Die Anfänge Ferdinands I.* (Vienna/Leipzig, 1907).

Bautier, Robert-Henri, *The economic development of medieval Europe* (London, 1971).

Beemelmans, Wilhelm, *Die Verfassung und Verwaltung der Stadt Ensisheim im sechzehnten Jahrhundert* (Beiträge zur Landes- und Volkskunde von Elsaß-Lothringen, 35) (Strasbourg, 1908).

Bergier, Jean-François, 'Commerce et politique du blé à Genève aux XV et XVIe siècles', *Schweizerische Zeitschrift für Geschichte*, 14 (1964), 521–50.

Berry, B. J. L., and Allan Pred, *Central place studies: A bibliography of theory and applications* (Philadelphia, 1961).

*Bevölkerung und Wirtschaft der Regio* (Schriften der Regio, 1) (Basel, 1965).

Billerey, Michel, 'Le Pays Montbéliard, carrefour historique entre l'Alsace, la Franche-Comté et la Suisse', in *Trois provinces de l'Est: Lorraine, Alsace, Franche-Comté* (Publications de la Société Savante d'Alsace et des Régions de l'Est: Grandes Publications, 6) (Strasbourg/Paris, 1967), 311–21.

Bischoff, Georges, 'Belfort au XVe siècle—une duchesse et des comptes', in Baradel *et al.*, *Histoire de Belfort*, 75–96.

—— *Gouvernés et gouvernants en Haute-Alsace à l'époque autrichienne: Les États des pays antérieurs des origines au milieu du XVI siècle* (Publications de la Société Savante d'Alsace et des Régions de l'Est: Grandes Publications, 20) (Strasbourg, 1982).

—— 'La Guerre du Haut-Mundat: Un épisode oublié de l'histoire d'Alsace', *Annuaire de la Société d'Histoire des Régions de Thann-Guebwiller*, 13 (1979–80), 77–89.

—— 'Die markanten Züge des österreichischen Elsaß', in Maier and Press, *Vorderösterreich*, 271–83.

—— *Recherches sur la puissance temporelle de l'abbaye de Murbach (1229–1525)* (Publications de la Société Savante d'Alsace et des Régions de l'Est: Recherches et Documents, 22) (Strasbourg, 1975).

—— 'Un symbole de l'Alsace autrichienne: Belfort du début du XVIe siècle à la Guerre de Trente Ans', in Baradel *et al.*, *Histoire de Belfort*, 97–121.

Bissegger, Alfred, *Die Silberversorgung der Basler Münzstätte bis zum Ausgang des 18. Jahrhunderts* (Basel, 1917).

Blanchard, Ian, 'The continental European cattle trades, 1400–1600', *Economic History Review*, 2nd series, 39 (1986), 427–60.

Boesch, Bruno, 'Der alemannische Sprachraum im Bereich des heutigen Baden-Württemberg: Ein geschichtlicher Überblick', in Günther Haselier, Eberhard Gönner, Meinrad Schaab, and Robert Uhland (eds.), *Bausteine zur geschichtlichen Landeskunde von Baden-Württemberg* (Stuttgart, 1979), 71–84.

*Bibliography*

Bosch, Reinhold, 'Der Kornhandel der Nord-, Ost-, Innerschweiz und der ennetbirgischen Vogteien im 15. und 16. Jahrhundert' (Diss. phil. Zürich, 1913).

*La Bourgeoisie alsacienne: Études d'histoire sociale* (Publications de la Société Savante d'Alsace et des Régions de l'Est: Grandes Publications 5) (Strasbourg, 1967).

Brady, T. A., Jr., *Protestant politics: Jakob Sturm (1489–1553) and the German Reformation* (Atlantic Highlands, NJ, 1995).

—— *Ruling class, regime and Reformation at Strasbourg, 1520–1550* (Studies in Medieval and Renaissance Thought, 22) (Leiden, 1978).

—— *Turning Swiss: Cities and Empire, 1450–1550* (Cambridge, 1985).

Braun, Rudolf, *Industrialisierung und Volksleben: Die Veränderungen der Lebensformen in einem ländlichen Industriegebiet vor 1800*, 2nd edn. (Göttingen, 1979).

Brenner, Robert, 'Agrarian class structure and economic development in pre-industrial Europe', in Aston and Philpin, *Brenner debate*, 10–63.

—— 'The agrarian roots of European capitalism', ibid. 213–317.

Brieger, Rudolf, *Die Herrschaft Rappoltstein: Ihre Entstehung und Entwicklung* (Beiträge zur Landes- und Volkskunde von Elsaß-Lothringen, 31) (Strasbourg, 1907).

Buszello, Horst, and Hans Schadek, 'Alltag der Stadt—Alltag der Bürger: Wirtschaftskrisen, soziale Not und neue Aufgaben der Verwaltung zwischen Bauernkrieg und Westfälischem Frieden', in Heiko Haumann and Hans Schadek (eds.), *Geschichte der Stadt Freiburg im Breisgau*, ii. *Vom Bauernkrieg bis zum Ende der habsburgischen Herrschaft* (Stuttgart, 1994), 69–152.

Büttner, Heinrich, 'Geschichte des Elsaß I', in idem, *Geschichte des Elsaß I: Politische Geschichte des Landes von der Landnahmezeit bis zum Tode Ottos III.*, and *Ausgewählte Beiträge zur Geschichte des Elsaß in Früh- und Hochmittelalter*, ed. Traute Endemann (Sigmaringen, 1991), 25–182.

Cahn, Julius, *Der Rappenmünzbund: Eine Studie zur Münz- und Geld-Geschichte des oberen Rheinthales* (Heidelberg, 1901).

Calmet, Augustin, *Histoire ecclesiastique et civile de Lorraine*, ii (Nancy, 1728).

Christaller, Walter, *Central places in Southern Germany*, trans. Carlisle W. Baskin (Englewood Cliffs, NJ, 1966).

—— *Das Grundgerüst der räumlichen Ordnung in Europa: Die Systeme der europäischen Zentralen Orte* (Frankfurter Geographische Hefte, 24. 1) (Frankfurt am Main, 1950).

—— *Die zentralen Orte in Süddeutschland: Eine ökonomisch-geographische Untersuchung über die Gesetzmäßigkeit der Verbreitung und Entwicklung der Siedlungen mit städtischer Funktion* (Jena, 1933).

Clark, Peter, and Paul Slack, *English towns in transition 1500–1700* (London/Oxford/New York, 1976).

Croot, Patricia, and David Parker, 'Agrarian class structure and the development of capitalism: France and England compared', in Aston and Philpin, *Brenner Debate*, 79–90.

Daveau, Suzanne, *Les Régions frontalières de la montagne jurassienne: Étude de géographie humaine* (Institut des Études Rhodaniennes de l'Université de Lyon: Mémoires et Documents, 14) (Lyon, 1959).

Debard, Jean-Marc, *Les Monnaies de la principauté de Montbéliard du XVIe au XVIIe siècle: Essai de numismatique et d'histoire économique* (Annales Littéraires de l'Université de Besançon, 220: Cahiers d'Études Comtoises, 26) (Paris, 1980).

Dege, Wilfried, *Zentralörtliche Beziehungen über Staatsgrenzen untersucht am südlichen Oberrheingebiet* (Bochumer Geographische Arbeiten) (Paderborn, 1979).

Dickinson, R. E., *City and region: A geographical interpretation* (London, 1964).

—— *City region and regionalism: A geographical contribution to human ecology* (London, 1947).

—— *The regions of Germany* (London, 1945).

Dietrich, Christian, *Die Stadt Zürich und ihre Landgemeinden während der Bauernunruhen von 1489 bis 1525* (Europäische Hochschulschriften, 3rd series, 229) (Frankfurt am Main/Bern/New York, 1985).

Dirlmeier, Ulf, 'Mittelalterliche Zoll- und Stapelrechte als Handelshemmnisse', in Hans Pohl (ed.), *Die Auswirkungen von Zöllen und anderen Handelshemmnissen auf Wirtschaft und Gesellschaft vom Mittelalter bis zur Gegenwart: Referate der 11. Arbeitstagung der Gesellschaft für Sozial- und Wirtschaftsgeschichte vom 9. bis 13. April 1985 in Hohenheim (Vierteljahrschrift für Sozial- und Wirtschaftsgeschichte*, suppl. 80) (Stuttgart, 1987), 19–39.

Dodgshon, Robert A., *The European past: Social evolution and spatial order* (Houndmills, Hants/London, 1987).

Dollinger, Philippe, 'La Ville libre à la fin du Moyen Âge (1350–1482)', in Livet and Rapp, *Histoire de Strasbourg*, ii. 99–175.

Dopsch, Alfons, 'Die Weststaatspolitik der Habsburger im Westen ihres Großreiches (1477–1526)', in *Gesamtdeutsche Vergangenheit: Festgabe für Heinrich Ritter von Srbik zum 60. Geburtstag am 10. November 1938* (Munich, 1938), 55–62.

Dotzauer, Winfried, *Die deutschen Reichskreise in der Verfassung des Alten Reiches und ihr Eigenleben (1500–1806)* (Darmstadt, 1989).

Doucet, Roger, 'Le Grand Parti de Lyon au XVIe siècle', *Revue historique*, 171 (1933), 473–513; 172 (1933), 1–41.

Dubled, Henri, 'Ville et village en Alsace au Moyen Âge: Essai de definitions, critères de distinction', in *La Bourgeoisie alsacienne*, 57–69.

Dubler, Anne-Marie, 'Das Fruchtwesen der Stadt Basel von der Reformation bis 1700', *Jahresbericht des Staatsarchivs Basel-Stadt*, 1968, suppl., 25–67.

—— *Handwerk, Gewerbe und Zunft in Stadt und Landschaft Luzern* (Luzerner Historische Veröffentlichungen, 14) (Lucerne/Stuttgart, 1982).

—— and Jean Jacques Siegrist, 'Wohlen: Geschichte von Recht, Wirtschaft und Bevölkerung einer frühindustrialisierten Gemeinde im Aargau', *Argovia*, 86 (1974), 5–709.

Duncker, Hermann, 'Das mittelalterliche Dorfgewerbe (mit Ausschluß der Nahrungsmittel-Industrie) nach den Weistumsüberlieferungen' (Diss. phil. Leipzig, 1903).

Eggers, Heinz, 'Der Grenzraum Nordelsaß-Südpfalz in Vergangenheit und Gegenwart', *Alemannisches Jahrbuch*, 1991/92, 41–60.

Ehmann, Eugen, *Markt und Sondermarkt: Zum räumlichen Geltungsbereich des Marktrechts im Mittelalter* (Nürnberger Werkstücke zur Stadt- und Landesgeschichte: Schriftenreihe des Stadtarchivs Nürnberg, 11) (Nuremberg, 1987).

Ehrensperger, Franz, 'Basels Stellung im internationalen Handelsverkehr des Spätmittelalters' (Diss. phil. Basel, 1972).

Ellerbach, J. B., *Der dreißigjährige Krieg im Elsaß. (1618–1648)*, i. *Vom Beginn des Krieges bis zum Abzug Mansfelds. (1618–1622)* (Carspach, 1912).

Englert, Hansjörg, 'Das Emmendinger Stadtrecht von 1590' (Diss. phil. Freiburg im Breisgau, 1973).

Epstein, Stephan R., 'Cities, regions, and the late medieval crisis: Sicily and Tuscany compared', *Past and Present*, 130 (1991), 3–50.

—— *An island for itself: Economic development and social change in late medieval Sicily* (Cambridge, 1989).

—— 'Regional fairs, institutional innovation, and economic growth in late medieval Europe', *Economic History Review*, 2nd series, 47 (1994), 459–82.

Eules, Susanne, *'der hafner gesellen lobliche bruderschaft.' Organisation der Hafnerbruderschaft und Erzeugnisse der Hafner des 15. bis 18. Jahrhunderts im Elsaß, Sundgau und Breisgau* (Artes Populares. Studia Ethnographica et Folkloristica, 22) (Frankfurt am Main/Bern/New York/Paris, 1991).

Febvre, Lucien, *Philippe II et la Franche-Comté*, new edn. (Paris, 1970).

—— *La Terre et l'évolution humaine: Introduction géographique à l'histoire*, 2nd edn. (Paris, 1938 printing).

Fester, Richard, *Markgraf Bernhard I. und die Anfänge des badischen Territorialstaates* (Neujahrsblätter der Badischen Historischen Kommission, 6) (Karlsruhe, 1896).

Fischer, Albert, 'Die Verdrängung der Münstertäler Melker von den herzoglich-lothringischen Hochweiden am Ende des 16. Jahrhunderts', *Annuaire de la Société d'Histoire du Val et de la Ville de Munster*, 45 (1991), 11–48.

Flamm, Hermann, *Der wirtschaftliche Niedergang Freiburgs i. Br. und die Lage des städtischen Grundeigentums im 14. und 15. Jahrhundert: Ein*

*Beitrag zur Geschichte der geschlossenen Stadtwirtschaft* (Volkswirt-schaftliche Abhandlungen der Badischen Hochschulen, 8, suppl. vol. 3) (Karlsruhe, 1905).

Frank, Theophil, 'Das Textilgewerbe der Stadt Freiburg i. Br. bis zum Ausgang des 16. Jahrhunderts' (Diss. phil Freiburg im Breisgau, 1912).

Fritze, Konrad, 'Probleme der Stadt-Land-Beziehungen im Bereich der wendischen Hansestädte nach 1370', *Hansische Geschichtsblätter*, 85 (1967), 38–57.

Fuchs, François-Joseph, 'Aspects du commerce de Strasbourg avec Mont-béliard et la Franche-Comté au XVIIe siècle', in *Trois provinces de l'Est. Lorraine, Alsace, Franche-Comté* (Publications de la Société Savante d'Alsace et des Régions de l'Est: Grandes Publications, 6) (Strasbourg/Paris, 1967), 109–17.

—— 'L'Espace économique rhénan et les relations commerciales de Stras-bourg avec le sud-ouest de l'Allemagne au XVIe siècle', in Alfons Schäfer (ed.), *Festschrift für Günther Haselier aus Anlaß seines 60. Geburtstages am 19. April 1974* (Oberrheinische Studien, 3) (Bretten, 1975), 289–325.

—— 'Une famille de négotiants banquiers du XVI siècle: Les Prechter de Strasbourg', *Revue d'Alsace*, 95 (1956), 146–94.

—— 'Les Foires et le rayonnement économique de la ville en Europe (XVI siècle)', in Livet and Rapp, *Histoire de Strasbourg*, ii. 259–361.

—— 'Richesse et faillite des Ingold, négotiants et financiers strasbourgeois du XVIe siècle', in *La Bourgeoisie alsacienne*, 203–23.

Füglister, Hans, *Handwerksregiment: Untersuchungen und Materialien zur sozialen und politischen Struktur der Stadt Basel in der ersten Hälfte des 16. Jahrhunderts* (Basler Beiträge zur Geschichtswissenschaft, 143) (Basel/Frankfurt am Main, 1981).

Geering, Traugott, *Handel und Industrie der Stadt Basel: Zunftwesen und Wirtschaftsgeschichte bis zum Ende des 17. Jahrhunderts* (Basel, 1886).

Gibert, André, *La Porte de Bourgogne et d'Alsace (Trouée de Belfort): Étude géographique* (Paris, 1930).

Gilissen, John, 'The notion of the fair in the light of the comparative method', in *La Foire* (Recueils de la Société Jean Bodin, 5) (Brussels, 1953), 333–42.

Gollut, Loys, *Les Mémoires historiques de la république séquanoise et des princes de la Franche-Comté de Bourgogne*, ed. C. Duvernoy and E. Bousson de Mairet (Arbois, 1846).

Gothein, Eberhard, *Die badischen Markgrafen im 16. Jahrhundert* (Neujahr-sblätter der Badischen Historischen Kommission, NS 13) (Heidelberg, 1910).

—— *Wirtschaftsgeschichte des Schwarzwaldes und der angrenzenden Land-schaften, i. Städte und Gewerbegeschichte* (Strasbourg, 1892).

Göttmann, Frank, *Getreidemarkt am Bodensee: Raum—Wirtschaft—Politik—Gesellschaft (1650–1810)* (Beiträge zur südwestdeutschen Wirtschafts- und Sozialgeschichte, 13) (St Katherinen, 1991).

—— Horst Rabe, and Jörn Sieglerschmidt, 'Regionale Transformation von Wirtschaft und Gesellschaft: Forschungen und Berichte zum wirtschaftlichen und sozialen Wandel am Bodensee vornehmlich in der frühen Neuzeit, 1: Theoretische und methodische Grundprobleme', *Schriften des Vereins für Geschichte des Bodensees und seiner Umgebung*, 102 (1984), 115–30.

Goubert, Pierre, 'The French peasantry of the seventeenth century', *Past and Present*, 10 (1956), 55–77.

Graf, Klaus, 'Aspekte zum Regionalismus in Schwaben und am Oberrhein im Spätmittelalter', in Kurt Andermann (ed.), *Historiographie am Oberrhein im späten Mittelalter und in der frühen Neuzeit* (Oberrheinische Studien, 7) (Sigmaringen, 1988), 127–64.

—— 'Das "Land" Schwaben im späten Mittelalter', in Peter Moraw (ed.), *Regionale Identität und soziale Gruppen im deutschen Mittelalter* (*Zeitschrift für historische Forschung*, suppl. 14) (Berlin, 1992), 127–64.

Gras, Christian, and Georges Livet (eds.), *Régions et régionalisme en France du XVIIIe siècle à nos jours* (Publications de la Société Savante d'Alsace et des Régions de l'Est: Grandes Publications, 13) (Paris, 1977).

Gschwind, Franz, *Bevölkerungsentwicklung und Wirtschaftsstruktur der Landschaft Basel im 18. Jahrhundert: Ein historisch-demographischer Beitrag zur Sozial- und Wirtschaftsgeschichte mit besonderer Berücksichtigung der langfristigen Entwicklung von Stadt (seit 1100) und Landschaft (seit 1500) Basel* (Quellen und Forschungen zur Geschichte und Landeskunde des Kantons Baselland, 15) (Liestal, 1977).

Guggisberg, Hans, *Basel in the sixteenth century: Aspects of the city republic before, during and after the Reformation* (St Louis, MO, 1982).

Habermann, Wolfgang, and Heinz Schlotmann, 'Der Getreidehandel in Deutschland im 14. und 15. Jahrhundert: Ein Literaturbericht', pt. 1, *Scripta Mercaturae*, 11: 2 (1977), 27–55.

Hall, Peter (ed.), and Carla M. Wartenberg (trans.), *Von Thünen's isolated state: An English edition of* Der isolierte Staat *by Johann Heinrich von Thünen* (Oxford, 1986).

Hanauer, Auguste, *Études économiques sur l'Alsace ancienne et moderne*, i. *Les monnaies* (Paris/Strasbourg, 1876).

Harvie, Christopher, *The rise of regional Europe* (London/New York, 1994).

Haselier, Günther, *Geschichte der Stadt Breisach am Rhein*, i. 1: *Von den Anfängen bis zum Jahr 1700* (Breisach, 1969).

Hauß, Heinrich, 'Das "alte" Baden und die Regio am Oberrhein', *Badische Heimat*, 76 (1996), 17–25.

Heiligenthal, Roman, *Grundlagen der Regionalplanung: Raumplanung und Staatsplanung* (Siedlungsstudien, 10) (Heidelberg, 1940).

Heitz, Gerhard, *Ländliche Leinenproduktion in Sachsen (1470–1555)* (Deutsche Akademie der Wissenschaften zu Berlin: Schriften des Instituts für Geschichte, 2nd series: Landesgeschichte, 4) (Berlin, 1961).

Hermann, Hans-Walter, 'Territoriale Verbindungen und Verflechtungen zwischen dem oberrheinischen und lothringischen Raum im Spätmittelalter', *Jahrbuch für westdeutsche Landesgeschichte*, 1 (1975), 129–76.

Herzog, Emile (ed.), *Inventaire sommaire des archives départementales antérieur à 1790: Archives civiles: Série I E, Seigneuries* (Colmar, 1952).

Hodges, Richard, *Primitive and peasant markets* (Oxford, 1988).

Hohenberg, Paul L., and Lynn Hollen Lees, *The making of urban Europe 1000–1950* (Cambridge, MA/London, 1985).

Holbach, Rudolf, *Frühformen von Verlag und Großbetrieb in der gewerblichen Produktion (13.–16. Jahrhundert)* (*Vierteljahrschrift für Sozial- und Wirtschaftsgeschichte*, suppl. 110) (Stuttgart, 1994).

Howiller, Alain, *Mémoires de midi: Les Mutations de l'Alsace (1960–1993)* (Strasbourg, 1993).

Hudson, Pat, *Regions and industries: A perspective on the Industrial Revolution in Britain* (Cambridge, 1989).

Huggle, F., *Geschichte der Stadt Neuenburg am Rhein* (Freiburg im Breisgau, 1876–81).

Hünnekens, Ludger, 'Neue Beiträge zur Emmendinger Stadtgeschichte', *Zeitschrift des Breisgau-Geschichtsvereins ('Schau-ins-Land')*, 105 (1986), 7–60.

Huter, Franz, 'Vorderösterreich und Österreich: Von ihren mittelalterlichen Beziehungen', in Metz, *Vorderösterreich*, 67–85.

Huttenlocher, Friedrich, 'Karte der naturräumlichen Gliederung von Baden-Württemberg', in *Historischer Atlas von Baden-Württemberg*, map II. 4: *Beiwort*.

Imbs[-Obermuller], Anne-Marie, 'Tableaux des corporations alsaciennes XIVe–XVIIIe siècles', in *Artisans et Ouvriers d'Alsace*, 35–45.

Irsigler, Franz, 'Kölner Wirtschaft im Spätmittelalter', in Hermann Kellenbenz (ed.), *Zwei Jahrtausende Kölner Wirtschaft*, i (Cologne, 1975), 217–319.

Jäger, Albert, 'Der Engedeiner Krieg im Jahre 1499, mit Urkunden', *Neue Zeitschrift des Ferdinandeums für Tirol und Vorarlberg*, 4 (1838), 1–227.

Jordan, Benoît, *Entre la gloire et la vertu: Les Sires de Ribeaupierre 1451–1585* (Publications de la Société Savante d'Alsace et des Régions de l'Est: Recherches [Textes] et Documents, 44) (Strasbourg, 1991).

Juillard, Étienne, *L'Europe rhénane: Géographie d'un grand espace* (Paris, 1968).

—— 'Paysans d'Alsace, paysans rhénans', in *Paysans d'Alsace* (Publications de la Société Savante d'Alsace et des Régions de l'Est: Grandes Publications, 7) (Strasbourg, 1959), 621–24.

Kähni, Otto, 'Die Landvogtei Ortenau', in Metz, *Vorderösterreich*, 491–503.

Kammerer, Odile, 'Le Carrefour alsacien-lorrain dans le grand commerce des XVe et XVIe siècles', in Jean-Marie Cauchies (ed.), *Aspects de la vie économique des pays bourguignons (1384–1559): Dépression ou prospérité?* (Publication du Centre Européen d'Études Bourguignonnes (XIVe–XVIe s.), 27: Rencontres de Douai (25 au 28 septembre 1986)) (Basel, 1987), 81–95.

—— 'Colmar et Fribourg à la fin du Moyen Âge: Convergences et divergences', *Annuaire de la Société d'Histoire et d'Archéologie de Colmar*, 37 (1990), 33–45.

—— 'Colmar ville-état et la puissante seigneurie des Ribeaupierre avant le XVIe siècle', in Jean-Marie Cauchies (ed.), *Les Relations entre États et principautés des Pays-Bays à la Savoie (XIVe–XVIe s.)* (Publication du Centre Européen d'Études Bourguignonnes, 32: Recontres de Montbéliard (26 au 29 septembre 1991)) (Neuchâtel, 1992), 99–113.

—— 'Échange et marchands à la fin du Moyen Âge dans l'Oberrhein', in *Le Marchand au Moyen Âge* (Société des Historiens Médiévistes de l'Enseignement Supérieur Public, 19e Congrès, Reims 1988) (Nantes, 1992), 137–53.

—— 'Le Haut Rhin entre Bâle et Strasbourg: A-t-il été une frontière mediévale?', in *Les Pays de l'entre-deux au Moyen Âge: Questions d'histoire des territoires d'Empire entre Meuse, Rhône et Rhin* (Actes du 113e Congrès National des Sociétés Savantes (Strasbourg, 1988), Section d'histoire médiévale et de philologie) (Paris, 1990), 171–93.

—— 'Der Oberrhein im Mittelalter: Zur Grenze nicht tauglich', *Alemannisches Jahrbuch*, 1993/94, 125–32.

—— 'Richesses publiques et capitaux privés: l'Exemple de Colmar à l'entrée des temps modernes (1350–1650)', *Revue d'Alsace*, 112 (1986), 83–106.

Kellenbenz, Hermann, 'Ländliches Gewerbe und bäuerliches Unternehmertum in Westeuropa vom Spätmittelalter bis ins XVIII. Jahrhundert', in *Deuxième Conférence Internationale d'Histoire Économique, Aix-en-Provence 1962* (École Pratique des Hautes Études—Sorbonne, Sixième Section: Sciences Économiques et Sociales, Congrès et Colloques, 7) (Paris/The Hague, 1965), 377–427.

—— 'Rural industries in the West from the end of the Middle Ages to the eighteenth century', in Peter Earle (ed.), *Essays in European economic history* (Oxford, 1974), 45–88.

Kiesel, Karl, *Petershüttly: Ein Friedensziel in den Vogesen* (Berlin, 1918).

Kießling, Rolf, 'Bürgerlicher Besitz auf dem Land—ein Schlüssel zu den Stadt-Land-Beziehungen im Spätmittelalter, aufgezeigt am Beispiel Augsburgs und anderer ostschwäbischer Städte', in Pankraz Fried (ed.), *Bayerisch-schwäbische Landesgeschichte an der Universität Augsburg 1975–1977: Vorträge, Aufsätze, Berichte* (Augsburger Beiträge zur Landesgeschichte Bayerisch-Schwabens, 1) (Sigmaringen, 1979), 121–40.

—— *Die Stadt und ihr Land: Umlandspolitik, Bürgerbesitz und Wirtschaftsgefüge in Ostschwaben vom 14. bis ins 16. Jahrhundert* (Städteforschung: Veröffentlichungen des Instituts für vergleichende Städtegeschichte in Münster, A 29) (Cologne/Vienna, 1989).

Kirchgässner, Bernhard, 'Zur Neuordnung der Währungsräume Südwestdeutschlands und der angrenzenden Eidgenossenschaft 1350–1500', in Hermann Aubin, Edith Ennen, Hermann Kellenbenz, Theodor Mayer, Friedrich Metz, Max Müller, and Josef Schmithüsen (eds.), *Beiträge zur Wirtschafts- und Stadtgeschichte: Festschrift für Hektor Ammann* (Wiesbaden, 1965), 312–32.

Köhler, Josef, 'Studien zum Problem des Regionalismus im späten Mittelalter' (Diss. phil. Würzburg, 1971).

Körner, Martin H., *Solidarités financières suisses aux seizième siècle* (Bibliothèque Historique Vaudoise, 66) (Lausanne, 1980).

Kramer, Hans, 'Die Beziehungen zwischen Vorderösterreich und Österreich in der Neuzeit', in Metz, *Vorderösterreich*, 87–110.

Kreutter, Franz, *Geschichte der k. k. Vorderösterreichischen Staaten*, i (St Blasien, 1790).

Krimm, Konrad, *Baden und Habsburg um die Mitte des 15. Jahrhunderts: Fürstlicher Dienst und Reichsgewalt im späten Mittelalter* (Veröffentlichungen der Kommission für geschichtliche Landeskunde in Baden-Württemberg, B 89) (Stuttgart, 1976).

Krüger, Herbert, 'Brücke, Fähre und Zoll im Rheinstromgebiet um 1500 (nach Sebastian Brants "Chronik über Teutsch land")', *Elsaß-Lothringisches Jahrbuch*, 21 (1943), 127–56.

Kulinat, Klaus, 'Regional planning in Baden-Württemberg', in Hans-Georg Wehling (ed.), *The German Southwest: Baden-Württemberg: History, politics, economy and culture* (Stuttgart/Berlin/Cologne, 1991), 140–67.

Langton, John, and Göran Hoppe, *Town and country in the development of early modern western Europe* (Historical Geography Research Series, 11) (Norwich, 1983).

Lauterbach, Klaus H., *Geschichtsverständnis, Zeitdidaxe und Reformgedanke an der Wende zum sechzehnten Jahrhundert: Das oberrheinische 'Buchli der hundert Capiteln' im Kontext des spätmittelalterlichen Reformbiblizismus* (Forschungen zur oberrheinischen Landesgeschichte, 33) (Freiburg im Breisgau/Munich, 1985).

—— 'Der "Oberrheinische Revolutionär" und Mathias Wurm von Geudertheim: Neue Untersuchungen zur Verfasserfrage', *Deutsches Archiv für Erforschung des Mittelalters*, 45 (1989), 109–72.

Leiser, Wolfgang, 'Zentralorte als Strukturproblem der Markgrafschaft Baden', in Maschke and Sydow, *Stadt umd Umland*, 1–19.

Lerner, Franz, 'Die Bedeutung des internationalen Ochsenhandels für die Fleischversorgung deutscher Städte im Spätmittelalter und der frühen Neuzeit', in Ekkehard Westermann (ed.), *Internationaler Ochsenhandel (1350–1750): Akten des 7th International Economic History Congress Edinburgh 1978* (Beiträge zur Wirtschaftsgeschichte, 9) (Stuttgart, 1979), 197–217.

Lhotsky, Alphons, *Das Zeitalter des Hauses Österreich: Die ersten Jahre der Regierung Ferdinands I. (1520–1527)* (Österreichische Akademie der Wissenschaften: Veröffentlichungen der Kommission für Geschichte Österreichs, 4 [Schriften des DDr. Franz-Josef Mayer-Gunthof-Fonds, 7]) (Vienna, 1971).

Livet, Georges, and Raymond Oberlé, *Histoire de Mulhouse des origines à nos jours (Collection Histoire des Villes d'Alsace)* (Strasbourg, 1977).

—— and Francis Rapp (eds.), *Histoire de Strasbourg des origines à nos jours*, ii. *Strasbourg des grandes invasions au XVIe siècle (Collection Histoire des Villes d'Alsace)* (Strasbourg, 1981).

Maier, Hans, and Volker Press (eds.), *Vorderösterreich in der frühen Neuzeit* (Sigmaringen, 1989).

Maschke, Erich, and Jürgen Sydow (eds.), *Stadt und Umland: Protokoll der X. Arbeitstagung des Arbeitskreises für südwestdeutsche Stadtgeschichtsforschung Calw 12.–14. November 1971* (Veröffentlichungen der Kommission für geschichtliche Landeskunde in Baden-Württemberg, B 82) (Stuttgart, 1974).

Mattmüller, Markus, *Bevölkerungsgeschichte der Schweiz*, pt. 1: *Die frühe Neuzeit, 1500–1700*, 2 vols. (Basel/Frankfurt am Main, 1987).

Mayer, Theodor, 'Der Staat der Herzöge von Zähringen', in idem, *Mittelalterliche Studien: Gesammelte Aufsätze* (Lindau/Constance, 1959), 350–64.

Meier, Thomas, *Handwerk, Hauswerk, Heimarbeit: Nicht-agrarische Tätigkeiten und Erwerbsformen in einem traditionellen Ackerbaugebiet des 18. Jahrhunderts (Zürcher Unterland)* (Zürich, 1986).

Melcher, Wilhelm, 'Die geistlichen und weltlichen Territorien in der Ortenau (Ihre Geschichte bis zur Auflösung 1803 bis 1806)', in Kurt Klein (ed.), *Land um Rhein und Schwarzwald: Die Ortenau in Geschichte und Gegenwart* (Kehl, 1978), 65–79.

Merkel, Rosemarie, 'Bemerkungen zur Bevölkerungsentwicklung der Stadt Freiburg zwischen 1390 und 1450', *Zeitschrift des Breisgau-Geschichtsvereins ('Schau-ins-Land')*, 108 (1989), 83–91.

Mertens, Dieter, 'Reich und Elsaß zur Zeit Maximilians I.: Untersuchungen zur Ideen- und Landesgeschichte im Südwesten des Reiches am Ausgang des Mittelalters' (Diss. habil. Freiburg im Breisgau, 1977).

Metz, Friedrich, 'Die burgundische Pforte', in idem, *Land und Leute*, 327–32.

—— 'Die elsässischen Städte: Die Grundlagen ihrer Entstehung und Entwicklung', ibid. 311–27.

—— 'Die Grenzen im Schwarzwald', ibid. 899–915.

—— 'Das Kinziggebiet als Brückenlandschaft', ibid. 896–99.

—— *Land und Leute: Gesammelte Beiträge zur deutschen Landes- und Volksforschung* (Stuttgart, 1961).

—— *Ländergrenzen im Südwesten* (Forschungen zur deutschen Landeskunde, 60) (Remagen, 1951).

—— 'Der Oberrhein als Grenze', in idem, *Land und Leute*, 238–54.

—— *Die Oberrheinlande* (Wrocław, 1925).

—— 'Der Südwesten', in idem, *Land und Leute*, 155–66.

—— *Vorderösterreich: Eine geschichtliche Landeskunde*, 2nd edn. (Freiburg im Breisgau, 1967).

—— 'Die vorderösterreichischen Lande', in idem, *Land und Leute*, 166–85.

Metz, Rudolf, 'Bergbau und Hüttenwesen in den Vorlanden', in Friedrich Metz, *Vorderösterreich*, 139–94.

Milizer, Klaus, 'Handel und Vertrieb rheinischer und elsässischer Weine über Köln im Spätmittelalter', in Alois Gerlach (ed.), *Weinbau, Weinhandel und Weinkultur: Sechstes Alzeyer Kolloquium* (Geschichtliche Landeskunde, 40) (Stuttgart, 1993), 165–85.

Mitterauer, Michael, 'Das Problem der zentralen Orte als sozial- und wirtschaftsgeschichtliche Forschungsaufgabe', in idem, *Markt und Stadt im Mittelalter. Beiträge zur historischen Zentralitätsforschung* (Monographien zur Geschichte des Mittelalters, 21) (Stuttgart, 1980), 22–51.

—— 'Typen und räumliche Verbreitung der mittelalterlichen Städte und Märkte in den österreichischen Ländern', ibid. 278–304.

Moore, Barrington, Jr., *Social origins of dictatorship and democracy: Lord and peasant in the making of the modern world* (Harmondsworth, 1969).

Müller, Karl Friedrich, *Geschichte der Getreidehandelspolitik, des Bäcker- und Müllergewerbes der Stadt Freiburg i. Breisgau im 14., 15. und 16. Jahrhundert* (Zeitschrift der Gesellschaft für Beförderung der Geschichts-, Altertums- und Volkskunde von Freiburg, dem Breisgau und den angrenzenden Landschaften, suppl. 3) (Freiburg im Breisgau, 1926).

Müller, Wolfgang, 'Studien zur Geschichte der Klöster St. Märgen und Allerheiligen, Freiburg i. Br.', *Freiburger Diözesan-Archiv*, 89 (1969), 5–129.

Münster, Sebastian, *Cosmographei* (Basel, 1550).

Nehlsen, Hermann, *Die Freiburger Familie Snewlin. Rechts- und sozialgeschichtliche Studien zur Entwicklung des mittelalterlichen Bürgertums* (Veröffentlichungen aus dem Archiv der Stadt Freiburg im Breisgau, 9) (Freiburg im Breisgau, 1967).

Nicholas, David M., 'Town and countryside: Social and economic tensions in fourteenth-century Flanders', *Comparative Studies in Society and History*, 10 (1968), 458–85.

Ogilvie, Sheilagh, 'Institutions and economic development in early modern central Europe', *Transactions of the Royal Historical Society*, 6th series, 5 (1995), 221–50.

Ohler, Norbert, *Von Grenzen und Herrschaften: Grundzüge territorialer Entwicklung im deutschen Südwesten* (Themen der Landeskunde: Veröffentlichungen aus dem Alemannischen Institut Freiburg im Breisgau, 4) (Bühl, 1989).

Pariset, Jean-Daniel, *Humanisme, Réforme et diplomatie: Les Relations entre la France et l'Allemagne au milieu du XVIe siècle d'après des documents inédits* (Publications de la Société Savante d'Alsace et des Régions de l'Est: Grandes Publications, 19) (Strasbourg, 1981).

Peyer, Hans Conrad, 'Gewässer und Grenzen in der Schweizergeschichte', in idem, *Gewässer, Grenzen und Märkte in der Schweizergeschichte* (Mitteilungen der Antiquarischen Gesellschaft in Zürich, 48. 3 (= 143. Neujahrsblatt) ) (Zürich, 1979), 5–17.

—— 'Die Märkte der Schweiz in Mittelalter und Neuzeit', ibid. 19–38.

Pfister, Christian, *Bevölkerung, Klima und Agrarmodernisierung 1525–1860: Das Klima der Schweiz von 1525–1860 und seine Bedeutung in der Geschichte von Bevölkerung und Landschaft*, ii (Bern, 1984).

Pickl, Othmar, 'Routen, Umfang und Organisation des innereuropäischen Handels mit Schlachtvieh im 16. Jahrhundert', in Alexander Novotny and Othmar Pickl (eds.), *Festschrift Hermann Wiesflecker zum sechzigsten Geburtstag* (Graz, 1973), 143–66.

Piguerre, Paul-Émile [= Miles], *Histoire de la France*, 1st edn. (Paris, 1550).

de Planhol, Xavier, with Paul Claval, *An historical geography of France* (Cambridge Studies in Historical Geography, 21) (Cambridge/Paris, 1994).

Pollard, Sidney, *Peaceful conquest: The industrialization of Europe 1760–1970* (Oxford, 1981).

Prak, Maarten, 'Le regioni nella prima Europa moderna', in *Regioni, culture e ancora regioni nella storia economica e sociale dell'Europa moderna, Proposte e Ricerche: Economia e Società nella Storia dell'Italia Centrale*, 35 (1995), 7–40.

Press, Volker, 'Baden und die badischen Kondominate', in Anton Schindling and Walter Ziegler (eds.), *Die Territorien des Reichs im Zeitalter der Reformation und Konfessionsbildung: Land und Konfession 1500–1650*, v. *Der Südwesten* (Katholisches Leben und Kirchenreform im Zeitalter der Glaubensspaltung, 53) (Münster, 1993), 124–66.

—— Vorderösterreich in der habsburgischen Reichspolitik des späten Mittelalters und der frühen Neuzeit', in Maier and Press, *Vorderösterreich*, 1–41.

Raeff, Marc, *The well-ordered police state: Social and institutional change through law in the Germanies and Russia 1600–1800* (New Haven/London, 1983).

Rapp, Francis, 'La Guerre des Paysans dans la vallée du Rhin supérieur: Quelques problèmes d'interprétation', in *Charles-Quint, le Rhin et la France: Droit savant et droit pénal à l'époque de Charles-Quint* (Publications de la Société Savante d'Alsace et des Régions de l'Est: Recherches et Documents, 17) (Strasbourg, 1973), 135–55.

—— 'Routes et voies de communication à travers les Vosges du XIIe au début du XVIe siècle', in *Les Pays de l'entre-deux au Moyen Âge: Questions d'histoire des territoires d'Empire entre Meuse, Rhône et Rhin* (Actes du 113e Congrès National des Sociétés Savantes (Strasbourg, 1988), Section d'histoire mediévale et de philologie) (Paris, 1990), 195–207.

—— 'Die soziale und wirtschaftliche Vorgeschichte des Bauernkriegs im Unterelsaß', in Bernd Moeller (ed.), *Bauernkriegs-Studien* (Schriften des Vereins für Reformationsgeschichte, 82. 2/83 [no. 189]) (Gütersloh, 1975), 29–45.

Rebel, Hermann, *Peasant classes: The bureaucratization of property and family relations under early Habsburg absolutism 1511–1636* (Princeton, NJ, 1983).

Reininghaus, Wilfried, *Gewerbe in der frühen Neuzeit* (*Enzyklopädie Deutscher Geschichte*, 3) (Munich, 1990).

Reuss, Rodolphe, *Die Hirsebreifahrt der Zürcher nach Straßburg 1576* (Zürich, 1976).

Rippmann, Dorothee, *Bauern und Städter. Stadt-Land-Beziehungen im 15. Jahrhundert: Das Beispiel Basel, unter besonderer Berücksichtigung der Nahmarktbeziehungen und der sozialen Verhältnisse im Umland* (Basler Beiträge zur Geschichtswissenschaft, 159) (Basel/Frankfurt am Main, 1990).

Rokkan, Stein, and Derek W. Urwin, *Economy, territory, identity: Politics of West European peripheries* (London/Beverly Hills/New Delhi, 1983).

Roos, Gisbert, 'Die geschichtliche Entwicklung des Bergbaus, insbesondere des Bergrechts im Elsaß und in Lothringen' (Diss. ing. Technische Universität Clausthal, 1974).

Rowan, Steven W. (ed.), 'Die Jahresrechnung eines Freiburger Kaufmanns 1487/88: Ein Beitrag zur Handelsgeschichte des Oberrheins, mit einem Nachwort von Berent Schwineköper', in Maschke and Sydow, *Stadt und Umland*, 227–77.

—— 'A Reichstag in the reform era: Freiburg im Breisgau, 1497–98', in idem and James A. Vann (eds.), *The old Reich: Essays on German political institutions 1495–1806* (Studies presented to the International Commission for the History of Representative and Parliamentary Institutions, 48) (Brussels, 1974), 33–57.

von Rundstedt, Hans-Gerd, *Die Regelung des Getreidehandels in den Städten Südwestdeutschlands und der deutschen Schweiz im späteren Mittelalter und im Beginn der Neuzeit* (*Vierteljahrschrift für Sozial- und Wirtschaftsgeschichte*, suppl. 10) (Stuttgart, 1930).

Russell, J.C., *Medieval regions and their cities* (Newton Abbot, 1972).

Schaab, Meinrad, 'Städtlein, Burg-, Amts- und Marktflecken Südwestdeutschlands in Spätmittelalter und früher Neuzeit', in Emil Meynen (ed.), *Zentralität als Problem der mittelalterlichen Stadtgeschichtsforschung* (Städteforschung: Veröffentlichungen des Instituts für vergleichende Städtegeschichte in Münster, A 8) (Cologne/Vienna), 1976), 219–71.

Schadek, Hans, and Karl Schmid (eds.), *Die Zähringer*, i. *Eine Tradition und ihre Erforschung*; ii. *Anstoß und Wirkung* (Veröffentlichungen zur Zähringer-Ausstellung, 1/2) (Sigmaringen, 1986).

Scheifele, Max, 'Flößerei und Holzhandel im Murgtal unter besonderer Berücksichtigung der Murgschifferfahrt: Ein Beitrag zur Wirtschafts-geschichte des Nordschwarzwaldes', in idem (ed.), *Die Murgschiffer-schaft: Geschichte des Floßhandels, des Waldes und der Holzindustrie im Murgtal* (Schriftenreihe der Landesforstverwaltung Baden-Württemberg, 66) (Stuttgart, 1988), 73–456.

Scherlen, Auguste, *Das Zunftwesen Colmars und der Umgebung* (Colmar, 1923).

Schib, Karl, 'Die vier Waldstädte', in Metz, *Vorderösterreich*, 375–99.

Schlageter, Albrecht, 'Der mittelalterliche Bergbau im Schauinslandrevier', pt. 1, *Schau-ins-Land*, 88 (1970), 125–71.

Schmidlin, Joseph, 'Der Visitationsstreit der Bischöfe von Basel mit der österreichischen Regierung um das Ober-Elsaß vor dem Dreißigjährigen Krieg', *Archiv für elsässische Kirchengeschichte*, 3 (1928), 115–58.

Schmoller, Gustav, *Die Strassburger Tucher- und Weberzunft: Urkunden und Darstellungen nebst Regesten und Glossar: Ein Beitrag zur Geschichte der deutschen Weberei und des deutschen Gewerberechts vom XIII.– XVII. Jahrhundert* (Strasbourg, 1897).

Schnell, Rüdiger, 'Deutsche Literatur und deutsches Nationalbewußtsein in Spätmittelalter und Früher Neuzeit', in Joachim Ehlers (ed.), *Ansätze und Diskontinuität deutscher Staatsbildung im Mittelalter* (Nationes: Historische und philologische Untersuchungen zur Entstehung der europäischen Nationen im Mittelalter, 8) (Sigmaringen, 1989), 247–319.

Schöller, Peter, 'Stadt und Einzugsgebiet: Ein geographisches Forschungs-problem und seine Bedeutung für Landeskunde, Geschichte und Kul-turrraumforschung', in idem (ed.), *Zentralitätsforschung* (*Wege der For-schung*, 301) (Darmstadt, 1972), 267–92.

Schöttler, Peter, 'The Rhine as an object of historical controversy in the inter-war years: Towards a history of frontier mentalities', *History Work-shop Journal*, 39 (1995), 1–21.

Schubring, Klaus, 'Die Neuformung der Oberrheinlande', in Horst Buszello (ed.), *Der Oberrhein in Geschichte und Gegenwart: Von der Römerzeit bis zur Gründung des Landes Baden-Württemberg* (Schriftenreihe der Pädagogischen Hochschule Freiburg, 1) (Freiburg im Breisgau, 1986), 40–52.

Schuler, Peter-Johannes, 'Die Bevölkerungsstruktur der Stadt Freiburg im Breisgau im Spätmittelalter—Möglichkeiten und Grenzen einer quanti-tativen Quellenanalyse', in Wilfried Ehbrecht (ed.), *Voraussetzungen und Methoden geschichtlicher Städteforschung* (Städteforschung: Veröffentli-chungen des Instituts für vergleichende Städtegeschichte in Münster, A 7) (Cologne/Vienna, 1979), 139–76.

Schultz, Helga, *Landhandwerk im Übergang vom Feudalismus zum Kapitalismus: Vergleichender Überblick und Fallstudie Mecklenburg-Schwerin* (Forschungen zur Wirtschaftsgeschichte, 21) (Berlin, 1984).

Schulz, Knut, *Handwerksgesellen und Lohnarbeiter. Untersuchungen zur oberrheinischen und oberdeutschen Stadtgeschichte des 14. bis 17. Jahrhunderts* (Sigmaringen, 1985).

—— 'Rheinschiffahrt und städtische Wirtschaftspolitik am Oberrhein im Spätmittelalter', in Erich Maschke and Jürgen Sydow (eds.), *Die Stadt am Fluß: 14. Arbeitstagung in Kehl 14.–16. 11. 1975* (Stadt in der Geschichte: Veröffentlichungen des Südwestdeutschen Arbeitskreises für Stadtgeschichtsforschung, 4) (Sigmaringen, 1978), 141–89.

Schüttenhelm, Joachim, *Der Geldumlauf im südwestdeutschen Raum vom Riedlinger Münzvertrag 1423 bis zur ersten Kipperzeit 1628: Eine statistische Münzfundanalyse unter Anwendung der elektronischen Datenverarbeitung* (Veröffentlichungen der Kommission für geschichtliche Landeskunde in Baden-Württemberg, B 108) (Stuttgart, 1987).

Schwineköper, Berent, 'Beobachtungen zum Lebensraum südwestdeutscher Städte im Mittelalter, insbesondere zum engeren und weiteren Einzugsbereich der Freiburger Jahrmärkte in der zweiten Hälfte des 16. Jahrhunderts', in Maschke and Sydow, *Stadt und Umland*, 29–53.

Scott, Tom, 'Economic conflict and co-operation on the Upper Rhine', in E. I. Kouri and Tom Scott (eds.), *Politics and society in Reformation Europe: Essays for Sir Geoffrey Elton on his sixty-fifth birthday* (London, 1987), 210–31.

—— 'Economic landscapes', in Bob Scribner (ed.), *Germany: A new social and economic history*, i. *1450–1630* (London/New York/Sydney/Auckland, 1995), 1–31.

—— *Freiburg and the Breisgau: Town–country relations in the age of Reformation and Peasants' War* (Oxford, 1986).

—— 'Der "Oberrheinische Revolutionär" und Vorderösterreich: Reformvorstellungen zwischen Reich und Territorium', in Norbert Fischer and Marion Kobelt-Groch (eds.), *Außenseiter zwischen Mittelalter und Neuzeit: Festschrift für Hans-Jürgen Goertz zum 60. Geburtstag* (Studies in Medieval and Reformation Thought, 61) (Leiden/New York, 1997), 47–63.

—— 'Die Territorialpolitik der Stadt Freiburg im Breisgau im ausgehenden Mittelalter', *Zeitschrift des Breisgau-Geschichtsvereins ('Schau-ins-Land')*, 102 (1983), 7–24.

—— and Bob Scribner, 'Urban networks', in Bob Scribner (ed.), *Germany: A new social and economic history*, i. *1450–1630* (London/New York/Sydney/Auckland, 1995), 113–43.

Scribner, Bob, 'Police and the territorial state in sixteenth-century Württemberg', in E. I. Kouri and Tom Scott (eds.), *Politics and society in Reformation Europe: Essays for Sir Geoffrey Elton on his sixty-fifth birthday* (London, 1987), 103–20.

Seidel, Karl Josef, 'Die Landgrafschaft im Breisgau und die Häuser Habsburg und Baden', *Zeitschrift für die Geschichte des Oberrheins*, 125 (1977), 381–87.

—— *Das Oberelsaß vor dem Übergang an Frankreich: Landesherrschaft, Landstände und fürstliche Verwaltung in Alt-Vorderösterreich (1602–1638)* (Bonner Historische Forschungen, 45) (Bonn, 1980).

Senti, Anton, 'Die Herrschaften Rheinfelden und Laufenburg', in Metz, *Vorderösterreich*, 401–30.

Sieber-Lehmann, Claudius, *Spätmittelalterlicher Nationalismus: Die Burgunderkriege am Oberrhein und in der Eidgenossenschaft* (Veröffentlichungen des Max-Planck-Instituts für Geschichte, 116) (Göttingen, 1995).

Siegrist, Jean Jacques, 'Beiträge zur Verfassungs- und Wirtschaftsgeschichte der Herrschaft Hallwil', *Argovia*, 64 (1952), 5–533.

—— 'Muri in den Freien Ämtern', i. 'Geschichte des Raumes der nachmaligen Gemeinde Muri vor 1798', ibid. 95 (1983), pp. i–xii, 1–292.

Sittler, Lucien, 'Le Commerce du vin de Colmar jusqu'en 1789', *Revue d'Alsace*, 89 (1949), 37–56.

—— 'Les Corporations et l'organisation du travail à Colmar jusqu'au début du XVIIe siècle', in *Artisans et Ouvriers d'Alsace*, 47–77.

—— 'Landwirtschaft und Gartenbau im alten Kolmar', *Elsaß-Lothringisches Jahrbuch*, 20 (1942), 71–94.

Sked, Allan, *Behavior and location: Foundation for a geographic and dynamic location theory*, i (Lund Series in Geography, B 27) (Lund, 1967).

Smith, Carol A., 'Exchange systems and the spatial distribution of elites: The organization of stratification in agrarian society', in idem (ed.), *Regional analysis*, 2 vols. (New York/San Francisco/London, 1976), ii. *Social systems*, 309–74.

—— 'Regional economic systems: Linking geographical models and socioeconomic problems', ibid. i. *Economic systems*, 3–63.

Sorg, Jean-Paul, 'Contribution à la recherche des fondements d'une sociologie régionale', *Revue des sciences sociales de la France de l'Est*, 16 (1988–89), 16–20.

—— 'La Régionalisme comme humanisme', ibid. 20 (1992–93), 98–103.

Speck, Dieter, *Die vorderösterreichischen Landstände im 15. und 16. Jahrhundert: Entstehung, Entwicklung und Ausbildung bis 1595/1602* (Veröffentlichungen aus dem Archiv der Stadt Freiburg im Breisgau, 29) 2 vols. (Freiburg im Breisgau/Würzburg, 1994).

Speiser, Béatrice, *Europa am Oberrhein: Der grenzüberschreitende Regionalismus am Beispiel der oberrheinischen Kooperation* (Schriften der Regio, 13) (Basel/Frankfurt am Main, 1993).

Stein, Wolfgang Hans, 'Formen der österreichischen und französischen Herrschaftsbildung im Elsaß im 16. und 17. Jahrhundert: Ein Vergleich', in Maier and Press, *Vorderösterreich*, 285–313.

Stenzel, Rüdiger, 'Die Städte der Markgrafen von Baden', in Jürgen Treffeisen and Kurt Andermann (eds.), *Landesherrliche Städte in Südwestdeutschland* (Oberrheinische Studien, 12) (Sigmaringen, 1994), 89–130.

Stinzi, Paul, 'Die Habsburger im Elsaß', in Metz, *Vorderösterreich*, 505–64.

Stolz, Otto, 'Zur Geschichte des Bergbaus im Elsaß im 15. und 16. Jahrhundert', *Elsaß-Lothringisches Jahrbuch*, 18 (1939), 116–71.

—— *Geschichtliche Beschreibung der ober- und vorderösterreichischen Lande* (Quellen und Forschungen zur Siedlungs- und Volkstumsgeschichte der Oberrheinlande, 40) (Karlsruhe, 1943).

—— 'Die Landsrettungen für Oberelsaß und Breisgau aus dem 16. Jahrhundert', *Elsaß-Lothringisches Jahrbuch*, 20 (1942), 181–99.

—— 'Die Verkehrsverbindungen des oberen Rhein- und Donaugebiets um die Mitte des 16. Jahrhunderts', *Zeitschrift für die Geschichte des Oberrheins*, 77 (NS 38) (1923), 60–88.

Strobel, Albrecht, *Agrarverfassung im Übergang: Studien zur Agrargeschichte des badischen Breisgaus vom Beginn des 16. bis zum Ausgang des 18. Jahrhunderts* (Forschungen zur oberrheinischen Landesgeschichte, 23) (Freiburg im Breisgau/Munich, 1972).

Taylor, P. J., *Political geography: World-economy, nation state and locality*, 2nd edn. (London, 1989).

von Thünen, J. H., *Der isolirte Staat in Beziehung auf Landwirthschaft und Nationalökonomie oder Untersuchungen über den Einfluß, den die Getreidepreise, der Reichthum des Bodens und die Abgaben auf den Ackerbau ausüben*, pt. 1, 2nd edn. (Rostock, 1842).

Tourneur-Aumont, J. M., 'L'Alsace et l'Alemanie: Origine et place de la tradition germanique dans la civilisation alsacienne (Études de géographie historique)', *Annales de l'Est*, 33 (1919), 1–225.

Treffeisen, Jürgen, 'Aspekte habsburgischer Stadtherrschaft im spätmittelalterlichen Breisgau', in idem and Kurt Andermann (eds.), *Landesherrliche Städte in Südwestdeutschland* (Oberrheinische Studien, 12) (Sigmaringen, 1994), 157–229.

Vetter, August, *Geisingen: Eine Stadtgründung der Edelfreien von Wartenberg* (Constance, 1964).

—— *Hüfingen* (Hüfingen, 1984).

Vidal de la Blache, Paul, 'Régions françaises', *Revue de Paris*, 15 Dec. 1910, 821–49.

de Villèle, Bruno, 'Belfort à la fin du Moyen Âge' (Diss. phil. Besançon, 1971).

Vogler, Bernard, 'Une alliance manquée: Strasbourg et les XIII cantons (1555–1789)', in *Cinq siècles des relations franco-suisses: Hommage à Louis-Edouard Roulet* (Neuchâtel, 1984), 111–21.

Vogt, Jean, 'Grandeur et décadence du marché de bétail de Cernay (Deuxième moitié du XVIe et début du XVIIe siècle)', *Annuaire de la Société d'Histoire des Régions de Thann-Guebwiller*, 1970–72, 131–38.

de Vries, Jan, *The Dutch rural economy in the Golden Age, 1500–1700* (New Haven/London, 1974).

—— 'On the modernity of the Dutch republic', *Journal of Economic History*, 33 (1973), 191–202.

Wackernagel, Rudolf, *Geschichte der Stadt Basel*, i (Basel, 1907).

Wallerstein, Immanuel, *The modern world-system*, ii. *Mercantilism and the consolidation of the European world-economy, 1600–1750* (New York/London/Toronto/Sydney/San Francisco, 1980).

Wellmer, Martin, 'Der vorderösterreichische Breisgau', in Metz, *Vorderösterreich*, 271–342.

Wickersheimer, Ernest, 'La Corporation des maçons et charpentiers du baillage du Kochersberg', in *Artisans et Ouvriers d'Alsace*, 199–203.

Wielandt, Friedrich, *Badische Münz- und Geldgeschichte* (Veröffentlichungen des Badischen Landesmuseums, 5) 3rd edn. (Karlsruhe, 1979).

—— 'Münzgeschichtliche Beziehungen zwischen Baden und dem Elsaß', *Elsaß-Lothringisches Jahrbuch*, 16 (1937), 57–74.

Wintzenberger, Daniel, *Nuw Reyse Büchlein* (Leipzig, 1579).

Wittmütz, Volkmar, *Die Gravamina der bayerischen Stände im 16. und 17. Jahrhundert als Quelle für die wirtschaftliche Situation und Entwicklung in Bayern* (Miscellanea Bavarica Monacensia, 26) (Munich, 1970).

Wolff, Christian, 'Le vignoble', in Jean-Michel Boehler, Dominique Lerch, and Jean Vogt (eds.), *Histoire de l'Alsace rurale* (Publications de la Société Savante d'Alsace et des Régions de l'Est: Grandes Publications, 24) (Strasbourg/Paris, 1983), 447–58.

Wunder, Gerhard, *Das Straßburger Gebiet: Ein Beitrag zur rechtlichen und politischen Geschichte des gesamten städtischen Territoriums vom 10. bis zum 20. Jahrhundert* (Schriften zur Verfassungsgeschichte, 3) (Berlin, 1965).

—— *Das Straßburger Landgebiet: Territorialgeschichte der einzelnen Teile des städtischen Herrschaftsbereichs vom 13. bis zum 18. Jahrhundert* (Schriften zur Verfassungsgeschichte, 5) (Berlin, 1967).

# Index